# Study Guide

for use with

# Financial Accounting
## A Business Perspective

Seventh Edition

Roger H. Hermanson
*Georgia State University*

James Don Edwards
*University of Georgia*

Boston   Burr Ridge, IL   Dubuque, IA   Madison, WI   New York   San Francisco   St. Louis
Bangkok   Bogotá   Caracas   Lisbon   London   Madrid
Mexico City   Milan   New Delhi   Seoul   Singapore   Sydney   Taipei   Toronto

## Irwin/McGraw-Hill

A Division of The McGraw·Hill Companies

Study Guide for use with
FINANCIAL ACCOUNTING: A BUSINESS PERSPECTIVE

234567890 CUS/CUS 09876543210

ISBN 0-256-24740-4


http://www.mhhe.com

# NOTE TO STUDENT

This Study Guide has been prepared to assist you in performing well in the accounting course you are taking.  For each chapter the Study Guide contains:

Learning Objectives
Reference Outline
Chapter Outline
Demonstration Problem
Solution to Demonstration Problem
Matching Questions
Completion Questions and Exercises
True-False Questions
Multiple Choice Questions
Solutions to all questions and exercises

We looked at our competitors' products and attempted to prepare the most comprehensive, student-oriented Study Guide in existence.  We hope you agree that we succeeded.

# TABLE OF CONTENTS

# THE ACCOUNTING ENVIRONMENT

## Learning Objectives

1. *Define accounting.*
2. *Describe the functions performed by accountants.*
3. *Describe employment opportunities in accounting.*
4. *Differentiate between financial and managerial accounting.*
5. *Identify several organizations that have a role in the development of financial accounting standards.*

---

## REFERENCE OUTLINE

# REVIEW OF INTRODUCTION

***Learning Objective 1***
*Define accounting.*

## ACCOUNTING DEFINED

1. Accounting is defined as "the process of identifying, measuring, and communicating economic information to permit informed judgments and decisions by the users of the information."[1]

***Learning Objective 2***
*Describe the functions performed by accountants.*

2. Accountants observe many events and identify and measure in financial terms those events considered evidence of economic activity. The economic events are recorded, classified, and summarized. Accountants report on economic events by preparing financial statements and special reports and often interpret these reports for others.

***Learning Objective 3***
*Describe employment opportunities in accounting.*

## EMPLOYMENT OPPORTUNITIES IN ACCOUNTING

3. Accounting is now recognized as an important profession and offers various types of employment.

## PUBLIC ACCOUNTING

4. The public accounting profession offers accounting and related services for a fee to companies, other organizations, and the general public.

   a. An accountant may become a certified public accountant (CPA) by passing an examination and meeting other requirements.

   b. Some CPAs are hired as auditors by companies to conduct an examination of their accounting and related records.

   c. Auditors give independent opinions or reports indicating whether or not the financial statements fairly report the economic performance of the business.

   d. CPAs also often provide expert advice on the preparation of federal, state, and city tax returns as well as on tax planning.

   e. Management advisory or consulting services are also performed by CPAs to provide clients with suggestions on how to improve their operations.

## PRIVATE (OR INDUSTRIAL) ACCOUNTING

5. Private or industrial accountants provide services for one business; they may or may not be CPAs.

   a. Some private accountants, regardless of whether or not they are CPAs, pass the Certified Management Accounting (CMA) exam.

   b. Some private accountants conduct internal audits to determine if policies and procedures established by the business are being followed; these accountants may pass the Certified Internal Auditors (CIA) exam.

---

[1] American Accounting Association, *A Statement of Basic Accounting Theory* (Evanston, IL, 1966), p.1.

## GOVERNMENTAL AND OTHER NOT-FOR-PROFIT ACCOUNTING

6. Other accountants, having similar educational backgrounds and training, may be employed by governmental agencies and other not-for-profit organizations.

## HIGHER EDUCATION

7. Academic accountants teach accounting courses, conduct scholarly and applied research, and perform services for the institution and the community.

***Learning Objective 4***
*Differentiate between financial and managerial accounting.*

## FINANCIAL ACCOUNTING VERSUS MANAGERIAL ACCOUNTING

8. Accounting is divided into two categories, financial and managerial accounting, based on the parties for whom the information is prepared.

## FINANCIAL ACCOUNTING

9. Financial accounting information is prepared for external users such as stockbrokers and creditors.

10. Financial accounting information relates to a company as a whole, while managerial accounting focuses on the parts of a company.

## MANAGERIAL ACCOUNTING

11. Managerial accounting provides special information for the managers of a company ranging from broad, long-range plans to detailed explanations.

***Learning Objective 5***
*Identify several organizations that have a role in the development of financial accounting standards.*

## DEVELOPMENT OF FINANCIAL ACCOUNTING STANDARDS

12. These organizations the American Institute of Certified Public Accountants, the Financial Accounting Standards Board, the Governmental Accounting Standards Board, the Securities and Exchange Commission, the American Accounting Association, the Financial Executives Institute, and the Institute of Management Accountants have each contributed to the development of generally accepted accounting principles (GAAP).

## AMERICAN INSTITUTE OF CERTIFIED PUBLIC ACCOUNTANTS (AICPA)

13. The AICPA Committee on Accounting Procedures issued 51 *Accounting Research Bulletins* recommending certain principles or practices during a 20-year period, ending in 1959.

14. The Committee's successor, the Accounting Principles Board (APB), issued 31 *Opinions* that CPAs generally are required to follow.

15. Through its monthly magazine, the *Journal of Accountancy,* the AICPA continues to influence the development of accounting standards and practices.

## FINANCIAL ACCOUNTING STANDARDS BOARD (FASB)

16. The Financial Accounting Standards Board replaced the Accounting Principles Board in 1973.

17. The FASB is an independent, seven-member, full-time board that has issued numerous (over 100) *Statements of Financial Accounting Standards.*

## GOVERNMENTAL ACCOUNTING STANDARDS BOARD (GASB)

18. The Governmental Accounting Standards Board was established in 1984 to develop new governmental accounting concepts and standards.

## SECURITIES AND EXCHANGE COMMISSION (SEC)

19. The SEC has the power to prescribe accounting practices for companies under its jurisdiction.

20. The SEC also indicates to the FASB the accounting topics it believes should be addressed and works closely with the accounting profession.

## AMERICAN ACCOUNTING ASSOCIATION (AAA)

21. The American Accounting Association is composed largely of accounting educators and has sought to encourage research and study into the concepts, standards, and principles of accounting on a theoretical level.

## FINANCIAL EXECUTIVES INSTITUTE (FEI)

22. Through its Committee on Corporate Reporting (CCR) and other means, the FEI is effective in influencing the decisions of the FASB, SEC, and other regulatory agencies.

## INSTITUTE OF MANAGEMENT ACCOUNTANTS (IMA)

23. Through its Management Accounting Practices (MAP) committee and other means, the IMA provides input on financial accounting standards to the FASB, SEC, and other regulatory agencies.

## OTHER ORGANIZATIONS

24. Other organizations, such as the Financial Analysts Federation, the Security Industry Associates, and CPA firms, provide input to the FASB.

## ETHICAL BEHAVIOR OF ACCOUNTANTS

25. Several accounting organizations have formulated codes of ethics that govern the behavior of their members.

## CRITICAL THINKING AND COMMUNICATION SKILLS

26. Accounting students need to work on developing critical thinking and communication skills.

## INTERNET SKILLS

27. It is important for accountants and students to be able to use the Internet to find relevant information.

## COMPLETION

1. Accounting is primarily an information system with three objectives to _____, _____ , and _____ economic information that is relevant to users for their decision-making needs.

2. The four major employment fields in accounting are ,_____ , _____ , _____ , and _____ .

3. Financial accounting information generally relates to a company as a _____ and is usually _____ in nature.

4. Accounting deals primarily with information regarding _____ activities of a business and is expressed in _____ terms.

5. Accountants who offer their services solely to a single profit-seeking organization are said to be in _____ or _____ accounting.

6. An independent, professional accountant, licensed by the state to practice as a certified public accountant (CPA), may offer clients three types of services, namely, _____, _____ , and _____ services.

7. The decisions that must be made by the management of a business generally fall into four major categories: (a) _____, (b) _____ (c) _____ , and (d) _____ decisions. That part of the accounting discipline called upon to provide information for such internal decision making is called _____ accounting.

8. The two tests that information supplied by managerial accountants must meet are:

   a. _____

   b. _____

9. The dominant influence over the past half century in the development of financial accounting standards is the _____.

10. A governmental agency having the power to prescribe the accounting practices of most large business corporations is the _____.

11. The major influence in the private sector in the development of new governmental accounting concepts and standards is the _____.

12. An accountant's most valuable asset is his or her _____.

13. Accountants in practice have generally been dissatisfied with accounting students' ability to think _____ and to _____ their ideas effectively in writing or orally.

# SOLUTIONS

1. identify; measure; communicate
2. public accounting; private accounting; governmental and other not-for-profit accounting; and higher education
3. whole; historical
4. economic; monetary
5. private or industrial
6. auditing; management advisory; tax
7. (a) financial, (b) resource allocation, (c) production, (d) marketing; managerial
8. *a*. It must be useful.
   *b*. It must not cost more to gather than it is worth (this test is known as the *cost/benefit test*).
9. American Institute of Certified Public Accountants
10. Securities and Exchange Commission
11. Governmental Accounting Standards Board
12. reputation
13. critically; communicate

# CHAPTER 1

# ACCOUNTING AND ITS USE IN BUSINESS DECISIONS

## Learning Objectives

1. Identify and describe the three basic forms of business organizations.
2. Distinguish among the three types of activities performed by business organizations.
3. Describe the contents and purposes of the income statement, statement of retained earnings, balance sheet, and statement of cash flows.
4. State the basic accounting equation and describe its relationship to the balance sheet.
5. Using the underlying assumptions or concepts, analyze business transactions and determine their effects on items in the financial statements.
6. Prepare an income statement, a statement of retained earnings, and a balance sheet.
7. Analyze and use the financial results – the equity ratio.

## REFERENCE OUTLINE

# CHAPTER OUTLINE

*Learning Objective 1:*
*Identify and describe the three basic forms of business organizations.*

## FORMS OF BUSINESS ORGANIZATIONS

1. A business organization is referred to as an accounting or business entity; the three basic forms of business organizations regarding ownership are single proprietorship, partnership, and corporation.

## SINGLE PROPRIETORSHIP

2. A single proprietorship is a business owned by one individual.
   a. This business is often managed by the owner.
   b. No legal formalities are necessary to organize a single proprietorship, and usually only a limited investment is required to begin operations.
   c. In a single proprietorship, the owner is solely responsible for all debts of the business.
   d. The business is considered an entity separate from the owner.

## PARTNERSHIP

3. A business owned by two or more persons associated as partners is a partnership.
   a. Partners often manage the business.
   b. A partnership agreement creates the partnership and sets forth the terms of the business.
      (1) The partnership agreement itemizes the duties of each partner, the initial investment of each partner, and the means of dividing profits or losses between partners.
      (2) A written partnership agreement is preferred over an oral agreement.
   c. Each partner may be held liable for all the debts of the partnership.

## CORPORATION

4. A corporation may be owned by a varying number of persons and is incorporated under the laws of a state.
   a. Owners of the corporation are called stockholders or shareholders.
   b. Stockholders elect a board of directors which then selects officers who manage the corporation.

*Learning Objective 2:*
*Distinguish among the three types of activities performed by business organizations.*

## TYPES OF ACTIVITIES PERFORMED BY BUSINESS ORGANIZATIONS

5. Instead of classifying business entities according to the type of ownership, they can be grouped according to the type of business activities they perform — service companies, merchandising companies, and manufacturing companies.
   a. Service companies perform such services as accounting, cleaning, or legal work for a fee.
   b. Merchandising companies buy goods that are ready for sale and sell them directly to customers.
   c. Manufacturing companies purchase materials and convert them into a different product for sale to other companies or to final customers.

***Learning Objective 3:***
*Describe the contents and purposes of the income statement, statement of retained earnings, balance sheet, and statement of cash flows.*

## FINANCIAL STATEMENTS OF BUSINESS ORGANIZATIONS

## THE INCOME STATEMENT

6. The income statement reports the profitability of a business organization for a stated period of time.
   a. An income statement may be called an earnings statement.
   b. An income statement indicates the revenues earned and the expenses incurred. The difference is net income (if revenues exceed expenses) or a net loss (if expenses exceed revenues.)
      (1) Revenues are defined as the inflow of assets resulting from the sale of products or the rendering of services to customers.
      (2) Expenses are the costs incurred to produce revenues.

## THE STATEMENT OF RETAINED EARNINGS

7. The statement of retained earnings explains the changes in retained earnings that occurred between two balance sheet dates.
   a. Usually these changes consist of adding net income and deducting dividends.
   b. Dividends are payments to the stockholders representing distributions of income.

## THE BALANCE SHEET

8. The balance sheet reflects the company's solvency. Solvency is the ability to pay debts as they become due.
9. A balance sheet lists the company's assets, liabilities, and stockholders' equity at a specific moment in time.
10. A balance sheet is sometimes called the statement of financial position.

## ASSETS

11. Assets are things of value owned by a company.
12. Assets are known as resources and include such items as cash, land, and buildings.

## LIABILITIES

13. Liabilities are debts or obligations owed by a company and usually must be paid by a specific date.
14. Liabilities include amounts owed suppliers for goods purchased with a promise to pay the amount owed at a later date.

## STOCKHOLDERS' EQUITY

15. Stockholders' equity reflects the owners' interest in a company.
16. Stockholders' equity is equal to assets minus liabilities.
17. Stockholders' equity consists of the owners' original investment in a company plus cumulative net income earned through operations minus total dividends distributed to the stockholders.

## THE STATEMENT OF CASH FLOWS

18. The statement of cash flows shows the cash inflows and cash outflows from operating activities, investing activities, and financing activities.
19. At this point in the course you do not need to know how to prepare a statement of cash flows. This statement is covered in detail in Chapter 16.

## THE FINANCIAL ACCOUNTING PROCESS

20. The process of accumulating data to include in financial statements reflects the relationship of assets, liabilities, and stockholders' equity.

***Learning Objective 4:***
*State the basic accounting equation and describe its relationship to the balance sheet.*

## THE ACCOUNTING EQUATION

21. The accounting equation is: Assets = Liabilities + Stockholders' Equity.
    a. The equation must always be in balance.
    b. The right-hand side of the equation (Liabilities + Stockholders' Equity) reflects the equities, since liabilities can be viewed as creditors' equity.
       (1) Equities are claims to or interests in assets.
       (2) The right side of the equation shows who provided the funds to acquire existing assets.

***Learning Objective 5:***
*Using the underlying assumptions or concepts, analyze business transactions and determine their effects on items in the financial statements.*

## ACCOUNTING ASSUMPTIONS

22. Accountants rely on five underlying assumptions or concepts.
    a. The *business entity concept* assumes that each business has an existence separate from its owners, creditors, customers, and employees.
    b. The *money measurement concept* refers to the form of common monetary unit of measure in which economic activity is initially recorded.
    c. The *exchange price (or cost)* indicates that most assets are recorded at their acquisition cost measured in terms of money paid.
    d. The *going-concern (continuity) concept* allows the accountant to assume the business entity will continue operations into the indefinite future unless strong evidence exists to the contrary.
    e. The *periodicity (time periods) concept* allows an entity's life to be subdivided into time periods for purposes of reporting its economic activities.

## ANALYSIS OF TRANSACTIONS

23. Exchanges of goods and services are called transactions.
    a. Transactions provide much of the raw data entered in an accounting process because a transaction is an observable event that occurred at an agree-upon price, which is objective.
    b. The evidence of the transaction is usually a source document.

## TRANSACTIONS AFFECTING ONLY THE BALANCE SHEET

24. Typical transactions affecting only the balance sheet are described below.
    a. Owners invested cash—Increase in cash (asset) and increase in capital stock account (stockholders' equity).
    b. Borrowed money—Increase in cash (asset) and increase in loan payable account (liability).
    c. Purchased equipment (or land) for cash—Increase in equipment (or land, both are assets) and decrease in cash (asset).
    d. Purchased equipment (or land) on credit—Increase in equipment (or land, both are assets) and increase in loan payable (liability).
    e. Paid liability—Decrease in cash (asset) and decrease in accounts or loan payable (liability).

## TRANSACTIONS AFFECTING THE INCOME STATEMENT AND/OR BALANCE SHEET

25. In its effort to use its assets to generate greater amounts of assets, a business typically encounters the following transactions involving revenue and expenses.
    a. Earned service revenue and received cash — Increase in cash (asset) and increase in revenue (retained earnings).
    b. Service revenue earned on account — Increase in accounts receivable (asset) and increase in revenue (retained earnings).
    c. Collected cash on accounts receivable — Increase in cash (asset) and decrease in accounts receivable (asset).
    d. Paid expenses such as wages or rent — Increase in expense (which decreases retained earnings) and decrease in cash (asset).
    e. Received bill for expense incurred during a period such as utilities — Increase in expense (which decreases retained earnings) and increase in accounts payable (liability).

## SUMMARY OF BALANCE SHEET AND INCOME STATEMENT TRANSACTIONS

26. Illustration 1.3 in the text shows the summary of all of the balance sheet and income statement transactions.

***Learning Objective 6:***
*Prepare an income statement, a statement of retained earnings, and a balance sheet.*

27. The income statement and statement of retained earnings can be prepared from the Retained Earnings column.
28. The balance sheet can be prepared using the column totals in the summary of transactions.

## DIVIDENDS PAID TO OWNERS (STOCKHOLDERS)

29. When owners (stockholders) receive assets (such as cash) from the company, the company's assets are decreased and the Dividends account is increased.
    a. Dividends do not appear on the income statement; they appear on the statement of retained earnings.
    b. Dividends are considered a distribution of earnings to the owner.

***Learning Objective 7:***
*Analyze and use the financial results — the equity ratio.*

## ANALYZING AND USING THE FINANCIAL RESULTS — THE EQUITY RATIO

30. The equity ratio is found by dividing stockholders' equity by total equities or total assets.
31. The higher the ratio, the more solvent the company. However, sometimes a lower ratio is an indication of higher profitability because borrowed funds can often earn a higher rate of earnings than the interest incurred.

# DEMONSTRATION PROBLEM

Asset, liability, and stockholders' equity titles for The Martin Service, Inc., are given in equation form below. At the left of the equation is a partial list of transactions completed during the month. Indicate the effect of each transaction on the items in the equation by writing a plus sign (+) below the item that is increased and a minus sign (-) below the item that is decreased.

| | Assets | | | | = Liabilities | + Stockholders' Equity | |
| --- | --- | --- | --- | --- | --- | --- | --- |
| | Cash | + Accts. Rec. | + Equipment | + Land | = Accts. Pay. | + Capital Stock | + Retained Earnings |
| 1. Stockholders invested cash by buying capital stock. | | | | | | | |
| 2. Purchased land for cash. | | | | | | | |
| 3. Performed services for cash customers. | | | | | | | |
| 4. Paid rent for month. | | | | | | | |
| 5. Purchased equipment on account. | | | | | | | |
| 6. Performed services for charge customers. | | | | | | | |
| 7. Paid for equipment purchased earlier on account. | | | | | | | |
| 8. Received payment from charge customers. | | | | | | | |
| 9. Sold equipment at cost for cash at no gain or loss. | | | | | | | |
| 10. Paid dividends to stockholders. | | | | | | | |
| 11. Returned defective equipment (purchased earlier) for cash. | | | | | | | |
| 12. Made cash payment for monthly wages. | | | | | | | |
| 13. Paid utilities for the period. | | | | | | | |

# SOLUTION TO DEMONSTRATION PROBLEM

| | Cash | + Accts. Rec. | + Equipment | + Land | = Accts. Pay. | + Capital Stock | + Retained Earnings |
|---|---|---|---|---|---|---|---|
| 1. Stockholders invested cash by buying capital stock. | + | | | | | + | |
| 2. Purchased land for cash. | − | | | + | | | |
| 3. Performed services for cash customers. | + | | | | | | + |
| 4. Paid rent for month. | − | | | | | | − |
| 5. Purchased equipment on account. | | | + | | + | | |
| 6. Performed services for charge customers. | | + | | | | | + |
| 7. Paid for equipment purchased earlier on account. | − | | | | − | | |
| 8. Received payment from charge customers. | + | − | | | | | |
| 9. Sold equipment at cost for cash at no gain or loss. | + | | − | | | | |
| 10. Paid dividends to stockholders. | − | | | | | | − |
| 11. Returned defective equipment (purchased earlier) for cash. | + | | − | | | | |
| 12. Made cash payment for monthly wages. | − | | | | | | − |
| 13. Paid utilities for the period. | − | | | | | | − |

Column group headers: Assets = Liabilities + Stockholders' Equity

# MATCHING

Referring to the items listed below, place the appropriate letter next to the corresponding description.

*a.* Accounting equation
*b.* Assets
*c.* Corporation
*d.* Dividends
*e.* Liabilities
*f.* Manufacturing company

*g.* Merchandising company
*h.* Net income
*i.* Net loss
*j.* Profitability
*k.* Salaries expense
*l.* Stockholders' equity/ Total equities

*m.* Service company
*n.* Single proprietorship
*o.* Solvency
*p.* Stockholders' equity
*q.* Transactions
*r.* Statement of cash flows

_____ 1. Ability to generate earnings.
_____ 2. Cash paid to stockholders as distribution of income.
_____ 3. Exchanges of goods and services that are objective and that occur at an agreed-upon price.
_____ 4. An organization owned by stockholders and managed by officers who generally are people other than the owners.
_____ 5. Land, buildings, cash, and other resources owned by the business.
_____ 6. This type of business acquires materials and converts them into products to sell to other companies or final customers.
_____ 7. Creditor's equity or claims on assets.
_____ 8. An organization owned by one individual who is solely responsible for all debts of the business.
_____ 9. The resulting figure when expenses exceed revenues.
_____ 10. This type of business acquires goods and sells them in the same form to customers.
_____ 11. Ability to pay debts as they become due.
_____ 12. Stockholders' equity = Assets – Liabilities is one form of this equation.
_____ 13. Shows cash inflows and cash outflows for a period of time.
_____ 14. Equity ratio.

# COMPLETION AND EXERCISES

1. The _____ _____ (sometimes called the statement of financial position) reflects a firm's solvency, while the _____ _____ shows profitability.

2. Accounting deals primarily with information regarding _____ activities of a business and is expressed in _____ terms.

3. _____, _____, and _____ are the three forms of ownership of business organizations.

4. The balance sheet of a business corporation usually shows three classes of items, namely *(a)* _____, *(b)* _____, and *(c)* _____ _____; while the income statement shows two classes, namely, *(a)* _____ and *(b)* _____.

5. In its most basic form, the accounting equation is simply _____ = _____.

   This is usually expanded to _____ = _____ + _____ _____.

6. Changes in the financial position of an organization are brought about by events, exchanges, and other real-world happenings that accountants measure and record and which they call _____.

7. To show your understanding of the effects of each of the named transactions on the assets, liabilities, and stockholders' equity of a business, fill in the blank in each column with either + (for increase), - (for decrease), or 0 (for no change).

|  | Assets | Liabilities | Stockholders' Equity |
|---|---|---|---|
| a. Stockholders invested cash in the business | _____ | _____ | _____ |
| b. Borrowed money from a bank.................. | _____ | _____ | _____ |
| c. Purchased equipment on credit ............... | _____ | _____ | _____ |
| d. Rendered services for cash........................ | _____ | _____ | _____ |
| e. Paid creditor in (c)..................................... | _____ | _____ | _____ |
| f. Paid monthly rent...................................... | _____ | _____ | _____ |
| g. Rendered services for which the customer promised to pay at a later date. | _____ | _____ | _____ |

8. Indicate, by letter, which of the above transactions would be reported in the income statement: _____, _____, and _____.

9. The inflows of assets for services rendered or goods delivered (as measured by the assets received from customers) are called _____, while the assets surrendered or consumed in this process are called _____.

10. The statement that shows the assets and equities of an entity as of a point in time is called the _____ _____.

11. The specific unit or organization for which accounting information is accumulated and reported is called the _____. The basis for valuation of assets in accounting is _____.

12. The _____ concept in accounting refers to the fact that the amounts entered in an accounting system are the objective money prices determined in the exchange process.

13. If expenses for a period exceed revenues for the same period, the entity is deemed to have suffered a _____ _____.

14. An income statement is prepared for a _____, while a balance sheet is prepared as of a _____.

15. Under the _____-_____ concept, the accountant assumes that a business will continue more or less indefinitely.

16. The _____ _____ is equal to stockholders' equity divided by

_____ _____.

17. The _____ _____ _____ _____ shows the cash inflows and cash outflows for a period of time.

18. Indicate the effect each of the following transactions has on the basic accounting equation by indicating one of the following:
   a. Decrease in an asset, decrease in a liability.
   b. Increase in an asset, increase in stockholders' equity.
   c. Increase in one asset, decrease in another asset.
   d. Increase in an asset, increase in a liability.
   e. None of the above.

   _____ 1. Purchased equipment on account.

   _____ 2. Returned an item of defective equipment purchased in (1).

   _____ 3. Paid cash to the supplier of equipment purchased in (1) for the remainder of the equipment.

   _____ 4. Received cash on account from customers.

   _____ 5. The stockholders invested additional cash in the business.

## TRUE-FALSE QUESTIONS

Indicate whether each of the following statements is true or false by inserting a capital "T" or "F" in the blank space provided.

_____ 1. Assets are generally recorded at cost because this amount is the objective price determined in the exchange process.

_____ 2. The laws of incorporation of each state require that the partnership agreement list the duties of each partner and the distribution of income and loss to the partners.

_____ 3. Liabilities represent things of value owned by the business and are also known as resources.

_____ 4. Each partner may be held liable for the actions of other partners when they are acting within the scope of the business.

_____ 5. All increases in cash and accounts receivable represent revenues, which increase retained earnings.

_____ 6. Cash is increased when an outstanding account receivable is collected.

_____ 7. A creditor of the partnership has a claim against an individual partner's personal assets if the partnership has no cash.

_____ 8. The creditors of an organization are the companies and individual customers who owe the business for goods and services purchased on account.

_____ 9. Claims to or interests in assets are referred to as equities.

_____ 10. For an exchange to occur that is recorded as a transaction in the accounting records, both sides of the accounting equation must be affected.

_____ 11. Another way to express the accounting equation is:
Assets – Stockholders' Equity = Liabilities.

_____ 12. Equities are composed of assets and stockholders' equity.

_____ 13. The accounting equation should be in balance only at the end of the year when the income of the period is determined.

_____ 14. The equity ratio is equal to stockholders' equity divided by total assets.

## MULTIPLE CHOICE QUESTIONS

For each of the following questions, indicate the best answer by circling the appropriate letter.

1. The purchase of equipment for cash would:
   A. Decrease an asset and decrease a liability.
   B. Increase an asset and increase a liability.
   C. Increase one asset and decrease another asset.
   D. Increase an asset and increase stockholders' equity.
   E. None of the above.

2. The payment of cash to the supplier of services previously accounted for as a purchase on account would:
   A. Increase an asset and increase a liability.
   B. Increase an asset and increase stockholders' equity.
   C. Increase one asset and decrease another asset.
   D. Decrease an asset and decrease a liability.
   E. None of the above

3. The return of defective equipment to the supplier before it is paid for would:
   A. Increase an asset and increase stockholders' equity.
   B. Decrease an asset and decrease a liability.
   C. Increase an asset and increase a liability.
   D. Increase one asset and decrease another asset.
   E. None of the above.

4. The receipt of cash on account from customers would:
   A. Decrease an asset and decrease a liability.
   B. Increase one asset and decrease another asset.
   C. Increase an asset and increase stockholders' equity.
   D. Increase an asset and increase a liability.
   E. None of the above.

5. Investment of additional cash in the business by the stockholders would:
   A. Decrease an asset and decrease a liability.
   B. Increase an asset and increase a liability.
   C. Increase an asset and increase stockholders' equity.
   D. Increase one asset and decrease another asset.
   E. None of the above.

6. In accounting, the resources of a business organization are called:

   A. Assets.
   B. Proprietorship.
   C. Creditors' equity.
   D. Stockholders' equity.
   E. None of the above.

7. The payment of business debts:

   A. Increases a liability account.
   B. Increases stockholders' equity.
   C. Has no effect on stockholders' equity.
   D. Increases assets.

8. If liabilities have increased by exactly the same amount that assets have increased, stockholders' equity will have:

   A. Remained the same.
   B. Decreased.
   C. Increased.
   D. Decreased more than increased.

9. A financial statement that has a date line similar to "For the month ended June 30, 19x1," is a(n):

   A. Schedule of accounts receivable.
   B. Balance sheet.
   C. Income statement.
   D. None of the above.

10. Gomex Company collected $600 of its $12,000 accounts receivable. How is the balance sheet affected?

   A. Cash increased $600, and Retained Earnings increased $600 because revenue was received.
   B. Accounts Receivable is decreased by $600, and Retained Earnings is decreased by $600.
   C. Total assets are decreased, but liabilities and stockholders' equity remain the same.
   D. There is no change in total assets, liabilities, or stockholders' equity.
   E. There is no change in any of the balance sheet items.

11. The statement of cash flows shows cash inflows and cash outflows from (select the false statement):

   A. Operating activities.
   B. Investing activities.
   C. Intangible activities.
   D. Financing activities.

# SOLUTIONS

## Matching

| | | | | |
|---|---|---|---|---|
| 1. | j | | 8. | n |
| 2. | d | | 9. | i |
| 3. | q | | 10. | g |
| 4. | c | | 11. | o |
| 5. | b | | 12. | a |
| 6. | f | | 13. | r |
| 7. | e | | 14. | l |

## Completion and Exercises

1. balance sheet; income statement
2. economic; monetary
3. Single proprietorship, partnership, and corporation
4. (a) assets; (b) liabilities; (c) stockholders' equity; (a) revenues; (b) expenses
5. Assets = Equities; Assets = Liabilities + Stockholders' equity
6. transactions
7.

| | Assets | Liabilities | Stockholders' Equity |
|---|---|---|---|
| a. | + | 0 | + |
| b. | + | + | 0 |
| c. | + | + | 0 |
| d. | + | 0 | + |
| e. | − | − | 0 |
| f. | − | 0 | − |
| g. | + | 0 | + |

8. (d), (f), and (g)
9. revenues; expenses
10. balance sheet
11. entity; cost
12. cost
13. net loss
14. period; date
15. going-concern
16. equity ratio; total equities
17. statement of cash flows
18. 1. d
    2. a
    3. a
    4. c
    5. b

## True-False Questions

1. T
2. F    The partnership agreement lists the duties of each partner and the income and loss distribution. Each state's laws of incorporation apply to corporations.
3. F    This statement is the definition of assets; liabilities are debts of the business.

4. T

5. F  Cash received from a customer on account does not necessarily represent revenue; revenue is recognized at the time the service is performed, not when cash is received. However, it is true that revenues increase retained earnings.

6. T

7. T

8. F  The creditors are the companies and individuals to whom debts of the company are owed. This statement describes customers.

9. T

10. F  A transaction may occur that involves only one side of the equation; for example, cash received from a customer in payment of an account receivable.

11. T

12. F  Equities are composed of liabilities (creditors' equity) and stockholders' equity.

13. F  The accounting equation should be in balance at all times.

14. T  The amount of total assets is equal to total stockholders' equity.

## Multiple Choice Questions

1. C

2. D

3. B

4. B

5. C

6. A

7. C  Cash is decreased and liabilities are decreased; thus, there is no effect on stockholders' equity.

8. A

9. C

10. D  Cash and accounts receivable are both assets, and total assets do not change.

11. C  The cash flow statement reports cash inflows and outflows from operating, investing, and financing activities.

# CHAPTER 2

# RECORDING BUSINESS TRANSACTIONS

*Learning Objectives*

1. *Use the account as the basic classifying and storage unit for accounting information.*
2. *Express the effects of business transactions in terms of debits and credits to different types of accounts.*
3. *List the steps in the accounting cycle.*
4. *Record the effects of business transactions in a journal.*
5. *Post journal entries to the accounts in the ledger.*
6. *Prepare a trial balance to test the equality of debits and credits in the journalizing and posting process.*
7. *Analyze and use the financial results — horizontal and vertical analysis.*

## REFERENCE OUTLINE

*Learning Objective 1:*
*Use the account as the basic classifying and storage unit for accounting information.*

## THE ACCOUNT AND RULES OF DEBIT AND CREDIT

1. Steps in recording and posting the effects of a business transaction are:
   a. The company enters into a business transaction.
   b. The business transaction is evidenced by a source document.
   c. The source document serves as the basis for preparing a journal entry.
   d. The journal entry is posted to accounts in the ledger.

## THE ACCOUNT

2. An account is used to classify and summarize measurements of business activity.
   a. Accounts are established where it is necessary to provide useful information about particular business items.
   b. A variety of formats can be used for accounts, such as a printed format in a bound book or an invisible encoding on magnetic tape.
   c. Every account format must provide for increases and decreases in that particular item.
   d. The number of accounts will vary in an accounting system.
   e. The primary requirement is that the account provide useful information.

## THE T-ACCOUNT

3. The T-account format is used in the textbook for illustration, with increases recorded on one side and decreases on the opposite side of the T-account.

*Learning Objective 2:*
*Express the effects of business transactions in terms of debits and credits to different types of accounts.*

## DEBITS AND CREDITS

4. Debits are entries on the left side of the ledger account.
   a. Dr. is the abbreviation, and another name for debit is "charge."
   b. A debit entry simply means an entry on the left side.
5. Credits are entries on the right side of the ledger account.
   a. Cr. is the abbreviation for a credit.
   b. The right side of *all* accounts is the credit side, and the left side is the debit side.

## DOUBLE-ENTRY PROCEDURE

6. *Increases* in *assets* are recorded on the debit, or left, side, while decreases are recorded on the credit, or right, side.
7. Since liabilities and stockholders' equity are on the opposite side (to assets) of the accounting equation, increases and decreases are recorded opposite to assets.
   a. Increases in liabilities and stockholders' equity are credits.
   b. Decreases in liabilities and stockholders' equity are debits.
8. Expenses and revenues theoretically could be recorded directly in the Retained Earnings account; but the volume of transactions involved prevents this approach from being recommended.
   a. Instead, expense and revenue ledger accounts are established.
      (1) Increases in revenues are recorded as credits and decreases as debits. (Note that revenues increase retained earnings.)
      (2) Increases in expenses are recorded as debits, and decreases as credits. (Note that expenses decrease retained earnings.)
9. Distributions of assets to the stockholders are recorded in a separate account and have the same effect as expenses on stockholders' equity.
   a. The Dividends account is increased by debits and decreased by credits.

## DETERMING THE BALANCE OF AN ACCOUNT

10. The balance of an account is determined by subtracting the smaller sum of the debit or credit side from the larger total; if the sum of the credits exceeds the debit total, the account has a credit balance.

## NORMAL BALANCES

11. The normal balances follow the pattern of increases in the account.

| Type of Account | Normal Balance |
|---|---|
| Assets | Debit |
| Expenses | Debit |
| Dividends | Debit |
| Liabilities | Credit |
| Stockholders' Equity | Credit |
| Revenue | Credit |

## RULES OF DEBIT AND CREDIT SUMMARIZED

12. The double-entry procedure, which keeps the accounting equation in balance, requires that an entry must have equal debit and credit amounts.

*Learning Objective 3:*
*List the steps in the accounting cycle.*

## THE ACCOUNTING CYCLE

13. The accounting cycle consists of a series of steps related to gathering, classifying, and reporting useful financial information. The steps in the accounting cycle and the chapter(s) in which they are discussed are given below along with when the steps are performed.

*Performed during Accounting Period*

a. Analyze transactions by examining source documents (Chapters 1 and 2).
b. Journalize transactions in the journal (Chapter 2).
c. Post journal entries to the accounts in the ledger (Chapter 2).

*Performed at End of Accounting Period*

d. Prepare a trial balance of the accounts (Chapter 2) and complete the work sheet (Chapter 4).
e. Prepare financial statements (Chapter 4).
f. Journalize and post adjusting entries (Chapters 3 and 4).
g. Journalize and post closing entries (Chapter 4).
h. Prepare a post-closing trial balance (Chapter 4).

*Learning Objective 4:*
*Record the effects of business transactions in a journal.*

## THE JOURNAL

14. A journal is a record of business transactions arranged in order of time.
a. A journal entry reflects the effects of a business transaction expressed in debits and credits.
b. A journal is called the book of original entry because each transaction is recorded here first.

# THE GENERAL JOURNAL

15. A general journal contains:
    a. Date column—the first entry on a page contains year, month, and day; for other entries, only the day is shown until the month changes.
    b. Account titles and explanation column—the first line shows the account debited and the second line shows the account credited. An explanation is included on the next line if needed.
    c. Posting reference column—shows the account number to which the debit or credit amount has been posted in the ledger.
    d. Debit column—where the debit amount is placed.
    e. Credit column—where the credit amount is placed.

# JOURNALIZING

16. Journalizing is the recording in terms of debits and credits of the effects on specific accounts of business information from source documents.

# FUNCTIONS AND ADVANTAGES OF A JOURNAL

17. The functions and advantages of using a journal are:
    a. Records each transaction in chronological order.
    b. Shows the analysis of each transaction in terms of debit and credit.
    c. Supplies an explanation of each transaction when necessary.
    d. Serves as a source for future reference to accounting transactions.
    e. Eliminates the need for lengthy explanations from the accounts.
    f. Makes possible posting to the ledger at convenient times.
    g. Assists in maintaining the ledger in balance because the debit(s) must always equal the credit(s) in each journal entry.
    h. Aids in tracing errors when the ledger is not in balance.

# THE LEDGER

18. The ledger contains all the company's accounts, which are classified into balance sheet accounts and income statement accounts.
    a. Balance sheet accounts are called *real* accounts because they are not subdivisions of other accounts.
    b. Income statement accounts are called *nominal* accounts because they are subdivisions of stockholders' equity accounts.
    c. A complete listing of all accounts in the ledger with their titles and account numbers is known as the *chart of accounts*.
    d. The typical sequencing of the accounts in the ledger is: assets, liabilities, stockholders' equity, dividends, revenues, and expenses.

# THE ACCOUNTING PROCESS IN OPERATION

19. The text contains a detailed illustration of the accounting process in operation.

# THE RECORDING OF TRANSACTIONS AND THEIR EFFECTS ON THE ACCOUNTS

20. Examples of transactions and their effects on accounts are given in the text.

# THE USE OF THREE-COLUMN LEDGER ACCOUNTS

21. In practice, companies normally use three-column ledger accounts rather than T-accounts.

*Learning Objective 5:*
*Post journal entries to the accounts in the ledger.*

22. Posting is recording in the ledger the information contained in the journal.
    a. Posting carries out the instructions in the journal.
    b. Posting may be made to a three-column ledger account, which has columns for debit, credit, and balance.

## CROSS-INDEXING (REFERENCING)

23. Cross-indexing is a means by which the journal and the ledger are tied together; it involves placing the account number in the journal's posting reference column and placing the journal page number in the ledger account.

## COMPOUND JOURNAL ENTRIES

24. A *compound journal entry* has more than one debit and/or credit, while a simple journal entry has only one debit and one credit.

## POSTING AND CROSS-INDEXING — AN ILLUSTRATION

25. Illustrations 2.6 and 2.7 in the text illustrate the journalizing and posting process.

*Learning Objective 6:*
*Prepare a trial balance to test the equality of debits and credits in the journalizing and posting process.*

## THE TRIAL BALANCE

26. A trial balance lists the ledger accounts and their debit and credit balances to determine that debits equal credits.
    a. A trial balance is a means of checking the equality of debits and credits.
    b. An inequality of debit and credit column totals signals an error; however, an error may be present even if these totals are equal.
    c. A trial balance may be prepared at any time, but one is usually prepared only before financial statements are prepared.

*Learning Objective 7:*
*Analyze and use the financial results — horizontal and vertical analysis.*

## ANALYZING AND USING THE FINANCIAL RESULTS — HORIZONTAL AND VERTICAL ANALYSIS

27. Horizontal analysis shows the calculation of dollar and/or percentage changes from one year to the next. Knowing the dollar amount and percentage of change in an amount is much more meaningful than merely knowing the amount at one point in time.

28. Vertical analysis shows the percentage that each item in a financial statement is of some significant total such as total assets or sales. Management performs horizontal and vertical analysis along with other types of analysis to help evaluate the wisdom of its past decisions and to plan for the future.

## DEMONSTRATION PROBLEM

Dexter Company informs you that the following business transactions occurred in 1999.

May 1 Stockholders exchanged $15,000 cash and equipment with a value of $4,000 for capital stock.

1 A building costing $39,000 and land costing $20,000 were purchased. Cash in the amount of $5,000 was paid and a mortgage note was given for the remainder.

2 Premiums for property insurance were paid in the amount of $1,500 for May.

3 Supplies costing $500 and equipment costing $6,000 were purchased on account.

15 Cash received for professional services performed, $5,600; other clients were billed for services in the amount of $2,430.

16 Paid cash to creditors on account, $1,800.

20 Returned portion of the supplies costing $240 since they were not of the proper grade.

22 Received $1,880 cash from clients on account.

31 Paid utility bill for May, $500.

31 Paid monthly salaries, $3,000.

31 Recorded additional amount owed by clients for services performed in May, $4,900; payment is due within 30 days.

*Required:*

a. Open three-column ledger accounts for Dexter Company using the following accounts:

| | |
|---|---|
| Cash | Mortgage Note Payable |
| Accounts Receivable | Capital Stock |
| Supplies on Hand | Service Revenue |
| Equipment | Salaries Expense |
| Buildings | Utilities Expense |
| Land | Insurance Expense |
| Accounts Payable | |

Use the account numbers shown in the chart of accounts on the inside cover of your text.

Record the above transactions in a general journal. (Omit explanations.)

b. Post the journal entries to the ledger accounts. (Omit explanations.)

c. Prepare a trial balance as of May 31, 1999.

d. Determine the following:

(1) Total revenue for the month.

(2) Total expenses for the month.

*a.*

# GENERAL JOURNAL

| Date | Account Titles and Explanation | Post. Ref. | Debit | Credit |
|------|-------------------------------|-----------|-------|--------|
|      |                               |           |       |        |
|      |                               |           |       |        |
|      |                               |           |       |        |
|      |                               |           |       |        |
|      |                               |           |       |        |
|      |                               |           |       |        |
|      |                               |           |       |        |
|      |                               |           |       |        |
|      |                               |           |       |        |
|      |                               |           |       |        |
|      |                               |           |       |        |
|      |                               |           |       |        |
|      |                               |           |       |        |
|      |                               |           |       |        |
|      |                               |           |       |        |
|      |                               |           |       |        |
|      |                               |           |       |        |
|      |                               |           |       |        |
|      |                               |           |       |        |
|      |                               |           |       |        |
|      |                               |           |       |        |
|      |                               |           |       |        |
|      |                               |           |       |        |
|      |                               |           |       |        |
|      |                               |           |       |        |
|      |                               |           |       |        |
|      |                               |           |       |        |
|      |                               |           |       |        |
|      |                               |           |       |        |
|      |                               |           |       |        |
|      |                               |           |       |        |
|      |                               |           |       |        |
|      |                               |           |       |        |
|      |                               |           |       |        |
|      |                               |           |       |        |
|      |                               |           |       |        |
|      |                               |           |       |        |
|      |                               |           |       |        |

*b.* _____

ACCOUNT NO.

| Date | Explanation | Post. Ref. | Debit | Credit | Balance |
|------|-------------|-----------|-------|--------|---------|
|      |             |           |       |        |         |
|      |             |           |       |        |         |
|      |             |           |       |        |         |
|      |             |           |       |        |         |
|      |             |           |       |        |         |
|      |             |           |       |        |         |
|      |             |           |       |        |         |
|      |             |           |       |        |         |
|      |             |           |       |        |         |
|      |             |           |       |        |         |
|      |             |           |       |        |         |
|      |             |           |       |        |         |
|      |             |           |       |        |         |

ACCOUNT NO.

| Date | Explanation | Post. Ref. | Debit | Credit | Balance |
|------|-------------|-----------|-------|--------|---------|
|      |             |           |       |        |         |
|      |             |           |       |        |         |
|      |             |           |       |        |         |
|      |             |           |       |        |         |
|      |             |           |       |        |         |
|      |             |           |       |        |         |
|      |             |           |       |        |         |
|      |             |           |       |        |         |

ACCOUNT NO.

| Date | Explanation | Post. Ref. | Debit | Credit | Balance |
|------|-------------|-----------|-------|--------|---------|
|      |             |           |       |        |         |
|      |             |           |       |        |         |
|      |             |           |       |        |         |
|      |             |           |       |        |         |

*b. (continued)*

ACCOUNT NO.

| Date | Explanation | Post. Ref. | Debit | Credit | Balance |
|------|-------------|------------|-------|--------|---------|
|  |  |  |  |  |  |
|  |  |  |  |  |  |

ACCOUNT NO.

| Date | Explanation | Post. Ref. | Debit | Credit | Balance |
|------|-------------|------------|-------|--------|---------|
|  |  |  |  |  |  |
|  |  |  |  |  |  |

ACCOUNT NO.

| Date | Explanation | Post. Ref. | Debit | Credit | Balance |
|------|-------------|------------|-------|--------|---------|
|  |  |  |  |  |  |
|  |  |  |  |  |  |

ACCOUNT NO.

| Date | Explanation | Post. Ref. | Debit | Credit | Balance |
|------|-------------|------------|-------|--------|---------|
|  |  |  |  |  |  |
|  |  |  |  |  |  |
|  |  |  |  |  |  |

ACCOUNT NO.

| Date | Explanation | Post. Ref. | Debit | Credit | Balance |
|------|-------------|------------|-------|--------|---------|
|  |  |  |  |  |  |
|  |  |  |  |  |  |

ACCOUNT NO.

| Date | Explanation | Post. Ref. | Debit | Credit | Balance |
|------|-------------|------------|-------|--------|---------|
|  |  |  |  |  |  |
|  |  |  |  |  |  |

ACCOUNT NO.

| Date | | Explanation | Post. Ref. | Debit | | Credit | | Balance | |
|---|---|---|---|---|---|---|---|---|---|
| | | | | | | | | | |
| | | | | | | | | | |
| | | | | | | | | | |

ACCOUNT NO.

| Date | | Explanation | Post. Ref. | Debit | | Credit | | Balance | |
|---|---|---|---|---|---|---|---|---|---|
| | | | | | | | | | |
| | | | | | | | | | |
| | | | | | | | | | |

ACCOUNT NO.

| Date | | Explanation | Post. Ref. | Debit | | Credit | | Balance | |
|---|---|---|---|---|---|---|---|---|---|
| | | | | | | | | | |
| | | | | | | | | | |

ACCOUNT NO.

| Date | | Explanation | Post. Ref. | Debit | | Credit | | Balance | |
|---|---|---|---|---|---|---|---|---|---|
| | | | | | | | | | |
| | | | | | | | | | |

*c.*

| | | | | | | | | | |
|---|---|---|---|---|---|---|---|---|---|
| | | | | | | | | | |
| | | | | | | | | | |
| | | | | | | | | | |
| | | | | | | | | | |
| | | | | | | | | | |
| | | | | | | | | | |
| | | | | | | | | | |
| | | | | | | | | | |
| | | | | | | | | | |
| | | | | | | | | | |
| | | | | | | | | | |
| | | | | | | | | | |
| | | | | | | | | | |
| | | | | | | | | | |
| | | | | | | | | | |
| | | | | | | | | | |
| | | | | | | | | | |
| | | | | | | | | | |
| | | | | | | | | | |

*d.*  (1)

(2)

*a.*

### DEXTER COMPANY
### General Journal

Page 1

| DATE | ACCOUNT TITLES AND EXPLANATIONS | POST REF. | DEBIT | CREDIT |
|------|----------------------------------|-----------|-------|--------|
| 1999 | | | | |
| May 1 | Cash | 100 | 15,000 | |
| | Equipment | 170 | 4,000 | |
| | Capital Stock | 300 | | 19,000 |
| 1 | Buildings | 140 | 39,000 | |
| | Land | 130 | 20,000 | |
| | Cash | 100 | | 5,000 |
| | Mortgage Note Payable | 218 | | 54,000 |
| 2 | Insurance Expense | 512 | 1,500 | |
| | Cash | 100 | | 1,500 |
| 3 | Supplies on Hand | 107 | 500 | |
| | Equipment | 170 | 6,000 | |
| | Accounts Payable | 200 | | 6,500 |
| 15 | Cash | 100 | 5,600 | |
| | Accounts Receivable | 103 | 2,430 | |
| | Service Revenue | 400 | | 8,030 |
| 16 | Accounts Payable | 200 | 1,800 | |
| | Cash | 100 | | 1,800 |
| 20 | Accounts Payable | 200 | 240 | |
| | Supplies on Hand | 107 | | 240 |
| 22 | Cash | 100 | 1,880 | |
| | Accounts Receivable | 103 | | 1,880 |
| 31 | Utilities Expense | 511 | 500 | |
| | Cash | 100 | | 500 |
| 31 | Salaries Expense | 507 | 3,000 | |
| | Cash | 100 | | 3,000 |
| 31 | Accounts Receivable | 103 | 4,900 | |
| | Service Revenue | 400 | | 4,900 |

*b.*

## DEXTER COMPANY
### General Ledger

### Cash        ACCOUNT NO. 100

| DATE | EXPLANATION | POST. REF. | DEBIT | CREDIT | BALANCE |
|---|---|---|---|---|---|
| 1999 | | | | | |
| May 1 | | G1 | 15,000 | | 15,000 Dr. |
| 1 | | G1 | | 5,000 | 10,000 Dr. |
| 2 | | G1 | | 1,500 | 8,500 Dr. |
| 15 | | G1 | 5,600 | | 14,100 Dr. |
| 16 | | G1 | | 1,800 | 12,300 Dr. |
| 22 | | G1 | 1,880 | | 14,180 Dr. |
| 31 | | G1 | | 500 | 13,680 Dr. |
| 31 | | G1 | | 3,000 | 10,680 Dr. |

### Accounts Receivable      ACCOUNT NO. 103

| DATE | EXPLANATION | POST. REF. | DEBIT | CREDIT | BALANCE |
|---|---|---|---|---|---|
| 1999 | | | | | |
| May 15 | | G1 | 2,430 | | 2,430 DR. |
| 22 | | G1 | | 1,880 | 550 DR. |
| 31 | | G1 | 4,900 | | 5,450 DR. |

### Supplies on Hand       ACCOUNT NO. 107

| DATE | EXPLANATION | POST. REF. | DEBIT | CREDIT | BALANCE |
|---|---|---|---|---|---|
| 1999 | | | | | |
| May 3 | | G1 | 500 | | 500 Dr. |
| 20 | | G1 | | 240 | 260 Dr. |

### Land          ACCOUNT NO. 130

| DATE | EXPLANATION | POST. REF. | DEBIT | CREDIT | BALANCE |
|---|---|---|---|---|---|
| 1999 | | | | | |
| May 1 | | G1 | 20,000 | | 20,000 Dr. |

### Buildings        ACCOUNT NO. 140

| DATE | EXPLANATION | POST. REF. | DEBIT | CREDIT | BALANCE |
|---|---|---|---|---|---|
| 1999 | | | | | |
| May 1 | | G1 | 39,000 | | 39,000 Dr. |

### Equipment        ACCOUNT NO. 170

| DATE | EXPLANATION | POST. REF. | DEBIT | CREDIT | BALANCE |
|---|---|---|---|---|---|
| 1999 | | | | | |
| May 1 | | G1 | 4,000 | | 4,000 Dr. |
| 3 | | G1 | 6,000 | | 10,000 Dr. |

## Accounts Payable
ACCOUNT NO. 200

| DATE | EXPLANATION | POST. REF. | DEBIT | CREDIT | BALANCE |
|------|-------------|------------|-------|--------|---------|
| 1999 | | | | | |
| May  3 | | G1 | | 6,500 | 6,500 Cr. |
| 16 | | G1 | 1,800 | | 4,700 Cr. |
| 20 | | G1 | 240 | | 4,460 Cr. |

## Mortgage Note Payable
ACCOUNT NO. 218

| DATE | EXPLANATION | POST. REF. | DEBIT | CREDIT | BALANCE |
|------|-------------|------------|-------|--------|---------|
| 1999 | | | | | |
| May  1 | | G1 | | 54,000 | 54,000 Cr. |

## Capital Stock
ACCOUNT NO. 300

| DATE | EXPLANATION | POST. REF. | DEBIT | CREDIT | BALANCE |
|------|-------------|------------|-------|--------|---------|
| 1999 | | | | | |
| May  1 | | G1 | | 19,000 | 19,000 Cr. |

## Service Revenue
ACCOUNT NO. 400

| DATE | EXPLANATION | POST. REF. | DEBIT | CREDIT | BALANCE |
|------|-------------|------------|-------|--------|---------|
| 1999 | | | | | |
| May 15 | | G1 | | 8,030 | 8,030 Cr. |
| 31 | | G1 | | 4,900 | 12,930 Cr. |

## Salaries Expense
ACCOUNT NO. 507

| DATE | EXPLANATION | POST. REF. | DEBIT | CREDIT | BALANCE |
|------|-------------|------------|-------|--------|---------|
| 1999 | | | | | |
| May 31 | | G1 | 3,000 | | 3,000 Dr. |

## Utilities Expense
ACCOUNT NO. 511

| DATE | EXPLANATION | POST. REF. | DEBIT | CREDIT | BALANCE |
|------|-------------|------------|-------|--------|---------|
| 1999 | | | | | |
| May 31 | | G1 | 500 | | 500 Dr. |

## Insurance Expense
ACCOUNT NO. 512

| DATE | EXPLANATION | POST. REF. | DEBIT | CREDIT | BALANCE |
|------|-------------|------------|-------|--------|---------|
| 1999 | | | | | |
| May  2 | | G1 | 1,500 | | 1,500 Dr. |

DEXTER COMPANY
Trial Balance
May 31, 1999

*Acct.*
*No.*

| | | | |
|---|---|---|---|
| 100 | Cash | $10,680 | |
| 103 | Accounts Receivable | 5,450 | |
| 107 | Supplies on Hand | 260 | |
| 130 | Land | 20,000 | |
| 140 | Buildings | 39,000 | |
| 170 | Equipment | 10,000 | |
| 200 | Accounts Payable | | $ 4,460 |
| 218 | Mortgage Note Payable | | 54,000 |
| 300 | Capital Stock | | 19,000 |
| 400 | Service Revenue | | 12,930 |
| 507 | Salaries Expense | 3,000 | |
| 511 | Utilities Expense | 500 | |
| 512 | Insurance Expense | 1,500 | |
| | | $90,390 | $90,390 |

d.  (1) $12,930
(2) $5,000 = ($3,000 + $500 + $1,500)

---

**MATCHING**

---

Referring to the terms listed below, place the appropriate letter next to the corresponding description.

| | | |
|---|---|---|
| a. Charge | g. Expenses | m. Simple journal entry |
| b. Compound journal entry | h. Journal | n. Trial balance |
| c. Credit side | i. Journalizing | o. Vertical analysis. |
| d. Cross-indexing | j. Nominal accounts | p. Horizontal analysis |
| e. Debit side | k. Posting | q. The accounting cycle |
| f. Double entry | l. Real accounts | |

_____ 1. Synonym for debt.

_____ 2. Cost of the use of services or consumption of assets for the purpose of generating revenue.

_____ 3. Entry involving more than one debit and/or credit.

_____ 4. Recording in the ledger the information contained in the journal.

_____ 5. Entering of a transaction in the book of original entry.

_____ 6. The right side of an account.

_____ 7. This procedure is related to the duality concept indicating that every transaction has a two-sided effect.

_____ 8. Revenue and expense accounts that appear on the income statement.

_____ 9. Placing of the ledger account numbers in the posting reference column of the journal and placing the journal page number in the posting reference column of the ledger account.

_____ 10. A chronological record of all business transactions that may also be called the book of original entry.

_____ 11.  Entry involving only one debit and one credit.

_____ 12.  Provides a proof of the arithmetic accuracy of the recording process by listing the ledger accounts and their debit or credit balances.

_____ 13.  Shows the calculation of dollar and/or percentage changes from one year to the next.

_____ 14.  Shows the percentage that each item in a financial statement is of some significant total such as total assets or sales.

_____ 15.  A series of steps performed during the accounting period to analyze, record, classify, summarize, and report useful financial information for the purpose of preparing financial statements.

## COMPLETION AND EXERCISES

1. The act of entering a transaction in a journal is called _____. After a transaction is so entered, it is _____ from the journal to the _____, at which time a process known as _____ _____ also takes place so that amounts in the accounts can be readily traced to the original record of each transaction.

2. Accountants do not speak in terms of increases and decreases. Rather, they use technical terminology. Thus, to _____ an account means to place an entry on the left side of the account; to _____ an account means to place an entry on the right side of the account.

3. The _____ _____ procedure requires that an entry has equal debits and credits, which keeps the accounting equation in balance.

4. For each of the following T-accounts, indicate on which side increases are recorded and on which side decreases are recorded:

| Assets | Liabilities | Stockholders' Equity |
|---|---|---|
|  |  |  |

5. From Question 4 it follows that assets, which appear on the left side of a balance sheet, will have balances on the _____ side of the account. Conversely, liabilities and stockholders'' equity items will appear on the right side of the balance sheet and have balances on the _____ side of the account.

6. Fill in the blanks below with the word _debits_ or _credits_:

| Type of account | Increased by | Decreased by |
|---|---|---|
| Asset............................. | _____ | _____ |
| Liability......................... | _____ | _____ |
| Stockholders' equity ................. | _____ | _____ |
| Revenue........................... | _____ | _____ |
| Expense ..................................... | _____ | _____ |

7. A _____ _____ contains a listing of the ledger accounts and their debit or credit balances to determine that _____ equal _____ in the recording process.

8. Collectively, all of the accounts in the accounting system are referred to as the _____. The list of accounts in an accounting system (often together with their numbers) is called the _____ _____ _____.

9. The basic unit in which data are stored in an accounting system is called an _____. These storage units should be so constructed as to readily receive money measurements of the _____ or _____ in the items for which they are established.

10. Whether or not an account is established is determined largely by whether or not it will provide _____ _____.

11. The difference between the amounts entered as increases in an account and those entered as decreases is called the _____ of the account.

12. Since revenues increase Retained Earnings and increases in Retained Earnings are recorded on the _____ side of the account, it follows that increases in revenues are recorded on the _____ side of the account.

13. Since expenses decrease Retained Earnings and since decreases in Retained Earnings are recorded on the _____ side of the account, it follows that increases in expenses are recorded on the _____ side of the account.

14. The financial accounting process has been shown to consist of eight steps, namely:

    1. _____

    2. _____

    3. _____

    4. _____

    5. _____

    6. _____

    7. _____

    8. _____

15. Prepare journal entries for the company that engaged in the following transactions:
    Jan.  1  Stockholders invested $10,000 cash in the business.
         10  Paid the rent for January, $100.
         13  Performed services for customers who promised to pay later, $125.
         20  Purchased equipment for $2,000 with a promise to pay later.
         30  Received payment for the services rendered on January 13.

### GENERAL JOURNAL

Page 1

| Date | Account Titles and Explanation | Post. Ref. | Debit | Credit |
|------|-------------------------------|------------|-------|--------|
|      |                               |            |       |        |
|      |                               |            |       |        |
|      |                               |            |       |        |
|      |                               |            |       |        |
|      |                               |            |       |        |
|      |                               |            |       |        |
|      |                               |            |       |        |
|      |                               |            |       |        |
|      |                               |            |       |        |
|      |                               |            |       |        |
|      |                               |            |       |        |
|      |                               |            |       |        |
|      |                               |            |       |        |
|      |                               |            |       |        |
|      |                               |            |       |        |
|      |                               |            |       |        |
|      |                               |            |       |        |
|      |                               |            |       |        |
|      |                               |            |       |        |
|      |                               |            |       |        |

16. Post the journal entries prepared in Question 15. Use the chart of accounts on the inside covers of your text to assign account numbers.

| Date | Explanation | Post. Ref. | Debit | Credit | Balance |
|------|-------------|------------|-------|--------|---------|
|      |             |            |       |        |         |
|      |             |            |       |        |         |
|      |             |            |       |        |         |
|      |             |            |       |        |         |
|      |             |            |       |        |         |
|      |             |            |       |        |         |

| Date | Explanation | Post. Ref. | Debit | Credit | Balance |
|------|-------------|------------|-------|--------|---------|
|      |             |            |       |        |         |
|      |             |            |       |        |         |

| Date | Explanation | Post. Ref. | Debit | Credit | Balance |
|------|-------------|------------|-------|--------|---------|
|      |             |            |       |        |         |
|      |             |            |       |        |         |
|      |             |            |       |        |         |

| Date | Explanation | Post. Ref. | Debit | Credit | Balance |
|------|-------------|------------|-------|--------|---------|
|      |             |            |       |        |         |
|      |             |            |       |        |         |
|      |             |            |       |        |         |

| Date | Explanation | Post. Ref. | Debit | Credit | Balance |
|------|-------------|------------|-------|--------|---------|
|      |             |            |       |        |         |
|      |             |            |       |        |         |
|      |             |            |       |        |         |

| Date | Explanation | Post. Ref. | Debit | Credit | Balance |
|------|-------------|------------|-------|--------|---------|
|      |             |            |       |        |         |
|      |             |            |       |        |         |
|      |             |            |       |        |         |

| Date | Explanation | Post. Ref. | Debit | Credit | Balance |
|------|-------------|-----------|-------|--------|---------|
|      |             |           |       |        |         |
|      |             |           |       |        |         |
|      |             |           |       |        |         |

17. A _____ is often called a book of original entry and contains a chronological record of the transactions of a business. Before a transaction can be entered in this book of original entry, its effects on the business must be determined and encoded in terms of _____ and _____.

18. The properties used by a business are known as _____; whereas the rights in the properties of a business are known as _____.

19. A sale made to a customer or client is recorded as an increase in a revenue account and an increase in an _____ account.

20. The total assets of the Miller Service Company are $22,000 and the total liabilities are $10,000. Therefore, the total stockholders' equity is $_____.

21. An entry on the left side of an account is known as a _____.

22. At the start of a year, a company had liabilities of $35,000 and stockholders' equity of $150,000. Net income for the year was $50,000, and $11,000 cash was distributed to the stockholders as dividends. Compute stockholders' equity at the end of the year and total assets at the beginning of the year.

Stockholders' equity at the end of year: _____

Total assets at beginning of year: _____

23. Explain each of the sets of debits and credits shown in the accounts below. There are 12 transactions to be explained. Each set is designated by the small letters to the left of the account.

### Cash

| | | | |
|------|--------|------|--------|
| (a) | 75,000 | (c) | 20,000 |
| (d) | 1,500  | (e) | 1,000  |
|     |        | (g) | 500    |
|     |        | (j) | 1,800  |
|     |        | (k) | 200    |

### Accounts Receivable

| | | | |
|------|--------|------|--------|
| (b) | 2,600 | (d) | 1,500 |
| (i) | 5,000 |     |       |

### Supplies

| | | | |
|------|------|------|------|
| (f) | 800 | (h) | 100 |

| Service Equipment | |
|---|---|
| (c) 20,000 | |
| (l) 40,000 | |

| Accounts Payable | |
|---|---|
| (g) 500 | (f) 800 |
| (h) 100 | (l) 40,000 |

| Capital Stock | |
|---|---|
| | (a) 75,000 |

| Service Revenue | |
|---|---|
| | (b) 2,600 |
| | (i) 5,000 |

| Salaries Expense | |
|---|---|
| (e) 1,000 | |

| Rent Expense | |
|---|---|
| (j) 1,800 | |

| Utilities Expense | |
|---|---|
| (k) 200 | |

24. At the beginning of 1999, the total assets of Hardy Corp were $2,500,000, the total liabilities were $1,500,000, and the stockholders' equity was $1,000,000. Hardy has earned $500,000 in 1999 and paid dividends of $50,000. The only transaction that affected Hardy's liability accounts was the redemption of its notes payable, $100,000. Compute total assets, total liabilities, and stockholders' equity at the end of the year.

25. Vitesse Semiconductor Corporation's 1996 annual report contained the following data:

(Dollars in thousands)

| | September 30 | | Increase or (Decrease) 1996 over 1995 | | Percentage of Total Assets September 30 | |
|---|---|---|---|---|---|---|
| | 1996 | 1995 | Dollars | % | 1996 | 1995 |
| Current assets: | | | | | | |
| Cash and equivalents | $ 52,436 | $ 6,315 | _____ | _____ | _____ | _____ |
| Receivables, net | 18,619 | 12,730 | _____ | _____ | _____ | _____ |
| Inventories | 9,959 | 9,895 | _____ | _____ | _____ | _____ |
| Prepaid expenses | 841 | 542 | _____ | _____ | _____ | _____ |
| Total current assets | $ 81,855 | $29,482 | _____ | _____ | _____ | _____ |
| Property, plant, and equipment, net | 17,892 | 11,862 | _____ | _____ | _____ | _____ |
| Other assets | 669 | 767 | _____ | _____ | _____ | _____ |
| Total assets | $100,416 | $42,111 | _____ | _____ | _____ | _____ |

Perform horizontal and vertical analysis on these data by filling in the blank spaces.

# TRUE-FALSE QUESTIONS

Indicate whether each of the following statements is true or false by inserting a capital "T" or "F" in the blank space provided.

_____ 1. Liabilities represent claims against the company's assets and may be in the form of accounts payable or notes payable.

_____ 2. Posting a transaction requires more knowledge than journalizing a transaction.

_____ 3. The primary function of the general ledger is to store transactions by account classification and to provide a balance for each account.

_____ 4. Since a particular journal entry has equal debits and credits, this entry must be correct.

_____ 5. A debit to the Dividends account would indicate an increase in expenses.

_____ 6. Expense accounts usually have debit balances and show the cost associated with producing revenue during an accounting period.

_____ 7. A purchase of land or equipment for cash would cause total assets to increase by the cost of the land or equipment.

_____ 8. One of the purposes of a ledger account is to record the complete effect of a transaction in one place.

_____ 9. Assets are recorded at cost for accounting purposes because cost is subjective and market value is objective.

_____ 10. Transactions are recorded in the journal in chronological order.

_____ 11. The trial balance would automatically reveal the following error: Land was purchased for cash but instead of crediting cash, the credit was made to Accounts Receivable.

_____ 12. Account numbers are entered in the posting reference column of the two-column general journal at the time the transactions are recorded in the ledger accounts.

_____ 13. If only two liability accounts are affected by a transaction, the balance of one account must be increased and the balance of the other decreased in recording this transaction.

_____ 14. The Office Equipment account normally has a credit balance.

_____ 15. Revenue is the difference between the selling price of a service and the cost of providing such service.

_____ 16. A trial balance proves that no errors were made in recording transactions, posting, and in preparing the trial balance.

_____ 17. A journal aids in the division of labor by allowing one person to journalize entries while another individual may post these entries.

_____ 18. Every transaction always affects two or more accounts in a double-entry accounting system.

_____ 19. All of the accounts of a specific business enterprise are referred to as a ledger.

_____ 20. Even though an expense is recognized on the income statement, it may not require an equivalent outlay of cash in that same period.

_____ 21. A general journal entry having two debits and a credit is a compound entry.

_____ 22. A purchase of an asset for immediate consumption that will not be paid for until next month would cause liabilities to increase and stockholders' equity to decrease this month.

_____ 23. A liability account normally has a debit balance.

_____ 24. A journal provides a complete collection of all of the accounts of an entity.

_____ 25. A cash expenditure for insurance and utilities would cause assets to increase but stockholders' equity to decrease.

_____ 26. The accounting cycle steps are all performed at the end of the accounting period.

_____ 27. Horizontal analysis shows the percentage that each item in a financial statement is of some significant total such as total assets or sales.

## MULTIPLE CHOICE QUESTIONS

For each of the following questions indicate the best answer by circling the appropriate letter.

1. The determination of periodic net income involves comparing (1) the revenue recognized during the period and (2) the expenses to be allocated to the period. This procedure is frequently referred to as:
   A. Cost accounting.
   B. Double-entry accounting.
   C. Balancing the accounts.
   D. Matching of revenues and expenses.
   E. None of these.

2. A company returned for credit a portion of the office supplies purchased previously for future use on credit. What entry is required?
   A. Debit Office Supplies on Hand; credit Cash.
   B. Debit Cash; credit Office Supplies on Hand and Office Equipment.
   C. Debit Accounts Payable; credit Office Supplies on Hand
   D. Debit Office Equipment; credit Office Supplies Expense.

3. A company purchased equipment for $1,000 cash; the journal entry to record this purchase is:
   A. Equipment......................................................................... 1,000
         Accounts Payable .......................................................              1,000
   B. Cash................................................................................... 1,000
         Equipment ..................................................................              1,000
   C. Supplies on Hand............................................................ 1,000
         Cash.............................................................................              1,000
   D. Equipment......................................................................... 1,000
         Capital.........................................................................              1,000
   E. None of the above.

4. A company received $600 for services performed in the current period. What is the entry?

| | | | |
|---|---|---|---|
| A. | Cash................................................................................... | 600 | |
| | Service Revenue ........................................................... | | 600 |
| B. | Accounts Receivable ..................................................... | 600 | |
| | Cash................................................................................. | | 600 |
| C. | Cash................................................................................... | 600 | |
| | Accounts Payable.......................................................... | | 600 |
| D. | Service Revenue............................................................. | 600 | |
| | Accounts Receivable..................................................... | | 600 |
| E. | None of the above. | | |

5. Which of the following is (are) descriptive of an asset?
   A. It is something of value because it can be used to produce products of the business.
   B. It has value because it has service potential.
   C. It is owned and/or under the control of the business.
   D. (A), (B), and (C) are all correct.

6. A company purchased office equipment and office supplies on credit from Doug Equipment Company. What is the entry?
   A. Debit Office equipment; credit Accounts Payable.
   B. Debit Equipment; credit Office Supplies Expense.
   C. Debit Office Equipment and Office Supplies on Hand; credit Cash.
   D. Debit Office Equipment, debit Office Supplies on Hand; credit Accounts Payable.

7. Expenses for an accounting period are:
   A. The costs of goods and/or services consumed in the earning of the revenue of the period.
   B. Former assets whose usefulness expired this period in the earning of revenues.
   C. Only the amounts actually paid for services used during the period.
   D. (A) and (B), but not (C).

8. Stockholders' equity is the term applied to which of the following?
   A. Amount of cash the stockholders invested in the company 10 years ago.
   B. Residual claim against the assets of the business after the total liabilities are deducted.
   C. Is also referred to as net worth.
   D. Residual cash of the business after the total liabilities are deducted.
   E. B and C are correct.

9. A law firm completed legal work for Public Service Company on credit. What entry should be made on the law firm's books?
   A. Debit Accounts Receivable; credit Legal Fees Revenue.
   B. Debit Legal Fees Revenue; credit Cash.
   C. Debit Cash; credit Capital Stock.
   D. Debit Cash; credit Legal Fees Revenue.

10. If $500 cash and a $2,000 note are given in exchange for a delivery truck for use in a business:
    A. The stockholders' equity is increased.
    B. Total assets are decreased.
    C. Total liabilities are decreased.
    D. None of the above.

11. Which of the following is *not* a business asset?
    A. Cash.
    B. Capital stock
    C. Equipment.
    D. Accounts receivable.
    E. All of the above are business assets.

12. A $150 debit to Office Equipment was entered in the account as a $150 credit. This error caused the trial balance to be out of balance by:
    A. $75
    B. $150
    C. $450
    D. $300
    E. None of these

13. Debit entries:
    A. Increase assets; and decrease expenses, liabilities, revenues, and stockholders' equity.
    B. Increase assets and stockholders' equity; and decrease expenses and revenues.
    C. Decrease assets and expenses; and increase liabilities, revenues, and stockholders' equity.
    D. Decrease assets and revenues; and increase expenses, liabilities, and stockholders' equity.
    E. Increase assets and expenses; and decrease liabilities, revenues, and stockholders' equity.

14. Which of the following statements about the accounting equation is *not* true?
    A. A transaction may add to both sides of the equation.
    B. A transaction may add to two items on the same side of the equation.
    C. A transaction may transfer between the terms on one side of the equation and have no effect on the other side of the equation.
    D. A transaction may subtract from both sides of the equation.

15. The type of analysis that shows the percentage that each item in a financial statement is of some significant total such as total assets or sales is called:
    A. Horizontal analysis
    B. Vertical analysis
    C. Balance sheet analysis
    D. None of the above

# SOLUTIONS

*Matching*

| | | | |
|---|---|---|---|
| 1. | a | 9. | d |
| 2. | g | 10. | h |
| 3. | b | 11. | m |
| 4. | k | 12. | n |
| 5. | i | 13. | p |
| 6. | c | 14. | o |
| 7. | f | 15. | q |
| 8. | j | | |

*Completion and Exercises*

1. Journalizing; posted; ledger; cross-indexing
2. Debit; credit
3. Double-entry
4.

| Assets | | Liabilities | | Stockholders' Equity | |
|---|---|---|---|---|---|
| increases | decreases | decreases | increases | decreases | increases |

5. left; right
6.

| Type of account | Increased by | Decreased by |
|---|---|---|
| Asset ........................................................ | Debits | Credits |
| Liability..................................................... | Credits | Debits |
| Stockholders' equity................................. | Credits | Debits |
| Revenue ..................................................... | Credits | Debits |
| Expense...................................................... | Debits | Credits |

7. trial balance; debits; credits
8. ledger; chart of accounts
9. account; increases; decreases
10. useful information
11. balance
12. right (credit); right (credit)
13. left (debit); left (debit)
14. The accounting cycle consists of the following steps:
    1. Analyze transactions by examining source documents.
    2. Journalize transactions in the journal.
    3. Post journal entries to the accounts in the ledger.
    4. Prepare a trial balance of the accounts and complete the work sheet.
    5. Prepare financial statements.
    6. Journalize and post adjusting entries.
    7. Journalize and post closing entries.
    8. Prepare a post-closing trial balance.

15.

| Date | Account Titles and Explanation | Post. Ref. | Debit | Credit |
|---|---|---|---|---|
| Jan. 1 | Cash ................................. | 100 | 10,000.00 | |
| | Capital Stock........................... | 300 | | 10,000.00 |
| | Cash invested in business. | | | |
| 10 | Rent Expense .............................. | 515 | 100.00 | |
| | Cash ...................................... | 100 | | 100.00 |
| | Rent for January 19__. | | | |
| 13 | Accounts Receivable.................... | 103 | 125.00 | |
| | Service Revenue ..................... | 400 | | 125.00 |
| | To record fees earned for services. | | | |
| 20 | Equipment ................................... | 170 | 2,000.00 | |
| | Accounts Payable.................... | 200 | | 2,000.00 |
| | Purchased equipment on credit. | | | |
| 30 | Cash ....................................... | 100 | 125.00 | |
| | Accounts Receivable.............. | 103 | | 125.00 |
| | Received cash on account. | | | |

16.                                    **Cash**                          ACCOUNT NO. 100

| Date | Explanation | Post. Ref. | Debit | Credit | Balance |
|---|---|---|---|---|---|
| 19-- | | | | | |
| Jan. 1 | | G1 | 10,000.00 | | 10,000.00 |
| 10 | | G1 | | 100.00 | 9,900.00 |
| 30 | | G1 | 125.00 | | 10,025.00 |

**Accounts Receivable**                ACCOUNT NO. 103

| Date | Explanation | Post. Ref. | Debit | Credit | Balance |
|---|---|---|---|---|---|
| 19-- | | | | | |
| Jan. 20 | | G1 | 125.00 | | 125.00 |
| | | G1 | | 125.00 | 0 |

**Equipment**                          ACCOUNT NO. 170

| Date | Explanation | Post. Ref. | Debit | Credit | Balance |
|---|---|---|---|---|---|
| 19-- | | | | | |
| Jan. 20 | | G1 | 2,000.00 | | 2,000.00 |

## Accounts Payable           ACCOUNT NO. 200

| Date | Explanation | Post. Ref. | Debit | Credit | Balance |
|------|-------------|------------|-------|--------|---------|
| 19-- | | | | | |
| Jan. 20 | | G1 | | 2,000.00 | 2,000.00 |

## Capital Stock           ACCOUNT NO. 300

| Date | Explanation | Post. Ref. | Debit | Credit | Balance |
|------|-------------|------------|-------|--------|---------|
| 19-- | | | | | |
| Jan. 1 | | G1 | | 10,000.00 | 10,000.00 |

## Service Revenue           ACCOUNT NO. 400

| Date | Explanation | Post. Ref. | Debit | Credit | Balance |
|------|-------------|------------|-------|--------|---------|
| 19-- | | | | | |
| Jan. 13 | | G1 | | 125.00 | 125.00 |

## Rent Expense           ACCOUNT NO. 515

| Date | Explanation | Post. Ref. | Debit | Credit | Balance |
|------|-------------|------------|-------|--------|---------|
| 19-- | | | | | |
| Jan. 10 | | G1 | 100.00 | | 100.00 |

17. journal; debit(s); credit(s)
18. assets; equities
19. asset
20. $12,000
21. debit
22. Stockholders' equity at end of year: $150,000 + $50,000 - $11,000 = $189,000
    Total assets at beginning of year: $35,000 + $150,000 = $185,000
23. (a) Investment of cash in business by stockholders.
    (b) Services performed on account.
    (c) Service equipment purchased for cash.
    (d) Cash collected on account.
    (e) Salaries paid in cash.
    (f) Supplies purchased on account.
    (g) Cash paid on accounts payable.
    (h) Supplies returned for credit.
    (i) Services performed on account.
    (j) Cash paid for rent expense.
    (k) Cash paid for utilities expense.
    (l) Service equipment purchased on account.
24. Stockholders' equity at the end of the year = $1,000,000 +$500,000 - $50,000 = $1,450,000
    Total liabilities = $1,500,000 - $100,000 = $1,400,000
    Total assets = $1,450,000 + $1,400,000 = $2,850,000

25. (Dollars in millions)

| | September 30 1996 | September 30 1995 | Increase or (Decrease) 1996 over 1995 | | Percentage of Total Assets 1996 | Percentage of Total Assets 1995 |
|---|---|---|---|---|---|---|
| | | | Dollars | % | | |
| Current assets: | | | | | | |
| Cash and equivalents | $52,436 | $ 6,315 | $46,121 | 730 | 52.2 | 15.0 |
| Receivables, net | 18,619 | 12,730 | 5,889 | 46 | 18.5 | 30.2 |
| Inventories | 9,959 | 9,895 | 64 | 1 | 9.9 | 23.5 |
| Other current assets | 841 | 542 | 299 | 55 | .8 | 1.3 |
| Total current assets | $81,855 | $29,482 | $52,373 | 178 | 81.5* | 70.0 |
| Property, plant, and equipment, net | 17,892 | 11,862 | 6,030 | 51 | 17.8 | 28.2 |
| Other assets | 669 | 767 | (98) | (13) | .7 | 1.8 |
| Total assets | $100,416 | $42,111 | $58,305 | 138 | 100.0 | 100.0 |

*Rounding difference

## True-False Questions

1. T
2. F  Journalizing requires the knowledge of determining the effect of the transaction on the accounting equation, while posting involves transferring the data from the journal to the proper accounts.
3. T
4. F  A wrong ledger account could have been used.
5. F  A debit to the Dividends account indicates payments of cash or other assets to the stockholders. Dividends are not expenses.
6. T
7. F  Total assets would remain unchanged because cash would decrease by the same amount land or equipment increased.
8. F  A journal records the complete effect of a transaction in one place.
9. F  Cost is objective, and market value is subjective.
10. T
11. F  The trial balance would be of limited assistance in locating this error because the total of the debit balances would equal the total of the credit balances. The trial balance does not call attention to errors of this type.
12. T  Account numbers are entered when the journal entries have been posted to ledger accounts.
13. T
14. F  Assets normally have debit balances.
15. F  Revenue is the selling price of a service; net income is the difference between revenue and expenses.
16. F  A trial balance only proves that debit balances equal credit balances.
17. T
18. T
19. T
20. T  Using the accrual system, expenses are recognized in the period in which incurred rather than when cash is paid.
21. T
22. T  An expense and a liability have been incurred; expenses decrease stockholders' equity.
23. F  A liability account normally has a credit balance.

24. F   A ledger provides a complete collection of all of the accounts of an entity; a journal provides a source of reference for the future by providing a chronological record of all financial events.

25. F   Assets would decrease by the amount of cash expenditure; stockholders' equity would decrease because of these expenses.

26. F   The first three steps are performed *throughout* the accounting period.

27. F   The description given was vertical analysis. Horizontal analysis shows the calculation of dollar and/or percentage changes from one year to the next.

## Multiple Choice Questions

1. D

2. C

3. E   The correct entry is to debit Equipment and credit Cash for $1,000.

4. A

5. D

6. D

7. D

8. E   There is no direct relationship between the amount of cash a company has and the balance in the stockholders' equity account.

9. A

10. D   Total assets are increased by $2,000 ($2,500 delivery truck - $500 cash given up), and total liabilities are increased by $2,000.

11. B   Capital stock is not a business asset.

12. D   $150 x 2 = $300 error; $150 that should have been there was missing from the debit side, while $150 that should not have appeared was included on the credit side.

13. E

14. B

15. B

# CHAPTER 3

# ADJUSTMENTS FOR FINANCIAL REPORTING

## *Learning Objectives*

1. *Describe the basic characteristics of the cash basis and the accrual basis of accounting.*
2. *Identify the reasons why adjusting entries must be made.*
3. *Identify the classes and types of adjusting entries.*
4. *Prepare adjusting entries.*
5. *Determine the effects of failing to prepare adjusting entries.*
6. *Analyze and use the financial results – trend percentages.*

## REFERENCE OUTLINE

# CHAPTER OUTLINE

*Learning Objective 1*
*Describe the basic characteristics of the cash basis and the accrual basis of accounting.*

## CASH VERSUS ACCRUAL BASIS ACCOUNTING

1. Using the cash basis of accounting, revenues are recognized when cash is received and expenses are recognized when cash is paid out.
    a. Small business firms and professional persons may account for their revenues and expenses on a cash basis.
    b. The cash basis of accounting is acceptable only if the results obtained approximate those obtained under the accrual basis of accounting.
2. Using the accrual basis of accounting, revenues are recognized when sales are made or services are performed, even though cash has not yet been received. Expenses are recognized when incurred, regardless of the time of cash payment. Adjusting entries are needed under the accrual basis of accounting to bring the accounts up to date for economic activity that has occurred but has not yet been recorded.

*Learning Objective 2:*
*Identify the reasons why adjusting entries must be made.*

## THE NEED FOR ADJUSTING ENTRIES

3. Adjusting entries are needed so that the income statement and balance sheet of an entity will be complete and accurate.
    a. In order to prepare financial statements, accountants arbitrarily divide an entity's life into time periods.
        (1) These time periods are normally equal in length and are called accounting periods.
        (2) A fiscal year or accounting year is an accounting period of one year.
            (a) A calendar year accounting period is a fiscal year that ends on December 31.
            (b) Other fiscal years continue for twelve consecutive months but do not end on December 31.
    b. This division of an entity's life into time periods requires the preparation of adjusting entries.
4. The need for adjusting entries is based on the matching principle, which requires that expenses incurred in producing revenues be deducted from the revenues they generated during an accounting period.
5. Adjusting entries must be prepared whenever financial statements are to be prepared.
    a. Adjusting entries may be recorded more frequently, but must be recorded annually in keeping with annual reporting.
    b. If monthly financial statements are prepared, monthly adjusting entries are required.

*Learning Objective 3:*
*Identify the classes and types of adjusting entries.*

## CLASSES AND TYPES OF ADJUSTING ENTRIES

6. Adjusting entries can be grouped into these two broad classes.
    a. Deferred items requiring two types of adjusting entries: asset/expense adjustments and liability/revenue adjustments.
    b. Accrued items requiring two types of adjusting entries: asset/revenue adjustments and liability/expense adjustments.

*Learning Objective 4:*
*Prepare adjusting entries.*

## ADJUSTMENTS FOR DEFERRED ITEMS

7. In the asset/expense group, adjusting entries for prepaid expenses and depreciation are recorded.
8. In the liability/revenue group, adjusting entries for unearned revenues are recorded.

## ASSET/EXPENSE ADJUSTMENTS—PREPAID EXPENSES AND DEPRECIATION

9. A prepaid expense is an asset awaiting assignment to expense and includes prepaid insurance, prepaid rent, supplies on hand, and depreciable assets.

## PREPAID INSURANCE

10. Prepaid Insurance (an asset) is recorded when the insurance policy premium is paid in advance.
    a. This asset expires with the passage of time and becomes an expense.
    b. Prepaid Insurance (an asset) is debited when the premium is paid, and Cash is credited.
    c. Insurance Expense is debited and Prepaid Insurance is credited at the end of the accounting period for the amount of insurance that has expired.

## PREPAID RENT

11. Prepaid Rent (an asset) is recorded when rent is paid in advance to cover more than one accounting period.
    a. Because facilities are being rented continuously through time, the expense is incurred continuously as time elapses, but the entry is not usually made until financial statements are to be prepared.
    b. Prepaid Rent (an asset) is debited and Cash is credited when payment is made in advance.
    c. Rent Expense is debited and Prepaid Rent is credited at the end of the accounting period for the amount of rent that has expired.

## SUPPLIES ON HAND

12. Supplies are often bought in large quantities and are assets until they are used.
    a. Supplies on Hand (an asset) is debited when the supplies are purchased, and Cash or Accounts Payable is credited.
    b. At the end of the period, the supplies on hand are counted, and an adjusting entry is made to reduce the account balance of Supplies on Hand to reflect the actual quantity on hand.
    c. Supplies Expense is debited and Supplies on Hand is credited for the amount of supplies used during the period.

## DEPRECIATION

13. Depreciation is an expense associated with the gradual use of depreciable assets such as buildings and machines.
    a. Depreciation expense is determined by dividing the asset cost less estimated salvage value by the asset's useful life.
    b. The useful life must be estimated in advance and represents the expected number of years the company plans to use the asset.
    c. Depreciation accounting is the process of recording depreciation expense.

*d.* Straight-line depreciation assigns the same amount of expense to each period of use. The formula is:

$$\frac{\text{Asset cost - Estimated salvage value}}{\text{Estimated years of useful life}} = \text{Annual depreciation}$$

   *e.* The adjusting entry involves debiting Depreciation Expense and crediting Accumulated Depreciation (a contra asset account).
   *f.* Book value, which is an asset's cost less accumulated depreciation, is shown in the balance sheet along with the asset's original cost and accumulated depreciation.

## LIABILITY/REVENUE ADJUSTMENTS—UNEARNED REVENUES

14. A liability called Unearned Revenue is recorded when assets are received before being earned.
   *a.* The liability account may be called Unearned Fees, Revenue Received in Advance, Advances by Customers, or Unearned Revenue.
   *b.* The seller is obligated to either refund the customer's money or provide the services.
   *c.* When cash is received in advance for future services, Cash is debited and Unearned Revenue is credited.
   *d.* After services are performed and revenue is earned, Unearned Revenue is debited and a revenue account is credited.

## ADJUSTMENTS FOR ACCRUED ITEMS

15. Accrued items require two types of adjusting entries:
   *a.* Asset/revenue adjustments are one group involving accrued assets.
   *b.* Liability/expense adjustments are the other group involving accrued liabilities.

## ASSET/REVENUE ADJUSTMENTS—ACCRUED ASSETS

16. Accrued assets are those assets that exist at the end of an accounting period but which have not yet been recorded.
   *a.* Accrued assets represent rights to receive payments that are not legally due at the balance sheet date.
   *b.* An adjusting entry recognizes these rights.
   *c.* Accrued assets adjustments may also be called accrued revenues adjustments.

## INTEREST REVENUE

17. At the end of an accounting period, interest may have been earned that has not been received. To record this interest it is necessary to debit Interest Receivable and credit Interest Revenue.

## UNBILLED TRAINING FEES

18. A company may perform services at the end of the accounting period and bill the customer in the next accounting period. To record this activity in the period in which the services were performed, the adjusting entry debits Accounts Receivable and credits Service Revenue.

## LIABILITY/EXPENSE ADJUSTMENTS—ACCRUED LIABILITIES

19. Accrued liabilities are those liabilities that exist at the end of an accounting period which have not yet been recorded, such as salaries earned by employees that have not been paid.
   *a.* Accrued liabilities represent obligations to make payments that are not legally due at the balance sheet date.

b. Salaries Expense is debited and Salaries Payable is credited in an adjusting entry to record salaries that are owed but are unpaid.

c. Accrued liabilities adjustments may also be called accrued expenses adjustments.

*Learning Objective 5:*
*Determine the effects of failing to prepare adjusting entries.*

EFFECTS OF FAILING TO PREPARE ADJUSTING ENTRIES

20. The following diagram shows the effect on net income and balance sheet items of failing to record each of the major types of adjusting entries:

| | *Failure to recognize* | *Effect on Net Income* | *Effect on balance sheet items* |
|---|---|---|---|
| a. | Consumption of the benefits of an asset (prepaid expense) | Overstates | Overstates assets<br>Overstates retained earnings |
| b. | Earning of previously unearned revenues | Understates | Overstates liabilities<br>Understates retained earnings |
| c. | Accrual of assets | Understates | Understates assets<br>Understates retained earnings |
| d. | Accrual of liabilities | Overstates | Understates liabilities<br>Overstates retained earnings |

*Learning Objective 6:*
*Analyze and use the financial results – trend percentages.*

ANALYZING AND USING THE FINANCIAL RESULTSXTREND PERCENTAGES

21. Trend percentages are calculated by dividing the amount for each year of an item by the amount of the same item in the base year.

$$\text{Trend percentage} = \frac{\text{Current year amount}}{\text{Base year amount}}$$

# DEMONSTRATION PROBLEM

Using the following information, prepare the adjusting entries in general journal form for the Beason Company as of December 31, 1999.

The Beason Company adjusts its books annually on December 31. Following are some of the accounts that appeared in the trial balance on December 31, 1999, *before* adjusting entries were made:

| | | |
|---|---:|---:|
| Cash in bank | $10,000 | |
| Buildings | 200,000 | |
| Accumulated depreciation—Buildings | | $15,000 |
| Office supplies on hand | 605 | |
| Prepaid advertising | 400 | |
| Prepaid insurance | 1,600 | |
| Utilities expense | 60 | |
| Prepaid rent | 5,000 | |
| Advertising expense | 1,080 | |
| Sales | | 20,400 |
| Unearned service fees | | 1,200 |

The following additional information is available:

1. Beason Company deposited $10,000 in a local bank. The deposit earns 6% interest annually, and the bank pays interest on the last day of the following months: February, May, August, and November.
2. On December 31, Beason Company has just finished a bookkeeping service for a client. Beason Company will bill the client $1,000 in January for the bookkeeping service.
3. The Beason Company purchased a two-year flood hazard insurance policy on September 1, 1999, paying the full two-year premium of $570 in advance.
4. The Beason Company rented an office space on November 1, 1999, at a monthly rental of $1,000, paying five months rent in advance. The five months rent was debited to an asset account.
5. On December 1, 1999, the Beason Company purchased advertising in the Global Morning News for two months for $400 paying for the space in advance.
6. Since the last payday, employees have earned an additional $250.
7. Two-thirds of the unearned service fees have been earned by December 31.
8. The building was purchased for $200,000 in early 1996. It has an estimated useful life of 40 years with no salvage value. Straight-line depreciation is used.
9. Office supplies on hand amount to $300.

GENERAL JOURNAL

| Date | Account Titles and Explanation | Post. Ref. | Debit | Credit |
|------|-------------------------------|-----------|-------|--------|
| | | | | |

# SOLUTION TO DEMONSTRATION PROBLEM

| 1. | Interest Receivable ($10,000 x .06 x 1/12) ............................................ | 50 | |
|---|---|---|---|
| | Interest Revenue .......................................................................... | | 50 |
| 2. | Accounts Receivable .............................................................................. | 1,000 | |
| | Service Revenue ........................................................................... | | 1,000 |
| 3. | Insurance Expense ($570 / 24 months) x 4 months ............................ | 95 | |
| | Prepaid Insurance ........................................................................ | | 95 |
| 4. | Rent Expense ($1,000 x 2 months) ....................................................... | 2,000 | |
| | Prepaid Rent ................................................................................. | | 2,000 |
| 5. | Advertising Expense .............................................................................. | 200 | |
| | Prepaid Advertising ...................................................................... | | 200 |
| | ($400 x 1/2 = $200) | | |
| 6. | Salaries Expense ..................................................................................... | 250 | |
| | Salaries Payable ........................................................................... | | 250 |
| 7. | Unearned Service Fees .......................................................................... | 800 | |
| | Service Fees Revenue ................................................................... | | 800 |
| | (1,200 x 2/3 = $800) | | |
| 8. | Depreciation Expense ($200,000 / 40 years) ....................................... | 5,000 | |
| | Accumulated Depreciation—Building ......................................... | | 5,000 |
| 9. | Office Supplies Expense ($605 - $300) ................................................. | 305 | |
| | Office Supplies on Hand .............................................................. | | 305 |

# MATCHING

Referring to the terms listed below, place the appropriate letter next to the corresponding description.

| | | | | | |
|---|---|---|---|---|---|
| *a.* | Accounting period | *f.* | Book value | *k.* | Fiscal year |
| *b.* | Accrued asset | *g.* | Calendar year | *l.* | Prepaid expense |
| *c.* | Accrual basis of accounting | *h.* | Cash basis of accounting | *m.* | Estimated salvage value |
| *d.* | Accumulated depreciation | *i.* | Depreciation | *n.* | Unearned revenue |
| *e.* | Adjusting entries | *j.* | Earned revenue | *o.* | Estimated useful life |

_____ 1. A plant asset's cost less its accumulated depreciation.

_____ 2. A period that begins on January 1 and ends on December 31.

_____ 3. Contra asset account.

_____ 4. An asset that will be assigned to expense at a later date.

_____ 5. A time period into which an entity's life is arbitrarily divided for financial reporting purposes.

_____ 6. Made at the end of an accounting period to reflect economic activity that has taken place but has not yet been recorded.

_____ 7. Recognizes revenues when cash is received and recognizes expenses when cash is paid out.

_____ 8. An asset that exists at the end of an accounting period but has not yet been recorded.

_____ 9. The expense resulting from a plant equipment's expiration of usefulness.

_____ 10. The estimated number of time periods that a company expects to make use of a plant asset.

_____ 11. A period of any twelve consecutive months used as an accounting period.

_____ 12. Cash received in advance for goods and services to be delivered at a later date.

## COMPLETION AND EXERCISES

1. Entries made to update the accounts prior to the preparation of financial statements for economic activity that has taken place but has not yet been recorded are called _____ entries.

2. One expense that would probably be recognized in the same period under both the modified cash basis and accrual basis of accounting is _____ _____.

3. Assume that a company received services from its employees in 1998 for which it had previously agreed it would pay $2,800. This sum was paid in 1999. The $2,800 would be treated as an expense of the year _____ under the cash basis accounting and of the year _____ under accrual basis accounting. Generally speaking, under cash basis accounting expenses are recognized in the accounting system when _____ _____.

4. Some small businesses, especially those rendering services, may employ _____ basis accounting. But most business firms use _____ basis accounting.

5. Assume that a consulting company rendered services for a client in 1998 and collected cash for those services in 1999. Under the cash basis of accounting, revenue would be recognized in _____, while under the accrual basis of accounting, revenue would be recognized in _____. Generally speaking, under the cash basis of accounting, revenue is recognized _____.

6. The two major classes of adjusting entries and the types of adjusting entries included in each class are:

   a.  _____

       _____

       Types of adjusting entries included in this class are: _____

       _____

   b.  _____

       _____

       Types of adjusting entries included in this class are: _____

       _____

7. Every adjusting entry will involve one account that is reported in the _____ _____ and another account that is reported in the _____ _____.

8. When depreciation is recorded, it is credited to a contra account called _____

_____ and reported in the _____ _____ as a

_____ from the depreciable asset to which it relates.

9. The process whereby the cost (less salvage value) of a long-lived asset used in a

business is allocated to the periods in which it is used is called _____

_____. The amount of cost allocated to each period is called _____

_____.

10. _____ _____ is subtracted from a plant asset's cost to derive its

_____ amount.

11. A liability that exists at the end of an accounting period, but which has not yet been

recorded is a/an _____ _____.

12. The Martin Company has a monthly payroll of $300,000, and its employees are paid

monthly on the first. The adjusting entry required on December 31 (the end of the

company's fiscal year) would involve a debit of $ _____ to the _____

_____ account and a credit of $_____ to the _____

_____ account.

13. The Folsom Company owns a warehouse that it leases to others for $1,000 per month,

which is collected in advance in semiannual installments on March 31 and September

30. The entry required to record the receipt of the advance payment of rent on

September 30 would involve a debit of $_____ to the _____ account and

a credit of $_____ to the _____ _____ _____

account.

14. Refer to the data in Question 13. If monthly adjusting entries are made, the entry required

on October 31 would consist of a debit to _____ _____ _____

and a credit to _____ _____ in the amount of $_____.

15. Assume that the six basic elements in accounting consist of assets, liabilities,

stockholders' equity, revenues, expenses, and net income. If the Martin Company in

Question 12 failed to make the required adjusting entry, its financial statements for the

period ending December 31 would show too much _____ _____

and _____ _____ and too little _____ and _____.

16. Refer to the data in Question 13. If financial statements are to be prepared for the period

ending October 31 and if the Folsom Company failed to make the required adjusting entry,

it would have overstated its _____ and understated its _____ ,

_____ _____ , and _____ _____.

17. James Call Company purchased $450 of store supplies during the quarter which were charged to an asset account. The beginning balance of store supplies on hand was $150. The end-of-quarter balance sheet showed store supplies on hand of $75. The amount charged to Store Supplies Expense and credited to Store Supplies on Hand is $_____.

18. A theater offered theater ticket books for use at future performances to its patrons at $50 per book for 5 tickets per book. During the year, 1,200 books were sold and this amount was erroneously credited to Theater Revenue. At the end of the period 2,400 tickets from the book sales had been turned in at the box office. The appropriate adjusting entry at the end of the period would be:

### GENERAL JOURNAL

| Date | Account Titles and Explanation | Post. Ref. | Debit | | Credit | |
|---|---|---|---|---|---|---|
| | | | | | | |
| | | | | | | |
| | | | | | | |
| | | | | | | |
| | | | | | | |
| | | | | | | |
| | | | | | | |
| | | | | | | |
| | | | | | | |
| | | | | | | |
| | | | | | | |

19. Standford Company started operations on December 1, 19__. Employees earn $85 per day and work a six-day week. There are 27 workdays in December. By the last payday in December (December 27), the employees had been paid $1,955.

Required:

Prepare the adjustment needed on December 31.

### GENERAL JOURNAL

| Date | Account Titles and Explanation | Post. Ref. | Debit | | Credit | |
|---|---|---|---|---|---|---|
| | | | | | | |
| | | | | | | |
| | | | | | | |
| | | | | | | |
| | | | | | | |
| | | | | | | |
| | | | | | | |
| | | | | | | |
| | | | | | | |

20. State the effect that each of the following would have on the amount of net income reported for 1998, 1999, and 2000, and on assets and liabilities as of 12/31/99. The firm's accounting period ends on December 31.

a. A collection in 1999 of $700 for services rendered in 1998 was credited to a revenue account instead of to Accounts Receivable in 1999.

b. The collection of $400 for services not yet performed as of December 31, 1999, was credited to a revenue account and not adjusted. The services are to be performed in 2000.

c. No adjustment was made for accrued salaries of $1,000 as of December 31, 1999.

_____

_____

_____

_____

_____

_____

_____

_____

_____

_____

_____

_____

_____

_____

_____

_____

_____

_____

_____

_____

_____

_____

_____

_____

21. Using the following information, prepare the adjusting entries in general journal form for the Brandon Company as of December 31, 1999.

The Brandon Company adjusts its books annually on December 31. Following are some of the accounts that appeared in the trial balance on December 31, 1999, *before* adjusting entries were made:

| | | |
|---|---:|---:|
| Buildings ............................................................................................ | $75,000 | |
| Accumulated DepreciationXBuildings ................................................ | | $12,500 |
| Office Supplies on Hand ..................................................................... | 445 | |
| Prepaid Advertising ............................................................................ | 960 | |
| Prepaid Insurance ............................................................................... | 1,600 | |
| Utilities Expense ................................................................................. | 60 | |
| Prepaid Rent ........................................................................................ | 900 | |
| Advertising Expense ........................................................................... | 1,080 | |
| Sales ..................................................................................................... | | 20,400 |
| Unearned Service Fees ........................................................................ | | 450 |

The following additional information is available:

a. The building has an estimated useful life of 15 years with no salvage value. Straight-line depreciation is used.
b. Office supplies on hand amount to $140.
c. The Brandon Company purchased a four-year fire insurance policy on July 1, 1999, paying the full four-year premium of $1,600 in advance.
d. The Brandon Company rented a warehouse on October 1, 1999, at a monthly rental of $300, paying three months rent in advance.
e. On December 1, 1999, the Brandon Company purchased advertising in the *Daily News* for three months for $960, paying for the space in advance.
f. Since the last payday, employees have earned an additional $600.
g. Two-thirds of the unearned service fees have been earned by December 31.

# GENERAL JOURNAL

| Date | Account Titles and Explanation | Post. Ref. | Debit | Credit |
|------|-------------------------------|-----------|-------|--------|
|      |                               |           |       |        |
|      |                               |           |       |        |
|      |                               |           |       |        |
|      |                               |           |       |        |
|      |                               |           |       |        |
|      |                               |           |       |        |
|      |                               |           |       |        |
|      |                               |           |       |        |
|      |                               |           |       |        |
|      |                               |           |       |        |
|      |                               |           |       |        |
|      |                               |           |       |        |
|      |                               |           |       |        |
|      |                               |           |       |        |
|      |                               |           |       |        |
|      |                               |           |       |        |
|      |                               |           |       |        |
|      |                               |           |       |        |
|      |                               |           |       |        |
|      |                               |           |       |        |
|      |                               |           |       |        |
|      |                               |           |       |        |
|      |                               |           |       |        |
|      |                               |           |       |        |
|      |                               |           |       |        |
|      |                               |           |       |        |
|      |                               |           |       |        |
|      |                               |           |       |        |
|      |                               |           |       |        |
|      |                               |           |       |        |
|      |                               |           |       |        |
|      |                               |           |       |        |
|      |                               |           |       |        |
|      |                               |           |       |        |
|      |                               |           |       |        |
|      |                               |           |       |        |
|      |                               |           |       |        |
|      |                               |           |       |        |
|      |                               |           |       |        |
|      |                               |           |       |        |
|      |                               |           |       |        |

22. Sun Microsystems, Inc., showed the following amounts of net income for the years 1994 through 1996:

(Dollars in thousands)

| | | Trend Percentage |
|---|---|---|
| 1994 | $195,824 | _____ |
| 1995 | 355,842 | _____ |
| 1996 | 476,388 | _____ |

Calculate the trend percentages using 1994 as the base year. What do you think of the prospects for the future?

## TRUE-FALSE QUESTIONS

Indicate whether each of the following statements is true or false by inserting a capital "T" or "F" in the blank space provided.

_____ 1. Transactions often overlap accounting periods.

_____ 2. Expenses from continuing transactions such as rent and insurance are usually only recorded at the end of accounting periods.

_____ 3. Every adjusting entry affects both a balance sheet and an income statement account.

_____ 4. Some assets represent services that will be used up over many accounting periods.

_____ 5. Consumption of supplies used in the business results in an expense.

_____ 6. An accrued liability results from a transaction in which a cash payment has been made but the expense has not been incurred.

_____ 7. Adjusting entries usually must be prepared prior to the preparation of financial statements.

_____ 8. The balances of any unearned revenue accounts appear as debits in the trial balance statement.

_____ 9. An expense may only be recognized and recorded if cash has been paid.

_____ 10. The maximum length of an accounting period is usually one month.

_____ 11. Adjusting entries divide amounts in accounts such as Supplies on Hand and Prepaid Insurance into their proper balance sheet and income statement components.

_____ 12. Wages paid in advance to an employee would be classified by the employer as an accrued expense.

_____ 13. The Prepaid Insurance account shows a debit of $450, representing the cost of a three-year fire insurance policy dated September 1. The adjusting entry on December 31 of the first year of insurance coverage is a debit to Insurance Expense and a credit to Prepaid Insurance for $50.

_____ 14. The purpose of adjusting entries is to compile all elements required to compute income or loss in one ledger account.

_____ 15. The effect on the income statement if the adjusting entry for depreciation was omitted would be to understate net income.

_____ 16. Adjusting entries are needed when the cost, expense, or revenue components of a transaction relate to more than one accounting period.

_____ 17. Some adjusting entries anticipate expenses that are to be incurred, but adjusting entries never anticipate revenues that are to be earned.

_____ 18. The proper adjusting entry to recognize the expiration of rent paid in advance is to debit Rent Expense and credit Prepaid Rent.

_____ 19. To prepare the adjusting entry for an accrued liability, an expense account is debited and a liability account is credited.

_____ 20. Expenses for which cash expenditures have not yet been made are still reported as expenses on the income statement under the accrual basis of accounting.

_____ 21. Adjusting entries are first entered in the journal and then are posted to the general ledger.

_____ 22. The following are all examples of expenses recognized in adjusting entries: salaries expense, depreciation expense, insurance expense, and dividends.

_____ 23. An adjusting entry may be the result of an expenditure that occurred many years ago.

_____ 24. Economic activity occurs continuously.

_____ 25. Under the accrual basis of accounting, revenue is recognized when cash is received, and expenses are recognized when cash is paid.

_____ 26. Trend percentages are calculated by dividing the amount for each year of an item by the amount of the same item in the base year.

## MULTIPLE CHOICE QUESTIONS

For each of the following questions, indicate the best answer by circling the appropriate letter.

1. Salaries incurred but unpaid at year-end would be classified on a financial statement as a(an):
   A. current asset.
   B. current liability.
   C. revenue.
   D. expense.
   E. other asset.

2. The Unearned Commission Fees account will normally have what type of balance?
   A. A negative balance
   B. A balance equal to salaries expense
   C. Credit balance
   D. Debit balance
   E. None of these.

3. The proper entry to recognize periodic depreciation of equipment is
   A. Depreciation ExpenseXEquipment ........................................................ XXX
        Equipment ................................................................................................ XXX
   B. Accumulated DepreciationXEquipment ................................................. XXX
        Depreciation ExpenseXEquipment ...................................................... XXX
   C. Accumulated DepreciationXEquipment ................................................. XXX
        Equipment ................................................................................................ XXX
   D. Equipment ................................................................................................. XXX
        Depreciation ExpenseXEquipment ...................................................... XXX
   E. None of these.

4. No adjustment was made for accrued wages on December 31, 1998. The amount of wages earned but not payable until the second week in January 1999, was $600. If this omission is not discovered before financial statements are prepared:
   A. 1998 net income will be overstated by $600.
   B. 1998 net income will be understated by $600.
   C. assets will not be affected.
   D. liabilities will be understated.
   E. (A), and (C), and (D) are all true.

5. Which one of the following entries would be made to record rent expired during the current accounting period, but paid in the prior period?

   A. Prepaid Rent ........................................................................................... XX
         Rent Expense ........................................................................................... XX
   B. Rent Expense ........................................................................................... XX
         Prepaid Rent ........................................................................................... XX
   C. Prepaid Rent ........................................................................................... XX
         Cash ........................................................................................... XX
   D. Rent Expense ........................................................................................... XX
         Rent Accrued ........................................................................................... XX
   E. None of the above.

6. On an income statement, which of the following groups of accounts would all be classified as expenses?
   A. Depreciation Expense, Rent Expense, Accumulated Depreciation
   B. Prepaid Insurance, Office Supplies Expense, Salaries Expense
   C. Service Revenue, Sales, Salaries Expense
   D. Office Supplies Expense, Rent Expense, Depreciation Expense

7. A company acquired supplies and, expecting to use them all in the current year, debited the full amount to the Office Supplies Expense account. At the end of the period, part of the supplies remained on hand. If no adjusting entry is made, the effect(s) on the balance sheet and the income statement is (are):
   A. revenue of the company will be overstated.
   B. net income and stockholders' equity will be overstated, while assets will be understated.
   C. assets, net income, and stockholders' equity will all be understated.
   D. net income and stockholders' equity will not be affected.
   E. None of the above are correct.

8. A magazine company received cash for subscriptions in August for magazines to be mailed in August 1998 through September 2001. It originally recorded the amount as revenue. On December 31, 1998, the correct adjusting entry will be:
   A. Unearned Advertising Fees
         Subscriptions Revenue
   B. Unearned Subscriptions Fees
         Subscriptions Revenue
   C. Subscriptions Revenue
         Unearned Subscriptions Fees
   D. Subscriptions Revenue
         Subscriptions Receivable
   E. None of the above.

9. Make an adjusting entry to record the office supplies used when an asset account was originally debited for office supplies purchased.
   A. Debit Retained Earnings; credit Office Supplies Expense.
   B. Debit Office Supplies Expense; credit Retained Earnings.
   C. Debit Office Supplies Expense; credit Office Supplies on Hand.
   D. Debit Office Supplies Expense; credit Cash.

10. The accrual basis of accounting operates on which of the following assumption(s)?
    A. Expenses are recorded *only* when they are paid for.
    B. Revenues are recorded *only* when cash is received for them.
    C. Expenses are recorded when they are incurred, regardless of the time of payment.
    D. Revenues are recorded when they are earned, regardless of the time when payment is received.
    E. (C) and (D) are correct.

11. An advertising agency received an $800 check on December 2 for services that it was to perform during December, January, and February. The agency recorded the check as a liability. One-fourth of the services were performed in December. The adjusting entry required on December 31 for the advertising agency was:
    A. Advertising Expense ........................................................... 200
          Unearned Advertising Fees ............................................. 200
    B. Advertising Expense ........................................................... 600
          Advertising Revenue ....................................................... 600
    C. Unearned Advertising Fees ............................................... 200
          Advertising Revenue ....................................................... 200
    D. Unearned Advertising Fees ............................................... 600
          Advertising Revenue ....................................................... 600
    E. None of these.

12. Depreciation:
    A. represents expired utility of a plant asset.
    B. may be caused in part by wear and tear from use.
    C. may be caused in part by obsolescence due to technological change.
    D. is a fund of cash available for replacing the asset when it is no longer useful.
    E. Items (A), (B), and (C) above.

13. Prepaid Rent is classified as a(an):
    A. liability.
    B. part of stockholders' equity.
    C. asset
    D. revenue.
    E. expense.

14. Insurance premiums received by an insurance company in advance of the coverage period would be classified by the insurance company as a(an):
    A. asset.
    B. liability.
    C. expense.
    D. revenue.

15. An example of a contra account is:
    A. Insurance Expense.
    B. Accumulated DepreciationXEquipment.
    C. Store Supplies Expense.
    D. Prepaid Rent.
    E. None of these.

16. If net income is $400,000 in 1998 and $500,000 in 1999 and 1998 is the base year, the trend percentage in 1999 is:
    A. 1.25
    B. .80
    C. 125
    D. 80
    E. 100

---

## SOLUTIONS

---

### Matching

| | | | |
|---|---|---|---|
| 1. | *f* | 7. | *h* |
| 2. | *g* | 8. | *b* |
| 3. | *d* | 9. | *i* |
| 4. | *l* | 10. | *o* |
| 5. | *a* | 11. | *k* |
| 6. | *e* | 12. | *n* |

### Completion and Exercises

1. adjusting

2. depreciation expense

3. 1999; 1998; they are paid for in cash

4. cash; accrual

5. 1999; 1998; when cash is received

6. (Note order is not important)
   *a.* Entries that relate to data previously recorded in the accounts (deferred items).
   Prepaid expenses, depreciation, and unearned revenue.
   *b.* Entries relating to activity on which nothing has been previously recorded in the accounts (accrued items).
   Accrued assets and accrued liabilities.

7. balance sheet; income statement

8. Accumulated Depreciation; balance sheet; deduction

9. depreciation accounting; depreciation expense

10. Salvage value; depreciable

11. accrued liability

12. $300,000; Salaries Expense; 300,000; Salaries Payable

13. $6,000; Cash; $6,000; Unearned Rental Fees

14. Unearned Rental Fees; Rent Revenue; $1,000

15. stockholders' equity; net income; liabilities; expenses.

16. Liabilities; revenues; net income; stockholders' equity.

17. $525 ($150 + $450 purchases = $600 available for use; $600 - $75 ending inventory = $525)

18. Theater Revenue .................................................................. 36,000
        Unearned Theater Ticket Fees ......................................          36,000

         1,200 x $50 =    $60,000    credited to Theater Revenue
                         - 24,000    Revenue earned
                         $36,000    Unearned Theater Ticket Fees

19. Salaries Expense ................................................................. 340
        Salaries Payable ..........................................................          340

         $2,295    (27 days x $85)
         -1,955    paid to employees
         $ 340    adjustment

20. *a.* Net income is overstated in 1999 by $700. Accounts Receivable (an asset) would be overstated as of 12/31/99 by $700 because the claim against the customer was not credited at the time of collection in 1999. There is no effect on liabilities or on 1998 net income.

    *b.* Revenue for 1999 is overstated, causing net income to be overstated by $400. In the following year, 2000, revenue and net income will be understated by $400 assuming the services are performed in that year. Liabilities are understated by $400 as of 12/31/99. There is no effect on assets.

    *c.* Net income for 1999 would be overstated by $1,000 because salaries expense is understated. The following year, 2000, net income would be understated by $1,000 since salaries expense would be overstated assuming all other salaries incurred in 2000 are correctly recognized. Salaries Payable (a liability) would be understated by $1,000 as of 12/31/99. There is no effect on assets.

21.  *a.* Depreciation ExpenseXBuildings ................................. 5,000
        Accumulated DepreciationXBuildings .......................................          5,000
        ($75,000 / 15 years)

    *b.* Office Supplies Expense ................................................ 305
        Office Supplies on Hand ............................................          305
        ($445 - $140)

    *c.* Insurance Expense ........................................................ 200
        Prepaid Insurance ......................................................          200
        [($1,600/4 years) = $400 x 1/2 year]

    *d.* Rent Expense ................................................................ 900
        Prepaid Rent ..............................................................          900

    *e.* Advertising Expense .................................................... 320
        Prepaid Advertising ...................................................          320
        ($960 x 1/3 = $320)

    *f.* Salaries Expense .......................................................... 600
        Salaries Payable ........................................................          600

    *g.* Unearned Service Fees ................................................ 300
        Service Revenue .........................................................          300
        (2/3 x $450 = $300)

22.                          *Trend Percentage*

|      |           |       |
|------|-----------|-------|
| 1994 | $195,824  | 100   |
| 1995 | 355,842   | 182   |
| 1996 | 476,388   | 243*  |

The prospects for continued growth in net income appear to be excellent.

*True-False Questions*

1. T

2. T  Rent and insurance expenses are incurred continuously; however, they are usually recorded through adjusting entries.

3. T

4. T

5. T

6. F  An accrued liability represents an obligation to make payments that are not legally due at the balance sheet date. No liability would result if cash has already been paid.

7. T

8. F  Unearned revenue accounts are liabilities and have credit balances.

9. F  Under the accrual basis of accounting, expenses only need be incurred (not paid) before they are recorded.

10. F  Normally the maximum length of an accounting period is one year.

11. T  This is the main purpose of adjusting entries.

12. F  Wages paid in advance to an employee would be classified as a prepaid expense.

13. T  $450/36 months = $12.50 insurance expense per month; $12.50 x 4 months = $50.

14. F  Entries other than adjusting entries are needed to record expenses and revenues during a period.

15. F  The adjusting entry to record depreciation recognizes an expense, which would decrease income. If this entry was omitted, income would be overstated.

16. T

17. F  Adjusting entries never anticipate expenses because they merely record expenses that have occurred; it is true that adjusting entries never anticipate revenues that are to be earned.

18. T

19. T

20. T

21. T

22. F  Dividends are not expenses.

23. T  Depreciation may result from an expenditure made many years ago.

24. T  Economic activity occurs continuously, which is why adjusting entries are needed before financial statements are prepared.

25. F  This statement describes the cash basis of accounting.

26. T

## Multiple Choice Questions

1. B  Salaries payable is a current liability.
2. C  Unearned Commission Fees is a liability and has a credit balance.
3. E  The proper entry is to debit Depreciation ExpenseXEquipment and credit Accumulated DepreciationXEquipment.
4. E
5. B
6. D  Accumulated Depreciation is a contra asset account; Prepaid Insurance is an asset; Service Revenue and Sales are revenue accounts.
7. C  The asset account, Supplies on Hand, will be understated and Supplies Expense will be overstated, which will understate net income and stockholders' equity.
8. C  The unearned subscription fees must be removed from the revenue account and placed in a liability account.
9. C
10. E  Both (C) and (D) are correct.
11. C
12. E
13. C  Prepaid Rent is an asset.
14. B  To the insurance company, insurance premiums received in advance would be classified as a liability until the period of coverage expires and the revenue is thereby earned.
15. B
16. C  ($500,000/$400,000) x 100

# COMPLETING THE
# ACCOUNTING CYCLE

## Learning Objectives

1. .Summarize the steps in the accounting cycle
2. Prepare a work sheet for a service company
3. Prepare an income statement, statement of retained earnings, and balance sheet using information contained in the work sheet
4. Prepare adjusting and closing entries using information contained in the work sheet
5. Prepare a post-closing trial balance
6. Describe the evolution of accounting systems
7. Prepare a classified balance sheet
8. Analyze and use the financial resultsXthe current ratio

## REFERENCE OUTLINE

# CHAPTER OUTLINE

*Learning Objective 1:*
*Summarize the steps in the accounting cycle*

## THE ACCOUNTING CYCLE SUMMARIZED

1. The accounting cycle consists of a series of steps related to gathering, classifying, and reporting useful financial information. The steps in the accounting cycle and the chapter(s) in which they are discussed are given below along with when the steps are performed.

   *Performed During Accounting Period*

   a. Analyze transactions by examining source documents (Chapters 1 and 2).
   b. Journalize transactions in the journal (Chapter 2).
   c. Post journal entries to the accounts in the ledger (Chapter 2).

   *Performed at End of Accounting Period*

   d. Prepare a trial balance of the accounts (Chapter 2) and complete the work sheet (Chapter 4).
   e. Prepare financial statements (Chapter 4).
   f. Journalize and post adjusting entries (Chapters 3 and 4).
   g. Journalize and post closing entries (Chapter 4).
   h. Prepare a post-closing trial balance (Chapter 4).

*Learning Objective 2:*
*Prepare a work sheet for a service company*

## THE WORK SHEET

2. A work sheet offers a convenient means for entering and summarizing information needed for making adjusting and closing entries and for preparing financial statements.
   a. A work sheet may be prepared each time financial statements are to be prepared.
   b. A work sheet is an internal statement and is not part of the formal accounting records.
   c. A work sheet may be prepared in various ways and is often prepared in pencil or using a computer spreadsheet program.

## THE TRIAL BALANCE COLUMNS

3. The work sheet usually contains Trial Balance columns; this avoids the preparation of a separate trial balance statement.
   a. The balances of the accounts are entered in the Trial Balance columns of the work sheet.
   b. The Trial Balance columns are totaled to check on equality of debit and credit totals.

## THE ADJUSTMENTS COLUMNS

4. Adjustments needed to bring the accounts up to date are entered in the Adjustments columns of the work sheet.
   a. The following steps can assist the accountant in determining the adjusting entries needed.
      (1) Examine adjusting entries made at the end of the preceding accounting period.
      (2) Examine the account titles appearing in the trial balance.
      (3) Examine various business documents to discover other assets, liabilities, expenses, and revenues that have not yet been recorded.
      (4) Specific questions may be directed to management or other personnel.

## THE ADJUSTED TRIAL BALANCE COLUMNS

5. All accounts having balances are extended to the Adjusted Trial Balance columns after entering adjustments on the work sheet.

## THE INCOME STATEMENT COLUMNS

6. Revenue and expense accounts appearing in the Adjusted Trial Balance columns are extended to the Income Statement columns. After subtotaling the debit and credit columns, the net income or net loss for the period is determined.
   a. If the debit subtotal exceeds the credit subtotal, a net loss has occurred.
   b. If the credit subtotal exceeds the debit subtotal, net income has been earned.

## THE STATEMENT OF RETAINED EARNINGS COLUMNS

7. The beginning balance in Retained Earnings, Dividends, and net income (or loss) are extended to the Statement of Retained Earnings columns. The ending balance in Retained Earnings is equal to the difference between the column totals.

## THE BALANCE SHEET COLUMNS

8. The amount for assets, liabilities, and capital stock listed in the Adjusted Trial Balance columns are extended to the Balance Sheet columns. The ending amount of retained earnings in the Statement of Retained Earnings column is extended to the credit Balance Sheet column if retained earnings is positive.

## LOCATING ERRORS

9. If the balance sheet column totals do not agree, work backward through the process used in preparing the work sheet.

*Learning Objective 3:*
*Prepare an income statement, statement of retained earnings, and balance sheet using information contained in the work sheet.*

## PREPARING FINANCIAL STATEMENTS FROM THE WORK SHEET

10. After the work sheet is completed, the information is used to prepare the financial statements.

## INCOME STATEMENT

11. The income statement can be prepared from data in the Income Statement columns in the work sheet.

## STATEMENT OF RETAINED EARNINGS

12. The statement of retained earnings shows the addition of the net income to the beginning Retained Earnings balance and the deduction of dividends to arrive at the ending Retained Earnings balance.
    a. A net loss is deducted from the beginning Retained Earnings account balance.
    b. The ending Retained Earnings balance is then carried forward to the balance sheet.
    c. The statement of retained earnings relates the income statement information to the balance sheet.

## BALANCE SHEET

13. The balance sheet is prepared from information contained in the Balance Sheet columns of the work sheet.

*Learning Objective 4:*
*Prepare adjusting and closing entries using information contained in the work sheet.*

## JOURNALIZING ADJUSTING ENTRIES

14. Adjusting entries that were entered on the work sheet must be entered in the general journal and posted to the appropriate ledger accounts.

## THE CLOSING PROCESS

15. The closing process transfers the balances in the revenue and expense accounts to Income Summary and then to Retained Earnings.
    a. Closing entries reduce revenue and expense account balances to zero.
    b. Closing entries are needed so that revenue and expense information for the current period will not be intermingled with information from all prior or future periods.

c. The balance in each revenue and expense account is transferred to the Income Summary account.
   (1) The Income Summary account is a clearing account used only at the end of the accounting period to summarize revenues and expenses for the period.
   (2) The Income Summary account does not appear on any financial statement.
   (3) The balance of the Income Summary account is transferred to the Retained Earnings account.
d. The Dividends account is closed to the Retained Earnings account.
   (1) The Dividends account is not closed to Income Summary.
   (2) Dividends have no effect on income and loss and are closed directly to Retained Earnings
e. Asset, liability, and stockholders' equity accounts are not closed during the closing process.

## STEP 1: CLOSING THE REVENUE ACCOUNT(S)

16. Because revenue accounts have credit balances, they must be debited to give them a zero balance.
    a. The revenue account is debited and the Income Summary account is credited in the closing process.

## STEP 2: CLOSING THE EXPENSE ACCOUNT(S)

17. Because expense accounts have debit balances, they must be credited to give them a zero balance.
    a. The expense accounts are credited and the Income Summary account is debited in the closing process.

## STEP 3: CLOSING THE INCOME SUMMARY ACCOUNT

18. After closing revenues and expenses to the Income Summary account, this account is closed to the Retained Earnings account.
    a. If revenues exceed expenses, income has been earned, and a closing entry debiting the Income Summary account and crediting the Retained Earnings account is needed.
    b. If instead, expenses exceed revenues, a loss has occurred, and a closing entry crediting the Income Summary account and debiting the Retained Earnings account is needed.

## STEP 4: CLOSING THE DIVIDENDS ACCOUNT

19. The Dividends account is closed by crediting this account and debiting the Retained Earnings account.
20. After the closing process is complete, all revenue, expense, Dividends, and Income Summary accounts have a zero balance.

*Learning Objective 5:*
*Prepare a post-closing trial balance.*

## POST-CLOSING TRIAL BALANCE

21. A post-closing trial balance is taken after revenue, expense, and Dividends accounts have been closed.
    a. Only asset, liability, and stockholders' equity accounts appear on the post-closing trial balance.
    b. The post-closing trial balance serves as a means of examining the accuracy of the closing process and ensures that the books are in balance at the start of the new accounting period.

*Learning Objective 6:*
*Describe the evolution of accounting systems.*

## ACCOUNTING SYSTEMS: FROM MANUAL TO COMPUTERIZED

22. The first manual double-entry accounting systems used one journal and one ledger. Special journals and subsidiary ledgers came into use to create more efficiency in the recording and posting process. "One write" systems and bookkeeping machines increased the efficiency.
23. Mainframe computers first started being used for accounting functions in the mid 1950s.
24. The microcomputer began being widely used for accounting purposes in the 1980s. The creation of inexpensive accounting software packages for the microcomputer has made it possible for even the smallest businesses to use a computerized accounting system.

## THE ROLE OF AN ACCOUNTING SYSTEM

25. An accounting system is a set of records and the procedures and equipment used to perform the accounting functions.

*Learning Objective 7:*
*Prepare a classified balance sheet.*

## THE CLASSIFIED BALANCE SHEET

26. A classified balance sheet divides the major categories of assets, liabilities, and stockholders' equity into more detailed classifications.
    a. An unclassified balance sheet has only major categories labeled as assets, liabilities, and stockholders' equity.
    b. Balance sheets may be presented in a vertical format, with assets appearing above liabilities and stockholders' equity.
    c. A horizontal format of the balance sheet shows assets on the left and liabilities and stockholders' equity on the right.

## CURRENT ASSETS

27. Current assets are cash and other assets that will be converted into cash or used up by the business in one year or one operating cycle, whichever is longer.

## LONG-TERM ASSETS

28. Long-term assets are assets that a business will have on hand or use for a relatively long period of time.

## PROPERTY, PLANT, AND EQUIPMENT

29. Property, plant, and equipment are assets acquired for use in a business rather than for resale.
    a. Property, plant, and equipment are also called plant assets or fixed assets.
    b. They are acquired for long-term use.
    c. Land, buildings, machinery, and accumulated depreciation are included in this classification.

## LONG-TERM INVESTMENTS

30. Long-term investments are often securities of another company held for long-term purposes.

## INTANGIBLE ASSETS

31. Intangible assets consist of noncurrent, nonmonetary, nonphysical assets of a business.

## CURRENT LIABILITIES

32. Current liabilities are debts that are due within one year or one operating cycle, whichever is longer.
    a. The payment of current liabilities requires the use of current assets.
    b. Accounts Payable, Notes Payable, and Salaries Payable are included in this category.

## LONG-TERM LIABILITIES

33. Long-term liabilities are not due for a relatively long period of time, usually more than a year.

## STOCKHOLDERS' EQUITY

34. Stockholders' equity shows the owners' interest in the business.

*Learning Objective 8:*
*Analyze and use the financial resultsXthe current ratio.*

## ANALYZING AND USING THE FINANCIAL RESULTSXTHE CURRENT RATIO

35. The current ratio indicates the short-term debt-paying ability of a company.
36. The current ratio is calculated by dividing current assets by current liabilities.

---

## DEMONSTRATION PROBLEM

---

The trial balance of the Charles Company at December 31, 1999, contains the following account balances. (The accounts are listed in alphabetical order to increase your skill in sorting amounts to the proper work sheet columns.)

### CHARLES COMPANY
### Trial Balance Account Balances

| | |
|---|---:|
| Accounts Payable | $15,000 |
| Accounts Receivable | 55,000 |
| Accumulated DepreciationXBuilding | 20,000 |
| Accumulated DepreciationXEquipment | 3,500 |
| Buildings | 120,000 |
| Capital Stock | 58,200 |
| Cash | 16,000 |
| Commissions Revenue | 58,000 |
| Dividends | 10,000 |
| Equipment | 35,000 |
| Land | 90,000 |
| Notes Payable | 10,000 |
| Salaries Expense | 55,000 |
| Prepaid Insurance | 2,400 |
| Retained Earnings, January 1, 1999 | 20,300 |
| Supplies on Hand | 3,500 |
| Unearned Management Fees | 204,000 |
| Utilities Expense | 2,100 |

a. Using the account balances given above and the additional information presented below, prepare a work sheet for the Charles Company. You do not need to include account numbers.
   Part *a.* (work sheet) appears on pages 108 and 109.
Additional data:
   1. Store supplies on hand at December 31 have a cost of $500.
   2. The balance in the Prepaid Insurance account represents the cost of a 12-month insurance policy beginning April 1, 1999. The company did not carry insurance from January through March 1999.
   3. Depreciation for the building is $2,000 and for the equipment, $1,000.
   4. The unearned management fees cover a 12-month management service of Charles Company from September 1, 1999, to August 31, 2000.
b. Prepare the adjusting and closing journal entries.

*b.*

## GENERAL JOURNAL

| Date | Account Titles and Explanation | Post. Ref. | Debit | Credit |
|------|-------------------------------|-----------|-------|--------|
|  |  |  |  |  |
|  |  |  |  |  |
|  |  |  |  |  |
|  |  |  |  |  |
|  |  |  |  |  |
|  |  |  |  |  |
|  |  |  |  |  |
|  |  |  |  |  |
|  |  |  |  |  |
|  |  |  |  |  |
|  |  |  |  |  |
|  |  |  |  |  |
|  |  |  |  |  |
|  |  |  |  |  |
|  |  |  |  |  |
|  |  |  |  |  |
|  |  |  |  |  |
|  |  |  |  |  |
|  |  |  |  |  |
|  |  |  |  |  |
|  |  |  |  |  |
|  |  |  |  |  |
|  |  |  |  |  |
|  |  |  |  |  |
|  |  |  |  |  |
|  |  |  |  |  |
|  |  |  |  |  |
|  |  |  |  |  |
|  |  |  |  |  |
|  |  |  |  |  |
|  |  |  |  |  |
|  |  |  |  |  |
|  |  |  |  |  |
|  |  |  |  |  |
|  |  |  |  |  |
|  |  |  |  |  |
|  |  |  |  |  |
|  |  |  |  |  |
|  |  |  |  |  |
|  |  |  |  |  |

# SOLUTION TO DEMONSTRATION PROBLEM

## CHARLES COMPANY
### Work Sheet
### For Year Ended December 31, 1999

| Account Name | Trial Balance Debit | Trial Balance Credit | Adjustments Debit | Adjustments Credit | Adjusted Trial Balance Debit | Adjusted Trial Balance Credit | Income Statement Debit | Income Statement Credit | Statement of Retained Earnings Debit | Statement of Retained Earnings Credit | Balance Sheet Debit | Balance Sheet Credit |
|---|---|---|---|---|---|---|---|---|---|---|---|---|
| Cash | 16,000 | | | | 16,000 | | | | | | 16,000 | |
| Accounts Receivable | 55,000 | | | | 55,000 | | | | | | 55,000 | |
| Supplies on Hand | 3,500 | | | (1) 3,000 | 500 | | | | | | 500 | |
| Prepaid Insurance | 2,400 | | | (2) 1,800 | 600 | | | | | | 600 | |
| Buildings | 120,000 | | | | 120,000 | | | | | | 120,000 | |
| Accumulated DepreciationXBuildings | | 20,000 | | (3) 2,000 | | 22,000 | | | | | | 22,000 |
| Equipment | 35,000 | | | | 35,000 | | | | | | 35,000 | |
| Accumulated DepreciationXEquipment | | 3,500 | | (3) 1,000 | | 4,500 | | | | | | 4,500 |
| Land | 90,000 | | | | 90,000 | | | | | | 90,000 | |
| Account Payable | | 15,000 | | | | 15,000 | | | | | | 15,000 |
| Notes Payable | | 10,000 | | | | 10,000 | | | | | | 10,000 |
| Unearned Management Fees | | 204,000 | 4) 68,000 | | | 136,000 | | | | | | 136,000 |
| Capital Stock | | 58,200 | | | | 58,200 | | | | | | 58,200 |
| Retained Earnings, January 1, 1999 | | 20,300 | | | | 20,300 | | | | 20,300 | | |
| Dividends | 10,000 | | | | 10,000 | | | | 10,000 | | | |
| Commissions Revenue | | 58,000 | | | | 58,000 | | 58,000 | | | | |
| Salaries Expense | 55,000 | | | | 55,000 | | 55,000 | | | | | |
| Utilities Expense | 2,100 | | | | 2,100 | | 2,100 | | | | | |
| | 389,000 | 389,000 | | | | | | | | | | |
| Management Fee Revenue | | | | (4)68,000 | | 68,000 | | 68,000 | | | | |
| Insurance Expense | | | (2) 1,800 | | 1,800 | | 1,800 | | | | | |
| Depreciation ExpenseXBuildings | | | (3) 2,000 | | 2,000 | | 2,000 | | | | | |
| Depreciation ExpenseXEquipment | | | (3) 1,000 | | 1,000 | | 1,000 | | | | | |
| Supplies Expense | | | (1) 3,000 | | 3,000 | | 3,000 | | | | | |
| | | | 75,800 | 75,800 | 392,000 | 392,000 | 64,900 | 126,000 | | | | |
| Net Income | | | | | | | 61,100 | | | 61,100 | | |
| | | | | | | | 126,000 | 126,000 | 10,000 | 81,400 | 317,100 | 245,700 |
| Retained Earnings, December 31, 1999 | | | | | | | | | 71,400 | | | 71,400 |
| | | | | | | | | | 81,400 | 81,400 | 317,100 | 317,100 |

*b.*

# CHARLES COMPANY
*Adjusting Entries*

1999

(1) December 31   Supplies Expense ............................................................   3,000

      Supplies on Hand .........................................................            3,000

      To record supplies expense.

(2)          31   Insurance Expense .........................................................   1,800

      Prepaid Insurance .......................................................            1,800

      Insurance expense for year.

(3)          31   Depreciation ExpenseXBuilding ..............................   2,000

      Depreciation ExpenseXEquipment .........................   1,000

      Accumulated DepreciationXBuilding .................            2,000

      Accumulated DepreciationXEquipment .............            1,000

      Depreciation expense for year.

(4)          31   Unearned Management Fees ......................................   68,000

      Management Fee Revenue .....................................            68,000

      To record management fees earned ($204,000/3).

*Closing Entries*

1999

     December 31   Management Fee Revenue ..........................................   68,000

      Commissions Revenue ................................................   58,000

      Income Summary .......................................................            126,000

      To close revenue accounts.

         31   Income Summary ..........................................................   64,900

      Salaries Expense ........................................................            55,000

      Utilities Expense .......................................................            2,100

      Supplies Expense ......................................................            3,000

      Insurance Expense ....................................................            1,800

      Depreciation ExpenseXBuilding ..........................            2,000

      Depreciation ExpenseXEquipment .....................            1,000

      To close expense accounts.

         31   Income Summary ..........................................................   61,100

      Retained Earnings .....................................................            61,100

      To close net income to Retained Earnings.

         31   Retained Earnings .......................................................   10,000

      Dividends ...................................................................            10,000

      To close the Dividends account.

# MATCHING

Referring to the terms listed below, place the appropriate letter(s) next to the corresponding description. A term can be used more than once.

a. Accrued assets
b. Accrued liabilities
c. Adjusting entries
d. Assets
e. Closing entries

f. Contra account
g. Income statement
h. Income Summary account
i. Prepaid expenses
j. Retained Earnings account

k. Statement of retained earnings
l. Work sheet
m. Current ratio
n. Accounting System

_____ 1. Accumulated depreciation.
_____ 2. Results from services that have been performed but have not yet been billed.
_____ 3. A statement showing changes in retained earnings.
_____ 4. Entries required at the end of the accounting period to clear out the temporary accounts.
_____ 5. Used to record the cost of office supplies used from inventory.
_____ 6. Classification(s) of accounts with debit balances remaining open after the accounting records are closed.
_____ 7. Is the account to which commissions earned is closed
_____ 8. Assets that exist at the end of an accounting period but have not yet been recorded.
_____ 9. Amounts owed for expenses incurred but not yet billed or due to be paid.
_____ 10. Used to record the cost of prepaid insurance that has expired.
_____ 11. Account subtracted from plant and equipment to arrive at book value.
_____ 12. The Dividends account is closed to this account.
_____ 13. The account's balance is subtracted from the balance of an associated account to show the appropriate balance.
_____ 14. After these entries are posted, revenue and expense accounts have a zero balance.
_____ 15. A form that provides a convenient way for summarizing information needed for preparing financial statements.
_____ 16. A set of records and the procedures and equipment used to perform accounting functions.
_____ 17. Current assets divided by current liabilities.

# COMPLETION AND EXERCISES

1. The financial accounting process has been shown to consist of eight steps, namely,

1. _____
2. _____
3. _____
4. _____
5. _____
6. _____
7. _____
8. _____

2. Depreciation expense is an _____ expense that is closed, at the end of the accounting year, to the _____ _____ account.

3. In the closing process or in closing the books, all revenue accounts are _____ and the _____ _____ account is _____. Similarly, all expense accounts are _____ and the _____ _____ account is _____.

4. After the closing entries have been prepared and posted, a _____ _____ _____ _____ is prepared as a means of checking upon the procedural accuracy of the process.

5. A _____ _____ is a large columnar sheet of paper used to summarize information needed to prepare the financial statements and the adjusting and closing entries.

6. Adjusting entries are entered in the _____ columns.

7. The Prepaid Insurance account has a debit balance of $2,500 in the Trial Balance columns. In the Adjustments columns, the account is credited for $1,200. The balance of the Prepaid Insurance account in the Adjusted Trial Balance column is a $_____ _____ (debit or credit) balance.

8. Expense and revenue account balances in the Adjusted Trial Balance columns are extended to the _____ _____ columns; asset, liability, capital stock and ending Retained Earnings account balances are extended to the _____ _____ columns. Beginning Retained Earnings and Dividends account balances are extended to the _____ _____ _____ _____ columns.

9. Net income appears in the _____ _____ debit column and the _____ __ _____ _____ credit column; a net loss appears in the _____ _____ credit column and the _____ __ _____ _____ debit column.

10. A statement of retained earnings summarizes changes in the _____ _____ account balance.

11. Use the information given below to complete the work sheet for B. B. Bean Company (on page 84). You do not need to show account numbers.

    *a.* Supplies on hand at December 31, 1999; $20.
    *b.* Rent expense for 1999; $60.
    *c.* Depreciation on equipment for 1999; $15

11. *(continued)*

## B. B. BEAN COMPANY
### Work Sheet
### For Year Ended December 31, 1999

| Account Name | Trial Balance | | Adjustments | | Adjusted Trial Balance | | Income Statement | | Statement of Retained Earnings | | Balance Sheet | |
|---|---|---|---|---|---|---|---|---|---|---|---|---|
| | Debit | Credit | Debit | Credit | Debit | Credit | Debit | Credit | Debit | Credit | Debit | Credit |
| Cash | 100 | | | | | | | | | | | |
| Accounts Receivable | 200 | | | | | | | | | | | |
| Supplies on Hand | 60 | | | | | | | | | | | |
| Prepaid Rent | 80 | | | | | | | | | | | |
| Equipment | 150 | | | | | | | | | | | |
| Accumulated Depr.XEquip. | | 60 | | | | | | | | | | |
| Accounts Payable | | 90 | | | | | | | | | | |
| Capital Stock | | 30 | | | | | | | | | | |
| Retained Earnings, 1/1/99 | | 70 | | | | | | | | | | |
| Dividends | 20 | | | | | | | | | | | |
| Service Revenue | | 650 | | | | | | | | | | |
| Salaries Expense | 200 | | | | | | | | | | | |
| Insurance Expense | 50 | | | | | | | | | | | |
| Utilities Expense | 30 | | | | | | | | | | | |
| Miscellaneous Expense | 10 | | | | | | | | | | | |
| | 900 | 900 | | | | | | | | | | |
| | | | | | | | | | | | | |
| | | | | | | | | | | | | |
| | | | | | | | | | | | | |
| | | | | | | | | | | | | |

12. Refer to Question 11. Prepare the adjusting entries (omit explanations).

## GENERAL JOURNAL

| Date | Account Titles and Explanation | Post. Ref. | Debit | Credit |
|------|-------------------------------|-----------|-------|--------|
|      |                               |           |       |        |
|      |                               |           |       |        |
|      |                               |           |       |        |
|      |                               |           |       |        |
|      |                               |           |       |        |
|      |                               |           |       |        |
|      |                               |           |       |        |
|      |                               |           |       |        |
|      |                               |           |       |        |
|      |                               |           |       |        |
|      |                               |           |       |        |
|      |                               |           |       |        |
|      |                               |           |       |        |

13. Refer to Question 11. Prepare the closing entries (omit explanations)

## GENERAL JOURNAL

| Date | Account Titles and Explanation | Post. Ref. | Debit | Credit |
|------|-------------------------------|-----------|-------|--------|
|      |                               |           |       |        |
|      |                               |           |       |        |
|      |                               |           |       |        |
|      |                               |           |       |        |
|      |                               |           |       |        |
|      |                               |           |       |        |
|      |                               |           |       |        |
|      |                               |           |       |        |
|      |                               |           |       |        |
|      |                               |           |       |        |
|      |                               |           |       |        |
|      |                               |           |       |        |
|      |                               |           |       |        |
|      |                               |           |       |        |
|      |                               |           |       |        |
|      |                               |           |       |        |
|      |                               |           |       |        |
|      |                               |           |       |        |
|      |                               |           |       |        |
|      |                               |           |       |        |
|      |                               |           |       |        |
|      |                               |           |       |        |
|      |                               |           |       |        |

14. Refer to Question 11. Prepare an income statement.

| | | | | | | | | | |
|---|---|---|---|---|---|---|---|---|---|
| | | | | | | | | | |
| | | | | | | | | | |
| | | | | | | | | | |
| | | | | | | | | | |
| | | | | | | | | | |
| | | | | | | | | | |
| | | | | | | | | | |
| | | | | | | | | | |
| | | | | | | | | | |
| | | | | | | | | | |
| | | | | | | | | | |
| | | | | | | | | | |
| | | | | | | | | | |

15. Refer to Question 11. Prepare a statement of retained earnings.

| | | | | | | | | | |
|---|---|---|---|---|---|---|---|---|---|
| | | | | | | | | | |
| | | | | | | | | | |
| | | | | | | | | | |
| | | | | | | | | | |
| | | | | | | | | | |
| | | | | | | | | | |
| | | | | | | | | | |
| | | | | | | | | | |
| | | | | | | | | | |
| | | | | | | | | | |
| | | | | | | | | | |
| | | | | | | | | | |

16. Refer to Question 11. Prepare a balance sheet.

17. After adjustment, selected account balances of the Adelaide Company are:

|  | Debits | Credits |
|---|---|---|
| Interest revenue ............................................................... | | $ 5,000 |
| Service revenue ............................................................... | | 40,000 |
| Service expense ............................................................... | $ 4,000 | |
| Salaries expense .............................................................. | 5,500 | |
| Delivery expense ............................................................. | 13,200 | |
| Dividends ......................................................................... | 5,000 | |

In journal form, give the entries required to close the books for the period

| Date | Account Titles and Explanation | Post. Ref. | Debit | Credit |
|---|---|---|---|---|
|  |  |  |  |  |
|  |  |  |  |  |
|  |  |  |  |  |
|  |  |  |  |  |
|  |  |  |  |  |
|  |  |  |  |  |
|  |  |  |  |  |
|  |  |  |  |  |
|  |  |  |  |  |
|  |  |  |  |  |
|  |  |  |  |  |
|  |  |  |  |  |
|  |  |  |  |  |
|  |  |  |  |  |
|  |  |  |  |  |
|  |  |  |  |  |
|  |  |  |  |  |
|  |  |  |  |  |
|  |  |  |  |  |

18. *a.* Illustrate how the Statement of Retained Earnings columns would be used. Assume a beginning balance in Retained Earnings of $15,000, net income for the year of $10,000, and dividends declared of $4,900.

*b.* If there was a credit balance of $9,000 in the Retained Earnings account as of the beginning of the year and a net loss of $6,750 for the year, show how these items would be treated.

| | | Statement of Retained Earnings | | Balance Sheet | |
|---|---|---|---|---|---|
| | | Debit | Credit | Debit | Credit |
| *a.* | | | | | |
| | | | | | |
| | | | | | |
| | | | | | |
| | | | | | |
| | | | | | |
| | | | | | |
| | | | | | |
| | | | | | |
| | | | | | |
| *b.* | | | | | |
| | | | | | |
| | | | | | |
| | | | | | |
| | | | | | |
| | | | | | |
| | | | | | |
| | | | | | |
| | | | | | |
| | | | | | |
| | | | | | |
| | | | | | |
| | | | | | |

19. You are given the following account balances. Prepare one entry to close the revenue accounts, prepare one entry to close the expense accounts, and prepare one entry to close out the balance in the Income Summary account.

| | | | |
|---|---|---|---|
| Service Revenue | 150,000 | Rental Revenue | 9,500 |
| Utilities Expense | 10,000 | Advertising Expense | 11,500 |
| Accumulated Depr.XBuildings | 50,000 | Delivery Expense | 2,000 |
| Salaries Expense | 72,000 | Salaries Payable | 8,000 |
| Depreciation Exp.XBuildings | 10,000 | Retained Earnings | 35,000 |

## GENERAL JOURNAL

| Date | Account Titles and Explanation | Post. Ref. | Debit | Credit |
|---|---|---|---|---|
| | | | | |
| | | | | |
| | | | | |
| | | | | |
| | | | | |
| | | | | |
| | | | | |
| | | | | |
| | | | | |
| | | | | |
| | | | | |
| | | | | |
| | | | | |
| | | | | |
| | | | | |
| | | | | |
| | | | | |
| | | | | |
| | | | | |
| | | | | |
| | | | | |
| | | | | |
| | | | | |
| | | | | |
| | | | | |
| | | | | |

20. The following account balances appeared in the Income Statement columns of the work sheet prepared for the Christabel Company for the year ended December 31, 19_.

| | Income Statement | |
| --- | --- | --- |
| | Debit | Credit |
| Interest Revenue ............................................................ | | 180,000 |
| Painting Revenue ............................................................ | | 280,000 |
| Advertising Expense ....................................................... | 1,800 | |
| Salaries Expense ............................................................. | 200,000 | |
| Utilities Expense ............................................................. | 3,500 | |
| Insurance Expense .......................................................... | 2,000 | |
| Rent Expense ................................................................... | 8,800 | |
| Supplies Expense ............................................................ | 3,000 | |
| Depreciation ExpenseXBuildings ................................. | 7,000 | |
| Interest Expense ............................................................. | 1,500 | |
| Rental Revenue ............................................................... | | 1,500 |
| Gas and Oil Expense ...................................................... | 700 | |
| | 228,300 | 461,500 |
| Net Income ...................................................................... | 233,200 | |
| | 461,500 | 461,500 |

Prepare the closing journal entries. Assume the Dividends account has a balance of $50,000 on December 31, 19_.

### GENERAL JOURNAL

| Date | Account Titles and Explanation | Post. Ref. | Debit | Credit |
| --- | --- | --- | --- | --- |
| | | | | |
| | | | | |
| | | | | |
| | | | | |
| | | | | |
| | | | | |
| | | | | |
| | | | | |
| | | | | |
| | | | | |
| | | | | |
| | | | | |
| | | | | |
| | | | | |
| | | | | |
| | | | | |
| | | | | |
| | | | | |
| | | | | |
| | | | | |
| | | | | |
| | | | | |
| | | | | |
| | | | | |

21. Four of the major column headings on a work sheet are Adjusted Trial Balance, Income Statement, Statement of Retained Earnings, and Balance Sheet. For each of the following items, determine under which major column heading it would appear and whether it would be a debit or credit.

|  | Adjusted Trial Balance | | Income Statement | | Statement of Retained Earnings | | Balance Sheet | |
|---|---|---|---|---|---|---|---|---|
|  | Dr. | Cr. | Dr. | Cr. | Dr. | Cr. | Dr. | Cr. |
| a. Supplies Expense |  |  |  |  |  |  |  |  |
| b. Accounts Receivable |  |  |  |  |  |  |  |  |
| c. Accounts Payable |  |  |  |  |  |  |  |  |
| d. Commissions Revenue |  |  |  |  |  |  |  |  |
| e. Salaries Expense |  |  |  |  |  |  |  |  |
| f. Retained Earnings (ending cr. Balance) |  |  |  |  |  |  |  |  |
| g. Service Revenue |  |  |  |  |  |  |  |  |
| h. Net Loss for the Year |  |  |  |  |  |  |  |  |

22. The Daphne Company reported net income of $25,750 for the current year. Examination of the work sheet and supporting data indicates that the following items were ignored.
1. A total of $750 of the Supplies on Hand represents supplies that were used.
2. Of the Prepaid Insurance, $1,200 has expired.
3. Depreciation on equipment acquired on July 1 amounts to $4,500.
4. Accrued salaries were $2,000 at December 31.
5. Delivery fees earned, $1,000. (Assume an Unearned Delivery Fees account was initially credited.)
   a. Based on the above information, what adjusting entries should have been made on December 31?
   b. What is the correct net income?

*a.*

## GENERAL JOURNAL

| Date | | Account Titles and Explanation | Post. Ref. | Debit | | | Credit | | |
|------|--|-------------------------------|------------|-------|--|--|--------|--|--|
| | | | | | | | | | |
| | | | | | | | | | |
| | | | | | | | | | |
| | | | | | | | | | |
| | | | | | | | | | |
| | | | | | | | | | |
| | | | | | | | | | |
| | | | | | | | | | |
| | | | | | | | | | |
| | | | | | | | | | |
| | | | | | | | | | |
| | | | | | | | | | |
| | | | | | | | | | |
| | | | | | | | | | |
| | | | | | | | | | |
| | | | | | | | | | |
| | | | | | | | | | |
| | | | | | | | | | |

*b.*

23. Digital Equipment Corporation is a world leader in implementing and supporting networked platforms and applications in multivendor environments. The July 1, 1995 and 1994 amounts (in thousands) for current assets and current liabilities as shown in its 1995 annual report were:

|  | 1995 | 1994 |
|---|---|---|
| Current Assets | $9,947,152 | $10,579,771 |
| Current Liabilities | $4,246,292 | $5,056,265 |

Calculate the current ratio at each of these dates and comment

1995: _____ = 1994: _____ =

Comment: _____

_____

_____

_____

---

## TRUE-FALSE QUESTIONS

Indicate whether each of the following statements is true or false by inserting a capital "T" or "F" in the blank space provided.

_____ 1. The account "Accounts Receivable" is closed to Income Summary in the closing process.

_____ 2. The company has earned income for the period if a debit is needed to close the Income Summary account.

_____ 3. An adjusting entry is needed to transfer the information in the individual revenue and expense accounts to the Income Summary account.

_____ 4. The purpose of the Income Summary account is to summarize all expenses and revenues of the period in one account.

_____ 5. An expense account is normally closed by debiting it.

_____ 6. The important role of the work sheet is to aid the accountant by bringing together all the data needed for preparing the financial statements.

_____ 7. In a classified balance sheet, net income for the period would be included in the total of stockholders' equity.

_____ 8. The Income Summary account reveals that an operating loss of $800 has been incurred. Before closing entries are posted, the Dividends account shows a balance of $460. The entry to close the Income Summary is a debit of $340 to the Retained Earnings account and a credit of $340 to Income Summary.

_____ 9. The Income Summary account has a debit balance before it is closed if there was net income for the period.

_____ 10. It is necessary to adjust the accounts each time financial statements are to be prepared.

_____ 11. Dividends are an expense because they reduce retained earnings.

_____ 12. The post-closing trial balance is prepared immediately after all adjustments have been journalized and posted.

_____ 13. If a company's expenses are greater than its revenues, retained earnings is increased.

_____ 14. Income Summary is an account that will not appear on any financial statement.

_____ 15. If the balance in Income Summary is a credit balance, this means that the organization has earned net income of this amount.

_____ 16. Following the adjusting and closing process, the revenue and expense accounts are the only accounts remaining open.

_____ 17. If a company reports net income for the current year, this amount will be shown on the work sheet in the debit Income Statement column and credit Statement of Retained Earnings column.

_____ 18. One of the purposes of closing entries is to prepare revenue and expense accounts for the recording of the next period's revenue and expenses.

_____ 19. Work sheets furnish in a convenient form the information required for the periodic financial statements.

_____ 20. When a work sheet's Income Statement debit column total exceeds the Income Statement credit column total, a loss is indicated.

_____ 21. The post-closing trial balance contains asset, liability, and stockholders' equity accounts.

_____ 22. Entering the adjustments in the Adjustments columns of a work sheet makes it unnecessary to record and post adjusting entries.

_____ 23. The adjusted trial balance contains only revenue and expense accounts.

_____ 24. An accounting system consists of a set of records and the procedures and equipment used to perform accounting functions.

_____ 25. On a classified balance sheet, Salaries Payable should be classified as a current liability.

_____ 26. A Note Payable due in eight years would be classified as part of current liabilities on a classified balance sheet.

_____ 27. The current ratio is calculated by dividing current liabilities by current assets.

## MULTIPLE CHOICE QUESTIONS

For each of the following questions, indicate the best answer by circling the appropriate letter.

1. The Trial Balance columns of the work sheet show store fixtures of $4,000. Estimated depreciation for the period is $400. The Store Fixtures amount in the Balance Sheet columns of the work sheet will be a:
   A. $3,600 debit.
   B. $3,600 credit.
   C. $4,400 debit.
   D. $4,000 debit.
   E. $4,000 credit.

2. Which of the following statements is incorrect?
   A. The work sheet eliminates the need for preparing and posting adjusting and closing journal entries.
   B. The work sheet serves as the basis for preparing the Income Statement.
   C. The work sheet serves as the basis for preparing the Balance Sheet.
   D. The work sheet serves as the basis for journalizing the adjusting entries.

3. If the debit subtotal of the Income Statement on the work sheet is $159,000 and the credit subtotal is $147,000, there is a:
   A. net income of $12,000.
   B. net loss of $12,000.
   C. net loss of $159,000.
   D. net income of $147,000.

4. Supplies on Hand are shown as $315 in the Trial Balance columns of the work sheet. The Adjustments columns show that $290 of these supplies were used during the month. The amount shown as Supplies on Hand in the Balance Sheet columns is a:
   A. $25 debit.
   B. $315 debit.
   C. $290 debit.
   D. $25 credit
   E. $290 credit.

5. The depreciation expense on office equipment was recorded by a debit to Depreciation Expense and a credit to Office Equipment. If statements are now prepared:
   A. net income and stockholders' equity are correct.
   B. the total dollar amount of total assets is correct but the details shown on the balance sheet are in error.
   C. total liabilities are correct.
   D. All of the above.
   E. (A) and (C), but not (B).

6. Salaries Expense before adjustment at September 30, the end of the fiscal year, has a balance of $140,000. The amount of accrued salaries is $3,100. The adjusting entry would be:

   A. Salaries Expense ............................................................................ 3,100
         Salaries Payable ......................................................................... 3,100
   B. Salaries Payable ............................................................................ 3,100
         Salaries Expense ......................................................................... 3,100
   C. Income Summary ............................................................................ 3,100
         Salaries Expense ......................................................................... 3,100
   D. Income Summary ............................................................................ 143,100
         Salaries Expense ......................................................................... 143,100
   E. None of these.

7. The closing entry for Salaries Expense in the previous question would be:
   A. Salaries Expense ............................................................................ 143,100
         Salaries Payable ......................................................................... 143,100
   B. Salaries Payable ............................................................................ 3,100
         Salaries Expense ......................................................................... 3,100
   C. Income Summary ............................................................................ 3,100
         Salaries Expense ......................................................................... 3,100
   D. Income Summary ............................................................................ 143,100
         Salaries Expense ......................................................................... 143,100
   E. None of these.

8. In adjusting and closing the books of Sally Smith Company at the end of the fiscal year, no provision was made for accrued sales salaries expense of $600. The effect of this omission was as follows:
   A. the assets on the balance sheet were the same regardless of the omission.
   B. stockholders' equity on the balance sheet is understated by $600.
   C. the liabilities reported on the balance sheet are overstated by $600.
   D. net income for the year was understated by $600.
   E. None of the preceding answers is correct.

9. Office Supplies on Hand shows up on the work sheet in the following columns, assuming office supplies expense must be deducted from the prepaid amount.
   A. Trial Balance, Adjustments, Adjusted Trial Balance, and Balance Sheet
   B. Income Statement and Adjustments
   C. Balance Sheet and Adjustments
   D. Balance Sheet and Income Statement

10. Murray Sporting Goods began business on January 1, 1999, with capital stock of $15,000. At December 31, 1999, assets amounted to $25,000 and liabilities were $6,000. Revenue from services during the year amounted to $30,000 and dividends were $8,000. The expenses of Murray Sporting Goods for 1999 amounted to:
    A. $10,000
    B. $18,000
    C. $26,000
    D. $19,000
    E. some other amount

11. Which of the following statements is <u>false</u>?
    A. Inclusion of special journals and subsidiary ledgers increased the efficiency of the manual accounting system.
    B. Microcomputers were used for accounting functions before mainframe computers.
    C. Even if special journals are used, the general journal is used.
    D. Many accounting software packages for use on a microcomputer are relatively inexpensive (under $500).

12. On a classified balance sheet, taxes payable should be classified as:
    A. Current asset.
    B. Property, plant, and equipment.
    C. Current liability.
    D. Long-term liability.
    E. Stockholders' equity.

13. If the subtotal of the income statement debit column is $250,000, the subtotal of the income statement credit column is $300,000, and the total of the Statement of Retained Earnings debit column is $475,000, what is the beginning balance in Retained Earnings? (Assume no dividends were declared.)
    A. $425,000
    B. $250,000
    C. $525,000
    D. $300,000
    E. None of the above.

14. If at the end of a period there is a debit balance in the Income Summary account, this means that:
    A. total assets have decreased during the period.
    B. the business has suffered a net loss during the period.
    C. revenues have exceeded expenses.
    D. dividends were greater than the income for the period.

15. Which of the following is true regarding the work sheet?
    A. It is a form that the accountant uses for his/her own aid and convenience.
    B. It assists in the orderly preparation of the adjusting entries and financial statements at the end of accounting periods.
    C. It can substitute for journals and ledgers.
    D. All of the above are true.
    E. Only (A) and (B) are true.

16. The current ratio:
    A. is a measure of long-term debt-paying ability.
    B. is found by dividing total assets by total liabilities.
    C. must be greater than 2:1 for a company to be able to pay its current liabilities.
    D. is a measure of short-term debt-paying ability.

*Matching*

| | | | |
|---|---|---|---|
| 1. | *f* | 10. | *c* |
| 2. | *a* | 11. | *f* |
| 3. | *k* | 12. | *j* |
| 4. | *e* | 13. | *f* |
| 5. | *c* | 14. | *e* |
| 6. | *d* and *i* | 15. | *l* |
| 7. | *h* | 16. | *n* |
| 8. | *a* | 17. | *m* |
| 9. | *b* | | |

*Completion and Exercises*

1. The accounting cycle consists of the following steps:
    1. Analyze transactions by examining source documents.
    2. Journalize transactions in the journal.
    3. Post journal entries to the accounts in the ledger.
    4. Prepare a trial balance of the accounts and complete the work sheet.
    5. Prepare financial statements.
    6. Journalize and post adjusting entries.
    7. Journalize and post closing entries.
    8. Prepare a post-closing trial balance.
2. operating; Income Summary
3. debited; Income Summary; credited; credited; Income Summary; debited
4. post-closing trial balance
5. work sheet
6. Adjustments
7. $1,300 debit
8. Income Statement; Balance Sheet; Statement of Retained Earnings
9. Income Statement; Statement of Retained Earnings; Income Statement; Statement of Retained Earnings
10. Retained Earnings
11. See page 100 for worksheet.
12. *a.* Supplies Expense ............ 40
       Supplies on Hand ............ 40
    *b.* Rent Expense ............ 60
       Prepaid Rent ............ 60
    *c.* Depreciation ExpenseXEquipment ............ 15
       Accumulated DepreciationXEquipment ............ 15

# B. B. BEAN COMPANY
## Work Sheet
### For Year Ended December 31, 1999

11.

| Account Name | Trial Balance | | Adjustments | | Adjusted Trial Balance | | Income Statement | | Statement of Retained Earnings | | Balance Sheet | |
|---|---|---|---|---|---|---|---|---|---|---|---|---|
| | Debit | Credit | Debit | Credit | Debit | Credit | Debit | Credit | Debit | Credit | Debit | Credit |
| Cash | 100 | | | | 100 | | | | | | 100 | |
| Accounts Receivable | 200 | | | | 200 | | | | | | 200 | |
| Supplies on Hand | 60 | | | (a) 40 | 20 | | | | | | 20 | |
| Prepaid Rent | 80 | | | (b) 60 | 20 | | | | | | 20 | |
| Equipment | 150 | | | | 150 | | | | | | 150 | |
| Accumulated Depr.XEquip. | | 60 | | (c) 15 | | 75 | | | | | | 75 |
| Accounts Payable | | 90 | | | | 90 | | | | | | 90 |
| Capital Stock | | 30 | | | | 30 | | | | | | 30 |
| Retained Earnings, 1/1/99 | | 70 | | | | 70 | | | | 70 | | |
| Dividends | 20 | | | | 20 | | | | 20 | | | |
| Service Revenue | | 650 | | | | 650 | | 650 | | | | |
| Salaries Expense | 200 | | | | 200 | | 200 | | | | | |
| Insurance Expense | 50 | | | | 50 | | 50 | | | | | |
| Utilities Expense | 30 | | | | 30 | | 30 | | | | | |
| Miscellaneous Expense | 10 | | | | 10 | | 10 | | | | | |
| | 900 | 900 | | | | | | | | | | |
| Supplies Expense | | | (a) 40 | | 40 | | 40 | | | | | |
| Rent Expense | | | (b) 60 | | 60 | | 60 | | | | | |
| Depreciation Expense—Equip. | | | (c) 15 | | 15 | | 15 | | | | | |
| | | | 115 | 115 | 915 | 915 | 405 | 650 | | | | |
| Net Income | | | | | | | 245 | | | 245 | 490 | 195 |
| | | | | | | | 650 | 650 | 295 | | | |
| Retained Earnings, 12/31/99 | | | | | | | | | 315 | 315 | | 295 |
| | | | | | | | | | | | 490 | 490 |

13.

*Closing Entries*

| | | | |
|---|---|---|---|
| *a.* | Service Revenue ............................................................... | 650 | |
| | Income Summary ......................................................... | | 650 |
| *b.* | Income Summary ............................................................... | 405 | |
| | Salaries Expense ......................................................... | | 200 |
| | Insurance Expense ...................................................... | | 50 |
| | Utilities Expense ........................................................ | | 30 |
| | Miscellaneous Expense .............................................. | | 10 |
| | Supplies Expense ........................................................ | | 40 |
| | Rent Expense .............................................................. | | 60 |
| | Depreciation ExpenseXEquipment ............................ | | 15 |
| *c.* | Income Summary ............................................................... | 245 | |
| | Retained Earnings ...................................................... | | 245 |
| *d.* | Retained Earnings ............................................................ | 20 | |
| | Dividends .................................................................... | | 20 |

14.

**B. B. BEAN COMPANY**
**Income Statement**
**For the Year Ended December 31, 1999**

| | | |
|---|---|---|
| Revenues: | | |
| Service revenue ........................................................................... | | $650 |
| Expenses: | | |
| Salaries expense .......................................................................... | $200 | |
| Insurance expense ....................................................................... | 50 | |
| Utilities expense .......................................................................... | 30 | |
| Miscellaneous expense ................................................................ | 10 | |
| Supplies expense ......................................................................... | 40 | |
| Rent expense ............................................................................... | 60 | |
| Depreciation expenseXequipment ............................................... | 15 | 405 |
| Net income .................................................................................. | | $245 |

15.

**B. B. BEAN COMPANY**
**Statement of Retained Earnings**
**For the Year Ended December 31, 1999**

| | |
|---|---|
| Retained earnings, January 1, 1999 .............................................. | $ 70 |
| Add: Net income ......................................................................... | 245 |
| Total .................................................................................... | $315 |
| Less: Dividends ........................................................................... | 20 |
| Retained earnings, December 31, 1999 ......................................... | $295 |

16.

**B. B. BEAN COMPANY**
**Balance Sheet**
**December 31, 1999**
*Assets*

| | | |
|---|---:|---:|
| Cash ............................................................................................ | | $100 |
| Accounts receivable ................................................................... | | 200 |
| Supplies on hand ....................................................................... | | 20 |
| Prepaid rent ............................................................................... | | 20 |
| Equipment .................................................................................. | $150 | |
| Less: Accumulated depreciationXequipment .......................... | 75 | 75 |
| Total assets | | $415 |

*Liabilities and Stockholders' Equity*

| | | |
|---|---:|---:|
| Liabilities: | | |
| Accounts payable ................................................................... | | $ 90 |
| Stockholders' equity: | | |
| Capital stock ......................................................................... | $ 30 | |
| Retained earnings, December 31, 1999 ................................. | 295 | |
| Total stockholders' equity ................................................. | | 325 |
| Total liabilities and stockholders' equity ................................. | | $415 |

*Closing Entries*

| | | |
|---|---:|---:|
| 17. Service Revenue ........................................................................ | 40,000 | |
| Interest Revenue ....................................................................... | 5,000 | |
| Income Summary .................................................................. | | 45,000 |
| To close the revenue accounts. ................................................ | | |
| | | |
| Income Summary ....................................................................... | 22,700 | |
| Service Expense ................................................................... | | 4,000 |
| Salaries Expense ................................................................. | | 5,500 |
| Delivery Expense ................................................................ | | 13,200 |
| To close the expense accounts. | | |
| | | |
| Income Summary ....................................................................... | 22,300 | |
| Retained Earnings ............................................................... | | 22,300 |
| To close the Income Summary account. ................................... | | |
| | | |
| Retained Earnings ..................................................................... | 5,000 | |
| Dividends .............................................................................. | | 5,000 |
| To close the Dividends account. ............................................... | | |

18.

a.

| | Statement of Retained Earnings | | Balance Sheet | |
|---|---|---|---|---|
| | Debit | Credit | Debit | Credit |
| Retained Earnings, Jan. 1 | | 15,000 | | |
| Net income for the year | | 10,000 | | |
| Dividends | 4,900 | | | |
| Retained Earnings, Dec. 31 | 20,100 | | | 20,100 |
| | 25,000 | 25,000 | | |

b.

| | Statement of Retained Earnings | | Balance Sheet | |
|---|---|---|---|---|
| | Debit | Credit | Debit | Credit |
| Retained Earnings, Jan. 1 | | 9,000 | | |
| Net loss for the year | 6,750 | | | |
| Retained Earnings, Dec. 31 | 2 250 | | | 2,250 |
| | 9,000 | 9,000 | | |

*Closing Entries*

19. Service Revenue ................................................................ 150,000
     Rental Revenue ................................................................ 9,500
         Income Summary ....................................................... 159,500
    To close revenue accounts.

    Income Summary ............................................................. 105,500
         Salaries Expense ......................................................... 72,000
         Depreciation ExpenseXBuildings ............................ 10,000
         Advertising Expense .................................................. 11,500
         Utilities Expense ........................................................ 10,000
         Delivery Expense ...................................................... 2,000
    To close expense accounts.

    Income Summary ............................................................. 54,000
         Retained Earnings ..................................................... 54,000
    To close Income Summary account.

20.

## CHRISTABEL COMPANY
### *Closing Entries*

| | | | |
|---|---|---|---|
| 19_ | | | |
| December 31 | Interest Revenue ........................................................ | 180,000 | |
| | Painting Revenue ....................................................... | 280,000 | |
| | Rental Revenue ........................................................... | 1,500 | |
| | Income Summary ............................................ | | 461,500 |
| | To close the revenue accounts | | |
| | | | |
| 31 | Income Summary ........................................................ | 228,300 | |
| | Advertising Expense ........................................... | | 1,800 |
| | Salaries Expense .................................................. | | 200,000 |
| | Utilities Expense ................................................. | | 3,500 |
| | Insurance Expense ............................................... | | 2,000 |
| | Rent Expense ....................................................... | | 8,800 |
| | Supplies Expense ................................................. | | 3,000 |
| | Depreciation ExpenseXBuildings ................. | | 7,000 |
| | Interest Expense ................................................. | | 1,500 |
| | Gas and Oil Expense .......................................... | | 700 |
| | To close the expense accounts. | | |
| | | | |
| 31 | Income Summary ........................................................ | 233,200 | |
| | Retained Earnings ............................................. | | 233,200 |
| | To close net income to Retained Earnings. | | |
| | | | |
| 31 | Retained Earnings ..................................................... | 50,000 | |
| | Dividends .......................................................... | | 50,000 |
| | To close the Dividends account. | | |

21.

| | | Adjusted Trial Balance | | Income Statement | | Statement of Retained Earnings | | Balance Sheet | |
|---|---|---|---|---|---|---|---|---|---|
| | | Dr. | Cr. | Dr. | Cr. | Dr. | Cr. | Dr. | Cr. |
| a. | Supplies Expense | X | | X | | | | | |
| b. | Accounts Receivable | X | | | | | | X | |
| c. | Accounts Payable | | X | | | | | | X |
| d. | Commissions Revenue | | X | | X | | | | |
| e. | Salaries Expense | X | | X | | | | | |
| f. | Retained Earnings (ending cr. balance) | | | | | | X | | X |
| g. | Service Revenue | | X | | X | | | | |
| h. | Net Loss for the Year* | | | | X | X | | | |

*The net loss figure actually represents an excess of debits over credits in the Income Statement columns. It appears in the credit column only so that the debit and credit columns will balance. It is then transferred to the debit side of the Statement of Retained Earnings column.

22.  *a.* The following adjusting journal entries should have been made at December 31.

1.  Supplies Expense .................................................. 750
        Supplies on Hand ................................................. 750
    To record supplies used.

2.  Insurance Expense .................................................. 1,200
        Prepaid Insurance ................................................. 1,200
    To record insurance expense.

3.  Depreciation ExpenseXEquipment ............................. 4,500
        Accumulated DepreciationXEquipment ................ 4,500
    To record depreciation for half a year.

4.  Salaries Expense .................................................. 2,000
        Salaries Payable ................................................. 2,000
    To record accrued salaries.

5.  Unearned Delivery Fees .................................................. 1,000
        Delivery Fees Revenue ................................................. 1,000
    To record delivery fee earned.

*b.* Correct net income is $18,300, computed as follows:

| | |
|---|---:|
| Reported net income ................................................. | $25,750 |
| Add: Total delivery fees earned ................................ | 1,000 |
| | $26,750 |

Less:

| | | |
|---|---:|---:|
| Supplies expense ................................................. | $ 750 | |
| Insurance expense ................................................. | 1,200 | |
| Depreciation expenseXequipment ............................ | 4,500 | |
| Salaries expense ................................................. | 2,000 | 8,450 |
| Correct net income ................................................. | | $18,300 |

23. Current ratios

$$1995: \quad \frac{9,947,152}{4,246,292} = 2.34 \qquad 1994: \quad \frac{10,579,771}{5,056,265} = 2.09$$

The current ratio has increased from 2.09 to 2.34 in one year. This increase would generally be viewed favorably by analysts.

### True-False Questions

1.  F  Accounts Receivable is a current asset, and assets are not closed.
2.  T
3.  F  This statement describes a closing entry.
4.  T
5.  F  Expenses are closed by debiting Income Summary and crediting the expense account.
6.  T
7.  T  Net income would be included in total Retained Earnings, but would not be separately identified.
8.  F  The correct entry would be a debit to Retained Earnings and a credit to Income Summary in the amount of $800. The Dividends account would be closed directly to Retained Earnings.
9.  F  The Income Summary account would have a credit balance before closing.
10. T

11. F Dividends are a distribution of assets, not an expense of the company.
12. F The post-closing trial balance is prepared after the closing entries have been journalized and posted.
13. F
14. T
15. T Revenues are recorded on the credit side of the Income Summary account and expenses are debits.
16. F Assets, liabilities, and stockholders' equity accounts remain open. Revenue and expense accounts are closed.
17. T
18. T
19. T
20. T
21. T
22. F Posting should not be made from the work sheet; journal entries are the source from which postings to the ledger are made.
23. F The adjusted trial balance contains assets, liabilities, stockholders' equity, and revenue and expense accounts.
24. T
25. T
26. F A note payable due in eight years would be classified as a long-term liability.
27. F The current ratio is calculated by dividing current assets by current liabilities.

## Multiple Choice Questions

1. D There also will be an Accumulated Depreciation account showing the total depreciation taken on the store fixtures since their acquisition.
2. A Adjusting and closing entries must still be entered in the journal and posted to the ledger; postings cannot be made directly from the work sheet.
3. B $159,000 expenses - $147,000 revenues = $12,000 net loss.
4. A $315 - $290 expense = $25 Supplies on Hand.
5. D
6. A
7. D
8. A The omitted journal entry would be a debit to Sales Salaries Expense and a credit to Sales Salaries Payable of $600; assets are not involved in this entry.
9. A
10. B
$25,000 12-31 assets
- 6,000 12-31 liabilities
$19,000 12-31 stockholders' equity

$30,000 revenues
-8,000 dividends
-4,000 increase in stockholders' equity during year
$18,000 expenses
11. B Mainframes were used for accounting functions in the 1950s, while the microcomputer came into use 20 to 30 years later.
12. C
13. A $300,000 - $250,000 = $50,000 income; $475,000 - $50,000 income = $425,000.
14. B
15. E
16. D

*Chapter 4 Demonstration Problem*

a.

## CHARLES COMPANY
### Work Sheet
#### For Year Ended December 31, 1999

| | Account Name | Trial Balance | | Adjustments | |
|---|---|---|---|---|---|
| | | Debit | Credit | Debit | Credit |
| 1 | | | | | |
| 2 | | | | | |
| 3 | | | | | |
| 4 | | | | | |
| 5 | | | | | |
| 6 | | | | | |
| 7 | | | | | |
| 8 | | | | | |
| 9 | | | | | |
| 10 | | | | | |
| 11 | | | | | |
| 12 | | | | | |
| 13 | | | | | |
| 14 | | | | | |
| 15 | | | | | |
| 16 | | | | | |
| 17 | | | | | |
| 18 | | | | | |
| 19 | | | | | |
| 20 | | | | | |
| 21 | | | | | |
| 22 | | | | | |
| 23 | | | | | |
| 24 | | | | | |
| 25 | | | | | |
| 26 | | | | | |
| 27 | | | | | |
| 28 | | | | | |
| 29 | | | | | |
| 30 | | | | | |
| 31 | | | | | |
| 32 | | | | | |
| 33 | | | | | |
| 34 | | | | | |
| 35 | | | | | |
| 36 | | | | | |
| 37 | | | | | |
| 38 | | | | | |
| 39 | | | | | |
| 40 | | | | | |
| 41 | | | | | |

## Chapter 4 Demonstration Problem (continued)

| Adjusted Trial Balance | | Income Statement | | Statement of Retained Earnings | | Balance Sheet | | |
|---|---|---|---|---|---|---|---|---|
| Debit | Credit | Debit | Credit | Debit | Credit | Debit | Credit | |
| | | | | | | | | 1 |
| | | | | | | | | 2 |
| | | | | | | | | 3 |
| | | | | | | | | 4 |
| | | | | | | | | 5 |
| | | | | | | | | 6 |
| | | | | | | | | 7 |
| | | | | | | | | 8 |
| | | | | | | | | 9 |
| | | | | | | | | 10 |
| | | | | | | | | 11 |
| | | | | | | | | 12 |
| | | | | | | | | 13 |
| | | | | | | | | 14 |
| | | | | | | | | 15 |
| | | | | | | | | 16 |
| | | | | | | | | 17 |
| | | | | | | | | 18 |
| | | | | | | | | 19 |
| | | | | | | | | 20 |
| | | | | | | | | 21 |
| | | | | | | | | 22 |
| | | | | | | | | 23 |
| | | | | | | | | 24 |
| | | | | | | | | 25 |
| | | | | | | | | 26 |
| | | | | | | | | 27 |
| | | | | | | | | 28 |
| | | | | | | | | 29 |
| | | | | | | | | 30 |
| | | | | | | | | 31 |
| | | | | | | | | 32 |
| | | | | | | | | 33 |
| | | | | | | | | 34 |
| | | | | | | | | 35 |
| | | | | | | | | 36 |
| | | | | | | | | 37 |
| | | | | | | | | 38 |
| | | | | | | | | 39 |
| | | | | | | | | 40 |
| | | | | | | | | 41 |

# CHAPTER 5

# ACCOUNTING THEORY UNDERLYING FINANCIAL ACCOUNTING

## Learning Objectives

1. *Identify and discuss the underlying assumptions or concepts of accounting.*
2. *Identify and discuss the major principles of accounting.*
3. *Identify and discuss the modifying conventions (or constraints) of accounting.*
4. *Describe the conceptual framework project of the Financial Accounting Standards Board.*
5. *Describe the recommendations for meeting the information needs of investors and creditors.*
6. *Discuss the nature of a company's summary of significant accounting policies in its annual report.*

---

### REFERENCE OUTLINE

---

## CHAPTER OUTLINE

*Learning Objective 1:*
*Identify and discuss the underlying assumptions or concepts of accounting.*

### UNDERLYING ASSUMPTIONS OR CONCEPTS

1. Accounting theory is a set of basic concepts or assumptions and related principles or standards that explain and guide the accountant's actions in identifying, measuring, and communicating economic information.

### BUSINESS ENTITY

2. An entity is a specific unit for which accounting information is gathered. An entity has an existence apart from its owners, creditors, employees, other businesses and interested parties.

### GOING CONCERN (CONTINUITY)

3. The going concern (continuity) assumption is that the entity will continue to operate indefinitely unless there is strong evidence that the entity will terminate.

    *a.* If liquidation (the process of termination) appears likely, the going concern assumption is no longer used.

    *b.* The going concern assumption is used to justify the use of historical costs rather than market values in measuring assets because market value has limited value to an entity that intends to use rather than sell its assets.

### MONEY MEASUREMENT

4. Instead of quantification of business transactions in terms of other measurements, money terms are used. Money measurement provides accountants with a common unit of measure in reporting on economic activity.

### STABLE DOLLAR

5. The stable dollar assumption is that fluctuations in the value of the dollar may be ignored because they are insignificant.

### PERIODICITY (TIME PERIODS)

6. According to the periodicity assumption, an entity's life can be subdivided into time periods for purposes of reporting on the entity's economic activities.

    *a.* The periodicity assumption requires the use of the accrual basis of accounting and leads to approximations requiring the exercise of judgment.

    *b.* Estimates must often be made of such things as expected uncollectible accounts and useful lives of depreciable assets.

## OTHER BASIC CONCEPTS

7. Other basic concepts include general-purpose financial statements, substance over form, consistency, double-entry, and articulation.

## GENERAL-PURPOSE FINANCIAL STATEMENTS

8. General-purpose financial statements are presented to external parties and top-level internal managers. The statements try to meet the common needs of these and other users by showing the results of the financial accounting process.

## SUBSTANCE OVER FORM

9. Accountants should always record the economic substance of a transaction rather than be guided by the legal form of the transaction.

## CONSISTENCY

10. Consistency requires a company to use the same accounting principles and reporting practices through time.

    *a.* The consistency concept bars indiscriminate switching of principles or methods every year.

    *b.* The consistency concept does not bar a change in principles if the information needs of users are better served by the change.

## DOUBLE ENTRY

11. Every transaction has a two-sided effect on each company or party engaging in the transaction.

## ARTICULATION

12. Financial statements are fundamentally related and articulate with each other.

## MEASUREMENT IN ACCOUNTING

13. Accounting is defined as a measurement process because the accountant measures the assets, liabilities, and stockholders' equity of an accounting entity.

## MEASURING ASSETS AND LIABILITIES

14. Cash is measured at its specified amount. Notes and accounts receivable are measured at expected cash inflows, allowing for possible uncollectibles. Inventories, prepaid expenses, plant assets, and intangibles are measured at their historical cost. Liabilities are measured in terms of the cash that will be paid or the value of services that will be performed to satisfy the liabilities.

## MEASURING CHANGES IN ASSETS AND LIABILITIES

15. While some changes in assets and liabilities are easily measured, the accountant must rely on the matching principle and other principles in other exchanges.

*Learning Objective 2:*
*Identify and discuss the major principles of accounting.*

## THE MAJOR PRINCIPLES

16. The accounting profession relies upon generally accepted accounting principles (GAAP) in recording changes in assets, liabilities, and stockholders' equity.

## EXCHANGE PRICE (OR COST) PRINCIPLE

17. According to the exchange price principle, transfers of resources are recorded at prices agreed on by the parties at the time of exchange. This principle determines the following three issues:

    a. What goes into the accounting systemsXtransaction data.

    b. When it is recordedXat the time of exchange.

    c. The amountsXexchange prices at which assets, liabilities, stockholders' equity, revenues, and expenses are recorded.

## MATCHING PRINCIPLE

18. Under the matching principle, net income of a period is determined by associating or relating revenues earned in a period with the expenses incurred to generate the revenues.

## REVENUE RECOGNITION PRINCIPLE

19. According to the revenue recognition principle, revenue should be earned and realized before it is recognized and recorded.

    a. Under the realization principle, revenue is recognized only after the seller acquires the right to receive payment from the buyer.

    b. There are several advantages to recognizing revenue at time of sale including the following:

        (1) Delivery of goods is an observable event.

        (2) Revenue is measurable.

        (3) Risk of loss due to price decline or destruction of the goods has passed to the buyer.

        (4) Revenue has been earned or substantially earned.

        (5) Expenses and net income can be determined because the revenue has been earned.

    c. The disadvantage of recognizing revenue at time of sale is that the revenue might not be recorded in the period in which most of the activity creating it occurred.

## EXCEPTIONS TO THE REALIZATION PRINCIPLE

20. Practical considerations may cause accountants to vary the point of revenue recognition from the point of sale.

    ### RECEIPT OF CASH

    a. Cash collection as point of revenue recognition is known as the cash basis of accounting; the cash basis is acceptable primarily in service organizations.

    ### INSTALLMENT BASIS

    b. The installment basis may be used when the selling price of goods sold is to be collected in installments and considerable doubt exists as to collectibility.

        (1) Gross margin on an installment sale is recognized in proportion to the cash collected on the receivable.

        (2) The installment basis of revenue recognition may be used for tax purposes only in very limited circumstances.

    ### REVENUE RECOGNITION ON LONG-TERM CONSTRUCTION PROJECTS

    c. Revenue from a long-term construction project can be recognized under either the completed-contract method or the percentage-of-completion method.

        (1) The completed-contract method recognizes revenue on long-term projects in the period in which the project is completed.

            (a) Costs incurred on the project are carried forward in an inventory account called Construction in Process and are charged to expense in the period in which revenue is recognized.

(b) It can be argued that it is unreasonable to wait in recognizing revenue because revenue-producing activities have been performed during each year of construction.

(2) Under the percentage-of-completion method, revenue is recognized based on the estimated stage of completion of a long-term project.

## REVENUE RECOGNITION AT COMPLETION OF PRODUCTION

d. Recognizing revenue at the time of product completion is referred to as the production basis and it is considered acceptable for certain precious metals and for many farm products.

    (1) Arguments in support of the production basis for revenue recognition include the following:

        (a) Homogeneous nature of the products.

        (b) Products can usually be sold at their market prices.

        (c) Difficulties sometimes are encountered in determining unit production costs.

    (2) Inventory is debited and a revenue account is credited for the expected selling price of the goods at the time of production or extraction.

## EXPENSE RECOGNITION PRINCIPLE

21. Expenses are incurred voluntarily to produce revenue.

    a. Most assets used in operating a business are measured in terms of historical cost.

    b. The matching principle implies that a relationship exists between expenses and revenues and this timing of expense recognition is guided by the concepts of product costs and period costs.

    c. Product costs are incurred in the acquisition or manufacture of goods and are carried forward in inventory accounts as long as the goods are on hand; product costs become expenses when the goods are sold.

    d. Period costs are expensed in the period in which incurred because they cannot be traced to specific revenues.

## GAIN AND LOSS RECOGNITION PRINCIPLE

22. Gains may be recorded only when realized, but losses should be recorded when they first become evident. Losses are usually involuntary.

## FULL DISCLOSURE PRINCIPLE

23. Information that is important enough to influence the decisions of an informed user of the statements should be disclosed.

*Learning Objective 3:*
*Identify and discuss the modifying conventions (or constraints) of accounting.*

## MODIFYING CONVENTIONS

24. Modifying conventions are customs emerging from accounting practice that alter results that would be obtained from a strict application of accounting principles. These conventions include cost-benefit, materiality, and conservatism.

    a. The cost-benefit consideration states that the benefits of using information should exceed the costs of providing it.

    b. The materiality convention allows the accountant to deal with unimportant items in a theoretically incorrect manner simply because it is more convenient and less expensive to handle them this way.

    c. The conservatism convention means being cautious or prudent and making certain that any errors in estimates tend to understate rather than overstate net assets and net income.

*Learning Objective 4:*
*Describe the conceptual framework project of the Financial Accounting Standards Board.*

## CONCEPTUAL FRAMEWORK PROJECT OF THE FINANCIAL ACCOUNTING STANDARDS BOARD

25. The debate over the exact nature of the basic concepts and related principles comprising accounting theory has surfaced with the Financial Accounting Standards Board (FASB) issuing concepts statements.

## OBJECTIVES OF FINANCIAL REPORTING

26. According to the FASB, the three overriding objectives of financial reporting are:
    a. To provide information that is useful to present and potential investors and creditors and other users in making rational investment, credit, and similar decisions.
    b. To provide information to help present and potential investors, creditors, and other users in assessing the amounts, timing, and uncertainty of prospective cash receipts.
    c. To provide information about the economic resources of an enterprise, the claims to those resources, and the effects of transactions, events, and circumstances that change its resources and claims to those resources.

## QUALITATIVE CHARACTERISTICS

27. Qualitative characteristics are those characteristics which accounting information should possess to be useful; included in these characteristics are relevance, reliability, and comparability.

### RELEVANCE
    a. Information has relevance if it is pertinent to a decision and makes a difference to someone who does not already have the information.

### RELIABILITY
    b. Information has reliability when it faithfully depicts for users what it purports to represent; reliability of information depends upon its representational faithfulness, verifiability, and neutrality.
    c. Information has verifiability when it can be substantially duplicated by independent measures using the same measurement methods.
    d. Neutrality in accounting information means that the information should be free of measurement method bias.

### COMPARABILITY AND CONSISTENCY
    e. In order for comparability in financial information to exist, differences and similarities that are real are noted.
        (1) Consistency leads to comparability of financial information for a single company through time.
        (2) Comparability between companies is harder to achieve because the same activities may be accounted for in different ways.

### PERVASIVE CONSTRAINTS
    f. The two pervasive constraints faced in providing useful information are the cost/benefit analysis and materiality.

## THE BASIC ELEMENTS OF FINANCIAL STATEMENTS

28. The FASB has defined several technical terms that are likely to have a major impact upon financial accounting.

*Learning Objective 5:*
*Describe the information needs of investors and creditors.*

MEETING THE INFORMATION NEEDS OF INVESTORS AND CREDITORS

29. The AICPA Special Committee on Financial Reporting issued a report on recommendations for meeting the information needs of investors and creditors. These recommendations are quoted in the text from the report.

*Learning Objective 6:*
*Discuss the nature of a company's summary of significant accounting policies in its annual report.*

SUMMARY OF SIGNIFICANT ACCOUNTING POLICIES

30. The text showed a summary of the significant accounting policies of The Walt Disney Company. These policies cover such items as consolidation policy, what is included in cash and cash equivalents, inventory methods used, amortization policy for intangible assets, and depreciation method(s) used.

31. Knowing these policies helps users of the financial statements to interpret the financial statements.

---

## DEMONSTRATION PROBLEM

Give the letter of the item that indicates the accounting concept or principle that is applied for each item below of Watson, Inc. An item may be used more than once.

A.  Stable monetary unit (money measurement)       D.  Periodicity        G.  Continuity of
B.  QuantifiabilityXobjective evidence              E.  Historical cost        lifeXgoing
C.  Consistency                                     F.  Business entity        concern

_____ 1.  The balance sheet shows an investment in an art painting at its cost of $50,000; however, an art dealer has indicated he could find a museum that would pay $75,000 since the price index has shown a rapid rise during the five years since the purchase of the painting.

_____ 2.  Sum-of-the-years'-digits depreciation is recorded at the end of each accounting period.

_____ 3.  This concept assumes that a business enterprise is separate and distinct from the persons who supply its assets.

_____ 4.  Store equipment costing $500 at the time of purchase is shown at its book value of $300 even though its market value is only $250.

_____ 5.  Equipment purchases costing $50,000 are not charged to expense in the period purchased.

_____ 6.  Inventories are reported using the same method each period rather than changing the method from period to period.

_____ 7.  A liability is established at the end of each year for the estimated number of cents-off coupons issued as part of the current year's advertising campaign that will be redeemed next year.

_____ 8.  Periodic payments of $2,250 per month for services of J. Reed, who owns all the stock of the company, are reported as salary; additional amounts are reported as dividends.

_____ 9.  Cash received for magazine subscriptions to be delivered for the next two years is reported as a liability.

_____ 10.  The accounting equation is an expression of this concept.

_____ 11.  Prepaid insurance of $600 is shown on the balance sheet as an asset even though the chance of obtaining a premium refund is slim.

_____ 12.  A memorandum entry indicating the additional shares received is made when a stock split is declared by a company in which Watson, Inc., holds 100 shares of stock acquired at a cost of $80. The total current market value of the stock is $95.

_____ 13. Physical counts of merchandise on hand, bank statements indicating the amount of cash in bank, and invoices for purchases support accounting transactions.

_____ 14. The declining value of the unit of measurement due to inflation is not recognized in the ledger accounts.

_____ 15. Application of this concept involves the revenue recognized during the period and the expired costs to be allocated to the period.

---

## SOLUTION TO DEMONSTRATION PROBLEM

| | | | | | |
|---|---|---|---|---|---|
| 1. | E | 6. | C | 11. | G |
| 2. | D | 7. | D | 12. | E |
| 3. | F | 8. | F | 13. | B |
| 4. | G, E | 9. | D | 14. | A |
| 5. | D | 10. | F | 15. | D |

---

## MATCHING

Referring to the items listed below, place the appropriate letter next to the corresponding description.

a. Cash basis
b. Entity
c. Expense
d. Installment sales
e. Liquidation

f. Loss
g. Modifying conventions
h. Summary of significant accounting policies

i. Period costs
j. Product costs
k. Revenue

_____ 1. Procedure of accounting when revenues and expenses are recorded at the time of cash collection and payment.

_____ 2. Selling and administrative costs comprise this cost classification because these costs cannot be traced to specific revenues.

_____ 3. Conservatism is an example of this.

_____ 4. Inventory costs, freight, and other costs incurred in the acquisition or manufacture of goods.

_____ 5. Asset expiration that is incurred voluntarily to produce revenue.

_____ 6. Sales of merchandise under terms that allow the buyer to make equal periodic payments over an extended period of time.

_____ 7. Asset expiration that is incurred involuntarily and does not create revenue.

_____ 8. The process of termination of an entity.

_____ 9. A specific unit for which accounting information is gathered.

_____ 10. The inflow of assets from the sale of goods and services to customers.

_____ 11. Assists users in interpreting the financial statements.

## COMPLETION AND EXERCISES

1. Give three advantages of recognizing revenue at the time of sale.

   a. _____

   _____

   b. _____

   _____

   c. _____

   _____

2. A disadvantage of recognizing revenue at the time of sale is that _____

   _____

   _____

3. Give two arguments in support of the use of the production basis for recognizing revenue.

   a. _____

   _____

   b. _____

   _____

4. In financial accounting, substance is to be emphasized over form. This concept means that

   _____

   _____

5. An item is considered to be material if _____

   _____

6. The basic ideas that make the accounting practices followed by different accountants fairly similar are called_____ _____ _____ _____.

7. An underlying assumption of accounting that has not been true in some years is the assumption that the _____ _____ _____ _____ unit of measure.

8. Accounting measurements are characterized by approximation and judgment from application of the _____ basis of accounting which is required if the activities of an enterprise are to be reflected in _____ _____ _____.

9. The primary data entered in the accounting system are _____

   _____.

10. In general, in accounting, net income is determined through a process of _____ revenues and expenses by _____ _____.

11. In general, revenue must be _____ and _____ before it is recorded in the accounts. Revenue is considered realized at the _____ _____ _____ for merchandise transactions and when _____ _____ _____ for service transactions.

12. In specified, limited circumstances, it is considered acceptable to recognize revenue

    a. _____

    b. _____

    c. _____

13. In accounting for expenses, a line of distinction is usually drawn between _____ costs and _____ costs. The former are expensed when the _____ ____ _____; the latter are expensed in the _____ _____ _____ _____.

14. Neutrality essentially means that accounting information should not be _____ .

15. Financial reporting is, according to the FASB, intended primarily for informed _____ and _____ to aid them in making _____ and _____ _____. It also seeks to help these parties assess the prospects of receiving _____ from their investments or loans to an enterprise. Because they affect cash inflows and outflows, financial statements should provide information about the _____ _____, _____ _____ , and _____ of an enterprise.

16. Relevance and verifiability are examples of _____ _____ which accounting information should possess to be useful.

17. The president of Finance Company asks you to determine the amount of revenue earned by his company for 1999. The following statements relate to 1999 data:

    1. Cash sales were $140,000.

    2. Credit sales were $250,000 of which $180,000 was collected. Included in the $250,000 was a sale to John Smith in the amount of $15,000; John Smith has since declared bankruptcy and Finance Company has written off his account. Also included in the $250,000 is a sale to Control Company in the amount of $10,000; it appears now that $6,000 of the $10,000 must be written off as uncollectible.

    3. Cash of $66,000 was collected in 1999 on sales made in 1998.

    4. Machinery with an original cost of $9,000 and accumulated depreciation of $5,600 was sold for $4,000. Cash of $1,800 was collected with an 8% note of $2,200 signed also.

Required: Determine the revenue earned in 1999:

18. Kramer Company had reported net income amounts for 1998 of $180,000 and 1999 of $95,000. No adjusting entries were made at either year-end for any of the transactions given below:
    1. On January 1, 1998, a machine costing $65,000 and having an estimated useful life of 10 years and a salvage value of $5,000 was put into service. The machine was debited to the Machinery account.
    2. The Service Supplies on Hand account balance on December 31, 1998, is $4,600. A count of the supplies on December 31, 1998, showed that only $2,800 of supplies were actually on hand. No purchases of supplies were made during 1999. A count of the supplies showed that $700 of supplies were on hand at December 31, 1999.
    3. Painting services performed in December 1998 in the amount of $22,000 were not billed until January 1999. A debit to Cash and a credit to Service Revenue when payment was received in January is the only transaction that was recorded.
    4. A truck was rented on April 1, 1998. Prepaid Rent was debited when cash of $12,000 was paid on that date to cover a two-year period.

    Required: Compute the correct net income for 1998 and 1999, beginning with the net income amounts as reported. Show the effects of each correction (adjustment) for each year using a plus or a minus to indicate whether reported income should be increased or decreased as a result of the correction. Your final net income for each year should be the correct amount after adding or deducting the adjustments.

# TRUE-FALSE QUESTIONS

Indicate whether each of the following statements is true or false by inserting a capital "T" or "F" in the blank space provided.

_____ 1. The cash basis of accounting is acceptable primarily in enterprises that do not have substantial credit transactions or inventories.

_____ 2. The completed-contract method recognizes revenues at the point of sale.

_____ 3. Period costs are carried in inventory accounts as long as the goods are on hand.

_____ 4. The consistency principle implies that a relationship exists between expenses and revenues.

_____ 5. The historical cost approach to recording accounting data has been severely criticized in periods of high inflation because often the income statement reports income when the economic value of the owner's investment has declined.

_____ 6. The completed-contract method is a method of recognizing revenue on long-term projects in which no revenue is recognized until the period in which the project is completed.

_____ 7. Period costs are costs incurred in the acquisition or manufacture of goods.

_____ 8. Materiality is a modifying convention which allows the accountant to deal with immaterial items in a theoretically incorrect but expedient manner.

_____ 9. The percentage-of-completion method recognizes revenue at the point of sale.

_____ 10. Losses are asset expirations which are incurred voluntarily to produce revenue.

_____ 11. The matching principle provides that net income of a period can be determined by associating the revenues earned in a period with the expenses incurred to generate the revenues.

_____ 12. One of the reasons for recognizing revenue at the time of sale is that the risk of loss due to price decline or destruction of the goods is passed to the buyer.

_____ 13. The installment basis of revenue recognition is acceptable only when a high degree of certainty exists as to the collectibility of the installments.

_____ 14. The cash basis of accounting recognizes revenues when cash is collected.

_____ 15. Recognizing revenue at the time of completion of production is called the installment basis of accounting.

_____ 16. Most assets used in operating a business are measured in terms of current cost.

_____ 17. The practice of conservatism tends to understate rather than overstate net assets and net income.

_____ 18. The stable dollar assumption is that fluctuations in the value of the dollar are significant and may not be ignored.

_____ 19. Many accounting measurements are estimates and involve approximation and judgment.

_____ 20. Under the transactions approach used in financial accounting, every transaction has a single effect upon each party engaging in it.

_____ 21. The AICPA Special Committee on Financial Reporting was appointed because of increasing concerns about the relevance and usefulness of financial reporting.

# MULTIPLE CHOICE QUESTIONS

For each of the following questions indicate the best answer by circling the appropriate letter.

1. This convention is used as a response to the uncertainty faced in the environment in which accounting is practiced.
   - A. Matching
   - B. Conservatism
   - C. Materiality
   - D. Neutrality
   - E. Relevance

2. A company uses the straight-line method of depreciation in 1996. In 1997, the company decides to change to a different method of depreciation. This procedure violates the rule of:
   - A. the matching principle.
   - B. consistency.
   - C. the cost principle.
   - D. periodicity.

3. Qualitative characteristics include:
   - A. relevance.
   - B. timeliness.
   - C. predictive value.
   - D. All of the above.
   - E. None of the above.

4. The required disclosures to financial statements may be in all of the following except:
   - A. notes to the financial statements.
   - B. special communications or reports.
   - C. a special letter to the Board of Directors.
   - D. the body of the financial statements.

5. When information is free of measurement method bias, it is said to be:
   - A. neutral.
   - B. verifiable.
   - C. reliable.
   - D. None of the above.

6. Some of the advantages of recognizing revenue at the time of sale are that:
   - A. delivery of goods is an observable event.
   - B. revenue is measurable.
   - C. risk of loss due to price decline or destruction of the goods has passed to the buyer.
   - D. All of the above.

7. Which of the following is a generally accepted accounting principle?
   - A. The exchange price (or cost) principle
   - B. The matching principle
   - C. The realization principle
   - D. All of the above.
   - E. Only (B) and (C).

8. Which of the following accounts requires a substantial amount of judgment by the accountant?
   A. Cash
   B. Accounts Receivable
   C. Depreciation
   D. Notes

9. .Under the accrual basis of accounting, revenues are recorded when:
   A. received and expenses are recorded when incurred.
   B. received and expenses are recorded when paid.
   C. services are rendered or products sold, and expenses are recorded when incurred.
   D. services are rendered or products sold, and expenses are recorded when paid.

10. Consistency generally:
    A. requires a company to use the same accounting principles as other companies in the same industry.
    B. requires a company to use the same accounting principles and reporting practices through time.
    C. bars indiscriminate switching of principles or methods.
    D. (B) and (C) above.

11. Under the realization principle:
    A. revenue is recognized after the seller acquires the right to receive payment from the buyer.
    B. revenue is not recognized until after payment is received from the buyer.
    C. (A) and (B) above.
    D. None of the above.

12. The percentage-of-completion method is a:
    A. revenue recognition procedure in which the gross margin on an installment sale is recognized in proportion to the cash collected on the receivable.
    B. method of recognizing revenue based on the estimated stage of completion of a long-term project.
    C. means of allowing greater comparability of the financial statements of a single company through time since the effects of price-level changes are removed.
    D. means of reflecting the purchasing power of the dollar relative to that of the base year by using the reciprocal of the price index.
    E. None of the above.

13. Historical cost accounting:
    A. measures accounting transactions in terms of the actual dollars expended or received.
    B. is a set of basic concepts and assumptions and related principles that explain and guide the accountant's actions in identifying, measuring, and communicating economic information.
    C. is supported by the stable dollar assumption which uses the current cost accounting approach.
    D. uses a general price index such as the Consumer Price Index in its valuation of assets.
    E. None of the above.

14. Under the production basis of revenue recognition, at the time of completion of production or extraction, the following journal entry is made:
    A. DebitXExpenses of Production or Extraction; CreditXRevenue account.
    B. DebitXAccounts Receivable; CreditXRevenue account.
    C. DebitXCost of Gold or Farm Products Sold; CreditXRevenue account.
    D. DebitXInventory account; CreditXRevenue account.
    E. None of the above.

## SOLUTIONS

### Matching

| | | |
|---|---|---|
| 1. *a* | 5. *c* | 9. *b* |
| 2. *i* | 6. *d* | 10. *k* |
| 3. *g* | 7. *f* | 11. *h* |
| 4. *j* | 8. *e* | |

### Completion and Exercises

1. The following are advantages of recognizing revenue at the time of sale.
    *a.* Delivery of goods is an observable event.
    *b.* Revenue is measurable.
    *c.* Risk of loss due to price decline or destruction of goods has passed to the buyer.
    *d.* Revenue has been earned or substantially earned.
    *e.* Expenses and net income can be determined because the revenue has been earned.
2. revenue might not be recorded in the period in which most of the activity creating it occurred.
3. Arguments for the production basis could include the following:
    *a.* homogeneous nature of the products
    *b.* products can usually be sold at their market prices
    *c.* difficulties are sometimes encountered in determining unit production costs
4. where economic substance and legal form conflict, economic substance is to be entered in the accounting system and reported.
5. knowledge of it would make a difference in the decision of an informed investor or creditor.
6. generally accepted accounting principles
7. dollar is a stable
8. accrual; periodic financial statements
9. exchange prices
10. matching; time periods
11. earned; realized; time of sale; services are rendered
12. *(a)* at completion of production; *(b)* when cash is received (installment method); *(c)* as production progresses
13. product; period; product is sold; period in which incurred
14. biased
15. investors; creditors; investment; credit decisions; cash; economic resources; economic obligations; earnings
16. qualitative characteristics

17.  $140,000
     + 250,000
     +    600
     $390,600      Revenue earned in 1999

The cash collected from 1998 sales is not included in 1999 revenues.

18.              *Explanation of Corrections*                              *1998*        *1999*

Reported net income ................................................................    $180,000     $95,000
To correct error in accounting for:
   1.  Depreciation:
      ($65,000 - $5,000) / 10 years = $6,000
      For 1998 ..........................................................................     -6,000
      For 1999 ..........................................................................                  -6,000
   2.  Service Supplies:
      Correct expense for 1998 ($4,600 - $2,800) .................     -1,800
      Correct expense for 1999 ($2,800 - $700) ....................                  -2,100
  3.     Service revenue:
      For 1998:
      Reported ........................................................ $      0
      Correct amount ..........................................    22,000
      Necessary correction ...................................................    +22,000
      For 1999:
      Reported ........................................................$22,000
      Correct amount ..........................................        0
      Necessary correction ...................................................                 -22,000
4.Truck rental:
      Correct expense for 1998
      ($12,000/2 x :year) .....................................................     -4,500
      Correct expense for 1999
      ($12,000/2) ...................................................................                  -6,000
Correct Net Income ................................................................    $189,700     $58,900

## True-False Questions

1. T
2. T  The sale occurs when the project is completed and delivered.
3. F  This statement describes product costs.
4. F  The matching principle implies that a relationship exists between expenses and revenues.
5. T
6. T
7. F  Product costs are incurred in the acquisition or manufacture of goods.
8. T
9. F  Revenue is recognized as work is completed.
10. F  Losses are usually incurred involuntarily; this statement describes expenses.
11. T
12. T
13. F  A high degree of uncertainty must exist.
14. T
15. F  Under the installment basis, revenue is recognized as cash is collected.
16. F  Most assets are measured in terms of historical costs.

17. T
18. F   The stable dollar assumption is that fluctuations in the value of the dollar are insignificant and may be ignored.
19. T
20. F   Transactions have a dual effect.
21. T

*Multiple Choice Questions*

1. B
2. B
3. D
4. C
5. A
6. D
7. D   The exchange price, matching, and realization principles are all GAAP.
8. C   The accountant must make a decision regarding the following: depreciation method, estimated useful life, amount to capitalize including freight, installation costs, cash discount deductions available, and estimated salvage value.
9. C
10. D
11. A
12. B
13. A
14. D

# MERCHANDISING TRANSACTIONS: INTRODUCTION TO INVENTORIES AND CLASSIFIED INCOME STATEMENT

## Learning Objectives

1. Record journal entries for sales transactions involving merchandise.
2. Describe briefly cost of goods sold and the distinction between perpetual and periodic inventory procedures.
3. Record journal entries for purchase transactions involving merchandise.
4. Describe the freight terms and record transportation costs.
5. Determine cost of goods sold.
6. Prepare a classified income statement.
7. Analyze and use the financial resultsXgross margin percentage.
8. Prepare a work sheet and closing entries for a merchandising company (Appendix).

## REFERENCE OUTLINE

---

## CHAPTER OUTLINE

---

TWO INCOME STATEMENTS COMPAREDXSERVICE COMPANY AND
MERCHANDISING COMPANY

1. A merchandising company's income statement is more involved since inventories must be included on its income statement.

*Learning Objective 1:*
*Record journal entries for sales transactions involving merchandise.*

SALES REVENUES

2. Sales revenue is earned from sales of merchandise to final consumers or to other companies.

RECORDING GROSS SALES

3. A sales transaction consists of the transfer of legal ownership, or passage of title, of goods from one party to another.
   a. The sales transaction is usually accompanied by physical delivery of the goods.
   b. A revenue account entitled Sales is credited when a sale is made; cash is debited if payment is received or Accounts Receivable is debited for sales on account.
   c. An invoice is prepared by the seller of the merchandise and sent to the buyer; it contains the details of a sale.
      (1) The invoice contains such items as the number of units sold, unit price, total price billed, terms of sale, and manner of shipment.
      (2) An invoice is called a sales invoice by the seller and a purchase invoice by the buyer.
   d. The following justifications exist for recording revenue at the time of sale:
      (1) Legal title to the goods has passed and the goods are now the responsibility and property of the buyer.
      (2) The selling price of the goods has been established.
      (3) The seller's obligation has been completed.
      (4) The goods have been exchanged for another asset such as cash or accounts receivable.
      (5) The costs incurred can be determined.
   e. The number for net sales must be examined before it is relied upon. Seasonal changes may affect net sales from one quarter to the next.

DETERMINING GROSS SELLING PRICE WHEN COMPANIES OFFER TRADE DISCOUNTS

4. Trade discounts are deductions from the list or catalog price of merchandise to arrive at the gross sales or invoice price.
   a. Trade discounts may be shown on the seller's invoice, but they are not recorded in the buyer's or seller's books.
   b. Trade discounts are used by various industries for a number of purposes.
      (1) Trade discounts are used to reduce the cost of catalog publications because separate discount lists can be distributed at less cost than reprinting a catalog.
      (2) Trade discounts can be used to grant quantity discounts.
      (3) Trade discounts facilitate the quotation of different prices to different types of customers, such as retailers and wholesalers.
   c. A chain discount occurs when a list price is subject to several trade discounts.

## RECORDING DEDUCTIONS FROM GROSS SALES

5. Sales discounts and sales returns and allowances are two common deductions from gross sales that are recorded in contra accounts to the Sales account.

## SALES DISCOUNTS

6. The terms of the cash discount vary among industries, but all cash discounts are offered as an incentive for early payment and are a deduction from the gross sales price to arrive at actual cost of the purchase.

   a. To the seller, a cash discount is a sales discount.

   b. To the buyer, a cash discount is a purchase discount.

   c. Cash discount terms of 2/10, n/30 mean that a discount of 2 percent of the gross sales price of the merchandise may be taken if payment is made within ten days following the invoice date. Otherwise, the gross sales price is due 30 days from the invoice date.

   d. A 2/E.O.M., n/60 cash discount means a 2 percent discount may be deducted if the invoice is paid by the end of the month of the date of sale. The gross sales or invoice amount is due 60 days from the date of the invoice.

   e. A 2/10/E.O.M., n/60 cash discount means a 2 percent discount may be deducted if the invoice is paid by the 10th day of the month following the date of sale. The gross sales or invoice amount is due 60 days from the date of the invoice.

   f. The Sales Discount account is a contra revenue account to Sales and is shown as a deduction from gross sales in the income statement.

## SALES RETURNS AND ALLOWANCES

7. Merchandise returned by the buyer is recorded in a Sales Returns and Allowances account, which is a contra revenue account to Sales.

   a. If cash has already been paid by the buyer for goods returned, the debit is to Sales Returns and Allowances and the credit is to Cash.

      (1) If the purchase was paid for in the discount period, only the net amount would be returned to the customer. The entry would be a debit to Sales Returns and Allowances and a credit to Sales Discounts (for the discount taken on the returned merchandise) and a credit to Cash.

      (2) The credit to Sales Discounts reduces the balance of that account.

   b. If the customer had not paid for the merchandise being returned, the debit is to Sales Returns and Allowances and the credit is to Accounts Receivable.

## REPORTING NET SALES IN THE INCOME STATEMENT

8. Rather than report the details of the net sales computation with Sales Discounts and Sales Returns and Allowances deducted from Gross Sales, the income statement may only indicate the net sales.

*Learning Objective 2:*
*Describe briefly cost of goods sold and the distinction between perpetual and periodic inventory procedures.*

## COST OF GOODS SOLD

9. Cost of goods sold indicates the cost to the seller of the goods sold to the buyer of the merchandise. This is a section of the classified income statement.

   a. Merchandise inventory is the quantity of goods on hand and available for sale at any given time.

   b. Cost of goods sold is determined by computing the cost of beginning inventory plus the net cost of goods purchased less the ending inventory.

## TWO PROCEDURES FOR ACCOUNTING FOR INVENTORIES

10. Perpetual inventory procedure and periodic inventory procedure comprise two procedures for accounting for inventory. Perpetual inventory procedure will be covered in the next chapter.

a. Under periodic inventory procedure, the cost of merchandise sold and the cost of merchandise on hand are determined *only* at the end of the accounting period.

b. Periodic inventory procedure is more often used by companies selling low value items because there is less control over inventory under this approach.

*Learning Objective 3:*
*Record journal entries for purchase transactions involving merchandise.*

## PURCHASES OF MERCHANDISE

11. The Purchases account under periodic inventory procedure is used to record the cost of merchandise purchased.

a. Increases to the Purchases account are recorded as debits and the credit is to Cash (if payment is made) or to Accounts Payable (if payment will be made later).

b. The Purchases account is shown in the Income Statement debit column of the work sheet and as part of the Cost of Goods Sold section of the classified income statement.

## DEDUCTIONS FROM PURCHASES

12. Deductions from purchases to arrive at net purchases include purchase discounts and purchase returns and allowances, which are recorded in contra accounts to the Purchases account.

## PURCHASE DISCOUNTS

13. The buyer may be able to take a purchase discount on the merchandise bought when the credit terms specify that a discount can be deducted when the invoice is paid within a stated time period.

a. The Purchase Discounts account is a contra account to Purchases that reduces the recorded gross invoice cost of the purchase to the price actually paid.

b. The entry to record purchase discounts is to debit Accounts Payable and to credit Cash and Purchase Discounts.

## INTEREST RATE IMPLIED IN CASH DISCOUNTS

14. All cash discount terms can be converted to their approximate annual interest rates to determine whether or not a company should take advantage of discounts by using cash or borrowing.

## PURCHASE RETURNS AND ALLOWANCES

15. Because management of the company may want to know the amounts of returns and allowances taken on goods purchased, a separate Purchase Returns and Allowances account is used to accumulate these.

a. The Purchase Returns and Allowances account is a contra account to the Purchases account and is shown on the Income Statement as a deduction from Purchases.

b. The Purchase Returns and Allowances account normally has a credit balance.

*Learning Objective 4:*
*Describe the freight terms and record transportation costs.*

## TRANSPORTATION COSTS

16. There are various terms used to indicate whether the buyer or seller pays for the costs incurred to deliver the merchandise purchased to the buyer.

a. The term ``FOB shipping point" means "free on board at shipping point," and the buyer incurs all transportation costs after the merchandise is loaded at the point of shipment.

b. The term ``FOB destination" means the seller bears the transportation charges and the goods are shipped to their destination without the buyer incurring the delivery charge.

c. Passage of title is a legal term used to indicate transfer of legal ownership of goods.

d. The term ``freight prepaid" is used when the seller pays the freight at the time of shipment.

e. The term "freight collect" is used when the buyer pays the freight bill upon the arrival of the goods

MERCHANDISE INVENTORIES

17. Merchandise inventory is the cost of goods on hand that are available for sale.
   a. The beginning inventory cost is already known because it is the balance of the Merchandise Inventory account at the end of the prior period.
   b. The ending inventory cost is determined under the periodic inventory procedure by taking a physical count of goods on hand and multiplying them times their cost.
      (1) Goods delivered on consignment should not be recorded as sold because the owner has shipped these goods to another party who is trying to sell them for the owner.
      (2) If passage of title has occurred, merchandise in transit must be recorded as a purchase by the buyer and included in inventory.

DETERMINING COST OF GOODS SOLD

18. The relationship between the items used in determining cost of goods sold is as follows
   a. Beginning inventory + Net cost of purchases = Cost of goods available for sale
   b. Cost of goods available for sale - Ending inventory = Cost of goods sold

LACK OF CONTROL UNDER PERIODIC INVENTORY PROCEDURE

19. Periodic inventory procedure provides little control over inventory as this method assumes that any items not included in the physical count of inventory have been sold.

CLASSIFIED INCOME STATEMENT

20. Revenues and expenses are the only two categories on an unclassified income statement. The classified income statement divides revenues and expenses into operating and nonoperating items.
   a. A classified income statement separates operating expenses into selling and administrative expenses.
   b. A classified income statement is also known as a multiple-step income statement.
   c. An income statement for a merchandising company usually has four sections.
      (1) Operating revenuesXsales and sales contra accounts.
      (2) Cost of goods sold.
      (3) Operating expenses.
      (4) Nonoperating revenues and expensesXother revenues and other expenses.
   d. Gross margin is the excess of net sales over cost of goods sold.
   e. Management chooses which type of income statement their company will use to present financial data, classified or unclassified. The decision may be based on cost or on which type of income statements are used by other companies in their industry.

IMPORTANT RELATIONSHIPS IN THE INCOME STATEMENT

21. The important relationships in the income statement of a merchandising firm can be summarized in the following equations:
   a. *Net sales* = Gross sales - (Sales returns and allowances + Sales discounts).
   b. *Net purchases* = Purchases - (Purchase returns and allowances + Purchase discounts).
   c. *Net cost of purchases* = Net purchases + Transportation-in.
   d. *Cost of goods sold* = Beginning inventory + Net cost of purchases - Ending inventory.
   e. *Gross margin* = Net sales - Cost of goods sold.
   f. *Net income from operations* = Gross margin - Operating (selling & administrative) expenses.
   g. *Net income* = Net income from operations + Nonoperating revenues - Nonoperating expenses.

*Learning Objective 7:*
*Analyze and use the financial ratio - gross margin percentage.*

## ANALYZING AND USING THE FINANCIAL RESULTSXGROSS MARGIN PERCENTAGE

22. Gross Margin Percentage = Gross Margin/Net Sales.
    a. The gross margin percentage indicates the amount of sales dollars that are available to cover expenses and produce income.
    b. Gross margin is often watched by management to see if trends can be explained. Sara Lee Corporation even has a statement in its annual report concerning this fact.

*Learning Objective 8:*
*Prepare a work sheet and closing entries for a merchandising company (Appendix).*

## APPENDIX: THE WORK SHEET FOR A MERCHANDISING COMPANY

23. A merchandising company's work sheet contains several steps in addition to those in preparing a service company's work sheet.

## COMPLETING THE WORK SHEET

24. Each account must be entered into the appropriate column(s) in the work sheet.
    a. All revenue accounts and contra purchases accounts are carried to the Income Statement credit column.
    b. All expense accounts, contra revenue accounts, beginning inventory, purchases, and transportation-in are carried to the Income Statement debit column.
    c. The ending merchandise inventory is entered in the Income Statement credit column and the Balance Sheet debit column.

## FINANCIAL STATEMENTS FOR A MERCHANDISING COMPANY

25. After the work sheet has been completed, the financial statements are prepared from data appearing in the Income Statement, Statement of Retained Earnings, and Balance Sheet columns.

## INCOME STATEMENT

26. The focus in a merchandising company's income statement is on the determination of cost of goods sold.

## STATEMENT OF RETAINED EARNINGS

27. The statement of retained earnings summarizes the transactions affecting the Retained Earnings account balance.

## BALANCE SHEET

28. The merchandising company's balance sheet differs from the service company's balance sheet only because of the addition of Merchandise Inventory as a current asset.

## CLOSING ENTRIES

29. Closing entries may be prepared directly from the work sheet using information appearing in the Income Statement Columns.
    a. Merchandise Inventory (ending balance), Sales, Purchase Discounts, and Purchase Returns and Allowances accounts are debited and Income Summary is credited for the total.
    b. Merchandise Inventory (beginning balance), Sales Discounts, Sales Returns and Allowances, Purchases, Transportation-in, Selling Expense, and Administration Expense accounts are credited and Income Summary is debited for the total.
    c. The balance of Income Summary is closed to the Retained Earnings account just as in a service company.
    d. The dividends account is closed to the Retained Earnings account just as in a service company.

# DEMONSTRATION PROBLEM

The May 1999 transactions and data given below are for Recall Company (which uses periodic inventory procedure):

May   1   Recall Company was organized as a corporation. John Recall invested the following assets in the business for capital stock: $210,000 cash; $80,000 of merchandise; and $50,000 of land.

5   The company purchased and paid cash for merchandise having a gross cost of $90,000, from which a 2% cash discount was granted.

8   Cash of $2,100 was paid to a trucking company for delivery of the merchandise purchased May 5. The goods were sold FOB shipping point.

14   The company sold merchandise on account, $150,000; terms 2/10, n/30.

16   Of the merchandise sold May 14, $6,600 was returned for credit.

19   Salaries for services received were paid as follows: to office employees, $6,600; and to salespersons, $17,400.

23   The company collected the amount due on $60,000 of the accounts receivable arising from the sales of May 14.

25   The company purchased and paid cash for merchandise costing $72,000 gross, less a 2% cash discount.

28   Of the merchandise purchased May 25, $12,000 gross was returned to the vendor, who gave Recall Company a check for the proper amount.

28   A trucking company was paid $1,500 for delivery to Recall Company of the goods purchased May 25. The goods were sold FOB shipping point.

29   The company sold merchandise on account, $7,200; terms 2/10, n/30.

30   Cash sales were $36,000 gross, less a 2% cash discount.

30   Cash of $48,000 was received from the sales of May 14.

31   Paid store rent for May, $9,000.

Additional data:

The inventory on hand at the close of business on May 31 was $139,400 at cost.

Required:

a.   Prepare journal entries for the transactions.
b.   Post the journal entries to the proper ledger accounts.
c.   Prepare a classified income statement and a statement of retained earnings for the month ended May 31, 1999.
d.   Prepare a classified balance sheet as of May 31, 1999.

## RECALL COMPANY
## GENERAL JOURNAL

Page ____

| Date | Account Titles and Explanation | Post. Ref. | Debit | Credit |
|------|-------------------------------|-----------|-------|--------|
|  |  |  |  |  |
|  |  |  |  |  |
|  |  |  |  |  |
|  |  |  |  |  |
|  |  |  |  |  |
|  |  |  |  |  |
|  |  |  |  |  |
|  |  |  |  |  |
|  |  |  |  |  |
|  |  |  |  |  |
|  |  |  |  |  |
|  |  |  |  |  |
|  |  |  |  |  |
|  |  |  |  |  |
|  |  |  |  |  |
|  |  |  |  |  |
|  |  |  |  |  |
|  |  |  |  |  |
|  |  |  |  |  |
|  |  |  |  |  |
|  |  |  |  |  |
|  |  |  |  |  |
|  |  |  |  |  |
|  |  |  |  |  |
|  |  |  |  |  |
|  |  |  |  |  |
|  |  |  |  |  |
|  |  |  |  |  |
|  |  |  |  |  |
|  |  |  |  |  |
|  |  |  |  |  |
|  |  |  |  |  |
|  |  |  |  |  |
|  |  |  |  |  |
|  |  |  |  |  |
|  |  |  |  |  |
|  |  |  |  |  |
|  |  |  |  |  |
|  |  |  |  |  |
|  |  |  |  |  |
|  |  |  |  |  |
|  |  |  |  |  |

## RECALL COMPANY
## GENERAL JOURNAL

a.

Page ____

| Date | Account Titles and Explanation | Post. Ref. | Debit | Credit |
|------|-------------------------------|------------|-------|--------|
|      |                               |            |       |        |
|      |                               |            |       |        |
|      |                               |            |       |        |
|      |                               |            |       |        |
|      |                               |            |       |        |
|      |                               |            |       |        |
|      |                               |            |       |        |
|      |                               |            |       |        |
|      |                               |            |       |        |
|      |                               |            |       |        |
|      |                               |            |       |        |
|      |                               |            |       |        |
|      |                               |            |       |        |
|      |                               |            |       |        |
|      |                               |            |       |        |
|      |                               |            |       |        |
|      |                               |            |       |        |
|      |                               |            |       |        |
|      |                               |            |       |        |
|      |                               |            |       |        |
|      |                               |            |       |        |

b.

### Cash

ACCOUNT NO.

| Date | Explanation | Post. Ref. | Debit | Credit | Balance |
|------|-------------|------------|-------|--------|---------|
|      |             |            |       |        |         |
|      |             |            |       |        |         |
|      |             |            |       |        |         |
|      |             |            |       |        |         |
|      |             |            |       |        |         |
|      |             |            |       |        |         |
|      |             |            |       |        |         |
|      |             |            |       |        |         |
|      |             |            |       |        |         |

b. (continued)

## Accounts Receivable                              ACCOUNT NO.

| Date | Explanation | Post. Ref. | Debit | Credit | Balance |
|------|-------------|------------|-------|--------|---------|
|      |             |            |       |        |         |
|      |             |            |       |        |         |
|      |             |            |       |        |         |
|      |             |            |       |        |         |
|      |             |            |       |        |         |

## Merchandise Inventory                            ACCOUNT NO.

| Date | Explanation | Post. Ref. | Debit | Credit | Balance |
|------|-------------|------------|-------|--------|---------|
|      |             |            |       |        |         |
|      |             |            |       |        |         |
|      |             |            |       |        |         |

## Land                                             ACCOUNT NO.

| Date | Explanation | Post. Ref. | Debit | Credit | Balance |
|------|-------------|------------|-------|--------|---------|
|      |             |            |       |        |         |
|      |             |            |       |        |         |
|      |             |            |       |        |         |

## Capital Stock                                    ACCOUNT NO.

| Date | Explanation | Post. Ref. | Debit | Credit | Balance |
|------|-------------|------------|-------|--------|---------|
|      |             |            |       |        |         |
|      |             |            |       |        |         |
|      |             |            |       |        |         |

## ACCOUNT NO.

| Date | Explanation | Post. Ref. | Debit | Credit | Balance |
|------|-------------|------------|-------|--------|---------|
|      |             |            |       |        |         |
|      |             |            |       |        |         |
|      |             |            |       |        |         |

*b. (continued)*

| Date | Explanation | Post. Ref. | Debit | Credit | Balance |
|------|-------------|------------|-------|--------|---------|
|      |             |            |       |        |         |
|      |             |            |       |        |         |
|      |             |            |       |        |         |
|      |             |            |       |        |         |
|      |             |            |       |        |         |

| Date | Explanation | Post. Ref. | Debit | Credit | Balance |
|------|-------------|------------|-------|--------|---------|
|      |             |            |       |        |         |
|      |             |            |       |        |         |
|      |             |            |       |        |         |

| Date | Explanation | Post. Ref. | Debit | Credit | Balance |
|------|-------------|------------|-------|--------|---------|
|      |             |            |       |        |         |
|      |             |            |       |        |         |
|      |             |            |       |        |         |

| Date | Explanation | Post. Ref. | Debit | Credit | Balance |
|------|-------------|------------|-------|--------|---------|
|      |             |            |       |        |         |
|      |             |            |       |        |         |
|      |             |            |       |        |         |

| Date | Explanation | Post. Ref. | Debit | Credit | Balance |
|------|-------------|------------|-------|--------|---------|
|      |             |            |       |        |         |
|      |             |            |       |        |         |

*b. (concluded)*

ACCOUNT NO.

| Date | | Explanation | Post. Ref. | Debit | | | Credit | | | Balance | | |
|------|--|-------------|-----------|-------|--|--|--------|--|--|---------|--|--|
| | | | | | | | | | | | | |
| | | | | | | | | | | | | |
| | | | | | | | | | | | | |

ACCOUNT NO.

| Date | | Explanation | Post. Ref. | Debit | | | Credit | | | Balance | | |
|------|--|-------------|-----------|-------|--|--|--------|--|--|---------|--|--|
| | | | | | | | | | | | | |
| | | | | | | | | | | | | |
| | | | | | | | | | | | | |
| | | | | | | | | | | | | |

ACCOUNT NO.

| Date | | Explanation | Post. Ref. | Debit | | | Credit | | | Balance | | |
|------|--|-------------|-----------|-------|--|--|--------|--|--|---------|--|--|
| | | | | | | | | | | | | |
| | | | | | | | | | | | | |
| | | | | | | | | | | | | |
| | | | | | | | | | | | | |

ACCOUNT NO.

| Date | | Explanation | Post. Ref. | Debit | | | Credit | | | Balance | | |
|------|--|-------------|-----------|-------|--|--|--------|--|--|---------|--|--|
| | | | | | | | | | | | | |
| | | | | | | | | | | | | |
| | | | | | | | | | | | | |
| | | | | | | | | | | | | |

# RECALL COMPANY
## Income Statement
### For the Year Ended _____ 31, 19__

| | | | | | | | | | | | | | | |
|---|---|---|---|---|---|---|---|---|---|---|---|---|---|---|
| Operating revenues: | | | | | | | | | | | | | | |
| | | | | | | | | | | | | | | |
| | | | | | | | | | | | | | | |
| | | | | | | | | | | | | | | |
| | | | | | | | | | | | | | | |
| Cost of goods sold: | | | | | | | | | | | | | | |
| | | | | | | | | | | | | | | |
| | | | | | | | | | | | | | | |
| | | | | | | | | | | | | | | |
| | | | | | | | | | | | | | | |
| | | | | | | | | | | | | | | |
| | | | | | | | | | | | | | | |
| | | | | | | | | | | | | | | |
| | | | | | | | | | | | | | | |
| | | | | | | | | | | | | | | |
| Operating expenses: | | | | | | | | | | | | | | |
| | | | | | | | | | | | | | | |
| | | | | | | | | | | | | | | |
| | | | | | | | | | | | | | | |
| | | | | | | | | | | | | | | |
| | | | | | | | | | | | | | | |
| | | | | | | | | | | | | | | |
| | | | | | | | | | | | | | | |
| | | | | | | | | | | | | | | |
| | | | | | | | | | | | | | | |

*c. (concluded)*

**RECALL COMPANY**

**Statement of Retained Earnings**

**For the Year Ended            31, 19**

|  |  |  |  |
|---|---|---|---|
|  |  |  |  |
|  |  |  |  |
|  |  |  |  |
|  |  |  |  |
|  |  |  |  |
|  |  |  |  |

*d.*

**RECALL COMPANY**

**Balance Sheet**

**31, 19**

| Assets |  |  |  |  |  |
|---|---|---|---|---|---|
| Current assets: |  |  |  |  |  |
|  |  |  |  |  |  |
|  |  |  |  |  |  |
|  |  |  |  |  |  |
|  |  |  |  |  |  |
| Property, plant, and equipment: |  |  |  |  |  |
|  |  |  |  |  |  |
|  |  |  |  |  |  |
| **Liabilities and Stockholders' Equity** |  |  |  |  |  |
|  |  |  |  |  |  |
|  |  |  |  |  |  |
|  |  |  |  |  |  |
|  |  |  |  |  |  |
|  |  |  |  |  |  |
|  |  |  |  |  |  |
|  |  |  |  |  |  |
|  |  |  |  |  |  |
|  |  |  |  |  |  |
|  |  |  |  |  |  |
|  |  |  |  |  |  |
|  |  |  |  |  |  |

# SOLUTION TO DEMONSTRATION PROBLEM

*a.*

## RECALL COMPANY
## GENERAL JOURNAL

| Date 1999 | Account Titles and Explanation | Debit | Credit |
|---|---|---|---|
| May 1 | Cash | 210,000 | |
| | Merchandise Inventory | 80,000 | |
| | Land | 50,000 | |
| | Capital Stock | | 340,000 |
| | Stock issued for assets invested in business by John Recall. | | |
| 5 | Purchases | 90,000 | |
| | Purchase Discounts | | 1,800 |
| | Cash | | 88,200 |
| | Purchased merchandise for cash, less 2% ($90,000 x 0.98 = $88,200). | | |
| 8 | Transportation-In | 2,100 | |
| | Cash | | 2,100 |
| | Transportation on May 5 purchases. | | |
| 14 | Accounts Receivable | 150,000 | |
| | Sales | | 150,000 |
| | Sales on account; terms 2/10, n/30. | | |
| 16 | Sales Returns and Allowances | 6,600 | |
| | Accounts Receivable | | 6,600 |
| | Sales returned. | | |
| 19 | Office Salaries Expense | 6,600 | |
| | Sales Salaries Expense | 17,400 | |
| | Cash | | 24,000 |
| | Paid salaries. | | |
| 23 | Cash | 58,800 | |
| | Sales Discounts | 1,200 | |
| | Accounts Receivable | | 60,000 |
| | Collections on account. | | |
| 25 | Purchases | 72,000 | |
| | Purchase Discounts | | 1,440 |
| | Cash | | 70,560 |
| | Cash purchases. | | |
| 28 | Cash | 11,760 | |
| | Purchase Discounts | 240 | |
| | Purchase Returns and Allowances | | 12,000 |
| | Returned cash purchases. | | |
| 28 | Transportation-In | 1,500 | |
| | Cash | | 1,500 |
| | Transportation on purchases of May 25. | | |

*a. (concluded)*

**RECALL COMPANY**
**GENERAL JOURNAL**

Page 2

| Date | Account Titles and Explanation | Debit | Credit |
|---|---|---|---|
| 1999 | | | |
| May 29 | Accounts Receivable ................................................................. | 7,200 | |
| |     Sales ....................................................................................... | | 7,200 |
| |     Sales on account; terms 2/10, n/30. | | |
| 30 | Cash ......................................................................................... | 35,280 | |
| | Sales Discounts ....................................................................... | 720 | |
| |     Sales ....................................................................................... | | 36,000 |
| |     Cash sales, less 2%. | | |
| 30 | Cash ......................................................................................... | 48,000 | |
| |     Accounts Receivable ............................................................ | | 48,000 |
| |     Collections on account. | | |
| 31 | Rent Expense ........................................................................... | 9,000 | |
| |     Cash ....................................................................................... | | 9,000 |
| |     Rent for May. | | |

*b.*

**Cash**

| Date | Explanation | Post. Ref. | Debit | Credit | Balance |
|---|---|---|---|---|---|
| 1999 | | | | | |
| May 1 | Stock issued for assets | G1 | 210,000 | | 210,000 |
| 5 | Purchases | G1 | | 88,200 | 121,800 |
| 8 | Transportation-in | G1 | | 2,100 | 119,700 |
| 19 | Salaries | G1 | | 24,000 | 95,700 |
| 23 | Collections on accounts receivable | G1 | 58,800 | | 154,500 |
| 25 | Purchases | G1 | | 70,560 | 83,940 |
| 28 | Purchase returns | G1 | 11,760 | | 95,700 |
| 28 | Transportation-in | G2 | | 1,500 | 94,200 |
| 30 | Sales | G2 | 35,280 | | 129,480 |
| 30 | Collections on accounts receivable | G2 | 48,000 | | 177,480 |
| 31 | Rent | G2 | | 9,000 | 168,480 |

**Accounts Receivable**

| Date | Explanation | Post. Ref. | Debit | Credit | Balance |
|---|---|---|---|---|---|
| 1999 | | | | | |
| May 14 | Sales | G1 | 150,000 | | 150,000 |
| 16 | Sales returns | G1 | | 6,600 | 143,400 |
| 23 | Collections | G1 | | 60,000 | 83,400 |
| 29 | Sales | G2 | 7,200 | | 90,600 |
| 30 | Collections | G2 | | 48,000 | 42,600 |

*b. (continued)*

### Merchandise Inventory

| Date | Explanation | Post. Ref. | Debit | Credit | Balance |
|------|-------------|------------|-------|--------|---------|
| 1999 | | | | | |
| May 1 | Stock issued for assets | G1 | 80,000 | | 80,000 |

### Land

| Date | Explanation | Post. Ref. | Debit | Credit | Balance |
|------|-------------|------------|-------|--------|---------|
| 1999 | | | | | |
| 1 | Stock issued for assets | G1 | 50,000 | | 50,000 |

### Capital Stock

| Date | Explanation | Post. Ref. | Debit | Credit | Balance |
|------|-------------|------------|-------|--------|---------|
| 1999 | | | | | |
| 1 | Stock issued for asset | G1 | | 340,000 | 340,000 |

### Sales

| Date | Explanation | Post. Ref. | Debit | Credit | Balance |
|------|-------------|------------|-------|--------|---------|
| 1999 | | | | | |
| May 14 | On account | G1 | | 150,000 | 150,000 |
| | On account | G2 | | 7,200 | 157,200 |
| | Cash | G2 | | 36,000 | 193,200 |

### Sales Returns and Allowances

| Date | Explanation | Post. Ref. | Debit | Credit | Balance |
|------|-------------|------------|-------|--------|---------|
| 1999 | | | | | |
| May 16 | On account | G1 | 6,600 | | 6,600 |

### Sales Discounts

| Date | Explanation | Post. Ref. | Debit | Credit | Balance |
|------|-------------|------------|-------|--------|---------|
| 1999 | | | | | |
| May 23 | On account | G1 | 1,200 | | 1,200 |
| 30 | For cash sales | G2 | 720 | | 1,920 |

### Purchases

| Date | Explanation | Post. Ref. | Debit | Credit | Balance |
|------|-------------|------------|-------|--------|---------|
| 1999 | | | | | |
| May 5 | Cash | G1 | 90,000 | | 90,000 |
| 25 | Cash | G1 | 72,000 | | 162,000 |

## Purchase Returns and Allowances

| Date | Explanation | Post. Ref. | Debit | Credit | Balance |
|------|-------------|------------|-------|--------|---------|
| 1999 | | | | | |
| May 28 | Cash | G1 | | 12,000 | 12,000 |

## Purchase Discounts

| Date | Explanation | Post. Ref. | Debit | Credit | Balance |
|------|-------------|------------|-------|--------|---------|
| 1999 | | | | | |
| May 5 | For cash purchases | G1 | | 1,800 | 1,800 |
| 25 | For cash purchases | G1 | | 1,440 | 3,240 |
| 28 | Purchase return | G1 | 240 | | 3,000 |

## Transportation-In

| Date | Explanation | Post. Ref. | Debit | Credit | Balance |
|------|-------------|------------|-------|--------|---------|
| 1999 | | | | | |
| May 8 | Cash | G1 | 2,100 | | 2,100 |
| 28 | Cash | G2 | 1,500 | | 3,600 |

## Sales Salaries Expense

| Date | Explanation | Post. Ref. | Debit | Credit | Balance |
|------|-------------|------------|-------|--------|---------|
| 1999 | | | | | |
| May 19 | Cash | G1 | 17,400 | | 17,400 |

## Rent Expense

| Date | Explanation | Post. Ref. | Debit | Credit | Balance |
|------|-------------|------------|-------|--------|---------|
| 1999 | | | | | |
| May 31 | Cash—rent for May | G2 | 9,000 | | 9,000 |

## Office Salaries Expense

| Date | Explanation | Post. Ref. | Debit | Credit | Balance |
|------|-------------|------------|-------|--------|---------|
| 1999 | | | | | |
| May 19 | Cash | G1 | 6,600 | | 6,600 |

*c.*

## RECALL COMPANY
### Income Statement
### For the Year Ended May 31, 1999

Operating revenues:

| | | | |
|---|---|---|---|
| Gross sales | | | $193,200 |
| Less: Sales returns and allowances | | $ 6,600 | |
| Sales discounts | | 1,920 | 8,520 |
| Net sales | | | $184,680 |

Cost of goods sold:

| | | | |
|---|---|---|---|
| Merchandise inventory, May 1, 1999 | | | $ 80,000 |
| Purchases | | $162,000 | |
| Less: Purchase returns and allowances | $12,000 | | |
| Purchase discounts | 3,000 | 15,000 | |
| Net purchases | | $147,000 | |
| Add: Transportation-in | | 3,600 | |
| Net cost of purchases | | | 150,600 |
| Cost of goods available for sale | | | $ 230,600 |
| Less: Merchandise inventory, May 31, 1999 | | | 139,400 |
| Cost of goods sold | | | 91,200 |
| Gross margin | | | $ 93,480 |

Operating expenses:

| | | | |
|---|---|---|---|
| Selling expenses: | | | |
| Sales salaries | | $ 17,400 | |
| Rent | | 9,000 | |
| Total selling expenses | | $ 26,400 | |
| Administrative expenses: | | | |
| Office salaries | | 6,600 | |
| Total operating expenses | | | 33,000 |
| Net income | | | $ 60,480 |

## RECALL COMPANY
### Statement of Retained Earnings
### For the Year Ended May 31, 1999

| | |
|---|---|
| Retained earnings, May 1, 1999 | $ 0 |
| Net income for the month | 60,480 |
| Retained earnings, May 31, 1999 | $ 60,480 |

*d.*

## RECALL COMPANY
### Balance Sheet
### May 31, 1999
*Assets*

Current assets:

| | | |
|---|---|---|
| Cash | $168,480 | |
| Accounts receivable | 42,600 | |
| Merchandise inventory | 139,400 | |
| Total current assets | | $350,480 |
| Property, plant, and equipment: | | |
| Land | | 50,000 |
| Total assets | | $400,480 |

*Liabilities and Stockholders' Equity*

Stockholders' equity:

| | | |
|---|---|---|
| Capital stock | | $340,000 |
| Retained earnings | | 60,480 |
| Total liabilities and stockholders' equity | | $400,480 |

# MATCHING

Referring to the terms listed below, place the appropriate letter next to the corresponding description. A term may be used more than once.

| | | |
|---|---|---|
| a. FOB shipping point | f. Freight collect | k. Debit |
| b. Freight prepaid | g. Purchase discounts | l. Cost of goods sold |
| c. Chain discount | h. Operating revenues | m. Gross margin |
| d. Sales discounts | i. Nonoperating revenues | n. Selling expenses |
| e. FOB destination | j. Credit | o. Administrative expenses |

_____ 1. The term used when the buyer incurs all transportation costs after the merchandise is loaded at the point of shipment.

_____ 2. This term is used when the buyer pays the freight bill upon arrival of the goods.

_____ 3. This term is applied when a list price is subject to several trade discounts.

_____ 4. Cash discounts as recorded on the books of the buyer.

_____ 5. The term used when goods are shipped to their destination without charge to the buyer.

_____ 6. This term is used when the seller pays the freight at the time of shipment.

_____ 7. Revenues generated by the major activities of the business.

_____ 8. The term used when the seller bears all the transportation charges.

_____ 9. The normal balance of the Purchase Discounts account.

_____ 10. Net Sales - Cost of goods sold.

_____ 11. Expenses incurred in performing and facilitating the marketing effort.

_____ 12. Beginning inventory + Net purchases - Ending inventory.

_____ 13. Operating expenses incurred in the overall management of a business.

_____ 14. Advertising Expense, Warehousing and Handling Expense, and Salaries ExpenseXMarketing Managers are grouped into this category.

_____ 15. Are deducted along with purchase returns and allowances from gross purchases to arrive at net purchases.

# COMPLETION AND EXERCISES

1. When using periodic inventory procedure, how is the amount of the ending inventory determined?

   _____

   _____

   _____

2. Although cash discounts are offered to induce prompt payment of an account, they are theoretically viewed as _____ from revenue by the seller and from cost by the buyer.

3. The two basic inventory procedures are _____ and _____.

4. Suppose that A sold $1,500 of merchandise to B on July 26 under terms of 3/10, n/30. State exactly what is meant by these terms in these circumstances.

_____

_____

_____

_____

_____

_____

5. Use the data in Question 4 and assume that B returned $300 of the merchandise to A and then paid the balance of the invoice within the discount period. In the space below, give the necessary entries on B's books for the purchase, the return, and the payment. (Assume B uses periodic inventory procedure.)

| Date | Account Titles and Explanation | Post. Ref. | Debit | Credit |
|------|-------------------------------|-----------|-------|--------|
|      |                               |           |       |        |
|      |                               |           |       |        |
|      |                               |           |       |        |
|      |                               |           |       |        |
|      |                               |           |       |        |
|      |                               |           |       |        |
|      |                               |           |       |        |
|      |                               |           |       |        |
|      |                               |           |       |        |
|      |                               |           |       |        |
|      |                               |           |       |        |
|      |                               |           |       |        |
|      |                               |           |       |        |

6. Typically, _____ discounts are not recorded by either the buyer or the seller.

7. If A purchased $750 of goods under terms 2/10, n/30, FOB destination, freight of $75 prepaid, A would pay the seller $_____ if A paid the invoice on these goods within the discount period.

8. Using the following information, prepare the necessary closing entries for the Barker Company.

| | |
|---|---|
| Sales ...................................................................... __ | $68,000 |
| Merchandise inventory, 1/1 ................................................. | 16,000 |
| Merchandise inventory, 12/31 ............................................... | 20,800 |
| Purchases ................................................................. | 44,000 |
| Purchase discounts ........................................................ | 800 |
| Purchase returns and allowances .......................................... | 1,600 |
| Transportation-in ......................................................... | 2,400 |
| Selling expenses .......................................................... | 3,600 |
| Administrative expenses ................................................... | 3,040 |

8. (concluded)

| Date | Account Titles and Explanation | Post. Ref. | Debit | Credit |
|---|---|---|---|---|
|  |  |  |  |  |
|  |  |  |  |  |
|  |  |  |  |  |
|  |  |  |  |  |
|  |  |  |  |  |
|  |  |  |  |  |
|  |  |  |  |  |
|  |  |  |  |  |
|  |  |  |  |  |
|  |  |  |  |  |
|  |  |  |  |  |

9. Use the information in Question 8 to prepare an income statement.

_____

_____

| | | | | | |
|---|---|---|---|---|---|
|  |  |  |  |  |  |
|  |  |  |  |  |  |
|  |  |  |  |  |  |
|  |  |  |  |  |  |
|  |  |  |  |  |  |
|  |  |  |  |  |  |
|  |  |  |  |  |  |
|  |  |  |  |  |  |
|  |  |  |  |  |  |
|  |  |  |  |  |  |
|  |  |  |  |  |  |
|  |  |  |  |  |  |
|  |  |  |  |  |  |

10. A disadvantage of periodic inventory procedure is that losses from shrinkage, deterioration, and shoplifting are _____

_____

11. The following information is given:

| Invoice Date | List Price | Trade Discounts | Credit Terms | Date Paid |
|---|---|---|---|---|
| May 21 | $700 | 10%, 15% | 2/10, n/30 | June 17 |

The amount to be recorded as the selling price is _____. The amount that was

actually paid is _____.

12. In taking a physical inventory, care should be exercised to exclude _____ _____

_____ and _____ _____.

13. C sold $1,200 of merchandise to D under terms 2/5, n/30, FOB destination, freight of

$60 prepaid. The transportation company would receive payment from _____ who

would charge (debit) the amount paid to _____.

14. If the terms in Question 13 had been FOB shipping point, freight collect, the

transportation company would receive payment from _____ who would charge it to

_____.

15. E sold merchandise to F, list price $8,000, less 50 percent and 20 percent, under terms of

2/10, n/30, FOB shipping point, freight of $80 collect. If F paid E within the discount

period, F would send a check in the amount of $_____.

16. A purchased merchandise from B, invoice price, $1,250; terms 2/10, n/30. A returned
$250 of the merchandise and then paid the balance due on the invoice after the discount
period had expired. Give the entries required on A's books.

| Date | Account Titles and Explanation | Post. Ref. | Debit | Credit |
|---|---|---|---|---|
|  |  |  |  |  |
|  |  |  |  |  |
|  |  |  |  |  |
|  |  |  |  |  |
|  |  |  |  |  |
|  |  |  |  |  |
|  |  |  |  |  |
|  |  |  |  |  |
|  |  |  |  |  |
|  |  |  |  |  |
|  |  |  |  |  |
|  |  |  |  |  |

17. The income statement of a merchandising company generally has four major sections, namely:

a. _____

b. _____

c. _____

d. _____

18. Distinguish between an operating expense and a nonoperating expense.

_____

_____

_____

_____

_____

_____

19. Accounts that appear on the work sheet of a merchandising company that do not appear on that of a service company are the following (in any order):

*a.* _____    *f.* _____

*b.* _____    *g.* _____

*c.* _____    *h.* _____

*d.* _____    *i.* _____

*e.* _____

20. Determine the missing amounts in the following data. The individual cases are not related.

| | | | | | |
|---|---|---|---|---|---|
| Sales ............................. | $32,000 | $ ? *(b)* | $72,000 | $32,000 | $64,000 |
| Gross margin .............. | 8,000 | 24,000 | ? *(c)* | 8,000 | 8,000 |
| Purchases ................... | 48,000 | 40,000 | 32,000 | 40,000 | ? *(e)* |
| Beginning inventory .. | ? *(a)* | 8,000 | 32,000 | 8,000 | 32,000 |
| Ending inventory ....... | 40,000 | 16,000 | 8,000 | ? *(d)* | 16,000 |
| Answers ...................... | $_____ | $_____ | $_____ | $_____ | $_____ |

The subtotals of the income statement columns of a work sheet are $344,000 debit and $352,000 credit.

What is the amount of the income or loss? (Indicate whether income or loss.) $ _____ *(f)*

The subtotal of the balance sheet debit column of the same work sheet is $160,000. What is the subtotal of the balance sheet credit column? ........................................ $_____ *(g)*

21. Generally, a sale consists of the transfer of _____ _____ to goods accompanied by actual _____ to the customer.

22. The sales revenue (or net sales revenue) of a firm is usually equal to sales less _____ _____, _____ _____, and _____ _____. Its amount is

important because it represents an approximate measure of the flow of _____ into a firm from its operations.

23. Give two reasons why the accountant finds recording revenue at the time of sale attractive.

    1._____

    _____

    2._____

    _____

24. The following data pertain to a particular purchase:

    Date of invoice ................................................... August 23
    List price .......................................................... $2,500
    Trade discount ................................................... 40%
    Prepaid freight ................................................... $125
    Terms ............................................................... 2/10, n/30 FOB Shipping Point

    a. When the invoice is received from the vendor, the purchaser should expect the total of the invoice to be what amount? ................................................... $ _____

    b. What is the last day on which the purchaser may make payment and still be entitled to the cash discount? ................................................... _____

    c. What is the amount of the cash discount that can be taken if the invoice is paid within the discount period? ................................................... $ _____

25. Determine the amount to be paid in full settlement of each of the following invoices assuming that the credit memorandum was received prior to payment and that the invoices were paid within the discount period.

    | Purchase Invoice: | (a) | (b) |
    |---|---|---|
    | Merchandise ........................................... | $2,160 | $2,304 |
    | Transportation ........................................ | $72 Prepaid | |
    | Terms .................................................... | FOB Shipping Point 2/10, n/30 | FOB Destination 1/10, n/30 |
    | | | |
    | Credit memorandum: | | |
    | Merchandise ........................................... | $84 | $156 |

    Amount to be paid in full settlement ........ $ _____        $_____

26. If Company A has net sales of $500,000 and gross margin of $200,000, its gross margin percentage is _____%.

Indicate whether each of the following statements is true or false by inserting a capital "T" or "F" in the blank space provided.

_____ 1. Sales Returns and Allowances is debited and Income Summary is credited in the closing entry.

_____ 2. Trade discounts are terms that allow deductions to customers if they pay their bills within a definite period of time.

_____ 3. The Purchase Returns and Allowances account normally has a credit balance.

_____ 4. Cash discounts taken on goods acquired for resale should be debited to a Sales Discounts account.

_____ 5. Periodic inventory procedure provides more control over inventory than does perpetual inventory procedure.

_____ 6. A cash discount is synonymous with a trade discount.

_____ 7. Buyers determine their cash discount on the total amount of the invoice, including the freight charge under the terms FOB shipping point when the seller prepays the freight.

_____ 8. Using periodic inventory procedure, the cost of goods sold is reflected in the balance of the Purchases account.

_____ 9. An error that understates the ending inventory will overstate net income in the year of the error.

_____ 10. Typically, neither a trade discount nor a cash discount is recorded by seller or buyer.

_____ 11. Assume that inventory was not counted and was omitted from the Merchandise Inventory account at year-end; this omission would cause inventory and retained earnings on the balance sheet to be understated because cost of goods sold would be understated.

_____ 12. The merchandise inventory amount in the Balance Sheet debit column of the work sheet is the ending inventory.

_____ 13. Cost of goods sold is the net cost of purchases of the period adjusted for any difference between beginning and ending inventories.

_____ 14. An income statement that separates revenues and expenses into operating and nonoperating items is called a classified or multiple-step income statement.

_____ 15. The work sheet of a merchandising company eliminates the need for adjusting and closing journal entries.

_____ 16. Using the credit terms 2/10, n/30 means that the buyer may deduct 10 percent of the amount of the invoice if payment is made by the 2nd of the following month.

_____ 17. Cash discounts are substantial reductions from the list price granted to retailers and wholesalers in differing amounts to reflect a variety of quantities purchased.

_____ 18. A company's cost of goods sold would be $42,400 for a period in which purchases were $28,000, beginning inventory was $14,400 and ending inventory was zero.

_____ 19. Sales would be $120,000 for a company based on the following: Beginning inventoryX$28,800; ending inventoryX$32,000; cost of goods soldX$64,000; gross margin on salesX$40,000.

_____ 20. In a sale of merchandise, the buyer should receive an invoice from the seller.

_____ 21. With trade discounts of 20%, 10%, and 5% and a list price of $150, the sale should be recorded in the journal as $102.60.

_____ 22. If the accountant mistakenly places a revenue account balance in the Balance Sheet credit column instead of the Income Statement credit column of the work sheet, the work sheet columns will still balance.

_____ 23. Merchandise on consignment should not appear as inventory on the consignee's balance sheet.

_____ 24. The balances of the Purchase Returns and Allowances account and the Purchase Discounts account are subtracted from Purchases on the income statement to show cost of goods available for sale.

_____ 25. Consigned goods should be included in the owner's inventory even though the owner may have delivered them to another party.

_____ 26. Management chooses which type of income statement their company will use to present financial data, classified or unclassified.

_____ 27. Gross margin percentage is equal to gross margin divided by net income.

---

## MULTIPLE CHOICE QUESTIONS

For each of the following questions, indicate the best answer by circling the appropriate letter.

1. In the income statement:
   A. operating expenses are usually classified as either "Administrative Expenses" or "Selling Expenses."
   B. ending inventory is added to purchases to determine cost of goods available for sale.
   C. "Net Income from Operations" and "Net Income" are synonymous.
   D. the amount shown as "Net Sales" includes all cash sales plus only those charge sales for which cash has been received.
   E. expenses are subtracted from revenues to determine the balance of the Retained Earnings capital account.

2. If merchandise purchased cost $35,000, what was the company's cost of goods sold if beginning inventory was $12,600 and ending inventory was $26,600?
   A. $49,000
   B. $74,200
   C. $21,000
   D. None of these.

3. Which of the following correctly describes the cost of goods sold section of the income statement under periodic inventory procedure?
   A. Beginning Inventory + Purchases + Transportation-In - Purchase Discounts + Ending Inventory
   B. Beginning Inventory - Purchases + Transportation-In - Purchase Discounts - Ending Inventory
   C. Beginning Inventory + Purchases - Transportation-In - Purchase Discounts + Ending Inventory
   D. Beginning Inventory + Purchases - Transportation-In - Purchase Discounts - Ending Inventory
   E. None of the above.

4. Cost of goods sold refers to:
   A. purchases plus beginning inventory.
   B. cost of goods available for sale less ending inventory.
   C. cost prices that are identified with the items which were sold during the period.
   D. net sales less gross margin.
   E. All of the above except A.

5. The entry on the books of the seller to record the return of merchandise sold on account for which no payment has been received is:
   A. Sales
      Accounts Receivable
   B. Accounts Receivable
      Sales Returns and Allowances
   C. Sales Returns and Allowances
      Cash
   D. Sales Returns and Allowances
      Sales
   E. None of these.

6-7.  In the following equations identify the item designated by X.

6. Merchandise Inventory (Beginning) + X = Cost of goods available for sale. What does X represent?
   A. Purchase discounts
   B. Net cost of purchases
   C. Cost of goods sold
   D. Ending inventory
   E. None of these.

7. Net sales - X = Gross margin. What does "X" represent?
   A. Net purchases
   B. Net profit
   C. Ending inventory
   D. Cost of goods sold
   E. None of these.

8. An Account Payable of $180 is subject to a 2 percent discount if paid within the 60-day discount period. Part of the entry to record this payment within the discount period would be a:
   A. credit to Accounts Payable of $180
   B. credit to Accounts Payable of $176.40
   C. debit to Accounts Payable of $180
   D. credit to Cash of $180
   E. debit to Purchases Discount of $3.60

9. Determine the amount to be paid in full settlement of the invoice, assuming that credit for returns and allowances was received prior to payment and that the invoice was paid within the discount period. Merchandise $1,560, Transportation $60, Returns and Allowances $120, and terms FOB shipping point, 1/10, n/30, freight prepaid.
   A. $1,485.00
   B. $1,485.60
   C. $1,356.00
   D. $1,470.00
   E. None of these.

10. Partial closing entries for Brown Company are given below.

| | | |
|---|---|---|
| Commissions Earned | 4,000 | |
| Merchandise Inventory | 2,800 | |
|     Income Summary | | 6,800 |

The debit item of $2,800 is:
A. the cost of the ending inventory.
B. the cost of the beginning inventory.
C. the cost of purchases made during the period.
D. the cost of goods available for sale during the period.
E. None of the above.

11-13. Given the following information, answer Questions 11-13:
Purchases X $66,000
Operating Expenses X $21,000
Ending Inventory X $18,000
Net Income X $15,000
Cost of Goods Sold X $81,000

11. What is the beginning inventory?
A. $99,000
B. $33,000
C. $84,000
D. $18,000

12. What is the gross margin?
A. $99,000
B. $15,000
C. $36,000
D. $6,000

13. What are sales?
A. $99,000
B. $33,000
C. $117,000
D. $96,000

14. Merchandise on hand July 1 was $4,050; purchases during July were $21,150; delivery expense was $525; transportation-in was $1,125; purchase returns were $450; inventory, July 31, was found to be $4,650. The Cost of Goods Sold for the month of July was:
A. $21,225
B. $25,875
C. $20,700
D. $30,525
E. $21,750

15. In the income statement, the inventory that was on hand at the beginning of the period is treated as a(n):
A. asset item.
B. addition in the computation of cost of goods sold.
C. deduction from purchases.
D. direct deduction from gross sales.

# SOLUTIONS

*Matching*

| | | | | |
|---|---|---|---|---|
| 1. *a* | 4. *g* | 7. *h* | 10. *m* | 13. *o* |
| 2. *f* | 5. *e* | 8. *e* | 11. *n* | 14. *n* |
| 3. *c* | 6. *b* | 9. *j* | 12. *l* | 15. *g* |

*Completion and Exercises*

1. Units of inventory (obtained by physical counts) are multiplied by prices obtained from vendor's invoices and the extensions summed to arrive at the total cost of the inventory.
2. deductions (or reductions)
3. perpetual; periodic
4. B can deduct $45 (0.03 x $1,500) from the $1,500 amount of the invoice for these goods if B pays on or before August 5. Otherwise, B must pay $1,500 by August 25.

5.
| | | |
|---|---|---|
| Purchases | 1,500 | |
|     Accounts Payable | | 1,500 |
|   To record purchase on account. | | |
| | | |
| Accounts Payable | 300 | |
|     Purchase Returns and Allowances | | 300 |
|   To record return of merchandise to vendor. | | |
| | | |
| Accounts Payable | 1,200 | |
|     Purchase Discounts ($1,200 x .03) | | 36 |
|     Cash | | 1,164 |
|   To record payment of invoice. | | |

6. trade
7. $735 = $750 - ($750 x 0.02)

8.
| | | |
|---|---|---|
| Merchandise Inventory | 20,800 | |
| Purchase Discounts | 800 | |
| Purchase Returns and Allowances | 1,600 | |
| Sales | 68,000 | |
|     Income Summary | | 91,200 |
| | | |
| Income Summary | 69,040 | |
|     Purchases | | 44,000 |
|     Transportation-In | | 2,400 |
|     Merchandise Inventory | | 16,000 |
|     Selling Expenses | | 3,600 |
|     Administrative Expenses | | 3,040 |

9.

## BARKER COMPANY
### Income Statement
### For the Year Ended December 31, 19__

| | | | |
|---|---|---|---|
| Sales | | | $68,000 |
| Cost of goods sold: | | | |
| Merchandise inventory, 1/1 | | $16,000 | |
| Purchases | $44,000 | | |
| Less: Purchase discounts | $ 800 | | |
| Purchase returns and allowances | 1,600 | 2,400 | |
| Net purchases | | $41,600 | |
| Add: Transportation-in | | 2,400 | |
| Net cost of purchases | | 44,000 | |
| Cost of goods available for sale | | $60,000 | |
| Less: Merchandise inventory, 12/31 | | 20,800 | |
| Cost of goods sold | | | 39,200 |
| Gross margin | | | $28,800 |
| Operating expenses: | | | |
| Selling expenses | | $ 3,600 | |
| Administrative expenses | | 3,040 | 6,640 |
| Net income | | | $22,160 |

10. buried in cost of goods sold (when the cost of the ending inventory is deducted from total goods available for sale)

11. $535.50; $535.50

12. goods not owned; nonsalable goods

13. C; Delivery Expense (or Transportation-Out) (or Freight Expense)

14. D; Transportation-In

15. $3,136 (which is 98 percent of $3,200). The gross selling price is: $8,000 x .50 x .80 = $3,200. The transportation company would collect $80 from F.

16.

| | | |
|---|---|---|
| Purchases | 1,250 | |
| Accounts Payable | | 1,250 |
| To record invoice price of goods purchased. | | |
| | | |
| Accounts Payable | 250 | |
| Purchase Returns and Allowances | | 250 |
| To record return of merchandise. | | |
| | | |
| Accounts Payable | 1,000 | |
| Cash | | 1,000 |
| To record payment of invoice after discount has expired. | | |

17. (a) operating revenues (sales); (b) cost of goods sold; (c) operating expenses; (d) nonoperating revenues and nonoperating expenses.

18. An operating expense is an expense incurred in carrying out a company's major activity, such as salespersons' salaries. A nonoperating expense is an expense incurred that relates only remotely (or not at all) to a company's main line of activity, such as interest expense.

19. a. Merchandise Inventory      f. Sales
    b. Purchases      g. Sales Returns and Allowances
    c. Purchase Returns and Allowances      h. Sales Discounts
    d. Purchase Discounts      i. Delivery Expense
    e. Transportation-In

20. *(a)* $16,000; *(b)* $56,000; *(c)* $16,000; *(d)* $24,000; *(e)* $40,000; *(f)* $8,000 income; *(g)* $152,000
21. legal title; delivery
22. sales discounts, sales returns; sales allowances; assets
23. Any two of the following reasons could be given:
    1. Legal title to the goods has passed and the goods are now the responsibility and property of the buyer.
    2. The selling price of the goods has been established.
    3. The seller's part of the contract has been completed.
    4. The goods have been exchanged for another asset such as cash or accounts receivable.
    5. The costs incurred can be determined.
24. *a.* $1,625 [($2,500 x .60) + $125]
    *b.* September 2
    *c.* $30 ($1,500 x .02)

25.

| | | |
|---|---:|---:|
| Purchase ........................................ | $2,160.00 | $2,304.00 |
| Less return .................................... | 84.00 | 156.00 |
| | $2,076.00 | $2,148.00 |
| Transportation ............................. | 72.00 | — |
| | $2,148.00 | $2,148.00 |
| Discount ....................................... | 41.52 | 21.48 |
| | $2,106.48 | $2,126.52 |

26. 40%.

## True-False Questions

1. F Sales Returns and Allowances is a contra sales account and has a debit balance; to clear this account leaving it with a zero balance requires a credit in the closing entry.
2. F This describes cash discounts.
3. T This is a contra purchases account and will have a balance opposite to the Purchases account.
4. F Cash discounts taken on goods acquired for resale should be credited to a Purchase Discounts account.
5. F
6. F A cash discount is offered as an inducement to pay invoices early and trade discounts are deductions from list price.
7. F Cash discounts are not allowed on freight charges.
8. F The Purchases account balance shows the gross cost of merchandise acquired during the period; cost of goods sold is determined by subtracting ending inventory from the total cost of goods available for sale.
9. F Understated inventory will cause the cost of goods sold to be overstated, which causes net income to be understated.
10. F Cash discounts are recorded by both parties; but trade discounts are not recorded by either buyer or seller.
11. F It is true that inventory and retained earnings would be understated, but cost of goods sold would be overstated due to the omission.
12. T
13. T
14. T
15. F Postings cannot be made from the work sheet to the ledger.
16. F The buyer may deduct 2 percent from the invoice if payment is made within 10 days of the invoice date.

17. F This describes trade discounts.
18. T
19. F Sales would be $104,000; $64,000 cost of goods sold + $40,000 gross margin from sales = $104,000 Sales.
20. T
21. T Note that the trade discounts cannot be added and 35 percent applied to the $150 invoice price. Instead each discount must be applied separately in any order.
22. T But net income will be misstated.
23. T The consignee does not have title to the goods. Title remains with the consignor.
24. F This calculation would show Net Purchases.
25. T Consigned goods should be included in the owner's inventory because these are goods delivered to another party who will attempt to sell the goods for a commission. The consigned goods remain the property of the owner until sold by the consignee.
26. T
27. F Gross margin percentage is equal to gross margin divided by net sales.

## Multiple Choice Questions

1. A
2. C $35,000 Purchases + $12,600 Beginning Inventory - $26,600 Ending Inventory = $21,000 Cost of Goods Sold.
3. E Under the periodic inventory procedure, the cost of goods sold section is composed of: Beginning Inventory + Purchases + Transportation-In minus Purchase Discounts *minus* Ending Inventory.
4. E
5. E The correct entry is to debit Sales Returns and Allowances and to credit Accounts Receivable.
6. B
7. D
8. C The credit would be to Cash, $176.40 and to Purchase Discounts, $3.60.
9. B $1,560 Merchandise - $120 Returns and Allowances = $1,440; $1,440 - $14.40 Discount + $60 Transportation = $1,485.60.
10. A
11. B $81,000 Cost of Goods Sold + $18,000 Ending Inventory = $99,000; $99,000 - $66,000 Purchases = $33,000 Beginning Inventory
12. C $15,000 Net Income + $21,000 Operating Expenses = $36,000 Gross Margin
13. C $36,000 Gross Margin + $81,000 Cost of Goods Sold = $117,000 Sales
14. A $4,050 Beginning Merchandise Inventory + $21,150 Purchases + $1,125 Transportation-In - $450 Purchase Returns = $25,875 Cost of Goods Available for Sale; $25,875 - $4,650 Ending Inventory = $21,225 Cost of Goods Sold
15. B

# CHAPTER 7

# MEASURING AND REPORTING INVENTORIES

## Learning Objectives

1. *Explain and calculate the effects of inventory errors on certain financial statement items.*
2. *Indicate which costs are properly included in inventory.*
3. *Calculate cost of ending inventory and cost of goods sold under the four major inventory costing methods using periodic and perpetual inventory procedures.*
4. *Explain the advantages and disadvantages of the four major inventory costing methods.*
5. *Record merchandise transactions under perpetual inventory procedure.*
6. *Apply net realizable value and the lower-of-cost-or-market method to inventory.*
7. *Estimate cost of ending inventory using the gross margin and retail inventory methods.*
8. *Analyze and use the financial results - inventory turnover ratio.*

## REFERENCE OUTLINE

---

## CHAPTER OUTLINE

---

### INVENTORIES AND COST OF GOODS SOLD

1. Merchandise inventory is the quantity of goods on hand and available for sale at any specific time.
2. Inventory is often the largest and most important asset owned by a merchandising company.

*Learning Objective 1:*
*Explain and calculate the effects of inventory errors on certain financial statement items.*

### IMPORTANCE OF PROPER INVENTORY VALUATION

3. Proper inventory valuation is important because it affects cost of goods sold, which is used to calculate a company's net income.
4. Since net income affects retained earnings, incorrect inventory amounts affect both the reported ending inventory and retained earnings on the balance sheet.
5. Because assets are listed in the order of liquidity, inventories usually follow cash and receivables on the balance sheet.
6. An accurate valuation of ending inventory is necessary to reflect the proper net income for the period, since the ending inventory is deducted from cost of goods available for sale to yield cost of goods sold.
    a. If ending inventory is overstated, current and total assets will be overstated, and cost of goods sold will be understated, with a resulting overstatement of gross margin, net income, and retained earnings.
    b. If ending inventory is misstated, that misstatement is carried forward into the next year.

### DETERMINING INVENTORY COST

7. To obtain proper inventory valuation, the costs to be included in inventory must be determined, and the costs to be assigned to items sold must be calculated.

*Learning Objective 2:*
*Indicate which costs are properly included in inventory.*

### TAKING A PHYSICAL INVENTORY

8. Taking a physical inventory is distinct from pricing an inventory and is not, strictly speaking, an accounting function.
    a. Taking an inventory is the procedure of obtaining the physical quantities of the goods on hand by counting, weighing, measuring, and estimating.
    b. Accuracy should be the goal throughout the entire process of inventory taking.

### COSTS INCLUDED IN INVENTORY COST

9. Inventory cost includes all the necessary outlays to obtain the goods and place them in condition and in the desired location for sale to customers. Inventory cost includes the following costs:
    a. Seller's invoice price, less purchase discounts.
    b. Cost of the buyer's insurance on the goods while in transit.
    c. Transportation charges when borne by the buyer.
    d. Handling costs.

### INVENTORY VALUATION UNDER CHANGING PRICES

10. Merchandise inventory is valued at historical cost, which is the purchase price.

## METHODS OF DETERMINING INVENTORY COST

11. These four methods can be used to determine the cost of inventory: specific identification, FIFO, LIFO, and weighted-average methods.

## COMPARISON OF PERPETUAL AND PERIODIC INVENTORY PROCEDURES

12. Perpetual inventory procedure is often used to enhance internal control.
    a. Using perpetual inventory procedure, there are no purchases or purchase-related accounts.
    b. The Merchandise Inventory account is used to record inventory purchased for resale.
    c. At the time of sale, Merchandise Inventory is credited, leaving a balance showing the cost of inventory on hand.
    d. The Cost of Goods Sold account is updated every time a sale is made.
13. Under periodic inventory procedure, the Purchases, Purchase Discounts, and Purchase Returns and Allowances accounts are used to record purchases and subsequent adjustments.
    a. The Merchandise Inventory account is not adjusted until the end of the period.
    b. Goods not in ending inventory are assumed to have been sold.
    c. The cost of goods sold under periodic procedure is determined only at the end of the period during the closing process.
14. More businesses are using perpetual inventory procedure due to recent developments of inventory management software packages.

## PERPETUAL INVENTORY RECORDS

15. Perpetual inventory cards can show the maximum and minimum number of units the company wishes to stock at any given time in addition to reflecting quantity and cost of items purchased and sold.

*Learning Objective 3:*
*Calculate cost of ending inventory and cost of goods sold under the four major inventory costing methods using periodic and perpetual inventory procedures.*

## SPECIFIC IDENTIFICATION

16. Specific identification assigns the specific actual cost to each unit. Identification is usually made through means of a serial number or identification tag.

## FIFO (FIRST-IN, FIRST-OUT) UNDER PERIODIC PROCEDURE

17. The first-in, first-out (FIFO) method assumes that the first units acquired are the first sold; ending inventory is valued at the most recent purchase prices.
    a. At the end of the year, the physical count is taken and then valued by starting with the most recent purchase and going back through the year until all of the ending inventory has been assigned a cost.
    b. Cost of goods sold = Cost of goods available for sale – Cost of ending inventory.

## LIFO (LAST-IN, FIRST-OUT) UNDER PERIODIC PROCEDURE

18. The last-in, first-out (LIFO) method assumes that the last units acquired are the first units sold; cost of goods sold is the cost of the latest goods acquired.
    a. To compute the cost of ending inventory, begin with the beginning inventory cost and continue listing purchases until enough units have been listed to equal the number in ending inventory.
    b. Cost of goods sold = Cost of goods available for sale – Cost of ending inventory.

## WEIGHTED-AVERAGE UNDER PERIODIC PROCEDURE

19. The weighted-average method also uses actual costs; units sold and in inventory are all costed at the average figure.
    a. Under periodic procedure, the weighted-average unit cost is computed at the end of the period: Weighted-average unit cost = (Total cost of purchases + Cost of beginning inventory) / (Units purchased + Units in beginning inventory).

# FIFO UNDER PERPETUAL INVENTORY PROCEDURE

20. The Merchandise Inventory account will reflect the most recent purchases at any given time. Each time a sale occurs, the items sold are assumed to be the earliest ones acquired.

   a. Under the FIFO method, the use of perpetual and periodic inventory procedures will result in the same total costs for ending inventory and cost of goods sold.

# LIFO UNDER PERPETUAL INVENTORY PROCEDURE

21. The inventory composition and balance are updated with each purchase and sale. Each time a sale occurs, the items sold are assumed to be the most recent ones purchased.

# WEIGHTED-AVERAGE UNDER PERPETUAL INVENTORY PROCEDURE

22. Under perpetual procedure, the weighted-average unit cost (often called the moving weighted-average) is computed after each purchase: Weighted-average unit cost = (Total cost of goods available for sale) / (Total units available for sale).

*Learning Objective 4:*
*Explain the advantages and disadvantages of the four major inventory costing methods.*

# ADVANTAGES AND DISADVANTAGES OF SPECIFIC IDENTIFICATION

23. An advantage of specific identification is that cost of goods sold and ending inventory are stated at the actual cost of specific units sold and on hand.

24. Disadvantages of specific identification include:

   a. Earnings may be manipulated if different units of a given product have different costs.

   b. Relatively homogeneous units are included in inventory at different prices.

   c. In many cases, the method is too costly to apply.

# ADVANTAGES AND DISADVANTAGES OF FIFO

25. FIFO's advantages include:

   a. It is easy to apply.

   b. The assumed flow of costs usually corresponds with the actual physical flow of goods.

   c. No manipulation of income is possible.

   d. The balance sheet correctly reflects the approximate current market value of the inventory.

26. FIFO's disadvantages include:

   a. The recognition of "paper" profits.

   b. Heavier tax burden if used for tax purposes in a period of rising prices.

# ADVANTAGES AND DISADVANTAGES OF LIFO

27. LIFO's advantages include:

   a. Income exists only if sales revenues are sufficient to cover all expenses and the cost of replacing the units sold, provided replacement occurs before the end of the period.

   b. Since prices have risen almost constantly for decades, LIFO avoids recognizing inventory or paper profits.

   c. When prices are rising, income taxes are lower when LIFO is used.

28. LIFO's disadvantages include:

   a. LIFO often matches cost of goods *not* sold against revenues.

   b. In a period of rising prices, inventory is often grossly understated.

   c. Income can be manipulated by speeding up or delaying replacement purchases.

# ADVANTAGES AND DISADVANTAGES OF WEIGHTED-AVERAGE

29. Inventory is not understated as much as under LIFO, but does not necessarily reflect current values as under FIFO.

30. Although income can be manipulated, the effects of buying or not buying are lessened due to the averaging process.

## DIFFERENCES IN COSTING METHODS SUMMARIZED

31. The choice of inventory method affects cost of goods sold, inventory cost, and gross margin.
    a. There is no single correct method because all four methods are acceptable.
    b. Companies are required to disclose the inventory method used. The method is chosen by management.

## CHANGING INVENTORY METHODS

32. Even though companies may generally change inventory methods, switching of methods periodically would violate the accounting principle of consistency.
    a. Accounting information is more useful when it is gathered using the same methods, period after period.
    b. When a change in inventory costing methods is made, the change must be fully disclosed in a footnote to the financial statements.

*Learning Objective 5:*
*Record merchandise transactions under perpetual inventory procedure.*

## JOURNAL ENTRIES UNDER PERPETUAL INVENTORY PROCEDURE

33. The entries required under perpetual inventory procedure as described below do not include a Purchases account.
    a. Purchases of merchandise involve a debit to Merchandise Inventory and a credit to Cash or Accounts Payable (if payment is to be made later).
    b. At the time of sale, Cost of Goods Sold is debited and Merchandise Inventory is credited for the cost. Accounts Receivable (or Cash) is debited and Sales is credited for the retail price of the goods sold.
    c. At year-end when a physical inventory is taken and compared with perpetual records, any shortages are debited to Loss from Inventory Shortage and credited to Merchandise Inventory.
    d. There are no purchases or purchase related accounts to be closed, and only cost of goods sold requires a closing entry.

## DEPARTURES FROM COST BASIS OF INVENTORY MEASUREMENT

34. When the utility of inventory items is less than the cost of those items, departures from historical cost are justified.

*Learning Objective 6:*
*Apply net realizable value and the lower-of-cost-or-market method to inventory.*

## NET REALIZABLE VALUE

35. Damaged, obsolete, or shopworn goods should be carried in inventory at not more than net realizable value, which is the estimated selling price of an item less all costs to complete and dispose of it.
    a. Inventory is written down from cost to net realizable value by debiting a loss account and crediting Merchandise Inventory.
    b. If net realizable value exceeds cost, the item continues to be carried at cost.

## LOWER-OF-COST-OR-MARKET (LCM) METHOD

36. The lower-of-cost-or-market method values inventory at the lower of (1) its historical cost or (2) its current market value.
    a. "Market" is current replacement cost in terms of the quantity usually purchased.
    b. Using LCM, inventory is written down to market value when that value is less than the cost of the item.

    *c.* The method is based on the assumption that if purchase prices fall, sales prices will also fall.

## LCM APPLIED

37. LCM can be applied to each inventory item, to each inventory class, or to total inventory.
    *a.* LCM is often disclosed in the notes of the financial statements.

*Learning Objective 7:*
*Estimate cost of ending inventory using the gross margin and retail inventory methods.*

## ESTIMATING INVENTORY

38. A company using periodic inventory may wish to estimate its inventory for a number of reasons:
    *a.* To obtain an inventory cost figure for use in monthly or quarterly financial statements without taking a physical inventory.
    *b.* To compare with physical inventories to determine whether shortages exist.
    *c.* To determine the amount recoverable from an insurance company when inventory is destroyed by fire or has been stolen.

## GROSS MARGIN METHOD

39. The gross margin method is a procedure for estimating inventory cost in which estimated cost of goods sold, which is determined by deducting estimated gross margin from sales, is deducted from cost of goods available for sale.
    *a.* This method is used to estimate monthly inventories, to verify a previously determined ending inventory amount, or to estimate the cost of goods destroyed or stolen.
    *b.* This method assumes that the gross margin rate is stable from period to period.
    *c.* Estimated gross margin is computed by applying the gross margin rate to the sales figure.
    *d.* Sales - Estimated gross margin = Estimated cost of goods sold.
    *e.* (Beginning inventory + Net cost of purchases) - Estimated cost of goods sold = Estimated ending inventory.

## RETAIL INVENTORY METHOD

40. The retail method can also be used to estimate ending inventory.
    *a.* A cost/price ratio is determined by relating cost of goods available for sale to the retail price of goods available for sale.
    *b.* Ending inventory is determined at retail price by subtracting sales from goods available for sale at retail.
    *c.* Cost of ending inventory = Cost/Price ratio x Ending inventory at retail.

*Learning Objective 8:*
*Analyze and use the financial results - inventory turnover ratio.*

## ANALYZING AND USING THE FINANCIAL RESULTS—INVENTORY TURNOVER

41. Inventory Turnover Ratio = Cost of Goods Sold / Average Inventory
42. The inventory turnover ratio measures the efficiency of the firm in managing and selling inventory. It gauges the liquidity of the firm's inventory.

Mark Company had 3,000 units of Article AX 25 in its end-of-the-year inventory. Its beginning inventory, year's purchases, and year's sales of Article AX 25 were as follows:

| Jan. 1 | Beg. inv. | 1,000 units @ $14.20 | May 3 | Sale | 2,800 units |
|---|---|---|---|---|---|
| Apr. 14 | Purchase | 3,000 units @ $14.80 | June 25 | Sale | 3,200 units |
| June 2 | Purchase | 5,000 units @ $15.58 | July 15 | Sale | 2,000 units |
| Oct. 28 | Purchase | 4,000 units @ $15.60 | Nov. 5 | Sale | 4,000 units |
| Dec. 15 | Purchase | 2,000 units @ $15.92 | | | |

Required:

a. Using the information given above, compute the ending inventory and the cost of goods sold under each of the following methods using perpetual procedure.
   1. FIFO
   2. LIFO
   3. Weighted-average

b. Compute the ending inventory and the cost of goods sold under each of the following methods using periodic procedure:
   1. FIFO
   2. LIFO
   3. Weighted-average

c. In analyzing your answers for a. and b., explain the effect of price inflation on the inventory costing method used.

## SOLUTION TO DEMONSTRATION PROBLEM

*a.* The ending inventory consists of:

|  | Units |
|---|---|
| Beginning inventory | 1,000 |
| Purchases | 14,000 |
| Goods available for sale | 15,000 |
| Sales | 12,000 |
| Ending inventory | 3,000 |

1. Ending inventory and cost of goods sold under FIFO using perpetual procedure:

| | Purchased | | | Sold | | | Balance | | |
|---|---|---|---|---|---|---|---|---|---|
| Date | Units | Unit Cost | Total Cost | Units | Unit Cost | Total Cost | Units | Unit Cost | Total Cost |
| Beg. Inv. | | | | | | | 1,000 | $14.20 | $14,200 |
| Apr. 14 | 3,000 | $14.80 | $44,400 | | | | 1,000 | 14.20 | 14,200 |
| | | | | | | | 3,000 | 14.80 | 44,400 |
| May 3 | | | | 1,000 | $14.20 | $14,200 | | | |
| | | | | 1,800 | 14.80 | 26,640 | 1,200 | 14.80 | 17,760 |
| June 2 | 5,000 | 15.58 | 77,900 | | | | 1,200 | 14.80 | 17,760 |
| | | | | | | | 5,000 | 15.58 | 77,900 |
| June 25 | | | | 1,200 | 14.80 | 17,760 | | | |
| | | | | 2,000 | 15.58 | 31,160 | 3,000 | 15.58 | 46,740 |
| July 15 | | | | 2,000 | 15.58 | 31,160 | 1,000 | 15.58 | 15,580 |
| Oct. 28 | 4,000 | 15.60 | 62,400 | | | | 1,000 | 15.58 | 15,580 |
| | | | | | | | 4,000 | 15.60 | 62,400 |
| Nov. 5 | | | | 1,000 | 15.58 | 15,580 | | | |
| | | | | 3,000 | 15.60 | 46,800 | 1,000 | 15.60 | 15,600 |
| Dec. 15 | 2,000 | 15.92 | 31,840 | | | | 1,000 | 15.60 | 15,600 |
| | | | | | | | 2,000 | 15.92 | 31,840 |
| Cost of goods sold | | | | 12,000 | | $183,300 | | | |

Ending inventory = (1,000 x $15.60) + (2,000 x $15.92) = $47,440

*a. (continued)*

2. Ending inventory and cost of goods sold under LIFO using perpetual procedure:

| Date | Purchased Units | Purchased Unit Cost | Purchased Total Cost | Sold Units | Sold Unit Cost | Sold Total Cost | Balance Units | Balance Unit Cost | Balance Total Cost |
|---|---|---|---|---|---|---|---|---|---|
| Beg. Inv. | | | | | | | 1,000 | $14.20 | $14,200 |
| Apr. 14 | 3,000 | $14.80 | $44,400 | | | | 1,000 | 14.20 | 14,200 |
| | | | | | | | 3,000 | 14.80 | 44,400 |
| May 3 | | | | 2,800 | $14.80 | $41,440 | 1,000 | 14.20 | 14,200 |
| | | | | | | | 200 | 14.80 | 2,960 |
| June 2 | 5,000 | 15.58 | 77,900 | | | | 1,000 | 14.20 | 14,200 |
| | | | | | | | 200 | 14.80 | 2,960 |
| | | | | | | | 5,000 | 15.58 | 77,900 |
| June 25 | | | | 3,200 | 15.58 | 49,856 | 1,000 | 14.20 | 14,200 |
| | | | | | | | 200 | 14.80 | 2,960 |
| | | | | | | | 1,800 | 15.58 | 28,044 |
| July 15 | | | | 1,800 | 15.58 | 28,044 | | | |
| | | | | 200 | 14.80 | 2,960 | 1,000 | 14.20 | 14,200 |
| Oct. 28 | 4,000 | 15.60 | 62,400 | | | | 1,000 | 14.20 | 14,200 |
| | | | | | | | 4,000 | 15.60 | 62,400 |
| Nov. 5 | | | | 4,000 | 15.60 | 62,400 | 1,000 | 14.20 | 14,200 |
| Dec. 15 | 2,000 | 15.92 | 31,840 | | | | 1,000 | 14.20 | 14,200 |
| | | | | | | | 2,000 | 15.92 | 31,840 |
| Cost of goods sold | | | | 12,000 | | $184,700 | | | |

Ending inventory = (1,000 x $14.20) + (2,000 x $15.92) = $46,040

*a. (concluded)*

3. Ending inventory and cost of goods sold under weighted-average using perpetual procedure:

| Date | Units | Purchased Unit Cost | Purchased Total Cost | Units | Sold Unit Cost | Sold Total Cost | Units | Balance Unit Cost | Balance Total Cost |
|---|---|---|---|---|---|---|---|---|---|
| Beg. Inv. | | | | | | | 1,000 | $14.20 | $14,200 |
| Apr. 14 | 3,000 | $14.80 | $44,400 | | | | 4,000 | 14.65[a] | 58,600 |
| May 3 | | | | 2,800 | $14.65 | $41,020 | 1,200 | 14.65 | 17,580 |
| June 2 | 5,000 | 15.58 | 77,900 | | | | 6,200 | 15.40[b] | 95,480 |
| June 25 | | | | 3,200 | 15.40 | 49,280 | 3,000 | 15.40 | 46,200 |
| July 15 | | | | 2,000 | 15.40 | 30,800 | 1,000 | 15.40 | 15,400 |
| Oct. 28 | 4,000 | 15.60 | 62,400 | | | | 5,000 | 15.56[c] | 77,800 |
| Nov. 5 | | | | 4,000 | 15.56 | 62,240 | 1,000 | 15.56 | 15,560 |
| Dec. 15 | 2,000 | 15.92 | 31,840 | | | | 3,000 | 15.80[d] | 47,400 |
| Cost of goods sold | | | | 12,000 | | $183,340 | | | |

Ending inventory = (3,000 x $15.80) = $47,400

[a] $58,600/4,000 = $14.65  [b] $95,480/6,200 = $15.40  [c] $77,800/5,000 = $15.56  [d] $47,400/3,000 = $15.80

*b.* 1. Ending inventory and cost of goods sold under FIFO using periodic procedure:

| *Ending Inventory:* Date | Units | Unit Cost | Total Cost | *Cost of Goods Sold:* | |
|---|---|---|---|---|---|
| Dec. 15 purchase | 2,000 | $15.92 | $31,840 | Total cost | $230,740 |
| Oct. 28 purchase | 1,000 | 15.60 | 15,600 | Less: Ending inventory | 47,440 |
| | 3,000 | | $47,440 | Cost of goods sold | $183,300 |

2. Ending inventory and cost of goods sold under LIFO using periodic procedure:

| *Ending Inventory:* Date | Units | Unit Cost | Total Cost | *Cost of Goods Sold:* | |
|---|---|---|---|---|---|
| Beg. Inv. | 1,000 | $14.20 | $14,200 | Total cost | $230,740 |
| Apr. 14 purchase | 2,000 | 14.80 | 29,600 | Less: Ending inventory | 43,800 |
| | 3,000 | | $43,800 | Cost of goods sold | $186,940 |

3. Ending inventory and cost of goods sold under weighted-average using periodic procedure:

| Date | Units | Unit Cost | Total Cost |
|---|---|---|---|
| Beg. Inv. | 1,000 | $14.20 | $14,200 |
| Apr. 14 purchase | 3,000 | 14.80 | 44,400 |
| June 2 purchase | 5,000 | 15.58 | 77,900 |
| Oct. 28 purchase | 4,000 | 15.60 | 62,400 |
| Dec. 15 purchase | 2,000 | 15.92 | 31,840 |
| | 15,000 | | $230,740 |

Weighted-average unit cost = $230,740/15,000 = $15.3827

Ending inventory = $15.3827 x 3,000 = $46,148

Cost of goods sold = $230,740 - $46,148 = $184,592

*c.* In a period of rising prices, as experienced by Mark Company, LIFO gives a higher cost of goods sold and a lower ending inventory than FIFO. Weighted-average costing tends to average out the effects of price increases and decreases.

# MATCHING

Referring to the terms listed below, place the appropriate letter next to the corresponding description. A letter may be used more than once.

a. FIFO
b. Gross margin method
c. LIFO
d. Net realizable value

e. Lower-of-cost-or-market method
f. Retail inventory method
g. Specific identification
h. Weighted-average

i. Inventory or "paper" profits
j. Perpetual inventory procedure
k. Periodic inventory procedure

_____ 1. A method of pricing inventory under which the costs of the latest goods acquired are the first costs charged to cost of goods sold.

_____ 2. An inventory pricing method that assigns known actual costs to particular units of product.

_____ 3. A method of estimating the cost of inventory based on past relationships and used when a physical inventory cannot be taken or would be too costly or inconvenient to take.

_____ 4. A method of pricing inventory under which the costs of the first goods acquired are the first costs charged to cost of goods sold.

_____ 5. Estimated selling price of merchandise less estimated costs to complete and dispose of the goods.

_____ 6. A method of pricing inventory that takes into consideration declines but not increases in the utility of goods.

_____ 7. A method of pricing inventory that usually yields an inventory cost that falls between the amounts that would be computed using FIFO or LIFO.

_____ 8. A procedure for estimating the cost of ending inventory by applying a cost/price ratio to the ending inventory at sales prices.

_____ 9. A portion of the net income computed under FIFO that is considered fictitious by LIFO supporters because it must be reinvested in inventory.

_____ 10. Damaged, obsolete, or shopworn goods should be carried at an amount that does not exceed this value.

_____ 11. Under this procedure of accounting for inventory, there is no Purchases account because all entries involving merchandise purchased for resale are entered in the Merchandise Inventory account.

_____ 12. Under this procedure of accounting for inventory, there are Purchases, Purchase Returns and Allowances, and Purchase Discounts accounts.

# COMPLETION AND EXERCISES

1. When the perpetual inventory method is being used, the accountant debits _____ _____ and credits Accounts Payable (or Cash) when goods are purchased and debits Cost of Goods Sold and credits _____ _____ when goods are sold, along with the proper sales entry.

2. When prices are rising, LIFO inventory is _____ (higher or lower) than FIFO inventory at the end of the year. This will cause the cost of goods sold under LIFO to be _____ (higher or lower) than under FIFO, and accordingly the net income will be _____ (higher or lower) under LIFO.

3. Describe two recognized methods of estimating the cost of ending inventory.

a. _____

_____

_____

b. _____

_____

4. Assuming periodic inventory procedure, what effect would an understatement of ending inventory have on the different items on the financial statements?

| *Balance Sheet* | *Income Statement* |
|---|---|
| Current Assets _____ | Cost of Goods Sold _____ |
| Total Assets _____ | Gross Margin _____ |
| Retained Earnings _____ | Net Income _____ |
| Total Liabilities and Retained Earnings _____ | |

5. What is included in the cost of inventory?

_____

_____

_____

_____

_____

_____

6. When is the specific identification method of inventory valuation most applicable?

_____

_____

_____

7. Both _____-_____ , _____-_____ and _____-_____ , _____-_____ methods of inventory valuation are assumptions as to the flow of costs.

8. Following is a summary of beginning inventory, purchases, and sales. At what amount would the inventory be priced assuming the first-in, first-out method is used under perpetual inventory procedure?

| | | |
|---|---|---|
| Beg. Inv., Jan. 1 | 2,400 | units @ $8.80 |
| Purchases: | | |
| Jan. 8 | 5,600 | units @ $9.00 |
| Mar. 15 | 2,000 | units @ $9.10 |
| July 28 | 2,800 | units @ $9.50 |
| Nov. 30 | 400 | units @ $9.70 |
| Sales: | | |
| Feb. 13 | 3,000 | units |
| June 9 | 2,800 | units |
| Sept. 22 | 1,400 | units |

9. At what amount would the inventory in the preceding question be priced if the last-in, first-out method were used under perpetual inventory procedure?

10. Under FIFO, net income exists if revenues are sufficient to cover the _____ cost of the units of inventory sold.

11. Under LIFO, net income exists if revenues are sufficient to cover the _____ cost of the units of inventory sold, provided new units are acquired before the end of the accounting period.

12. The principle argument for _____ is that this method more precisely matches costs and revenues in current terms.

13. During a period of rising prices, _____ will give a higher net income figure.

14. Below is a record of beginning inventory and purchases. Compute the ending inventory under the weighted-average method assuming periodic inventory procedure if a physical count showed 150 units on hand at the end of the month.

| | | | |
|---|---|---|---|
| Inventory on May 1 ........................... | 75 | units at $10.00 | = $ 750.00 |
| Purchases: | | | |
| May 10 ............................................. | 50 | units at $10.50 | = 525.00 |
| May 15 ............................................. | 25 | units at $10.30 | = 257.50 |
| May 25 ............................................. | 100 | units at $10.10 | = 1,010.00 |
| | 250 | | $2,542.50 |

15. What is the cost of goods sold in the example in Question 14?

16. The lower-of-cost-or-market method uses market values only to the extent that these

values are _____ than historical cost.

17. The Mia Company has three different products in its inventory at December 31, 1999 which have costs and current market value as follows:

| Item | Cost | Market |
|---|---|---|
| A ........................................................ ...................... | $ 5,000 | $5,500 |
| B ........................................................ ...................... | 15,000 | 14,750 |
| C ........................................................ ...................... | 12,500 | 12,875 |

If each product is priced at the lower-of-cost-or-market, the inventory is $_____.

If the total is priced at the lower-of-cost-or-market, the inventory is $_____.

18. Concerning the gross margin method of estimating inventory, what assumption must be correct for this method to be satisfactory?

_____

_____

19. To apply the gross margin method, the rate of gross margin on sales is multiplied by

_____ _____ to arrive at gross margin. The gross margin is then subtracted from

net sales to arrive at _____ _____ _____ _____ _____. This

figure is then subtracted from _____ _____ _____ _____

_____ _____ to arrive at ending inventory.

20. Use the following information and the retail inventory method to estimate the ending inventory at cost:

|  | Cost | Retail |
|---|---|---|
| Beginning inventory | $ 44,000 | $ 70,000 |
| Purchases, net | 550,000 | 920,000 |
| Sales | | 900,000 |

21. Under perpetual inventory procedure, what journal entries are required to record a sale of merchandise on account?

_____

_____

_____

_____

22. The D Company's gross margin rate has been 37.5 percent for each of the past three years. R needs financial statements for the period ending February 14, 1999. You are given the following data:

| | |
|---|---|
| Inventory, January 1 | $45,000 |
| Net cost of purchases through February 14 | 32,000 |
| Net sales through February 14 | 80,000 |

Compute the estimated cost of the February 14, 1999, inventory.

| | | | | | | | | | | | | |
|---|---|---|---|---|---|---|---|---|---|---|---|---|
| | | | | | | | | | | | | |
| | | | | | | | | | | | | |
| | | | | | | | | | | | | |
| | | | | | | | | | | | | |
| | | | | | | | | | | | | |
| | | | | | | | | | | | | |
| | | | | | | | | | | | | |
| | | | | | | | | | | | | |
| | | | | | | | | | | | | |
| | | | | | | | | | | | | |
| | | | | | | | | | | | | |

23. The Computational Error Company reported net income of $240,000 and $270,000 for 1998 and 1999. It was discovered later that the ending inventory for 1998 was understated by $28,000. Compute the correct net income for 1998 and 1999.

| | | | | | | | | | |
|---|---|---|---|---|---|---|---|---|---|
| | | | | | | | | | |
| | | | | | | | | | |
| | | | | | | | | | |
| | | | | | | | | | |
| | | | | | | | | | |
| | | | | | | | | | |
| | | | | | | | | | |

24. A company began an accounting period with 100 units of an item that cost $7.50 each. During the period it purchased 400 units of the item at $9 each and it sold 390 units. In the spaces below give the costs assigned to the ending inventory and to goods sold under each of the three assumptions using periodic inventory procedure:

|   |   | Ending Inventory | Cost of Goods Sold |
|---|---|---|---|
| 1. | The costs were assigned on a LIFO basis | $ _____ | $ _____ |
| 2. | The costs were assigned on a weighted-average cost basis | $ _____ | $ _____ |
| 3. | Costs were assigned on a FIFO basis | $ _____ | $ _____ |

25. Company A has the following financial information for 1999:

| | |
|---|---|
| Beginning inventory | $230,000 |
| Ending inventory | $300,000 |
| Cost of goods sold | $175,000 |

The inventory turnover ratio is equal to _____.

26. On July 10, 1999, the entire inventory of S Co. was destroyed by fire. You are to present a claim for insurance for the amount of the loss. In looking over the records you find the following data:

| | |
|---|---|
| Merchandise purchases, Jan. 1 to date | $470,000 |
| Sales returns | 3,750 |
| Purchase returns | 2,600 |
| Sales | 656,000 |
| Merchandise on hand, Jan. 1 | 120,000 |

Goods are generally marked up 33 α percent of cost which is 25 percent of sales price.

# TRUE-FALSE QUESTIONS

Indicate whether each of the following statements is true or false by inserting a capital "T" or "F" in the blank space provided.

_____ 1. When prices are rising, higher income will be reported using FIFO as compared with using LIFO.

_____ 2. If prices are steadily rising or falling, the use of the weighted-average method will yield a cost for inventory between those yielded by FIFO and LIFO.

_____ 3. Inventory costing methods can be changed at will to control reported net income.

_____ 4. The retail inventory method can be used at the end of any period except the end of the fiscal year.

_____ 5. Errors in determining the cost of the ending inventory lead to a balance sheet that does not balance and are thus readily observed.

_____ 6. An overstated ending inventory leads to understated net income.

_____ 7. An error in determining the cost of the ending inventory of a period generally results in misstated income for two periods.

_____ 8. Income cannot be manipulated by the timing of purchases if the FIFO method is used.

_____ 9. The gross margin method uses the gross margin rate of the current period in estimating the cost of inventory.

_____ 10. The net realizable value of an inventory item can never be greater than its expected selling price.

_____ 11. During a period of falling prices, FIFO yields the greatest cost of goods sold.

_____ 12. An advantage of using LIFO is that the balance sheet valuation for inventory is based on an up-to-date cost.

_____ 13. Inventory costs include only the seller's invoice price less any purchase discounts.

_____ 14. In a period of falling prices, FIFO will result in a higher net income figure than that resulting from LIFO.

_____ 15. Because of the importance of consistency, a company may not change inventory costing methods unless the prior method is one that is unacceptable to the accounting profession.

_____ 16. If the utility or value of inventory items is less than the cost of those items, departures from cost are justified.

_____ 17. The closing entries necessary under the perpetual and periodic inventory procedures do not differ because all expenses and revenues must be closed.

_____ 18. If the beginning inventory exceeds the ending inventory, the net income is overstated.

_____ 19. The two bases of inventory pricing most widely used are cost and lower-of-cost-or-market.

_____ 20. When the perpetual inventory method is used, it is never necessary to count merchandise on hand.

_____ 21. An overstatement of the beginning inventory will result in an overstatement of the net income for the period.

_____ 22. The gross margin method of determining an inventory produces precisely accurate results.

_____ 23. When the periodic method of inventory accounting is used, purchases are recorded in the Inventory account.

_____ 24. In a period of constant prices, FIFO and LIFO will give identical results.

_____ 25. When a company changes from one inventory costing method to another, the change must be fully disclosed in a footnote to the financial statements explaining the reasons for the change and the effect on net income.

_____ 26. The ending inventory and cost of goods sold will be the same under LIFO perpetual and LIFO periodic.

_____ 27. Whether or not a company uses the lower-of-cost-or-market method of valuing inventory is usually disclosed in a footnote to the financial statements.

---
## MULTIPLE CHOICE QUESTIONS
---

For each of the following questions, indicate the best answer by circling the appropriate letter.

1. The following principle requires a company to show in its financial statements by means of a footnote or other manner, the inventory costing method used:
   A. conservation principle.
   B. full-disclosure principle.
   C. consistency principle.
   D. business entity principle.
   E. stable monetary concept.

2. The system that continuously provides the cost of the inventory on hand is called:
   A. average cost.
   B. periodic.
   C. perpetual.
   D. gross profit.
   E. physical.

3. Smith & Olley Company for several years has maintained a 30 percent average gross margin on sales. Given the following data for 1999, what is the approximate inventory on December 31, 1999, computed by the gross margin method of estimating inventory?

|  | Cost |
| --- | --- |
| Inventory, January 1 ......................................... | $ 24,000 |
| Net cost of purchases ......................................... | 130,000 |
| Total ................................................................ | $154,000 |

Net sales at retail in 1999 were $180,000.
   A. $35,100
   B. $23,100
   C. $28,000
   D. $54,000
   E. $26,000

4. During a period of rising prices, which inventory costing method might be expected to give the lowest valuation for inventory on the balance sheet?
   A. LIFO
   B. FIFO
   C. Weighted-average cost
   D. Specific identification

5-7.The following inventory, purchases, and sales data are obtained:

|  | Units | Unit Cost | Total |
|---|---|---|---|
| Jan. 1 ............................................. | 20 | $2.00 | $40.00 |
| Purchases: | | | |
| Jan. 3 ............................................. | 8 | 2.10 | 16.80 |
| Jan. 15............................................ | 6 | 2.20 | 13.20 |
| Jan. 21............................................ | 10 | 2.25 | 22.50 |
| Jan. 30............................................ | 2 | 2.40 | 4.80 |
| | 46 | | |
| Sales: | | | |
| Jan. 8 | 10 | | |
| Jan. 17 | 7 | | |
| Jan. 24 | 9 | | |
| | 26 | | |

Perpetual inventory procedure is used.

5. If the weighted-average (moving average) method is used, what is the cost of ending inventory?
   A. $42.30
   B. $42.74
   C. $43.27
   D. $55.00

6. If instead, the first-in, first-out method is used, what is the cost of ending inventory?
   A. $47.40
   B. $39.90
   C. $44.70
   D. $40.50

7. If instead, the last-in, first-out method is used, what is the cost of ending inventory?
   A. $41.05
   B. $45.00
   C. $36.25
   D. $32.85

8. If the ending inventory is understated by $150, the cost of goods sold will be:
   A. overstated by $300
   B. overstated by $250
   C. overstated by $150
   D. understated by $250
   E. understated by $150

9. If the ending inventory is overstated by $100, the net income will be:
   A. understated by $200
   B. understated by $100
   C. overstated by $200
   D. overstated by $100
   E. None of these.

10-15. On January 1, 1999, Nichols Company's inventory of Item X consisted of 2,000 units that cost $8 each. During 1999 the company purchased 5,000 units of Item X at $10 each, and it sold 4,500 units. Periodic inventory procedure is used.

10. Cost of goods sold using FIFO is:
 A. $45,000
 B. $36,000
 C. $41,000
 D. None of these.

11. Cost of ending inventory using FIFO is:
 A. $25,000
 B. $20,500
 C. $37,500
 D. $53,500
 E. None of these.

12. Cost of goods sold using LIFO is:
 A. $20,000
 B. $36,000
 C. $45,000
 D. $25,000
 E. None of these.

13. Cost of ending inventory using LIFO is:
 A. $45,000
 B. $30,000
 C. $16,000
 D. $21,000
 E. None of these.

14. Cost of goods sold using weighted-average cost is:
 A. $45,000
 B. $42,429
 C. $20,250
 D. $25,000
 E. None of these.

15. Cost of ending inventory using weighted-average cost is:
 A. $21,000
 B. $25,500
 C. $23,572
 D. $16,000
 E. None of these.

16. For 1999, Johnson Company had the following:

| | |
|---|---|
| Beginning Inventory | $780,000 |
| Ending Inventory | $830,000 |
| Cost of Goods Sold | $215,000 |

The inventory turnover ratio is:
 A. .259
 B. .276
 C. .267
 D. .287
 E. None of these.

## SOLUTIONS

*Matching*

| 1. c | 7. h |
|---|---|
| 2. g | 8. f |
| 3. b | 9. i |
| 4. a | 10. d |
| 5. d | 11. j |
| 6. e | 12. k |

*Completion and Exercises*

1. Merchandise Inventory; Merchandise Inventory
2. Lower; higher; lower
3. (a) Gross margin method—this estimating procedure deducts estimated gross margin from sales to yield estimated cost of goods sold. Estimated cost of goods sold is subtracted from cost of goods available for sale to arrive at estimated inventory.
   (b) Retail inventory method—this estimating procedure applies a cost/price ratio to ending inventory stated at retail prices in order to estimate ending inventory at cost.

*Balance Sheet*

4. Current Assets—understated
   Total Assets—understated
   Retained Earnings—understated
   Total Liabilities and Retained Earnings—understated

*Income Statement*

Cost of Goods Sold—overstated
Gross Margin—understated
Net Income—understated

5. The cost of inventory includes all outlays necessary to acquire the goods, including the invoice price, insurance in transit, transportation charges, and handling costs. In theory, all costs incurred to acquire the goods and get them to their existing condition and location should be included in inventory.
6. The specific identification method is most applicable when the products bought and sold are large, readily identifiable, and of high unit value.
7. first-in, first-out; last-in, first-out
8. FIFO

| Date | Purchased Units | Purchased Unit Cost | Sold Units | Sold Unit Cost | Balance Units | Balance Unit Cost | Balance Total Cost |
|---|---|---|---|---|---|---|---|
| Jan. 1 Beg. Inv. | | | | | 2,400 | $8.80 | $21,120 |
| Jan. 8 | 5,600 | $9.00 | | | 2,400 | 8.80 | 21,120 |
| | | | | | 5,600 | 9.00 | 50,400 |
| Feb. 13 | | | 2,400 | $8.80 | | | |
| | | | 600 | 9.00 | 5,000 | 9.00 | 45,000 |
| Mar. 15 | 2,000 | 9.10 | | | 5,000 | 9.00 | 45,000 |
| | | | | | 2,000 | 9.10 | 18,200 |
| June 9 | | | 2,800 | 9.00 | 2,200 | 9.00 | 19,800 |
| | | | | | 2,000 | 9.10 | 18,200 |

|  | Purchased | | Sold | | Balance | | |
|---|---|---|---|---|---|---|---|
| Date | Units | Unit Cost | Units | Unit Cost | Units | Unit Cost | Total Cost |
| July 28 | 2,800 | 9.50 |  |  | 2,200 | 9.00 | 19,800 |
|  |  |  |  |  | 2,000 | 9.10 | 18,200 |
|  |  |  |  |  | 2,800 | 9.50 | 26,600 |
| Sept 22 |  |  | 1,400 | 9.00 | 800 | 9.00 | 7,200 |
|  |  |  |  |  | 2,000 | 9.10 | 18,200 |
|  |  |  |  |  | 2,800 | 9.50 | 26,600 |
| Nov. 30 | 400 | 9.70 |  |  | 800 | 9.00 | 7,200 |
|  |  |  |  |  | 2,000 | 9.10 | 18,200 |
|  |  |  |  |  | 2,800 | 9.50 | 26,600 |
|  |  |  |  |  | 400 | 9.70 | 3,880 |

FIFO - Ending inventory = (800 x $9.00) + (2,000 x $9.10) + (2,800 x $9.50)+ (400 x $9.70)
= $55,880

9. LIFO

|  | Purchased | | Sold | | Balance | | |
|---|---|---|---|---|---|---|---|
| Date | Units | Unit Cost | Units | Unit Cost | Units | Unit Cost | Total Cost |
| Jan.1 Beg. Inv. |  |  |  |  | 2,400 | $8.80 | $21,120 |
| Jan. 8 | 5,600 | $9.00 |  |  | 2,400 | 8.80 | 21,120 |
|  |  |  |  |  | 5,600 | 9.00 | 50,400 |
| Feb. 13 |  |  | 3,000 | $9.00 | 2,400 | 8.80 | 21,120 |
|  |  |  |  |  | 2,600 | 9.00 | 23,400 |
| Mar. 15 | 2,000 | 9.10 |  |  | 2,400 | 8.80 | 21,120 |
|  |  |  |  |  | 2,600 | 9.00 | 23,400 |
|  |  |  |  |  | 2,000 | 9.10 | 18,200 |
| June 9 |  |  | 2,000 | 9.10 | 2,400 | 8.80 | 21,120 |
|  |  |  | 800 | 9.00 | 1,800 | 9.00 | 16,200 |
| July 28 | 2,800 | 9.50 |  |  | 2,400 | 8.80 | 21,120 |
|  |  |  |  |  | 1,800 | 9.00 | 16,200 |
|  |  |  |  |  | 2,800 | 9.50 | 26,600 |
| Sept 22 |  |  | 1,400 | 9.50 | 2,400 | 8.80 | 21,120 |
|  |  |  |  |  | 1,800 | 9.00 | 16,200 |
|  |  |  |  |  | 1,400 | 9.50 | 13,300 |
| Nov. 30 | 400 | 9.70 |  |  | 2,400 | 8.80 | 21,120 |
|  |  |  |  |  | 1,800 | 9.00 | 16,200 |
|  |  |  |  |  | 1,400 | 9.50 | 13,300 |
|  |  |  |  |  | 400 | 9.70 | 3,880 |

LIFO - Ending inventory = (2,400 x $8.80) + (1,800 x $9.00) + (1,400 x $9.50) + (400 x $9.70)
= $54,500

10. historical
11. replacement
12. LIFO
13. FIFO
14. Weighted-average unit cost is $2,542.50 / 250 = $10.17
Ending inventory is 150 x $10.17 = $1,525.50

15. Cost of goods available for sale . $2,542.50
       Less: Ending inventory ............ 1,525.50
       Cost of goods sold ........................ $1,017.00

16. less

17. $32,250; $32,500

18. The assumption that the rate of gross margin realized is stable from period to period must be correct.

19. Net sales; estimated cost of goods sold; cost of goods available for sale

20.

| | Cost | Retail |
|---|---|---|
| Beginning inventory ..................................................................... | $ 44,000 | $ 70,000 |
| Purchases, net ............................................................................. | 550,000 | 920,000 |
| Goods available for sale .............................................................. | $594,000 | $990,000 |
| Cost/retail price ratio: $594,000 / $990,000 = 60% | | |
| Sales .......................................................................................... | | 900,000 |
| Cost of goods sold (60% x $900,000) .......................................... | 540,000 | |
| Ending inventory ........................................................................ | $ 54,000 | $ 90,000 |

21.

| | | |
|---|---|---|
| Accounts Receivable ................................................................... | xxxx | |
|     Sales.......................................................................................... | | xxxx |
| Cost of Goods Sold ...................................................................... | xxxx | |
|     Merchandise Inventory ........................................................... | | xxxx |

22. Goods available for sale = $45,000 (inventory) + $32,000 (net cost of purchases) = $77,000
    Less: Estimated cost of goods sold = $80,000 (net sales) - $30,000
      (gross margin on net sales: $80,000 x .375) =..................................... 50,000
      Estimated cost of February 14 inventory ............................................. $27,000

23. 1998: $240,000 (reported income) + $28,000 (error)  =   $268,000
    1999: $270,000 (reported income) - $28,000 (error)  =   $242,000

24.

| | Ending Inventory | Cost of Goods Sold |
|---|---|---|
| 1. | $840 | $3,510 |
| 2. | $957 | $3,393 |
| 3. | $990 | $3,360 |

25.

$$\frac{\$175,000}{(\$230,000+\$300,000)/2} = .66:1$$

26.

| | | |
|---|---|---|
| Inventory (beginning)................................................................ | | $120,000.00 |
| Purchases ................................................................................. | $470,000.00 | |
| Purchase Returns ...................................................................... | -2,600.00 | 467,400.00 |
| Cost of goods available for sale ............................................... | | $587,400.00 |
| Sales ........................................................................................ | $656,000.00 | |
| Sales Returns ............................................................................ | -3,750.00 | |
| Net sales .................................................................................. | $652,250.00 | |
| Less gross margin (25% x $652,250) ....................................... | -163,062.50 | 489,187.50 |
| Est. Ending Inventory at cost .................................................. | | $ 98,212.50 |

## True-False Questions

1. T    When prices are rising, the FIFO inventory method costs out the lower priced inventory as cost of goods sold resulting in a lower amount for cost of goods sold, which is applied against revenue to give net income.

2. T

3. F

4. F

5. F    The balance sheet may balance, but retained earnings and inventory will be over- or understated.

6. F    If ending inventory is overstated, the cost of goods sold is understated which results in an overstated net income.

7. T    This results because the ending inventory of one period is the following period's beginning inventory.

8. T

9. F

10. T    This applies more often to damaged and obsolete goods.

11. T

12. F    Under LIFO the ending inventory on the balance sheet reflects old costs because the current costs have been included in the cost of goods sold.

13. F    Inventory costs include other items besides the seller's invoice price, such as the cost of insurance while the goods are in transit, transportation charges, and handling costs.

14. F

15. F    While consistency is important, it does not mean a company can never make a change in an inventory costing method.

16. T

17. F    There are no purchases or purchase-related accounts to be closed under perpetual inventory procedure; only cost of goods sold requires a closing entry.

18. F    This comparison between beginning and ending inventory has no effect on the correctness of net income; it merely means that cost of goods sold may have exceeded the purchases.

19. T

20. F    At year-end or more frequently, a count of inventory is necessary to compare against the book record to determine if there are any differences that must be accounted for.

21. F    Net income would be understated.

22. F    The gross margin method is an estimating procedure.

23. F    Under periodic inventory method, purchases are recorded in a Purchases account.

24. T

25. T

26. F    Perpetual and periodic inventory procedures using LIFO will usually result in different ending inventory and cost of goods sold figures. However, the results will be equal using FIFO under both perpetual and periodic procedures.

27. T

1. B
2. C
3. C

| | |
|---|---:|
| Inventory, Jan. 1 ................................................................ | $ 24,000 |
| Net cost of purchases ...................................................... | 130,000 |
| Cost of goods available for sale .................................... | $154,000 |

Less estimated cost of goods sold:

| | | |
|---|---:|---:|
| Net sales ....................................................... | $180,000 | |
| Gross margin (30% x $180,000) ............................... | 54,000 | |
| Estimated cost of goods sold ........................................ | | 126,000 |
| Estimated inventory, December 31, 1999 ..................... | | $ 28,000 |

4. A
5. C

| | Units Acquired | | Units Sold | | | | Units | Unit Cost |
|---|---|---|---|---|---|---|---|---|
| Beg. inv. | 20 @ $2.00 | | | | | $40.00 | | |
| Jan. 3 | 8 @ 2.10 | | | | | +16.80 | $56.80 | 28 | $2.0286 |
| 8 | | | 10 @ | 2.0286 | -20.29 | 36.51 | 18 | |
| 15 | 6 @ 2.20 | | | | | +13.20 | 49.71 | 24 | 2.0713 |
| 17 | | | 7 @ | 2.0713 | -14.50 | 35.21 | 17 | |
| 21 | 10 @ 2.25 | | | | | +22.50 | 57.71 | 27 | 2.1374 |
| 24 | | | 9 @ | 2.1374 | -19.24 | 38.47 | 18 | |
| 30 | 2 @ 2.40 | | | | | +4.80 | $43.27 | 20 | |

+Purchases
- Sales

6. C

| | | | | Balance | | |
|---|---|---|---|---|---|---|
| | | Units | Unit Cost | Units | Unit Cost | |
| Jan. | 1 | 20 | $2.00 | 20 | $2.00 | |
| | 3 | +8 | 2.10 | 20 | 2.00 | |
| | | | | 8 | 2.10 | |
| | 8 | -10 | 2.00 | 10 | 2.00 | |
| | | | | 8 | 2.10 | |
| | 15 | +6 | 2.20 | 10 | 2.00 | |
| | | | | 8 | 2.10 | |
| | | | | 6 | 2.20 | |
| | 17 | -7 | 2.00 | 3 | 2.00 | |
| | | | | 8 | 2.10 | |
| | | | | 6 | 2.20 | |
| | 21 | +10 | 2.25 | 3 | 2.00 | |
| | | | | 8 | 2.10 | |
| | | | | 6 | 2.20 | |
| | | | | 10 | 2.25 | |
| | 24 | -3 | 2.00 | | | |
| | | -6 | 2.10 | 2 | 2.10 | |
| | | | | 6 | 2.20 | |
| | | | | 10 | 2.25 | |
| | 30 | +2 | 2.40 | 2 | 2.10 | $ 4.20 |
| | | | | 6 | 2.20 | 13.20 |
| | | | | 10 | 2.25 | 22.50 |
| | | | | 2 | 2.40 | 4.80 |
| | | | | | | $44.70 |

7. A

|  |  | Units | Unit Cost | Balance Units | Balance Unit Cost |  |
|---|---|---|---|---|---|---|
| Jan. | 1 | 20 | $2.00 | 20 | $2.00 |  |
|  | 3 | +8 | 2.10 | 20 | 2.00 |  |
|  |  |  |  | 8 | 2.10 |  |
|  | 8 | -8 | 2.10 |  |  |  |
|  |  | -2 | 2.00 | 18 | 2.00 |  |
|  | 15 | +6 | 2.20 | 18 | 2.00 |  |
|  |  |  |  | 6 | 2.20 |  |
|  | 17 | -6 | 2.20 |  |  |  |
|  |  | -1 | 2.00 | 17 | 2.00 |  |
|  | 21 | +10 | 2.25 | 17 | 2.00 |  |
|  |  |  |  | 10 | 2.25 |  |
|  | 24 | -9 | 2.25 | 17 | 2.00 |  |
|  |  |  |  | 1 | 2.25 |  |
|  | 30 | +2 | 2.40 | 17 | 2.00 | $34.00 |
|  |  |  |  | 1 | 2.25 | 2.25 |
|  |  |  |  | 2 | 2.40 | 4.80 |
|  |  |  |  |  |  | $41.05 |

8. C
9. D
10. C

| | | | |
|---|---|---|---|
| 2,000 | units @ $ 8 | = | $16,000 |
| 2,500 | units @ $ 10 | = | 25,000 |
| 4,500 | | | $41,000 |

11. A   2,500 units @ $10 = $25,000
12. C   4,500 units @ $10 = $45,000
13. D

| | | | |
|---|---|---|---|
| 2,000 | units @ $ 8 | = | $16,000 |
| 500 | units @ $10 | = | 5,000 |
| 2,500 | | | $21,000 |

14. B

| | | | |
|---|---|---|---|
| 2,000 | units @ $ 8 | = | $16,000 |
| 5,000 | units @ $ 10 | = | 50,000 |
| 7,000 | | | $66,000 |

$66,000/7,000 units = $9.4286

$9.4286 x 4,500 units = $42,428.70

15. C   $66,000 - $42,428.70 = $23,571.30
16. C   $215,000/[($780,000 + $830,000)/2]

# CHAPTER 8

# CONTROL OF CASH

## Learning Objectives

1. *Describe the necessity for and features of internal control.*
2. *Define cash and list the objectives sought by management in handling a company's cash.*
3. *Identify procedures for controlling cash receipts and disbursements.*
4. *Prepare a bank reconciliation and make necessary journal entries based on that schedule.*
5. *Explain why a company uses a petty cash fund, describe its operation, and make the necessary journal entries.*
6. *Analyze and use the financial results — quick ratio.*

---

## REFERENCE OUTLINE

# CHAPTER OUTLINE

*Learning Objective 1:*
*Describe the necessity for and features of internal control.*

INTERNAL CONTROL

1. An effective internal control structure includes an entity's plan of organization and all the procedures and actions taken by an entity to *(a)* protect its assets against theft and waste, *(b)* ensure compliance with company policies and federal law, *(c)* evaluate the performance of all personnel in the company so as to promote efficiency of operations, and *(d)* ensure accurate and reliable operating data and accounting reports.

PROTECTION OF ASSETS

2. One of a company's greatest concerns is the protection of its assets.

SEGREGATION OF EMPLOYEE DUTIES

3. Someone other than the employee responsible for safeguarding an asset must maintain the accounting records for that asset.

ASSIGNMENT OF SPECIFIC DUTIES TO EACH EMPLOYEE

4. When the responsibility for a particular work function is assigned to one employee, the company can quickly identify the responsible employee should a question or problem arise.

ROTATION OF EMPLOYEE JOB ASSIGNMENTS

5. Often, companies rotate job assignments to discourage employees from engaging in long-term schemes to steal from them; employees realize that if they steal from the company, the next employees assigned to their positions may discover the theft.

USE OF MECHANICAL DEVICES

6. Numerous mechanical devices, such as check protectors, cash registers, and time clocks, are used by companies, making it extremely difficult for employees to alter certain company documents and records.

COMPLIANCE WITH COMPANY POLICIES AND FEDERAL LAW

7. Internal control policies must be followed by employees, and those policies must satisfy the requirements of the Foreign Corrupt Practices Act.

EVALUATION OF PERSONNEL PERFORMANCE

8. Internal auditing can assist in evaluating how well company employees are doing their jobs.

ACCURACY OF ACCOUNTING RECORDS

9. Since source documents serve as documentation of business transactions, from time to time the validity of these documents should be checked. For added protection, a company should carry:
   a. Casualty insurance on assets.
   b. Fidelity bonds on employees

COMPONENTS OF INTERNAL CONTROL

10. According to the Committee of Sponsoring Organizations of the Treadway Commission, there are five components of an internal control structure. These components are:
   a. The control environment, which includes factors such as ethical values, management's philosophy, and the integrity of the employees of the corporation.
   b. Risk assessment of the risks (such as asset theft and waste, legal liability, inefficient operations, and inaccurate accounting reports) resulting from external and internal sources.

c. Control activities, which are procedures that employees must follow.
  d. Information and communication of the relevant information to employees and external parties such as stockholders.
  e. Monitoring of the effectiveness of the internal control structure.

## RESPONSIBILITY FOR INTERNAL CONTROL

11. Internal control is the responsibility of: (a) management; (b) the board of directors; and (c) auditors within the organization.

## INTERNAL CONTROL IN A COMPUTER ENVIRONMENT

12. Many of the same controls used in a manual system are used in a computerized system. Some additional controls are also necessary to limit access of unauthorized persons to the computers and software.

*Learning Objective 2:*
*Define cash and list the objectives sought by management in handling a company's cash.*

## CONTROLLING CASH

13. Many business transactions involve cash utilizing a checking account.
  a. By definition cash includes coins; currency; undeposited negotiable instruments such as checks, bank drafts, and money orders; amounts in checking and savings accounts; and demand certificates of deposit.
  b. Cash does not include stamps, IOUs, time certificates of deposit, or notes receivable.
  c. Petty Cash and Cash are the typical cash accounts.
  d. Management has the following objectives in regard to cash:
    (1) Account for all cash transactions accurately, so that correct information will be available regarding cash flows and balances.
    (2) Make certain there is enough cash available to pay bills as they come due.
    (3) Avoid holding too much idle cash because excess cash could be invested to generate income, such as interest.
    (4) Prevent loss of cash due to theft or fraud.

*Learning Objective 3:*
*Identify procedures for controlling cash receipts and disbursements.*

## CONTROLLING CASH RECEIPTS

14. All assets owned by the company must be protected from theft or mishandling, but cash requires additional care.
  a. Cash is more likely to be the object of theft because it is easily concealed.
  b. Cash is not readily identifiable and this makes it a likely target for thieves.
  c. Cash may be more desirable than other company assets because it can be quickly spent to acquire other things of value.
15. There are several basic principles for controlling cash receipts even though these may vary with each business.
  a. Records of all cash receipts should be prepared as soon as cash is received.
  b. All cash receipts should be deposited intact on the day received or the next business day.
    (1) Cash disbursements should not be made from cash receipts but only by check or from petty cash funds.
    (2) If refunds for returned merchandise are made from the cash register, refund tickets should be prepared and approved by a supervisor.
  c. The person who handles cash receipts should not record them in the accounting system.
  d. The person receiving cash should not also disburse cash.

## CONTROLLING CASH DISBURSEMENTS

16. There are basic control procedures for cash disbursements.
    a. All disbursements should be made by check or from petty cash.
    b. All checks should be serially numbered, and access to checks should be limited.
    c. Preferably, two signatures should be required on each check.
    d. If possible, the person who authorizes payment of a bill should not be allowed to sign checks.
    e. Approved invoices or vouchers should be required to support checks issued.
    f. The person authorizing disbursements should be certain that payment is in order and is made to the proper payee.
    g. When invoices and vouchers are paid, they should be stamped "paid" with the date and number of the check issued indicated.
    h. The person(s) who signed the checks should not have access to cancelled checks and should not prepare the bank reconciliation.
    i. A bank reconciliation should be prepared each month, preferably by a person who has no other cash duties.
    j. All voided and spoiled checks should be retained and marked *void* to prevent their unauthorized use.

## THE BANK CHECKING ACCOUNT

17. One of the services provided by a bank is a checking account, which is a balance maintained in a bank that is subject to withdrawal by the depositor on demand.

## THE SIGNATURE CARD

18. A new depositor completes a signature card, which provides the signatures of persons authorized to sign checks drawn upon an account.

## DEPOSIT TICKET

19. In making a bank deposit, the depositor prepares a deposit ticket, which is a form showing the date and the items constituting the deposit; in addition, the depositor's name, address, and bank account number are shown.

## CHECK

20. A check is a written order on a bank to pay a specific sum of money to the party designated as the payee by the party issuing the check.
    a. There are three parties to every bank check transaction:
       (1) The party issuing the check.
       (2) The bank on which the check is drawn.
       (3) The party to whose order the check is made payable.
    b. A remittance advice may be attached to a check informing the payee why the drawer of the check is making this payment.

## BANK STATEMENT

21. A bank statement is used by a bank to indicate the deposits and checks cleared during the period.
    a. Cancelled checks and original deposit tickets sometimes are returned with the bank statement.
    b. Debit memos and credit memos may also be returned with the bank statement.
       (1) Debit memos are forms used by banks to explain a deduction from the depositor's account. Note that the company's cash account is a liability to the bank, and if it wants to reduce that liability, a debit memo is used.
       (2) Credit memos explain additions to the account. Note that increases to the bank's liability accounts require credits.

c. The balance shown in the bank statement usually differs from the balance in the depositor's Cash in Bank ledger account. Reasons for the difference are:
    (1) Outstanding checks have not yet been deducted from the bank balance.
    (2) Deposits in transit have not yet been added to the bank balance.
    (3) Bank errors can occur in a depositor's account.
    (4) Service charges have not yet been recognized by the depositor and deducted from the Cash account balance.
    (5) NSF (Not Sufficient Funds) checks have not yet been deducted from the depositor's Cash account balance.
    (6) The bank may have collected a customer's note or received a wire transfer of funds, which is an inter-bank transfer of funds by telephone.
    (7) The depositor may have made errors by recording a check in the accounting records for a different amount from the actual figure.

*Learning Objective 4:*
*Prepare a bank reconciliation and make necessary journal entries based on that schedule.*

## BANK RECONCILIATION

22. A bank reconciliation is prepared to account for the difference between the two balances. Segregation of duties for internal control purposes must be considered in preparing a bank reconciliation. The employee who reconciles the account balances monthly should not be involved in making cash disbursements.
    a. Both the balance per the bank statement and the balance per the ledger account are adjusted to the true balance of expendable cash.
    b. The documents used are the bank statement and any accompanying debit and credit memoranda, returned checks, a list of checks issued, and a record of deposits made.
    c. After the reconciliation has been prepared, an adjusting entry is prepared to record the previously unrecorded items.

## CERTIFIED AND CASHIER'S CHECKS

23. A certified check is a check written, or drawn, by a depositor and taken to its bank for certification. The bank indicates that the depositor's balance is large enough to cover the check.
    a. The amount of the certified check is deducted immediately after certification from the depositor's checking account.
    b. The certified check then becomes a liability of the bank rather than the depositor.
24. A cashier's check is a check written, or drawn, by a bank made out to either the depositor or a third party after deducting the amount of the check from the depositor's account or receiving cash from the depositor.
25. Electronic fund transferring allows employees to have their payroll checks immediately deposited in their bank accounts. The money is transferred to the employees' accounts from the company's account through use of computers.

*Learning Objective 5:*
*Explain why a company uses a petty cash fund, describe its operation, and make the necessary journal entries.*

## PETTY CASH FUNDS
## ESTABLISHING THE FUND

26. Petty cash funds are usually established so small disbursements can be made from petty cash to avoid writing a check for each of these small payments.
    a. The entry to establish a petty cash fund is to debit Petty Cash and to credit Cash for the amount drawn.
    b. A petty cash cashier is responsible for the operation of the fund so that adequate control is maintained over cash disbursements.

## OPERATING THE FUND

27. A petty cash voucher is a form that indicates the amount and reason for a petty cash disbursement.
    a. A voucher should be prepared for each disbursement from the fund.
    b. Invoices for the expenditure should be stapled to the petty cash voucher.
    c. The person responsible for petty cash is accountable for having cash and petty cash vouchers equal to the total amount of the fund.

## REPLENISHING THE FUND

28. To replenish petty cash, a check is drawn for the amount that will restore the fund to its original amount.
    a. The journal entry is to debit expenses and assets for the amount disbursed and to credit Cash.
    b. Replenishments are made when the petty cash fund becomes low in currency and sometimes at the end of the accounting period.
    c. If the petty cash fund is found to be larger than needed, excess petty cash can be transferred back to the Cash account; then debit Cash and credit Petty Cash.
    d. Increases in the petty cash fund can be made by debiting Petty Cash and crediting Cash and transferring cash over to the individual responsible for the petty cash fund.

## CASH SHORT AND OVER

29. The petty cash fund must always be restored to its set amount, so the credit to Cash will always be for the difference between the set amount and the actual cash in the fund.
    a. Debits will be made for all items vouchered.
    b. Any discrepancy will be debited or credited to an account called Cash Short and Over.
       (1) The Cash Short and Over account is an expense or a revenue, depending upon whether it has a debit or credit balance.
       (2) Entries in the Cash Short and Over account may also be entered from other change-making funds such as those in the cash register.

*Learning Objective 6:*
*Analyze and use the financial results – quick ratio.*

## ANALYZING AND USING THE FINANCIAL RESULTS—QUICK RATIO

30. The quick ratio equals cash, marketable securities, and net receivables divided by current liabilities.
31. The quick ratio measures a company's short-term debt-paying ability.

## MATCHING

Referring to the terms listed below, place the appropriate letter next to the corresponding description.

| | | |
|---|---|---|
| a. Debit memo | f. Cash short and over | j. Remittance advice |
| b. Bank statement | g. NSF check | k. Bank reconciliation |
| c. Outstanding checks | h. Petty cash fund | l. Cancelled checks |
| d. Certificate of deposit | i. Petty cash voucher | m. Deposits in transit |
| e. Credit memo | | |

_____ 1. An interest-bearing deposit at a bank which can be withdrawn at will or on a fixed maturity date.

_____ 2. Form used by a bank to explain a deduction from the depositor's account.

_____ 3. Checks issued by the depositor that have not yet cleared the bank for payment.

_____ 4. Cash receipts entered in the depositor's accounts and put in the bank's night depository box. The bank will show the deposit on next month's statement.

_____ 5. A fixed amount of cash advanced to a custodian who will be reimbursed after making payments with the cash.

_____ 6. A statement issued by a bank describing activities in a depositor's account.

_____ 7. A form attached to a check informing the payee why the drawer of the check is making payment.

_____ 8. A check that the bank has refused to pay because the writer of the check does not have enough money in its account to cover the check.

_____ 9. A form explaining a payment made from a petty cash fund.

_____ 10. Form used by bank to explain an addition to the depositor's account.

_____ 11. This account may be either a revenue or an expense account, depending upon its balance.

## COMPLETION AND EXERCISES

1. What purposes are served through the use of an effective internal control structure?

    a. _____

    b. _____

    c. _____

    d. _____

2. Which groups have specific responsibilities regarding the internal control structure?

    a. _____

    b. _____

    c. _____

3. Give three objectives that management has in regard to cash.

    a. _____
       _____

    b. _____
       _____

    c. _____
       _____

4. Why do most firms exercise special care in safeguarding cash?

_____

_____

_____

_____

_____

5. What is the composition of cash?

_____

_____

_____

_____

_____

6. Give five reasons why the bank statement balance usually differs from the balance in the depositor's ledger account for cash. Categorize them as to which ones require entries on the depositor's books and which do not.
   a. Items that cause the bank statement to differ from the Cash ledger account that *do not* require an entry on the depositor's books.

   1. _____

   2. _____

   b. Items that cause the bank statement to differ from the Cash ledger account that *do* require an entry on the depositor's books.

   1. _____

   2. _____

   3. _____

7. List five basic control procedures for cash disbursements.

   1. _____

   _____

   2. _____

   _____

   3. _____

   _____

   4. _____

   _____

   5. _____

   _____

8. What is the purpose of the bank reconciliation?

_____

_____

_____

_____

_____

9. From the following information prepare a bank reconciliation for the Kelley Company:

Balance of Cash account on March 31, 1999 ..................................................... $30,373.08
Balance on March 31, 1999, bank statement .................................................... 34,314.32
Deposits in transit .......................................................................................... 2,021.44
Outstanding checks ........................................................................................ 4,774.68

The bank statement also contained the following information that had not been recorded on the books of Kelley Company:

The bank had collected a note for Kelley Company for $1,200.
The bank had charged Kelley Company $12 for servicing the account.

10. The Cash Short and Over account is a(n) _____ if it has a debit balance and a(n) _____ if it has a credit balance.

11. A _____ _____ _____ should be prepared for each disbursement from the petty cash fund.

12. A _____ _____ _____ _____ is an inter-bank transfer of funds by telephone.

13. At the time of replenishing, the $140 petty cash fund had $16.80 remaining and the following petty cash vouchers:

Stamps ......................................................................................................... $42.00
Transportation-in ......................................................................................... 70.00
Stationery ..................................................................................................... 9.80

What entry would be made to record the replenishment of the fund?

14. The Accounts Receivable clerk in the Davis Corporation is in charge of the petty cash fund. This is an example of poor _____ _____.

15. A deposit not yet credited by the bank is a _____ ___ _____.

16. Outstanding checks should be _____ _____ (deducted from or added to)

    the _____ (Cash ledger account or bank

    account) balance when a bank reconciliation is prepared.

17. A NSF check of your customer (returned by your bank) would be _____ _____
    (added to or deducted from) the Cash account during the preparation of the bank
    reconciliation.

18. On January 1, the Stockholm Company has a petty cash fund, which was established at
    $140. When the fund is found to contain only $15.54, it is replenished. Petty cash
    receipts are found for the following:

    | | |
    |---|---:|
    | Delivery Expense | $54.96 |
    | Transportation-In | 13.50 |
    | Office Supplies | 34.32 |
    | Miscellaneous Office Expense | 12.04 |

    Record the replenishment of the fund in journal form.

| Date | Account Titles and Explanation | Post. Ref. | Debit | Credit |
|---|---|---|---|---|
| | | | | |
| | | | | |
| | | | | |
| | | | | |
| | | | | |
| | | | | |
| | | | | |
| | | | | |
| | | | | |
| | | | | |
| | | | | |
| | | | | |
| | | | | |
| | | | | |
| | | | | |
| | | | | |
| | | | | |

19. Two weeks ago a company established a $75 petty cash fund. On December 15, there are $3 in cash and the following paid petty cash receipts in the petty cash box, transportation-in, $37.50 and postage, $34.50. In the space below give the entry to replenish the fund and increase its size to $150.

| Date | Account Titles and Explanation | Post. Ref. | Debit | Credit |
|------|-------------------------------|------------|-------|--------|
|      |                               |            |       |        |
|      |                               |            |       |        |
|      |                               |            |       |        |
|      |                               |            |       |        |
|      |                               |            |       |        |
|      |                               |            |       |        |
|      |                               |            |       |        |
|      |                               |            |       |        |
|      |                               |            |       |        |
|      |                               |            |       |        |
|      |                               |            |       |        |
|      |                               |            |       |        |
|      |                               |            |       |        |
|      |                               |            |       |        |

20. Data for Alexander Company are given below:
(1) A deposit placed in the bank's night depository after banking hours on May 31 appeared on the June bank statement; (2) but one placed there after hours on June 30 did not. Two checks, (3) No. 1010 and (4) 1013, were outstanding on May 31. Check No. 1010 was returned with the June bank statement but Check No. 1013 was not. (5) Check No. 1100 for $58 was incorrectly entered in the Cash Disbursements Journal and posted as though it were for $85. (6) Enclosed with the June bank statement was a debit memorandum for a bank service charge. (7) Also enclosed was a check received from a customer and deposited on June 23 but returned by the bank marked "Not sufficient funds." (8) Check No. 841, written on June 27, was not returned with the cancelled checks.

Required:

a. If an item in the foregoing list should not appear on the June bank reconciliation, ignore it. However, if an item should appear, enter its number in a set of parentheses below to show where it should be added or subtracted in preparing the reconciliation.

### ALEXANDER COMPANY
### Bank Reconciliation, June 30, 19—

Balance per bank statement ....$X,XXX    Balance per ledger .........................$X,XXX

Add:                                       Add:

        ( )                                        ( )

        ( )                                        ( )

        ( )                                        ( )

        ( )                                        ( )

Deduct:                             Deduct:

        ( )                                        ( )

        ( )                                        ( )

        ( )                                        ( )

        ( )                                        ( )

Adjusted balance          $X,XXX    Adjusted balance            $X,XXX

b. Certain reconciliation items require entries on the company's books. Place the numbers of these items within the following parentheses.

    ( ), ( ), ( ), ( ), ( ), ( ), ( ), ( ).

21. At August 31 of the current year, the Cash account of H. R. Johnson Co. reflected a balance of $9,543.20. This balance was determined after the cash register and the cash receipts journal had been posted. At the same date, the bank statement indicated a balance of $9,744.60. The following items were revealed in the comparison of the bank statement and the analysis of cancelled checks and bank notices:

  (1)  Bank service charges for August totaled $9.50.

  (2)  A check for $67 in payment of an account payable was erroneously recorded in the check register as $76.

  (3)  A deposit of $4,253.70, representing receipts of August 31, had been made too late to appear on the bank statement.

  (4)  Checks outstanding totaled $4,085.60.

  (5)  A check drawn for $25 had been erroneously charged by the bank as $250.

  (6)  The bank had collected for H. R. Johnson Co. $595 on a note left for collection.

    a.  Prepare a bank reconciliation.

    b.  Journalize the necessary entries assuming the accounts have not been closed.

---

## TRUE-FALSE QUESTIONS

---

Indicate whether each of the following statements is true or false by inserting a capital "T" or "F" in the blank space provided.

_____ 1. Cash includes certain undeposited negotiable instruments and demand certificates of deposit, among other items.

_____ 2. While a company must make sure that there is enough cash to pay bills, there is no problem holding excess cash.

_____ 3. All disbursements should be by check or from a petty cash fund.

_____ 4. The cash balance shown on the bank statement usually is not equal to the amount in the depositor's Cash account before reconciliation.

_____ 5. Outstanding checks will require an entry in the depositor's books after the bank reconciliation is prepared.

_____ 6. When certified, a check is a liability of the bank on which it is drawn.

_____ 7. If the Cash Short and Over account has a debit balance at the end of the accounting period, it will be treated as an expense on the income statement.

_____ 8. Petty Cash is credited when the petty cash fund is replenished.

_____ 9. The person who authorizes disbursements should also be the person who signs the checks.

_____ 10. Misappropriations of cash can occur just as easily before or after a record is made of the receipt.

_____ 11. All cash receipts should be deposited intact in the bank.

_____ 12. Cash disbursements should not be made from cash receipts.

_____ 13. The person who receives the cash should also record cash transactions in the accounting records.

_____ 14. Cash receipts and cash disbursements should be the function of one person to facilitate record keeping for cash.

_____ 15. Cash includes coin, currency, postdated checks, money orders, and money on deposit with banks.

_____ 16. In reconciling the bank account, the deposits in transit are deducted from the balance per ledger to determine the correct amount of cash owned by the depositor.

_____ 17. The Petty Cash account is debited for the establishment of the fund but is not credited for expenditures from the fund.

_____ 18. In a bank reconciliation, the total amount of outstanding checks is deducted from the cash balance per ledger amount.

_____ 19. Outstanding checks are ascertained by comparing the amounts in the Deposits column on the bank statement with a record of deposits in the cash receipts book.

_____ 20. On a bank reconciliation, the items found immediately below the "Balance, per bank statement" caption necessitate journal entries.

_____ 21. NSF checks should be deducted from the balance per bank statement on a bank reconciliation.

_____ 22. On the bank reconciliation, deposits in transit are added to the balance per ledger.

_____ 23. Postage stamps should be included in the Cash account balance.

_____ 24. Auditors use the internal control structure of a corporation to plan the audit and to determine the nature, timing, and extent of tests of account balances.

_____ 25. The employee who prepares the bank reconciliation should also be involved with making cash disbursements.

---

## MULTIPLE CHOICE

For each of the following questions, indicate the best answer by circling the appropriate letter.

1. The June 30 bank statement shows a balance of $648.86. A comparison with the check register shows that two checks, for $68.00 and $36.70 respectively, have not been paid by the bank. The receipts of June 30, amounting to $416.32, were not recorded by the bank as deposited until July 1. The correct checkbook balance for June 30 is:
   A. $337.24
   B. $1,169.88
   C. $960.48
   D. $832.64
   E. $209.40

2. Which of the following items would be least likely to be paid from petty cash?
   A. Postage
   B. Office supplies
   C. Office furniture addition
   D. Post office box rental

3. A petty cash fund has been established at $250. The petty cash cashier in balancing the records on June 30 lists the following items:

   | | | |
   |---|---|---|
   | (1) | Cash on hand | $ 98.20 |
   | (2) | Vouchers for merchandise purchased ........................................................ | 60.80 |
   | (3) | Vouchers for office supplies purchased .................................................. | 50.00 |
   | (4) | Vouchers for miscellaneous expenses ...................................................... | 41.00 |
   | | Total ........................................................................................................ | $250.00 |

   The entry to replenish the petty cash fund on June 30 would include:
   A. a debit to Petty Cash for $151.80
   B. a credit to Petty Cash for $151.80
   C. a credit to Cash for $151.80
   D. a credit to Purchases for $60.80
   E. None of these.

4. In reference to a check, the payee is:
   A. the one to whose order the check is drawn.
   B. the bank on which the check is drawn.
   C. the one who signs the check.
   D. None of the above.

5. If a customer's check is returned by the bank for lack of sufficient funds (NSF), the accountant should:
   A. debit Bad Checks and credit Cash.
   B. debit Accounts Receivable and credit Cash.
   C. file the check with Notes Receivable.
   D. debit Miscellaneous Expense and credit Cash.

6. As of March 1 of the current year, the Venture Company had outstanding checks of $15,000. During March the company issued an additional $57,000 of checks. As of March 31, the bank statement showed that $51,000 of checks had cleared the bank during the month. The amount of outstanding checks as of March 31 is:
   A. $9,000
   B. $6,000
   C. $21,000
   D. None of these.

7. In reference to a check, the drawer is:
   A. the one to whose order the check is drawn.
   B. the bank on which the check is drawn.
   C. the one who signs the check.
   D. None of the above.

Questions 8-10 assume the following:

| | |
|---|---|
| Balance per bank statement ................................... | $4,175.98 |
| Outstanding checks ................................................ | 1,544.99 |
| Balance per ledger ................................................. | 2,642.99 |
| Bank service charge ............................................... | 12.00 |

8. The adjusted cash balance is:
   A. $2,618.99
   B. $5,720.97
   C. $2,642.99
   D. $2,630.99

9. On the bank reconciliation, checks outstanding should be:
   A. deducted from balance per books.
   B. deducted from balance per bank statement.
   C. disregarded, as they have been entered in the cash disbursements journal.
   D. added to the balance per bank statement.

10. To record the bank service charge, which of the following accounts should be credited?
    A. Cash Short and Over
    B. Cash
    C. Petty cash
    D. None of these.

11. The quick ratio is used to measure:
    A. How quickly a company can sell its inventory.
    B. A company's short-term debt-paying ability.
    C. How profitable a company is.
    D. A company's long-term solvency.

---

## SOLUTIONS

---

*Matching*

| | | | |
|---|---|---|---|
| 1. | d | 7. | j |
| 2. | a | 8. | g |
| 3. | c | 9. | i |
| 4. | m | 10. | e |
| 5. | h | 11. | f |
| 6. | b | | |

*Completion and Exercises*

1. *a.* Protect assets against fraud and waste.
   *b.* Ensure compliance with company policies and federal law.
   *c.* Evaluate the performance of all personnel to promote efficiency of operations.
   *d.* Ensure accurate and reliable operating data and accounting reports.
2. *a.* Management.
   *b.* Board of Directors.
   *c.* Auditors (or Internal Auditors).
3. Any three of the following are objectives that management has in regard to cash.
   *a.* Account for all cash transactions accurately, so that correct information will be available regarding cash flows and balances.
   *b.* Make certain there is enough cash available to pay bills as they come due.
   *c.* Avoid holding too much idle cash because excess cash could be invested to generate income, such as interest.
   *d.* Prevent loss of cash due to theft or fraud.
4. Cash can easily be misappropriated since it can be concealed and it is not readily identifiable. It can also be used to acquire other things of value.

5. Cash is composed of those items commonly acceptable as a medium of exchange and also immediately convertible into money at face value. Cash includes the following: coins, currency, undeposited negotiable instruments (such as checks, bank drafts, and money orders), checking accounts, savings accounts, and demand certificates of deposit.

6. *a.* Items requiring no entry on the depositor's books would include:
   1. outstanding checks.
   2. deposits in transit.
   3. bank errors in depositor's account.

   *b.* Items requiring an entry on the depositor's books would include any of the following four:
   1. service charges.
   2. deductions for not sufficient funds (NSF) checks.
   3. nonroutine deposits such as collection of a customer's note by the bank or a wire-transfer of funds.
   4. errors made by the depositor.

7. Any five of the following are basic control procedures for cash disbursements.
   1. All disbursements should be made by check or from petty cash.
   2. All checks should be serially numbered, and access to checks should be limited.
   3. Preferably, two signatures should be required on each check.
   4. If possible, the person who authorizes payment of a bill should not be allowed to sign checks.
   5. Approved invoices or vouchers should be required to support checks issued.
   6. The person authorizing disbursements should be certain that payment is in order and is made to the proper payee.
   7. When invoices and vouchers are paid, they should be stamped "paid" with the date and number of the check issued indicated.
   8. The person(s) who signed the checks should not have access to cancelled checks and should not prepare the bank reconciliation.
   9. A bank reconciliation should be prepared each month, preferably by a person who has no other cash duties.
   10. All voided and spoiled checks should be retained and marked *void* to prevent their unauthorized use.

8. The purpose of a bank reconciliation is to account for the difference between the cash balance on the books and the depositor's balance at the bank as shown on the bank statement. Such a schedule concludes with the properly adjusted Cash account balance.

9.
**KELLEY COMPANY**
**Bank Reconciliation**
**March 31, 1999**

| | | | |
|---|---|---|---|
| Balance per bank statement, March 31, 1999 | $34,314.32 | Balance per ledger, March 31, 1999 | $30,373.08 |
| Add: Deposits in transit | 2,021.44 | Add: Note collected by bank | 1,200.00 |
| | $36,335.76 | | $31,573.08 |
| Less: Outstanding checks | 4,774.68 | Less: Bank charges | 12.00 |
| Adjusted Balance, March 31, 1999 | $31,561.08 | Adjusted Balance, March 31, 1999 | $31,561.08 |

10. expense; revenue
11. petty cash voucher
12. wire transfer of funds

| | | |
|---|---|---|
| 13. Stamps and Stationery ............................................... | 51.80 | |
| Transportation-In ............................................. | 70.00 | |
| Cash Short and Over ........................................ | 1.40 | |
| Cash ........................................................... | | 123.20 |

To record check drawn to replenish petty cash fund.

14. internal control
15. deposit in transit
16. deducted from; bank account
17. deducted from

| | | |
|---|---|---|
| 18. Delivery Expense ..................................................... | 54.96 | |
| Transportation-In ............................................ | 13.50 | |
| Office Supplies ................................................. | 34.32 | |
| Miscellaneous Office Expense ..................... | 12.04 | |
| Cash Short and Over ....................................... | 9.64 | |
| Cash ........................................................... | | 124.46 |
| 19. Petty Cash ................................................................ | 75.00 | |
| Postage Expense ............................................. | 34.50 | |
| Transportation-In ........................................... | 37.50 | |
| Cash ........................................................... | | 147.00 |

20. *a.*

**ALEXANDER COMPANY**
**Bank Reconciliation**
**June 30, 19—**

Balance per bank statement .....$X,XXX    Balance per ledger ...........................$X,XXX

Add:                                                    Add:

     (2)                                                      (5)
     ( )                                                      ( )
     ( )                                                      ( )
     ( )                                                      ( )

Deduct:                                                 Deduct:

     (4)                                                      (6)
     (8)                                                      (7)
     ( )                                                      ( )
     ( )                                                      ( )

Adjusted balance ......................$X,XXX    Adjusted balance ...........................$X,XXX

*b.* Items (5), (6), and (7) require entries on the company's books.

21. *a.*

**H. R. JOHNSON CO.**
**Bank Reconciliation**
**August 31, 19—**

| | | |
|---|---|---|
| Balance per bank statement .......................................... | | $9,744.60 |
| Add:    Deposit of August 31 not recorded by bank ............. | $4,253.70 | |
|           Bank error in charging check for $250 instead of $25 | 225.00 | 4,478.70 |
| | | $14,223.30 |
| Deduct: Outstanding checks ........................................... | | 4,085.60 |
| Adjusted balance ........................................................... | | $10,137.70 |
| Balance per ledger ........................................................ | | $9,543.20 |
| Add:    Proceeds of note collected by bank .......................... | $595.00 | |
|           Error in recording check .............................................. | 9.00 | 604.00 |
| | | $10,147.20 |
| Deduct: Bank service charges ...................................... | | 9.50 |
| Adjusted balance | | $10,137.70 |

| | | | |
|---|---|---|---|
| b. | Cash in Bank ................................................................... | 604.00 | |
| | Notes Receivable ........................................................ | | 595.00 |
| | Accounts Payable ........................................................ | | 9.00 |
| | Bank Service Charge ....................................................... | 9.50 | |
| | Cash in Bank .............................................................. | | 9.50 |

## True-False Questions

1. T
2. F  Good management of cash is important and companies do not wish to have idle ' cash on which no return is being earned.
3. T
4. T  Checks may have been written and deducted from the company's Cash ledger account, but may not have cleared the bank (these are outstanding checks) and some deposits may have been recorded as debits to the Cash account but are in transit to the bank.
5. F  Outstanding checks are ones that have been correctly recorded as credits to the Cash account, but have not yet cleared the bank.
6. T
7. T
8. F  Cash is credited and the related expenses and assets debited when the petty cash fund is replenished.
9. F  Different persons should have each of these responsibilities.
10. F  Misappropriations of cash more easily occur before a record is made of the receipt.
11. T
12. T
13. F
14. F  This violates good features of an internal control structure.
15. F  Postdated checks are not included as cash.
16. F  Deposits in transit are added to the balance per bank statement.
17. T  Expenditures from the fund are debited to the related expense or asset and credited to Cash.
18. F  These amounts have already been deducted from the Cash account.
19. F  Outstanding checks are ascertained by comparing the checks written per the Cash ledger account with the checks that have cleared the bank account as shown on the bank statement.
20. F  The items below the balance per ledger necessitate journal entries.
21. F  NSF checks should be deducted from the balance per ledger.
22. F  These deposits have already been debited to Cash.
23. F
24. T
25. F  These duties should be segregated for internal control purposes.

1. C  $648.86 - $68.00 - $36.70 + $416.32 = $960.48
2. C
3. C
4. A
5. B  The claim against the customer is established again.
6. C  $15,000 + $57,000 - $51,000 = $21,000
7. C
8. D  $2,642.99 - $12.00 = $2,630.99 or $4,175.98 - $1,544.99 = $2,630.99
9. B
10. B  The company has not recorded the bank service charge and must debit an expense and credit Cash.
11. B

# CHAPTER 9

# RECEIVABLES AND PAYABLES

## Learning Objectives

1. *Account for uncollectible accounts receivable under the allowance method.*
2. *Record credit card sales and collections.*
3. *Define liabilities, current liabilities, and long-term liabilities.*
4. *Define and account for clearly determinable, estimated, and contingent liabilities.*
5. *Account for notes receivable and payable, including calculation of interest.*
6. *Account for borrowing money using an interest-bearing note versus a noninterest-bearing note.*
7. *Analyze and use the financial results . accounts receivable turnover and the number of days' sales in accounts receivable.*

---

### REFERENCE OUTLINE

# CHAPTER OUTLINE

## ACCOUNTS RECEIVABLE

1. Accounts receivable (or trade receivables) are amounts due from customers for goods sold and services performed on account.
   a. The Accounts Receivable account should contain only amounts due from customers.
   b. Loans to officers, claims for tax refunds, and interest receivable are not included in accounts receivable.

*Learning Objective 1:*
*Account for uncollectible accounts receivable under the allowance method.*

## THE ALLOWANCE METHOD FOR RECORDING UNCOLLECTIBLE ACCOUNTS

2. Losses from customers' accounts that prove uncollectible are an operating (selling) expense and are referred to as Uncollectible Accounts Expense.
   a. The matching principle requires that the expense be matched against the revenue it generates.
   b. Estimates of uncollectible accounts are made through an adjusting entry by debiting Uncollectible Accounts Expense and crediting Allowance for Uncollectible Accounts.
   c. Net realizable value is the amount expected to be collected from accounts receivable, and is equal to recorded Accounts Receivable less the Allowance for Uncollectible Accounts.

## ESTIMATING UNCOLLECTIBLE ACCOUNTS

3. The percentage-of-sales method and the percentage-of-receivables method are two methods of estimating periodic uncollectible accounts.
   a. The percentage-of-sales method focuses attention on the income statement and the relationship of uncollectible accounts expense to current sales revenue.
   b. The percentage-of-receivables method focuses attention on the balance sheet and the relationship of the Allowance for Uncollectible Accounts to Accounts Receivable.

## PERCENTAGE-OF-SALES METHOD

4. The percentage-of-sales method is based on a ratio of prior years' actual uncollectible account losses to prior years' credit sales (or to total sales).
   a. The percentage is reviewed annually to see if it is still valid.
   b. Any existing balance in the Allowance for Uncollectible Accounts is ignored in calculating the amount of the year-end adjustment.

## PERCENTAGE-OF-RECEIVABLES METHOD

5. The percentage-of-receivables method estimates the percentage of period-end accounts receivable that might be uncollectible. The goal, or target, is to make the credit balance in the allowance account after adjustment equal to a certain percentage of accounts receivable.
   a. Any existing balance in the Allowance for Uncollectible Accounts before adjustment must be considered when adjusting for uncollectible accounts.
   b. One overall rate may be used or a different rate may be used for each age category of receivables.
   c. An aging schedule may be used under the percentage-of-receivables method to classify accounts receivable according to their age. An aging schedule reflects that, the older a receivable is, the more likely it will not be collected. On an aging schedule, accounts receivable are placed in categories of number of days past due.

## WRITE-OFF OF RECEIVABLES

6. To write off a customer's account, the Allowance for Uncollectible Accounts is debited and Accounts Receivable is credited. The credit is also posted to the specific customer's account in the subsidiary ledger.

## UNCOLLECTIBLE ACCOUNTS RECOVERED

7. If a customer pays the account and the company had previously written off the account under the assumption that it was uncollectible, the accounts receivable must be reinstated by reversing the original write-off entry.
   a. The entry to reinstate the account is to debit Accounts Receivable and credit Allowance for Uncollectible Accounts.
   b. The receipt of cash requires a debit to Cash and a credit to Accounts Receivable.
   c. Each debit or credit to Accounts Receivable is also posted to the customer's account in the subsidiary ledger.

*Learning Objective 2:*
*Record credit card sales and collections.*

## CREDIT CARDS

8. Credit cards that are used by customers to charge their purchases of goods and services enable companies to pass losses from uncollectible accounts on to banks or other credit card agencies.
   a. A fee ranging from 2% to 8% of sales price is charged for the credit card agency to absorb the bad debts.
   b. At the same time the card sale is made using a nonbank credit card, the seller debits Accounts Receivable—Credit Card Agency and Credit Card Expense and credits Sales. If a bank credit card is used, the debit is to Cash instead of Accounts Receivable.
   c. When payment for nonbank credit card receipts is received from the credit card agency, Cash is debited, and Accounts Receivable—Credit Card Agency is credited.

*Learning Objective 3:*
*Define liabilities, current liabilities, and long-term liabilities.*

## CURRENT VERSUS LONG-TERM LIABILITIES

9. Liabilities result from some past transaction and are obligations to pay cash, provide services, or deliver goods at some future time.
10. Current liabilities are obligations that are:
    a. payable within one year or one operating cycle, whichever is longer. An operating cycle is the time it takes to begin with cash and end with cash in producing revenues.
    b. debts that will be paid out of current assets or result in the creation of other current liabilities.
11. Long-term liabilities are obligations that do not qualify as current liabilities.

## TYPES OF CURRENT LIABILITIES

12. The three groups of current liabilities are: clearly determinable liabilities, estimated liabilities, and contingent liabilities.

*Learning Objective 4:*
*Define and account for clearly determinable, estimated, and contingent liabilities.*

## CLEARLY DETERMINABLE LIABILITIES

13. Clearly determinable liabilities, such as accounts payable, notes payable, and wages payable, are liabilities for which the existence of the liability and its amount are certain.

## ESTIMATED LIABILITIES

14. Estimated liabilities, such as estimated product warranty payable, have an existence that is certain but an amount of liability that can only be estimated.

## CONTINGENT LIABILITIES

15. Contingent liabilities have both an existence and an amount of liability that are uncertain.

*Learning Objective 5:*
*Account for notes receivable and payable, including calculation of interest.*

## NOTES RECEIVABLE AND NOTES PAYABLE

16. A promissory note is a written promise by a maker to pay a certain sum of money to the lender or payee on demand or on a specific date.

## INTEREST CALCULATION

17. Notes may be noninterest bearing or may bear interest at a rate specified on the face of the note. Interest is computed using the formula $I = P \times R \times T$, where $I$ is the interest, $P$ is the principal or face amount of the note, $R$ is the specified interest rate, and $T$ is the period of the note.

## DETERMINATION OF MATURITY DATE

18. The maturity date is specified in the note as one of the following:
    a. On demand.
    b. On a stated date.
    c. At the end of a stated period.

19. The maturity value is the amount that the maker must pay on a note on its maturity date, and maturity value includes principal and accrued interest.

## ACCOUNTING FOR NOTES IN NORMAL BUSINESS TRANSACTIONS

20. A note may be received when high-priced merchandise is sold or from the conversion of an overdue account receivable.

## DISHONORED NOTES

21. A note is dishonored if the maker fails to pay it at maturity.
    a. The payee may establish an account receivable and credit Notes Receivable.
    b. The note loses its negotiability when the maturity date has passed.
    c. If a firm has many notes receivable transactions, it may set up an allowance for uncollectible notes against which can be charged dishonored notes that are deemed uncollectible.
    d. If only part of a note is paid at maturity, the dishonored portion is treated as above.

## RENEWAL OF NOTES

22. Notes are frequently renewed rather than paid at their maturity date.

## ACCRUING INTEREST

23. Even though interest is usually recorded only at the maturity date, interest accrues on an interest-bearing note on a day-to-day basis.
    a. The adjusting entry needed to accrue interest on a note receivable is a debit to Interest Receivable and a credit to Interest Revenue.
    b. Interest Receivable is a current asset showing the asset for interest revenue earned but not yet collected.
    c. The adjusting entry needed to accrue interest on a note payable is a debit to Interest Expense and a credit to Interest Payable.
    d. Interest Payable is a current liability showing the liability for interest expense incurred but not yet paid.

*Learning Objective 6:*
*Account for borrowing money using an interest-bearing note versus a noninterest-bearing note.*

SHORT-TERM FINANCING THROUGH NOTES PAYABLE

24. Funds may be borrowed by signing either an interest-bearing note or a noninterest-bearing note.

INTEREST-BEARING NOTES

25. An interest-bearing note carries a stated interest rate and will mature on a specific date.

NONINTEREST-BEARING NOTES

26. A noninterest-bearing note does not have a stated interest rate that is applied to face value to calculate interest.
    a. The note is drawn for the maturity value and a bank discount is deducted.
    b. The proceeds are the amount received by the maker and are equal to the difference between the maturity value and the discount.
    c. Cash and Discount on Notes Payable are debited and Notes Payable is credited.
    d. Discount on Notes Payable is a contra account used to reduce Notes Payable from face value to book value.
        (1) Discount on Notes Payable is reported on the balance sheet as a deduction from the Notes Payable account.
        (2) Over time, this discount becomes interest expense.

*Learning Objective 7:*
*Analyze and use the financial results – accounts receivable turnover and the number of days' sales in accounts receivable.*

ANALYZING AND USING THE FINANCIAL RESULTS— ACCOUNTS RECEIVABLE TURNOVER AND NUMBER OF DAYS' SALES IN ACCOUNTS RECEIVABLE

27. Accounts receivable turnover is calculated by dividing net credit sales (or net sales) by average net accounts receivable.

28. The number of days' sales in accounts receivable (or average collection period) is calculated by dividing the number of days in the year (365) by the accounts receivable turnover.

29. Together, these ratios show the liquidity of accounts receivable and give some indication of their quality. Generally, the higher the accounts receivable turnover, the better, and the shorter the average collection period the better.

# DEMONSTRATION PROBLEM

Analysis of Green Company's ledger reveals that the January 1 credit balance in Allowance for Uncollectible Accounts was $1,800. During the month $2,025 of accounts receivable were written off as uncollectible; credit sales during the month totaled $300,000.

Required:

a. Prepare the adjusting entry to record the estimated uncollectible accounts for the month *and* give the January 31 balance in the Allowance for Uncollectible Accounts, after adjustment, assuming:

   (1) Analysis of the accounts receivable subsidiary ledger indicates a desired balance in Allowance for Uncollectible Accounts of $1,500.

   (2) Instead of (1), uncollectible accounts are estimated at one percent of credit sales.

b. Follow the same requirements as above except assume that on January 1 the Allowance for Uncollectible Accounts account had a credit balance of $2,790 and that January credit sales were $375,000.

## GENERAL JOURNAL

| Date | Account Titles and Explanation | Post. Ref. | Debit | Credit |
|---|---|---|---|---|
| *a.* (1) | | | | |
| | | | | |
| | | | | |
| | | | | |
| | | | | |
| | | | | |
| | | | | |
| | | | | |
| | | | | |
| (2) | | | | |
| | | | | |
| | | | | |
| | | | | |
| | | | | |
| | | | | |
| | | | | |
| *b.* (1) | | | | |
| | | | | |
| | | | | |
| | | | | |
| | | | | |
| | | | | |
| | | | | |
| | | | | |
| | | | | |
| (2) | | | | |
| | | | | |
| | | | | |
| | | | | |
| | | | | |
| | | | | |

# SOLUTION TO DEMONSTRATION PROBLEM

*a.* (1) Percentage-of-receivables method:

Uncollectible Accounts Expense ................................................................ 1,725
    Allowance for Uncollectible Accounts ............................................ 1,725

    $1,500  Desired credit balance
      225  Present debit balance ($2,025 - $1,800)
    $1,725  Required adjustment

    $1,500  Allowance for Uncollectible Accounts balance as of January 31.

  (2) Percentage-of-sales method:

Uncollectible Accounts Expense (1% x $300,000) ..................................... 3,000
    Allowance for Uncollectible Accounts ................................................ 3,000

    $2,775  Allowance for Uncollectible Accounts balance as of January 31
                ($3,000 credit - $225 debit balance)

*b.* (1) Uncollectible Accounts Expense ................................................................ 735
    Allowance for Uncollectible Accounts ................................................ 735

    $1,500  Desired credit balance
      765  Present credit balance ($2,790 - $2,025)
    $  735  Required adjustment

    $1,500  Allowance for Uncollectible Accounts balance as of January 31

  (2) Uncollectible Accounts Expense (1% x $375,000) ..................................... 3,750
    Allowance for Uncollectible Accounts ................................................ 3,750

    $4,515  Allowance for Uncollectible Accounts balance as of January 31 ($765 + $3,750)

# MATCHING

Referring to the terms listed below, place the appropriate letter next to the corresponding description.

*a.* Accounts Receivable
*b.* Aging
*c.* Allowance for Uncollectible Accounts
*d.* Credit cards
*e.* Clearly determinable liabilities
*f.* Long-term liabilities
*g.* Discount on Notes Payable

*h.* Maker
*i.* Maturity value
*j.* Maturity date
*k.* Payables
*l.* Payee
*m.* Percentage-of-accounts-receivable method
*n.* Percentage-of-sales method
*o.* Promissory note

*p.* Receivables
*q.* Uncollectible Accounts Expense
*r.* Uncollectible Accounts Recovered
*s.* Contingent liabilities
*t.* Estimated liabilities
*u.* Accounts receivable turnover

_____ 1. The date on which a note is due.

_____ 2. The principle of a note plus interest accrued to maturity date.

_____ 3. Sometimes erroneously called Prepaid Interest.

_____ 4. An unconditional written promise made by one person to another, signed by the maker, agreeing to pay on demand or at a definite time a sum certain in money to order or to bearer.

_____ 5. A method of estimating the expected amount of uncollectible accounts from a given period's credit sales.

_____ 6. Current liabilities for which the existence and amount are certain.

_____ 7. Plastic cards issued by certain banks and other credit agencies that permit their holders to charge purchases of goods or services.

_____ 8. The account that is debited when a dishonored note is recorded.

_____ 9. Liabilities that do not qualify as current liabilities because they mature in over one-year or one operating cycle, whichever is longer.

_____ 10. The person or party to whose order payment is promised or ordered on a note.

_____ 11. A contra account to Accounts Receivable designed to reduce gross accounts receivable to its net realizable value.

_____ 12. An operating expense a business incurs when it sells on credit and that results from nonpayment of accounts receivable.

_____ 13. Sums of money due to be received for any reason resulting from past transactions.

_____ 14. A method of determining the desired size of the allowance for uncollectible accounts and, indirectly, the uncollectible accounts expense for the period.

_____ 15. The person or party preparing and signing a note.

_____ 16. Sums of money due to be paid to other parties for any reason resulting from a past transaction.

_____ 17. A process of classifying accounts receivable according to their age in appraising the accounts for purposes of adjusting the balance in the Allowance for Uncollectible Accounts.

_____ 18. Have an existence that is certain but an amount of liability that can only be estimated.

_____ 19. Have both an existence and an amount of liability that are uncertain.

_____ 20. Net credit sales (or net sales) divided by average net accounts receivable.

1. The Allowance for Uncollectible Accounts is a _____ account to _____ _____ and shows _____ _____ .

2. The following information was taken from a trial balance:

> Accounts Receivable ......................................................... $25,500
> Allowance for Uncollectible Accounts ....................... 0

If the company's experience shows that 3% of its outstanding receivables (at year-end) will prove uncollectible, uncollectible accounts expense is $ _____ .

3. Give the two methods of estimating the amount of uncollectible accounts under the allowance method.

a. _____

b. _____

4. Assume that 3% of the $75,000 of accounts receivable is estimated to be uncollectible. A credit balance of $1,200 already exists in Allowance for Uncollectible Accounts. The _____ _____ _____ account should be debited, and the _____ _____ _____ _____ account should be credited for $ _____ in the end-of-period adjusting entry.

5. If an account for $450 is deemed to be uncollectible, the _____ _____ _____ _____ account should be debited and the _____ _____ account should be credited for $ _____ .

6. If $300 of the amount written off in Question 5 is collected (with no prospect of collecting the remainder) what entry(ies) would be made?

| Date | Account Titles and Explanation | Post. Ref. | Debit | Credit |
|------|-------------------------------|------------|-------|--------|
|  |  |  |  |  |
|  |  |  |  |  |
|  |  |  |  |  |
|  |  |  |  |  |
|  |  |  |  |  |
|  |  |  |  |  |
|  |  |  |  |  |
|  |  |  |  |  |

7. Of the $135,000 total credit sales for the year, $54,000 were made using a national nonbank credit card. Assume that an estimated 1 1/2% of non-credit-card sales are considered uncollectible. The end-of-period adjusting entry would include a debit to

_____ _____ _____ of $ _____.

8. Delta Company submitted sales invoices of $7,000 to the credit granting agency. The company received a check for $6,574 and the invoice for one sale of $80 made using a credit card, which the company had been notified was stolen. The company's only credit sales are made using credit cards. Give the journal entry for the above receipt of the check and return of the $80 invoice.

| Date | Account Titles and Explanation | Post. Ref. | Debit | | Credit | |
|------|-------------------------------|-----------|-------|---|--------|---|
|      |                               |           |       |   |        |   |
|      |                               |           |       |   |        |   |
|      |                               |           |       |   |        |   |
|      |                               |           |       |   |        |   |
|      |                               |           |       |   |        |   |
|      |                               |           |       |   |        |   |
|      |                               |           |       |   |        |   |
|      |                               |           |       |   |        |   |
|      |                               |           |       |   |        |   |

9. Scott Company sold a customer jewelry that is subject to a 5% sales tax and a 10% federal excise tax. The customer agreed to pay for the jewelry within 30 days. Record the sale of the jewelry, which has an invoice price of $5,000.

|  |  |  |  |  |  |  |
|--|--|--|--|--|--|--|
|  |  |  |  |  |  |  |
|  |  |  |  |  |  |  |
|  |  |  |  |  |  |  |
|  |  |  |  |  |  |  |
|  |  |  |  |  |  |  |

10. When sales taxes are remitted to the appropriate government agency, a retail store

debits _____ _____ _____ account and credits _____.

11. If a 90-day note is dated August 7, what is the due date?

12. In a commercial transaction, interest is commonly calculated on the basis of _____ days per year.

13. What is the interest on $300,000 for 60 days at 12%? _____

_____

14. What is a dishonored note? _____

_____

_____

15. Assume that on December 1, 1999, Power Company discounted its own $75,000 noninterest-bearing 90-day note at the bank. The discount rate is 10%. Give the entries required on December 1, December 31 (the end of the accounting period), and on the maturity date.

| Date | Account Titles and Explanation | Post. Ref. | Debit | Credit |
|------|-------------------------------|------------|-------|--------|
|  |  |  |  |  |
|  |  |  |  |  |
|  |  |  |  |  |
|  |  |  |  |  |
|  |  |  |  |  |
|  |  |  |  |  |
|  |  |  |  |  |
|  |  |  |  |  |
|  |  |  |  |  |
|  |  |  |  |  |
|  |  |  |  |  |
|  |  |  |  |  |
|  |  |  |  |  |
|  |  |  |  |  |
|  |  |  |  |  |
|  |  |  |  |  |
|  |  |  |  |  |
|  |  |  |  |  |

16. On June 1, Bounty Company discounted its own 60-day, noninterest-bearing note payable for $18,000 at Gotham Bank. The discount rate was 9%. Record in general journal form (a) the entry needed on June 1 and (b) the entry needed on the due date.

| Date | Account Titles and Explanation | Post. Ref. | Debit | | Credit | |
|------|-------------------------------|------------|-------|--|--------|--|
| a. | | | | | | |
| | | | | | | |
| | | | | | | |
| | | | | | | |
| | | | | | | |
| | | | | | | |
| b. | | | | | | |
| | | | | | | |
| | | | | | | |
| | | | | | | |
| | | | | | | |
| | | | | | | |

17. A customer gave Horace Company a $300,000, 6-month, 6% note on September 1. Prepare the adjusting entry on December 31.

| Date | Account Titles and Explanation | Post. Ref. | Debit | | Credit | |
|------|-------------------------------|------------|-------|--|--------|--|
| | | | | | | |
| | | | | | | |
| | | | | | | |
| | | | | | | |
| | | | | | | |

18. The term _____ is often used to include any sum of money due to be received as a result of a past transaction.

19. The term _____ is used to describe any amount of money due to be paid to any party resulting from a past transaction.

20. A customer gave a one-year note in payment of an account on September 1, 1999. If the annual interest amounts to $3,600 and is due on September 1, 2000, what is the adjusting entry required on December 31, 1999, to record the interest revenue earned?

| Date | Account Titles and Explanation | Post. Ref. | Debit | | Credit | |
|------|-------------------------------|------------|-------|--|--------|--|
| | | | | | | |
| | | | | | | |
| | | | | | | |
| | | | | | | |
| | | | | | | |

21. A company borrowed $37,500 on October 1 for 120 days with interest payable at the maturity of the loan at the rate of 12% per annum. Prepare the adjusting entry required on December 31.

| Date | Account Titles and Explanation | Post. Ref. | Debit | | | Credit | |
|------|-------------------------------|------------|-------|--|--|--------|--|
|  |  |  |  |  |  |  |  |
|  |  |  |  |  |  |  |  |
|  |  |  |  |  |  |  |  |
|  |  |  |  |  |  |  |  |
|  |  |  |  |  |  |  |  |
|  |  |  |  |  |  |  |  |
|  |  |  |  |  |  |  |  |
|  |  |  |  |  |  |  |  |

22. On October 3 a company discounted its own 30-day, noninterest-bearing note payable for $12,000 at First National Bank. The discount rate was 12%. Record in general journal form (a) the entry needed on October 3 and (b) the entry needed on the due date.

| Date | Account Titles and Explanation | Post. Ref. | Debit | | | Credit | |
|------|-------------------------------|------------|-------|--|--|--------|--|
| a. |  |  |  |  |  |  |  |
|  |  |  |  |  |  |  |  |
|  |  |  |  |  |  |  |  |
|  |  |  |  |  |  |  |  |
|  |  |  |  |  |  |  |  |
|  |  |  |  |  |  |  |  |
| b. |  |  |  |  |  |  |  |
|  |  |  |  |  |  |  |  |
|  |  |  |  |  |  |  |  |
|  |  |  |  |  |  |  |  |
|  |  |  |  |  |  |  |  |

23. Analysis of Oxford Company's ledger reveals that the July 1 credit balance in Allowance for Uncollectible Accounts was $750; credit sales during the month totaled $60,000.

Required:

a. Prepare the adjusting entry to record the estimated uncollectible accounts for the month and give the July 31 balance in the Allowance for Uncollectible Accounts. Based on last year's sales, uncollectible accounts are estimated at 1.5% of credit sales.

b. On August 1, Oxford Company decided that Dale's $1,500 account is uncollectible. What is the correct entry if Dale's account is written off?

c. On August 29, a $1,350 check is received from Dale. What are the correct entries in Oxford's book to record the payment? (No further payments from Dale are anticipated.)

| Date | Account Titles and Explanation | Post. Ref. | Debit | Credit |
|------|-------------------------------|-----------|-------|--------|
|      |                               |           |       |        |
|      |                               |           |       |        |
|      |                               |           |       |        |
|      |                               |           |       |        |
|      |                               |           |       |        |
|      |                               |           |       |        |
|      |                               |           |       |        |
|      |                               |           |       |        |
|      |                               |           |       |        |
|      |                               |           |       |        |
|      |                               |           |       |        |
|      |                               |           |       |        |
|      |                               |           |       |        |
|      |                               |           |       |        |
|      |                               |           |       |        |
|      |                               |           |       |        |
|      |                               |           |       |        |
|      |                               |           |       |        |
|      |                               |           |       |        |

24. The May Department Stores Company is one of the country's leading department store companies. In the company's 1995 annual report, the following data appeared:

| (In millions) | |
|---------------|---|
| Net sales | $10,507 |
| Net accounts receivable: | |
| 2/3/96 | 2,403 |
| 2/28/95 | 2,432 |

Required:
Determine the accounts receivable turnover and the number of days' sales in accounts receivable.

Indicate whether each of the following statements is true or false by inserting a capital "T" or "F" in the blank space provided.

_____ 1. Allowance for Uncollectible Accounts is shown in the Current Assets section of the balance sheet.

_____ 2. Every promissory note is an asset from the standpoint of the maker because the maker has a legal right to receive money.

_____ 3. Accounts receivable from officers should be shown separately in the balance sheet unless the receivables arose from sales and are collectible in accordance with the company's regular terms.

_____ 4. The entry providing for uncollectible accounts is an adjusting entry, but the entry writing off an uncollectible account may be made at any time that an account proves to be uncollectible.

_____ 5. The maker of a note is the party that has the legal obligation to pay money.

_____ 6. Under the allowance method, when an outstanding account receivable is written off, Allowance for Uncollectible Accounts is debited and Accounts Receivable is credited for the amount of the write-off.

_____ 7. Estimating uncollectible accounts is subject to errors, but the effects involved in not estimating are likely to be larger in most years and certainly larger in some years.

_____ 8. The Allowance for Uncollectible Accounts may at times have a debit balance.

_____ 9. When properly adjusted, the Allowance for Uncollectible Accounts will always have a credit balance.

_____ 10. Recoveries of accounts previously written off are, when an Allowance for Uncollectible Accounts is used, credited to Uncollectible Accounts Recovered.

_____ 11. One of the objectives sought through use of an allowance for uncollectible accounts is a proper matching of expense and revenue.

_____ 12. The sale of goods to a customer who charged them using a credit card usually leads to the recording of a credit card expense on the seller's books.

_____ 13. Clearly determinable liabilities have an existence that is certain but an amount that is uncertain.

_____ 14. Estimated product warranty payable is a contingent liability.

_____ 15. If Ron Hall gives Sue Jones a note for some merchandise he purchased from her, Ron is called the payee of the note.

_____ 16. Because it normally has a debit balance, the Discount on Notes Payable account should be reported in the balance sheet among the assets.

_____ 17. The due date of a 90-day note dated May 8 which Loan Company received from Bank Company on account is August 4.

_____ 18. After the year-end closing entries have been posted, the Allowance for Uncollectible Accounts will have no balance.

_____ 19. An excessive provision for uncollectible accounts will understate assets, net income, and retained earnings.

_____ 20. The number of days' sales in accounts receivable is calculated by dividing 365 by the accounts receivable turnover.

For each of the following questions, indicate the best answer by circling the appropriate letter.

1. In the balance sheet, the Allowance for Uncollectible Accounts account should be presented as a(an):
   A. part of stockholders' equity.
   B. liability.
   C. deduction from an asset.
   D. asset.
   E. None of these.

2. Which of the entries given below, made at the end of the accounting period, properly records the expense arising from estimated uncollectible accounts?
   A. Allowance for Uncollectible Accounts
        Uncollectible Accounts Expense
   B. Allowance for Uncollectible Accounts
        Accounts Receivable
   C. Uncollectible Accounts Expense
        Allowance for Uncollectible Accounts
   D. Accounts Receivable
        Allowance for Uncollectible Accounts
   E. None of these.

3. Unpaid interest on a note given to the bank would be classified by the maker of the note as:
   A. a prepaid expense.
   B. unearned revenue.
   C. an accrued asset.
   D. an accrued liability.

4. Interest deducted by a bank on a company's own discounted noninterest bearing note payable would be classified by the company as:
   A. a prepaid expense.
   B. a contra liability.
   C. an accrued asset.
   D. an accrued liability.

5. What are contingent liabilities?
   A. Liabilities that are due and payable within a year.
   B. Liabilities that are classified as long term on the balance sheet.
   C. Liabilities that are to be liquidated in periodic installments.
   D. Possible obligations that occur only if certain events occur in the future.
   E. All of the above.

6-7. Kilo Company received a $740,000, 6%, 90-day note dated March 8 on account from Swan Company.
   6. The due date of the note is:
   A. June 7.
   B. June 6.
   C. June 5.
   D. June 1.

7. The maturity value of the above note is:
   A. $751,100
   B. $740,000
   C. $759,500
   D. $784,400

8. The process of analyzing the trade receivable accounts according to their age is sometimes called:
   A. aging the receivables.
   B. reduction of receivables.
   C. the determination of which receivables to write off.
   D. extending the credit terms on your receivables.
   E. All of the above.

9. At year-end the accounts of the Stable Company show Accounts Receivable, $270,000; Allowance for Uncollectible Accounts (Cr.), $900; Sales, $1,590,000; and Sales Discounts, $20,250. At this time, the company decides to write off the account of the Shakey Corporation, $2,250. The Allowance for Uncollectible Accounts account is then to be adjusted to 4% of the outstanding receivables. The amount of uncollectible accounts expense recognized for the year is:
   A. $12,060
   B. $10,710
   C. $6,060
   D. $9,360
   E. $10,800

10. Which of the following methods of determining uncollectible accounts expense most closely matches expenses and revenues?
    A. Using a percentage of accounts receivable to estimate the allowance for uncollectible accounts.
    B. Estimating the allowance for uncollectible accounts by aging the accounts receivable.
    C. Debiting Uncollectible Accounts Expense with a percentage of credit sales for that period.
    D. None of the above.

11. Which of the following items is not used in calculating either the accounts receivable turnover or number of days' sales in accounts receivable?
    A. Net credit sales (or net sales)
    B. 365 days
    C. Average net accounts receivable
    D. Net cash sales

---

## SOLUTIONS

### Matching

| | | |
|---|---|---|
| 1. *j* | 8. *a* | 15. *h* |
| 2. *i* | 9. *f* | 16. *k* |
| 3. *g* | 10. *l* | 17. *b* |
| 4. *o* | 11. *c* | 18. *t* |
| 5. *n* | 12. *q* | 19. *s* |
| 6. *e* | 13. *p* | 20. *u* |
| 7. *d* | 14. *m* | |

*Completion and Exercises*

1. Contra; Accounts Receivable; the amount of outstanding accounts receivable that the company does not expect to collect in cash

2. $765

3. *(a)* percentage-of-sales; *(b)* percentage-of-accounts-receivable.

4. Uncollectible Accounts Expense; Allowance for Uncollectible Accounts; $1,050 [which is (0.03 x $75,000) - $1,200]

5. Allowance for Uncollectible Accounts; Accounts Receivable; $450

6.
| | | |
|---|---|---|
| Accounts Receivable | 300 | |
|     Allowance for Uncollectible Accounts | | 300 |

    To reverse part of original entry to write off an account receivable.

| | | |
|---|---|---|
| Cash | 300 | |
|     Accounts Receivable | | 300 |

    To record collection of $300 on account.

7. Uncollectible Accounts Expense; $1,215, [($135,000 - $54,000) x 0.015]

8. Delta Company

| | | |
|---|---|---|
| Cash | 6,574 | |
| Credit Card Expense | 346 | |
| Loss on Acceptance of Stolen Credit Card | 80 | |
|     Accounts Receivable (Credit Card Company) | | 7,000 |

    To record collection of credit card invoices, less discount, and return of one invoice for which stolen credit card was used.

9.
| | | |
|---|---|---|
| Accounts Receivable | 5,750 | |
|     Sales | | 5,000 |
|     Sales Tax Payable | | 250 |
|     Federal Excise Tax Payable | | 500 |

10. Sales Tax Payable, Cash

11.
| | | |
|---|---|---|
| Total note days | | 90 |
|     August — days | 31 | |
|     Date of note | 7 | |
| | 24 | |
|     September — days | 30 | |
|     October — days | 31 | 85 |
| Date due, November | | 5 |

12. 360

13. $6,000 [$300,000 x .12 x (60/360)]

14. A note is dishonored if the maker fails to pay at maturity.

15. Power Company

| | | | |
|---|---|---|---|
| Dec. 1 | Cash | 73,125.00 | |
| | Discount on Notes Payable ($75,000 x .10 x 90/360) | 1,875.00 | |
| |     Notes Payable | | 75,000.00 |

    To record discounting of own note at the bank.

| | | | |
|---|---|---|---|
| Dec. 31 | Interest Expense | 625.00 | |
| |     Discount on Notes Payable | | 625.00 |

    To record interest incurred on note.
    [$75,000 x .10 x(30/360)]

Mar. 1  Interest Expense ........................................................ 1,250.00
                Discount on Notes Payable .................................................... 1,250.00
            To record interest on note to maturity date.

        Notes Payable ......................................................... .............. 75,000.00
                Cash ...................................................................... ............ 75,000.00
            To record payment of note payable.

16. *a.*  June 1
        Cash ......................................................................... 17,730
        Discount on Notes Payable .......................................... 270
                Notes Payable ...................................................................... 18,000

    *b.*  July 31
        Notes Payable ........................................................... 18,000
        Interest Expense ........................................................ 270
                Cash ...................................................................... 18,000
                Discount on Notes Payable ...................................... 270

17. Horace Company
        Interest Receivable ..................................................... ............ 6,000
                Interest Revenue ..................................................... ............ 6,000
            To record interest earned from September 1 to December 31.
            [$300,000 x .06 x (4/12)]

18. receivables
19. payables
20.     Interest Receivable ..................................................... 1,200
                Interest Revenue ...................................................... 1,200
            To record interest earned from September 1 to December 31.
            [$3,600 x (4/12) = $1,200]

21.     Interest Expense ........................................................ 1,137.50
                Interest Payable ..................................................... 1,137.50
            To record accrued interest for 91 days (October, 30 days;
            November, 30 days; December, 31 days).
            $37,500 x .12 x (91/360) = $1,137.50

22. *a.*  Oct.  3  Cash .......................................................... 11,880
                Discount on Notes Payable ............................................. 120
                        Notes Payable ................................................................ 12,000

    *b.*  Nov. 2  Notes Payable ................................................... 12,000
                        Cash ...................................................................... 12,000

                Interest Expense ....................................................... 120
                        Discount on Notes Payable ..................................... 120

23. *a.*  Uncollectible Accounts Expense ...................................... 900
                Allowance for Uncollectible Accounts ................................... 900
            To record estimated uncollectible accounts.

        Balance at July 31 of Allowance for Uncollectible Accounts: $1,650

    *b.*  August 1
        Allowance for Uncollectible Accounts ............................................ 1,500
                Accounts Receivable—Dale ................................................... 1,500
            To write Dale's account off as uncollectible.

c. August 29

| | | |
|---|---:|---:|
| Accounts Receivable — Dale ............................................................... | 1,350 | |
|     Allowance for Uncollectible Accounts ..................................... | | 1,350 |
|     To reverse original write-off of Dale's account. | | |
| Cash ................................................................................................... | 1,350 | |
|     Accounts Receivable — Dale ...................................................... | | 1,350 |
|     To record collection of account. | | |

24. Accounts receivable turnover = \$10,507/[(\$2,403 + \$2,432) /2] = \$10,507/\$2,417.50 = 4.35

Number of days' sales in net accounts receivable = 365/4.35 = 83.91 days

## *True-False Questions*

1. T    This account is a contra asset to Accounts Receivable.
2. F    A promissory note is a liability to the maker because he or she has the legal obligation to pay money.
3. T    Accounts receivable from officers other than from normal sales are shown as other receivables.
4. T
5. T
6. T
7. T
8. T    A debit balance could occur when there have been more write-offs of specific accounts receivable than the estimate for uncollectibles credited to the Allowance for Uncollectible Accounts.
9. T
10. F    The credit is to Allowance for Uncollectible Accounts, and Accounts Receivable is debited.
11. T
12. T
13. F    Both their existence and amount are certain.
14. F    Estimated product warranty payable is an estimated liability.
15. F    Ron is called the maker of the note, and Sue Jones is the payee as she will receive cash.
16. F.    This account is reported on the balance sheet as a deduction from the Notes Payable account.
17. F    The due day is August 6. (May, 23 days; June, 30 days; July, 31 days; August, 6 days)
18. F    This account will have a credit balance as it is a contra asset and is not closed at the end of the period.
19. T
20. T

## *Multiple Choice Questions*

1. C    Allowance for Uncollectible Accounts is a contra asset and is deducted from Accounts Receivable.
2. C
3. D
4. B    Discount on Notes Payable becomes Interest Expense only as time passes.
5. D
6. B    (March, 23 days; April, 30 days; May, 31 days; June, 6 days)

7. A $740,000 + ($740,000 x .06 x 90/360) = $751,100.
8. A
9. A $270,000 Accounts Receivable - $2,250 write-off = $267,750. $267,750 x 4% = $10,710. $900 (cr. balance) Allowance for Uncollectible Accounts balance - $2,250 write-off = $1,350 debit balance. $10,710 + $1,350 debit balance = $12,060 needed credit to Allowance for Uncollectible Accounts.
10. C
11. D

# CHAPTER 10

# PROPERTY, PLANT, AND EQUIPMENT

## Learning Objectives

1. *List the characteristics of plant assets and identify the costs of acquiring plant assets.*
2. *List the four major factors affecting depreciation expense.*
3. *Describe the various methods of calculating depreciation expense.*
4. *Distinguish between capital and revenue expenditures for plant assets.*
5. *Describe the subsidiary records used to control plant assets.*
6. *Analyze and use the financial results — rate of return on operating assets.*

## REFERENCE OUTLINE

# CHAPTER OUTLINE

*Learning Objective 1:*
*List the characteristics of plant assets and identify the costs of acquiring plant assets.*

## NATURE OF PLANT ASSETS

1. Plant assets consist of land and depreciable property such as buildings, machinery, delivery equipment, and office equipment.
   a. The category "property, plant, and equipment" is often referred to as plant and equipment or plant assets.
   b. Proper recording of plant assets is important because of the effect on net income.
2. To be classified as a plant asset, an item must possess the following three attributes:
   a. It must be tangible (must be capable of being seen and touched).
   b. It must have a useful service life of more than one year.
   c. It must be used in business operations rather than held for resale to a customer.
3. Plant asset costs are an extreme form of prepaid expenses because the cost of these services must be allocated to the periods benefited.

## INITIAL RECORDING OF PLANT ASSETS

4. Plant assets usually are recorded initially at cost, which includes all normal, reasonable, and necessary expenditures made to place the asset in operating condition at its proper location.
   a. The initial plant asset cost includes repair and reconditioning costs for assets that were acquired in used or damaged condition.
   b. Unnecessary costs such as traffic fines that result from hauling machinery to a new plant are not part of the asset cost.

## LAND AND LAND IMPROVEMENTS

5. The cost of land includes the purchase price and costs such as attorney fees, cost of title search, and assessments for streets and sewers.
   a. Because land purchased as a building site is considered to have an unlimited life, it is not depreciable.
   b. Land improvements such as landscaping, driveways, parking lots, fences, and lighting and sprinkler systems are attachments that have limited lives and are depreciable.

## BUILDINGS

6. The cost of a purchased building includes the price of items such as remodeling costs, real estate broker commissions, and legal costs.

## GROUP PURCHASE OF ASSETS

7. Land and buildings might be purchased together.
   a. If land and buildings are purchased for a lump-sum amount, the total should be apportioned among the individual assets using appraised values to determine the portion of cost to assign to each asset.
   b. Separation of land and buildings is needed to record proper depreciation on the buildings.

## MACHINERY AND OTHER EQUIPMENT

8. The cost of machinery includes the net invoice price and items such as transportation charges, insurance in transit, and cost of installation.
   a. Discounts not taken are best viewed as losses and are not capitalized as part of an asset's cost.
   b. The cost of various types of equipment includes all costs necessary to place the equipment in a condition and location for use.

    *c.* Machinery cost does not include costs of removing and disposing of a replaced old machine that has been used in operations.

## SELF-CONSTRUCTED ASSETS

  9. When a company builds a plant asset for its own use, the cost would include the cost of materials and labor directly traceable to construction. Cost would also include incremental (extra) heat, light, power, and other indirect services related to construction.

## NONCASH ACQUISITIONS

10. Assets acquired in noncash exchanges are generally recorded at the fair market value of the securities or assets given up or the fair market value of the asset acquired, whichever is more clearly evident; but there are several asset valuation bases available.

## FAIR MARKET VALUE

    *a.* The plant asset may be recorded at its fair market value or the fair market value of what was given up, whichever is more clearly evident.

## APPRAISED VALUE

    *b.* If neither the plant asset acquired nor the noncash asset given up has a determinable fair market value, the exchange may be recorded at appraised value.
      (1) Appraised value is an expert's opinion as to what an item's market price would be if the item were sold.
      (2) Appraisals are often used to value works of art, rare books, and antiques

## BOOK VALUE

    *c.* Book value of an asset is its recorded cost less accumulated depreciation.
      (1) Book value is an acceptable basis only if there is no better basis available.
      (2) Book value of an old asset is usually not a valid indicator of the new asset's economic value.

## GIFTS OF PLANT ASSETS

11. Gifts of plant assets are generally recorded at their fair market value at the time of the donation or at an appraised value if a market value cannot be ascertained.
12. A city may give land to a company to build a factory that will provide jobs for local residents.
13. Gifts of plant assets are debited to an asset account and credited to the Retained Earnings account.

## DEPRECIATION OF PLANT ASSETS

14. Depreciation is the amount of plant asset cost allocated to each period benefiting from the asset's use.
    *a.* Depreciation is recorded on all plant assets except land, because these assets will eventually wear out or become so inadequate or obsolete that they will be sold or discarded.
    *b.* Depreciation is the allocation in a reasonable and systematic manner of the cost (or other basic value) of a plant asset to the periods comprising its useful life.
    *c.* The major causes of depreciation are:
      (1) Physical deterioration resulting from the use of the asset.
      (2) Inadequacy of asset resulting from its inability to produce enough products or provide enough services to meet current demand.
      (3) Obsolescence, which is its decline in usefulness brought on by invention and technological progress.

*Learning Objective 2:*
*List the four major factors affecting depreciation expense.*

## FACTORS AFFECTING DEPRECIATION

15. The following factors must be considered in determining depreciation:
    a. Cost of asset.
    b. Estimated salvage value of asset.
    c. Estimated useful life of asset.
    d. Depreciation method to use in depreciating the asset.

## COST OF ASSET

16. Cost is the amount of cash and/or cash equivalent given up to acquire the asset and place it in operating condition at its proper location.

## ESTIMATED SALVAGE VALUE

17. Estimated salvage value is the amount of money expected to be recoverable, less disposal costs, on the date a plant asset is scrapped, sold, or traded-in.
    a. Depreciable cost is acquisition cost less estimated salvage value.
    b. The accuracy of estimating salvage value varies among plant assets.

## ESTIMATED USEFUL LIFE

18. Estimated useful life is the period of time over which an asset is expected to provide services to the firm.
    a. Useful or economic life of an asset may differ from its physical life.
    b. Estimates of useful life are influenced by three factors: physical deterioration, inadequacy, and obsolescence.
       (1) Physical deterioration results from use, wear and tear, and the actions of the elements.
       (2) Inadequacy is the inability of a plant asset to produce enough products or provide enough services to meet current demands.
       (3) Obsolescence is the decline in usefulness of an asset brought about by invention and technological progress.

*Learning Objective 3:*
*Describe the various methods of calculating depreciation expense.*

## DEPRECIATION METHODS

19. Four common methods of depreciation exist, normally leaving a company free to adopt the method it believes most appropriate for its operations.

## STRAIGHT-LINE DEPRECIATION

20. Straight-line depreciation is one of the methods commonly used and allocates the same dollar amount of depreciation to each period:

Depreciation per period = (Cost - Estimated salvage value) / Number of accounting periods in estimated useful life.

## UNITS-OF-PRODUCTION (OUTPUT) METHOD

21. Units-of-production method often is used if usage is the dominant factor causing expiration of the asset:

Depreciation per unit = (Cost - Estimated salvage value) / Estimated total output over asset's life;

Depreciation per period = Depreciation per unit x Output for period in units.

## ACCELERATED DEPRECIATION METHODS—SUM-OF-THE-YEARS'-DIGITS AND DOUBLE-DECLINING-BALANCE METHODS

22. Accelerated depreciation methods record higher amounts of depreciation in the early years of an asset's life and lower amounts in the asset's later years.

a. A company may choose one of these two methods because the value of the benefits received from an asset decline with age.

b. Accelerated depreciation methods may also be used if the asset is of the high-technology type that is subject to rapid obsolescence.

c. Accelerated depreciation methods may also be used if repairs increase substantially in later years and depreciation and repairs together remain fairly constant over the asset's life.

## SUM-OF-THE-YEARS'-DIGITS METHOD

23. Sum-of-the-years'-digits method results in larger charges in the early years: Depreciation per period = (Cost - Estimated salvage value) x Ratio, the numerator of which is the number of years of life remaining from the beginning of the year in question and the denominator of which is the sum of the numbers from one through the estimated total life of the asset.

## DOUBLE-DECLINING-BALANCE METHOD

24. Double-declining-balance method results in larger amounts of depreciation being recorded in the early years of the asset's life: Depreciation per period = Net book value of asset at beginning of period x Double the straight-line rate of depreciation.

a. Salvage value is ignored in making annual calculations.

b. At the point where book value is equal to the estimated salvage value, no more depreciation is taken.

## PARTIAL-YEAR DEPRECIATION

25. When plant assets are acquired sometime during an accounting period, depreciation is usually computed to the nearest full month.

## CHANGES IN ESTIMATES

26. If original estimates of asset lives are proven incorrect, the revised annual depreciation will be based on the depreciable net book value remaining when the error is discovered.

## DEPRECIATION AND FINANCIAL REPORTING

27. *APB Opinion No. 12* requires that the amount of depreciation expense for the period be separately disclosed in the body of the income statement or in the footnotes. Companies usually report depreciation expense in the body of the income statement. Notes provide a detailed description of the depreciation methods used by the company.

## A MISCONCEPTION

28. The amount of accumulated depreciation does not represent funds available for replacing old plant assets with new assets.

## COSTS OR MARKET VALUES IN THE BALANCE SHEET

29. Under the going-concern concept, the assumption is made that the firm will remain in business and will use its plant assets in operations rather than sell them.

a. This assumption is the reason that market values are not considered relevant.

b. The going-concern concept is the justification for reporting remaining undepreciated costs rather than market values.

*Learning Objective 4:*
*Distinguish between capital and revenue expenditures for plant assets.*

## SUBSEQUENT EXPENDITURES (CAPITAL AND REVENUE) ON ASSETS

30. Expenditures that are directly related to plant assets are often made during the period of ownership at times other than the date of acquisition.

## EXPENDITURES CAPITALIZED IN ASSET ACCOUNTS

31. Betterments or improvements to existing plant assets are capital expenditures because they increase the quality of services obtained from the asset. Betterments add to the total service-rendering ability of the assets and are properly capitalizable as additions to asset accounts.

## EXPENDITURES CAPITALIZED AS CHARGES TO ACCUMULATED DEPRECIATION

32. Expenditures that merely extend the life of the asset beyond the original estimate are capitalized as charges to the accumulated depreciation accounts. This debit reduces the credit balance of this account. The remaining depreciable net book value is depreciated over the extended life remaining.

33. Sometimes expenditures for major repairs that do not extend the asset's life are charged to the accumulated depreciation account to avoid distorting one year's net income.

## EXPENDITURES CHARGED TO EXPENSE

34. Expenditures for ordinary repairs and part replacements are treated as periodic expenses.

35. The distinction between capital and revenue expenditures is primarily the length of the period of time benefited.

## ERRORS IN CLASSIFICATION

36. If the wrong account is debited for a capital expenditure, both the asset and the accumulated depreciation account would be misstated.

37. If an expenditure that should be expensed is capitalized, the effects are even more significant.

*Learning Objective 5:*
*Describe the subsidiary records used to control plant assets.*

## SUBSIDIARY RECORDS USED TO CONTROL PLANT ASSETS

38. General ledger accounts are maintained for each major class of plant assets.

39. The details concerning the plant assets are shown in subsidiary ledgers and records.

*Learning Objective 6:*
*Analyze and use the financial ratio — rate of return on operating assets.*

## ANALYZING AND USING FINANCIAL RESULTS—RATE OF RETURN ON OPERATING ASSETS

40. Rate of Return on Operating Assets = Net Operating Income/Operating Assets. The Rate of Return on Operating Assets indicates how effectively assets were used to produce a profit.

## DEMONSTRATION PROBLEM

On January 2, 1997, Joseph Company purchased a machine for $90,000 with an estimated useful life of five years and an estimated salvage value of $9,000. The machine was expected to produce 162,000 units. Production was 36,000 units in 1997, 27,000 units in 1998, and 43,200 units in 1999.

Complete the table using the four given methods to compute depreciation.

| Method | Annual Depreciation Expense 1997 | 1998 | 1999 | Accumulated Depreciation at the end of 1999 | Book Value at the end of 1999 |
|---|---|---|---|---|---|
| Straight-Line ....................................... | | | | | |
| Units-of-Production ............................ | | | | | |
| Sum-of-the-Years'-Digits .................... | | | | | |
| Double-Declining-Balance ................. | | | | | |

## SOLUTION TO DEMONSTRATION PROBLEM

| Method | Annual Depreciation Expense 1997 | 1998 | 1999 | Accumulated Depreciation at the end of 1999 | Book Value at the end of 1999 |
|---|---|---|---|---|---|
| Straight-Line ....................................... | $16,200 | $16,200 | $16,200 | $48,600 | $41,400 |
| Units-of-Production ............................ | 18,000 | 13,500 | 21,600 | 53,100 | 36,900 |
| Sum-of-the-Years'-Digits .................... | 27,000 | 21,600 | 16,200 | 64,800 | 25,200 |
| Double-Declining-Balance ................. | 36,000 | 21,600 | 12,960 | 70,560 | 19,440 |

Referring to the terms listed below, place the appropriate letters next to the corresponding description.

| | | |
|---|---|---|
| a. Accelerated depreciation | h. Extraordinary repairs | o. Estimated salvage value |
| b. Betterment (improvement) | i. Inadequacy | p. Obsolescence |
| c. Book value | j. Land improvements | q. Accelerated Cost Recovery Act |
| d. Capital expenditure | k. Plant and equipment | |
| e. Depreciable amount | l. Plant assets | r. Rate of return on operating assets |
| f. Depreciation | m. Physical deterioration | |
| g. Depreciation accounting | n. Revenue expenditure | |

_____ 1. Cost less salvage value.

_____ 2. The process of allocating a portion of the cost of a depreciable plant asset to the periods in which it provides benefits.

_____ 3. Cost less accumulated depreciation.

_____ 4. An alteration, addition to, or structural change in a depreciable asset that makes the asset more durable, productive, or efficient.

_____ 5. Improvements to real estate that have a limited life.

_____ 6. Tangible long-lived assets used in a business.

_____ 7. The amount expected to be recovered when a plant asset is disposed of.

_____ 8. An estimate, usually expressed in terms of cost, of the amount of service potential of a plant asset that expired during a period.

_____ 9. An accounting procedure under which the amounts of depreciation recorded in the early years of an asset's life are greater than those recorded in later years.

_____ 10. Inability of a plant asset to produce enough product to meet current demands.

_____ 11. Another term for plant and equipment.

_____ 12. An expenditure made on plant assets that is properly added to a plant asset account.

_____ 13. The decline in usefulness of a plant asset brought about by invention and technological progress.

_____ 14. A normal recurring expenditure made on a plant asset to keep it operating and that is believed to benefit only the current period.

_____ 15. The cost of overhauling or reconditioning a plant asset that increases its expected useful life.

_____ 16. The decline in usefulness of a plant asset resulting from wear and tear and the action of the elements.

_____ 17. The tax law governing depreciation for tax purposes.

_____ 18. Net operating income/operating assets.

## COMPLETION AND EXERCISES

1. From the following information, what is the yearly depreciation charge under the straight-line method?

   Cost of asset ......................................... $80,000
   Estimated salvage value ..................... 8,000
   Estimated useful life .......................... 12 years

2. From the following information, compute the depreciation for the current year under the units-of-production method.

   Cost of asset ......................................... $90,000
   Estimated salvage value ..................... 0
   Estimated production for entire life . 450,000 units
   Current year's production ................. 80,000 units

3. What is the *general* rule for determining the valuation to be placed on an exchange of noncash assets?

   _____

   _____

   _____

   _____

4. The major causes of depreciation are _____ _____ , _____ , and

   _____ .

5. Is the following statement true or false?  Why? Accountants depreciate assets so that the assets will be reported on the balance sheet at their current market values.

   _____

   _____

   _____

   _____

   _____

   _____

6. The _____-_____ method of depreciation allocates the same dollar amount of depreciation to each period in the estimated useful life of the asset.

7. The Bruce Company purchased a machine for $42,000 plus a 5-percent sales tax. Bruce paid for the machine in time to take advantage of a 2 percent discount. Transportation charges were $240, and installation and testing costs totaled $2,760. While being unloaded, the machine was dropped and damaged. It cost $300 to repair the damage. What is the cost of the machine? (Work space is provided below.)

8. The sum-of-the-years'-digits method of depreciation is suitable for those assets that have the greatest use _____ (early or late) in their lives. If used indiscriminately, this method would tend to _____ (overstate or understate) the asset values on the balance sheet.

9. If you assume the straight-line depreciation is correct, the sum-of-the-years'-digits method of depreciation is incorrect and will cause the net income during the early years of life to be _____ (understated or overstated), and during the later years of life to be _____ (understated or overstated).

10. To what are accountants referring when they use the term "plant assets"?

    _____

    _____

    _____

    _____

11. Plant assets can be broadly classified as _____ and _____

    _____.

12. What is included in the cost of plant assets?

    _____

    _____

    _____

    _____

    _____

13. The Sandra Company acquired land and a building at a lump-sum price of $540,000. The building is to be renovated and used by the company. According to competent appraisers, the land and the building have values of $240,000 and $360,000, respectively, on the acquisition date. A cost of _____ should be assigned to the land, and a cost of _____ should be assigned to the building.

14. Compute depreciation for each of the first two years of the asset's life under the double-declining-balance method.

   Cost of asset .......................................... $90,000
   Estimated salvage value ..................... 6,000
   Estimated useful life ........................... 10 years

15. Compute depreciation for the first year of the asset's life under the sum-of-the-years'-digits method.

   Cost of asset .......................................... $30,600
   Estimated salvage value ..................... 3,600
   Estimated useful life ........................... 8 years

16. A machine was acquired on September 1, 1997, at a cost of $72,000. It has an estimated salvage value of $5,400, and an estimated useful life of five years. The double-declining-balance method of depreciation is to be used. Compute depreciation for 1997 and 1998 assuming the accounting period ends on December 31.

17. A machine that cost $35,000 has an estimated salvage value of $5,000 and an estimated useful life of five years. The machine is being depreciated on a straight-line basis. At the beginning of the fourth year, it is estimated that the machine will last five more years with the same estimated salvage value. The revised annual depreciation charge is $_____.

18. Expenditures for additions to existing assets, such as betterments or improvements, should be charged to _____

19. If $900 is spent overhauling the engine in a machine, and, as a result, the machine will be used an additional two years beyond its original estimated life, what entry is necessary?

| Date | Account Titles and Explanation | Post. Ref. | Debit | Credit |
|------|-------------------------------|------------|-------|--------|
|      |                               |            |       |        |
|      |                               |            |       |        |
|      |                               |            |       |        |
|      |                               |            |       |        |
|      |                               |            |       |        |
|      |                               |            |       |        |

20. What effect will the engine overhaul in Question 19 have on periodic depreciation of the machine if the overhaul is accounted for as a debit to the accumulated depreciation account, but the original estimated useful life stays the same?

_____

_____

_____

_____

21. Assume the machine in Question 19 at acquisition had an estimated useful life of eight years, a cost of $5,800, and an estimated salvage value of $200. If the overhaul increased the machine's estimated useful life by one year and was made at the beginning of the eighth year, what will be the charge to depreciation expense for each of the last two years of the machine's useful life on a straight-line basis?

22. The main distinction between capital and revenue expenditures is _____

_____

23. Wendy Co., on April 1, 1997, debited to expense the $5,400 cost of installing a new machine. The machine had a cost (exclusive of installation costs) of $12,000 and an estimated useful life of 6 years. The company uses the straight-line method of depreciation. No salvage value is expected from the machine. State whether net income (ignoring income taxes) is overstated or understated for 1997. Compute the amount of the error.

24. Wakefield Co. bought a lot for $80,400 cash on which it intended to construct a new building. The company paid legal fees of $1,140 to cover costs of transfer of title and $6,900 to remove an old building. Prepare the journal entry to record the total cost of the land.

| Date | Account Titles and Explanation | Post. Ref. | Debit | Credit |
|------|-------------------------------|------------|-------|--------|
|      |                               |            |       |        |
|      |                               |            |       |        |
|      |                               |            |       |        |
|      |                               |            |       |        |
|      |                               |            |       |        |
|      |                               |            |       |        |
|      |                               |            |       |        |
|      |                               |            |       |        |
|      |                               |            |       |        |

25. Equipment was acquired on January 1, 1994, at a cost of $78,900. It has an estimated life of five years, an estimated salvage value of $900, and an estimated total of 40,000 service hours. Compute the depreciation for 1998 using each of the four methods.

   a. Straight-line method ......................................................................... _____

   b. Sum-of-the-years'-digits ................................................................. _____

   c. Double-declining-balance .............................................................. _____

   d. Service-hours method (assume it was used 6,000 hours) .................. _____
      (known as units-of-production method)

26. A description of depreciation methods used by a company can be found in which

   section of an annual report? _____

27. B Corporation has operating assets of $20,000,000 and net operating income of

   $5,000,000. B Corporation's rate of return on operating assets is _____%.

## TRUE-FALSE QUESTIONS

Indicate whether each of the following statements is true or false by inserting a capital "T" or "F" in the blank space provided.

_____ 1. One of the reasons for recording depreciation is to secure proper matching of costs and revenues.

_____ 2. The periodic expense associated with the use of land is called depreciation expense.

_____ 3. The basis of valuation or measurement of plant assets is called historical cost.

_____ 4. The price paid for a plant asset is actually a prepayment of an expense.

_____ 5. In general, plant assets should be recorded initially at their cash or cash equivalent price.

_____ 6. A firm that constructs a machine for its own use for $80,000 should record this machine at $90,000, the price that it would have to pay to purchase it.

_____ 7. In some situations, the depreciation recorded on one plant asset may be added to the cost of another asset.

_____ 8. Depreciation must be recorded on limited-life plant assets simply because the asset will not last indefinitely no matter how well it is maintained.

_____ 9. The cost of changing the oil and lubricating an auto is a revenue expenditure.

_____ 10. Treating a capital expenditure as an expense will overstate net income in the years after this action was taken.

_____ 11. Plant assets with a nominal cost may be charged to expense when acquired.

_____ 12. Failure to record depreciation will not affect the final determination of net income.

_____ 13. Freight paid by the buyer of a new machine should be included in the cost of the machine.

_____ 14. The sum-of-the-years'-digits method results in larger total depreciation expense than does the straight-line method.

_____ 15. Expenditures incurred on plant assets that extend the quantity of services beyond the original estimate but do not improve the quality of service are debited to the Accumulated Depreciation account.

_____ 16. When depreciation is to be computed individually on a substantial number of assets comprising a functional group, it is advisable to maintain a subsidiary ledger.

_____ 17. The purchase price of a fixed asset is a capital expenditure.

_____ 18. Depreciation is the process of periodically writing down an asset to arrive at its fair market value.

_____ 19. Depreciation Expense for the period must be separately disclosed in the body of the income statement or in the footnotes according to _APB Opinion No. 12._

_____ 20. Depreciation accounting automatically provides the cash required to replace plant assets as they wear out.

_____ 21. Depreciation expense does not require an equivalent outlay of cash in the period in which the expense is recorded.

_____ 22. The purpose of depreciation accounting is to provide funds for replacing fixed assets.

_____ 23. Depreciation is an estimate which reflects the cost of using up an asset.

_____ 24. The cost of the original installation of a machine should be credited to the Machinery account.

_____ 25. Land improvements should never be depreciated since they are attached to land.

_____ 26. Rate of return on operating assets indicates how effectively assets were used to produce sales.

## MULTIPLE CHOICE QUESTIONS

For each of the following questions, indicate the best answer by circling the appropriate letter.

1. A betterment represents:
   A. an ordinary repair.
   B. a revenue expenditure.
   C. a capital expenditure.
   D. None of the above.

2. The effect of recording a capital expenditure as a revenue expenditure is an:
   A. understatement of current year's expense.
   B. overstatement of current year's net income.
   C. understatement of subsequent year's net income.
   D. understatement of current year's net income.
   E. None of the above.

3. The credit balance in an Accumulated Depreciation account represents:
   A. a fund accumulated for the purpose of buying new assets.
   B. the amount of cost of plant assets expensed in the past.
   C. a long-term liability.
   D. None of the above.

4. The depreciation expense for a firm at the close of its first fiscal year, as determined by three different methods, is as follows: straight-line, $39,000; units-of-production, $28,860; and sum-of-the-years'-digits, $62,400. If the straight-line method is employed, the net income reported will be $85,800.
   What will be the amount of reported net income if the sum-of-the-years'-digits method is used?
   A. $124,800
   B. $114,660
   C. $62,400
   D. $91,260
   E. $52,260

5. Which of the following methods would be considered accelerated depreciation methods?
   A. Double-declining-balance method
   B. Sum-of-the-years'-digits method
   C. Straight-line method
   D. A and B
   E. All of the above.

6. An expenditure that is to be capitalized because of the benefit it will render in subsequent periods could be any of the following except a(n):
   A. capital expenditure.
   B. improvement.
   C. land improvement.
   D. revenue expenditure.

7. In the financial statements prepared at the end of the accounting period, the item "Accumulated depreciation" should appear:
   A. on the income statement as an expense.
   B. on the statement of retained earnings as a subtraction from net income.
   C. on the balance sheet as a liability.
   D. on the balance sheet as a deduction from the related asset.
   E. None of these.

8. An expenditure that should appear on the current income statement as an expense and a deduction from revenue is called a(n):
   A. operating revenue.
   B. revenue expenditure.
   C. capital expenditure.
   D. None of the above.

9. Dingle Company acquired a delivery truck for $30,600 on September 1, 1997. The truck has an estimated salvage value of $1,920 and an estimated useful life of eight years. The company operates on a calendar-year accounting period and uses double-declining-balance depreciation. What amounts of depreciation should be recorded for years 1997 and 1998 respectively?
   A. $1,221.86 and $4,887.43
   B. $2,550 and $7,650
   C. $2,550 and $7,012.50
   D. $1,275 and $3,825

10. The book value of an asset equals:
    A. fair market value.
    B. cost plus accumulated depreciation.
    C. cost minus estimated salvage value.
    D. fair market value less accumulated depreciation and estimated salvage value.
    E. None of the above.

Questions 11-14
Bell Company purchased a new machine having a $360 trade-in value which cost $3,600. It is estimated that the machine will have a four-year life and can produce 6,000 units of finished product during its service life. The machine produced 3,000 units during its first year of operation and 2,000 units during its second year of operation.

11. Straight-line depreciation per year is:
    A. $972
    B. $1,080
    C. $810
    D. $900
    E. None of these.

12. Sum-of-the-years'-digits depreciation for the second year is:
    A. $972
    B. $1,080
    C. $720
    D. $648
    E. None of the above.

13. Double-declining-balance depreciation for the second year is:
   A. $810
   B. $675
   C. $900
   D. $1,080
   E. None of these.

14. Units-of-production depreciation for the second year is:
   A. $1,200
   B. $810
   C. $900
   D. $1,080
   E. None of these.

15. Depreciation accounting is primarily for the purpose of:
   A. providing a fund to replace depreciable assets.
   B. showing conservative figures on the financial statements.
   C. providing a deduction for income tax purposes.
   D. revaluing assets whose fair market values have declined.
   E. systematically allocating the cost of depreciable assets against the revenues produced by those assets.

---

## SOLUTIONS

*Matching*

| | | |
|---|---|---|
| 1. *e* | 7. *o* | 13. *p* |
| 2. *g* | 8. *f* | 14. *n* |
| 3. *c* | 9. *a* | 15. *h* |
| 4. *b* | 10. *i* | 16. *m* |
| 5. *j* | 11. *l* | 17. *q* |
| 6. *k, l* | 12. *d* | 18. *r* |

*Completion and Exercises*

1. Depreciation per year = ($80,000 - $8,000) / 12 = $6,000
2. Depreciation per unit = $90,000/450,000 = $0.20 per unit; 80,000 units x $0.20 per unit = $16,000 depreciation for current year
3. The *general* rule is that of using the fair market value of the assets received or of the assets surrendered or securities issued, whichever is the more clearly evident.
4. physical deterioration; inadequacy; obsolescence
5. False. Accountants attempt to distribute in a systematic and rational manner the cost (or other basic value) less estimated salvage value of the plant asset over the estimated useful life of the asset in order to match the cost of the asset with the revenue produced by the asset.
6. straight-line
7. Invoice price including 5 percent sales tax ....................................... $44,100
    Less: 2 percent cash discount (on $42,000) ................................. ___840
    $43,260
    Transportation charges ........................................................................ 240
    Installation and testing costs ........................................................... _2,760_
    Cost of machine ................................................................................... $46,260

8. early; understate

9. understated; overstated.

10. Plant assets are the relatively long-lived tangible assets acquired for use in the operations of a business rather than for resale.

11. Land; depreciable property

12. The cost of a plant asset consists of all the normal and reasonable expenditures necessary to place the asset in its intended position in a usable condition. Cost is usually measured by the amount of cash and/or cash equivalent given up.

13. $216,000 found by [$540,000 x ($240,000 / $600,000)]
    $324,000 found by [$540,000 x ($360,000 / $600,000)]

14. First year: Depreciation = $90,000 x 0.20 = $18,000
    Second year: Depreciation = ($90,000 - $18,000) x 0.20 = $14,400

15. Sum-of-the-years'-digits = 8 + 7 + 6 + 5 + 4 + 3 + 2 + 1 = 36;
    or:  [n (n + 1)] /2  =  [8 (9)] /2  = 36

    Depreciation for first year = 8/36 x $27,000 = $6,000

16. 1997: Depreciation = $72,000 x 0.40 x 4/12 = $9,600
    1998: Depreciation = ($72,000 - $9,600) x .40 = $24,960

17. $2,400. ($35,000 - $5,000)/5 = $6,000; $35,000 - ($6,000 x 3) = $17,000; ($17,000 - $5,000)/5 = $2,400

18. the asset accounts.

19.     Accumulated Depreciation — Machinery .............................  900
            Cash (or Accounts Payable) .............................................  900
        Cost of overhauling machine engine.

20. The machine will still be depreciated over the same number of years, but the yearly charge to depreciation expense will be greater for the remaining years.

21. At the beginning of eighth year:

    | | |
    |---|---:|
    | Cost of machine .......................................................................... | $5,800 |
    | Less: Estimated salvage value ............................................... | 200 |
    | | $5,600 |
    | Less: Accumulated depreciation [($5,600/8) x 7] ............... | 4,900 |
    | Net depreciable book value before overhaul ........................... | $ 700 |
    | Cost of engine overhaul ................................................................ | 900 |
    | Net depreciable book value after overhaul.................................... | $1,600 |

    $1,600 / 2 remaining years of useful life = $800 depreciation per year.

22. the length of time that the expenditure will be beneficial.

23. 
    | | |
    |---|---:|
    | Expenses are overstated for the year 1995 ........................................ | $5,400 |
    | Depreciation that should have been recorded on the installation costs ($5,400/6) x 9/12 year ........................................................ | 675 |
    | Net income for 1997 is understated ................................................ | $4,725 |

24.     Land .......................................................................................... 88,440
            Cash ..................................................................................... 88,440

25. *a.* Straight-line method ($78,000 / 5) ..................................................... $15,600
    *b.* Sum-of-the-years'-digits (1/15 x $78,000) ................................. 5,200
    *c.* Double-declining-balance .......................................................... 4,090 *
    *d.* Service-hours method ................................................................ 11,700 **

          \*Declining-balance depreciation:

| | |
|---|---|
| 1994 (40% x $78,900) | $31,560 |
| 1995 (40% x $47,340) | 18,936 |
| 1996 (40% x $28,404) | 11,362 |
| 1997 (40% x $17,042) | 6,817 |
| 1998 (40% x $10,225) | 4,090 |

      \*\*$78,000 / 40,000 = $1.95 per service hour
       $1.95 x 6,000 = $11,700

26. Notes (footnotes) to the financial statements
27. 25%

### True-False Questions

1. T
2. F   Land is not a depreciable asset.
3. T
4. T   The expense associated with the use of a plant asset is called depreciation and it is recorded over the life of the plant asset.
5. T
6. F   The machine should be recorded at its cost of $80,000; the $10,000 savings will be recognized over the life of the machine due to less depreciation expense being recorded.
7. T   An example is when a truck is used in the construction of a building.
8. T
9. T
10. T   In the year of acquisition of the capital expenditure that is expensed, net income will be understated; then in later years, there will be no depreciation expense.
11. T   The principle of materiality allows this, as immaterial costs may be treated as revenue expenditures rather than capital expenditures.
12. F   Depreciation is an expense and will be closed to Income Summary the same as other expenses.
13. T
14. F   The total depreciation expense over the life of the asset will be the same whether the straight-line method or the sum-of-the-years'-digits method is used.
15. T
16. T
17. T   An asset account is debited.
18. F   Fair market value is determined by such factors as supply and demand in the market place, and it is not the purpose of depreciation to arrive at this figure.
19. T
20. F
21. T
22. F
23. T
24. F   This is a proper debit to the Machinery account.
25. F   Land improvements are attached to land but since they have limited lives they are subject to depreciation.

26. F Rate of return on operating assets indicates how effectively assets were used to produce a profit.

## Multiple Choice Questions

1. C
2. D Revenue expenditures are charged off in the current period; thus improperly reducing the current year's net income.
3. B
4. C $62,400 sum-of-the-years'-digits depreciation - $39,000 straight-line depreciation = $23,400 difference.
$85,800 income using straight-line depreciation - $23,400 difference = $62,400 income using sum-of-the-years'-digits depreciation.
5. D
6. D
7. D
8. B
9. C 1997: 25% x $30,600 x 4/12 months = $2,550
1998: 25% x ($30,600 - $2,550) = $7,012.50
10. E Book value is the cost of the asset less the balance in the related accumulated depreciation account.
11. C ($3,600 - $360) / 4 years = $810
12. A 3/10 x $3,240 = $972
13. C 1st year depreciation: 50% x $3,600 = $1,800
2nd year depreciation: 50% x ($3,600 - $1,800) = $900
14. D $3,240/6,000 units = $.54 per unit; $.54 x 2,000 units = $1,080
15. E

CHAPTER **11**

# PLANT ASSET DISPOSALS, NATURAL RESOURCES, AND INTANGIBLE ASSETS

*Learning Objectives*

1. *Calculate and prepare entries for the sale, retirement, and destruction of plant assets.*
2. *Describe and record exchanges of dissimilar and similar plant assets.*
3. *Determine the periodic depletion cost of a natural resource and calculate depreciation of plant assets located on extractive industry property.*
4. *Prepare entries for the acquisition and amortization of intangible assets.*
5. *Analyze and use the financial results — total assets turnover.*

## REFERENCE OUTLINE

# CHAPTER OUTLINE

## DISPOSAL OF PLANT ASSETS

1. When a plant asset is disposed of, the balances in the asset and related accumulated depreciation accounts must be removed.

*Learning Objective 1:*
*Calculate and prepare entries for the sale, retirement, and destruction of plant assets.*

## SALE OF PLANT ASSETS

2. When a plant asset is sold, the difference between the book value of the asset and the amount received represents the gain or loss on the sale.
   a. To record the sale, Cash and Accumulated Depreciation are debited and the plant asset account is credited.
   b. The difference is either a gain or loss on disposal of plant assets.

## RETIREMENT OF PLANT ASSETS WITHOUT SALE

3. If an asset is retired without sale, it must be removed from the accounts. If it has any salvage value, this value should be set up in a Salvaged Materials account.

## DESTRUCTION OF PLANT ASSETS

4. The loss resulting from any assets destroyed is reduced by any insurance proceeds received.

## EXCHANGES OF NONMONETARY ASSETS

5. Nonmonetary assets are inventories, property, plant, equipment, and other assets whose prices may change over time.
   a. When nonmonetary assets are exchanged, the recorded amount should be based on the fair value of the asset given up or the fair value of the asset received, whichever is clearly more evident.
   b. A loss resulting from the exchange is always recognized.
   c. Recognition of any gain resulting from the exchange depends on whether the assets exchanged are similar or dissimilar in nature.

*Learning Objective 2:*
*Describe and record exchanges of dissimilar and similar plant assets.*

## EXCHANGES OF DISSIMILAR PLANT ASSETS

6. When dissimilar plant assets are exchanged, both gains and losses are recognized. The new asset is recorded at its cash price, which is equal to the fair market value of the old asset at the time of the exchange plus the amount of cash paid.
   a. The new asset is recorded at the fair market value of the asset received or the asset given up, whichever is more clearly evident.
   b. If the cash price is not stated, the fair market value of the old asset plus any cash paid is used to record the new asset.
   c. The book value of the old asset is removed from the accounts by debiting the related accumulated depreciation and crediting the old asset.

## EXCHANGES OF SIMILAR PLANT ASSETS

7. When similar plant assets are exchanged, losses are recognized but gains are not recognized.
   a. If a loss is indicated on an exchange of similar plant assets, the loss is recognized and the new asset is recorded at its cash price.
   b. If a gain is indicated on an exchange of similar plant assets, the gain is not recognized and the new asset is recorded at the sum of the cash paid and the book value of the old asset.

## REMOVAL COSTS

8. Removal costs are incurred to dismantle and remove an old asset that has been used by the company.
   a. Removal costs are deducted from salvage proceeds to determine net salvage value.
   b. If removal costs exceed salvage proceeds, they increase the loss or reduce the gain recognized on disposal of a plant asset.
   c. Removal costs are not a cost of benefits expected from the new asset because they are costs of benefits already received.

## NATURAL RESOURCES

9. Mines, quarries, oil reserves, gas deposits, and timber stands are examples of natural resources or wasting assets.

10. Natural resources should be recorded in the accounts at the cost of acquisition plus the cost of development; they should be reported on the balance sheet at total cost less accumulated depletion. Oil and gas reserves cannot be measured exactly. Reserve estimates are subject to revision as additional data becomes available during the producing life of a reservoir.

*Learning Objective 3:*
*Determine the periodic depletion cost of a natural resource and calculate depreciation of plant assets located on extractive industry property.*

## DEPLETION

11. The amount of depletion recognized in a period is an estimate of the cost of the amount of resource removed during the period. Depletion is recorded by debiting the Depletion account and crediting either the resource account directly or an accumulated depletion account.

## DEPRECIATION OF PLANT ASSETS LOCATED ON EXTRACTIVE INDUSTRY PROPERTY

12. Depreciable plant assets located on extractive industry property should be depreciated over the shorter of the (1) physical life of the asset or (2) life of the natural resource. The units-of-production method is often used.

## INTANGIBLE ASSETS

13. Intangible assets are nonphysical and noncurrent assets that arise from exclusive privileges granted by governmental authority or by legal contract and superior entrepreneurial capacity or management know-how. Intangible assets include patents, copyrights, franchises, trademarks, goodwill, and leaseholds. Intangible assets can be quite substantial. For example, the majority of the total assets of Coca-Cola Enterprises are intangible assets.

*Learning Objective 4:*
Prepare entries for acquisition and amortization of intangible assets.

## ACQUISITION OF INTANGIBLE ASSETS

14. Intangible assets are initially recorded at their cost of acquisition.
   a. They should be amortized over the shortest of their economic useful life, their legal life, or 40 years.
   b. Only purchased intangibles are recorded in the accounting records.

## AMORTIZATION OF INTANGIBLE ASSETS

15. Amortization is the systematic write-off to expense of the cost of an intangible asset.
   a. All intangible assets are subject to amortization.
   b. Amortization is recorded by debiting Amortization Expense and crediting the intangible asset account. An Accumulated Amortization account could be used, but in most cases information gained would be insignificant.

c. Straight-line amortization must be used unless another method of amortization can be shown to be superior.

## PATENTS

16. A patent is a right granted by a government that gives the owner of the patent an exclusive right to manufacture, sell, lease, or benefit from an invention.
    a. The legal life of a patent is 17 years.
    b. Patents are recorded at cost if purchased.
    c. The Patent account should be debited for the cost of the first successfully defended patent infringement suit and for the cost of any competing patents that were purchased to ensure the revenue-generating capability of the purchased patent.

## COPYRIGHTS

17. A copyright gives exclusive right protection for writings, designs, and literary productions against being reproduced illegally.
    a. A copyright has a legal life equal to the life of the creator plus 50 years.
    b. Generally the cost of the copyright is expensed over the life of the first edition published.

## FRANCHISES

18. A franchise is a contract between two parties that grants the franchisee certain rights and privileges ranging from name identification to complete monopoly of service.
    a. A franchise also places certain restrictions on the company that purchased the franchise, such as the prices charged.
    b. If the franchise agreement specifies periodic payments to the grantor of the franchise, the Franchise Expense account should be debited.
    c. If instead the franchise agreement specifies a lump-sum payment be made to acquire the franchise, the cost should be recorded in an asset account entitled Franchise and amortized over the shorter of the useful life of the franchise or 40 years.

## TRADEMARKS; TRADE NAMES

19. Trademarks and trade names may be acquired that are used in conjunction with a particular product or company.
    a. A trademark is a symbol, design, or logo that is used in conjunction with a particular product or company.
    b. A trade name is a brand name under which a product is sold or a company does business.

## LEASES

20. A lease is a contract made between the renter (the lessee) and the owner (the lessor) of property to rent that property. The lessee obtains the right to possess and use the property.
    a. Rights granted under the lease are called a leasehold.
    b. Accounting for a lease depends on whether it is a capital lease or an operating lease.
        (1) A capital lease transfers to the lessee virtually all rewards and risks that accompany ownership of property.
            (a) A lease is a capital lease if it transfers ownership of the leased property to the lessee at the end of the lease term or contains a bargain purchase option that permits the lessee to buy the property at a price significantly below fair market value at the end of the lease term.
            (b) A capital lease is a means of financing property acquisitions and has the same economic impact as an installment purchase.
        (2) Operating leases are those leases that do not qualify as capital leases.
            (a) An operating lease does not transfer any of the rewards and risks of ownership to the lessee.

(b)  If the operating lease requires an immediate cash payment for a future year's occupancy, a Leasehold account, which is a long-term prepaid rent account, is debited. This Leasehold account is amortized when the services are received.

## LEASEHOLD IMPROVEMENTS

21. Leasehold improvements should be written off over the life of the lease or the life of the improvements, whichever is shorter.
    a.  Leasehold improvements are physical alterations made by the lessee to the leased property. These improvements are expected to yield benefits beyond the current accounting period.
    b.  Leasehold improvements made by a lessee usually become the property of the lessor after the lease has expired.
    c.  To amortize a leasehold improvement, Rent Expense or Leasehold Improvement Expense is debited and Leasehold Improvements is credited.

## GOODWILL

22. Goodwill is the intangible value attached to an entity because of its management's skill or know-how and a favorable reputation with customers.
    a.  A Goodwill account will appear in the accounting records only if goodwill has been bought and paid for in cash or other property.
    b.  Goodwill is determined to be the difference between the amount paid for the business and the fair market value of the assets purchased.

## REPORTING AMORTIZATION

23. Amortization expense on intangible assets appears as an operating expense on the income statement. Amortization of goodwill is not deductible for tax purposes.

*Learning Objective 5:*
*Analyze and use the financial resultsXtotal assets turnover.*

## ANALYZING AND USING THE FINANCIAL RESULTSXTOTAL ASSETS TURNOVER

24. Total Assets Turnover = Net Sales/Average Total Assets
25. This ratio indicates the efficiency with which a company uses its assets to generate sales.

---

## DEMONSTRATION PROBLEM

---

A machine that cost $15,900 and on which depreciation to date of $14,700 has been recorded is disposed of.

Required:

Prepare journal entries without explanations to record the disposition under each of the indicated circumstances:
a.  Sold for $1,200.
b.  Sold for $3,000.
c.  Sold for $900.
d.  Traded on a new, similar machine with a cash price of $21,000, trade-in allowance of $3,600, and the balance paid in cash.

|   |   |   |   |   |   |   |   |   |   |
|---|---|---|---|---|---|---|---|---|---|
| a. |   |   |   |   |   |   |   |   |   |
|   |   |   |   |   |   |   |   |   |   |
|   |   |   |   |   |   |   |   |   |   |
|   |   |   |   |   |   |   |   |   |   |
|   |   |   |   |   |   |   |   |   |   |
| b. |   |   |   |   |   |   |   |   |   |
|   |   |   |   |   |   |   |   |   |   |
|   |   |   |   |   |   |   |   |   |   |
|   |   |   |   |   |   |   |   |   |   |
| c. |   |   |   |   |   |   |   |   |   |
|   |   |   |   |   |   |   |   |   |   |
|   |   |   |   |   |   |   |   |   |   |
|   |   |   |   |   |   |   |   |   |   |
| d. |   |   |   |   |   |   |   |   |   |
|   |   |   |   |   |   |   |   |   |   |
|   |   |   |   |   |   |   |   |   |   |
|   |   |   |   |   |   |   |   |   |   |
|   |   |   |   |   |   |   |   |   |   |
|   |   |   |   |   |   |   |   |   |   |
|   |   |   |   |   |   |   |   |   |   |
|   |   |   |   |   |   |   |   |   |   |
|   |   |   |   |   |   |   |   |   |   |
|   |   |   |   |   |   |   |   |   |   |

| | | | | |
|---|---|---|---|---|
| *a.* | Cash ..................................................................... | 1,200 | |
| | Accumulated DepreciationXMachine ..................................... | 14,700 | |
| |    Machine ........................................................ | | 15,900 |
| *b.* | Cash ..................................................................... | 3,000 | |
| | Accumulated DepreciationXMachine ..................................... | 14,700 | |
| |    Machine ........................................................ | | 15,900 |
| |    Gain on Disposal of Plant Assets ......................... | | 1,800 |
| *c.* | Cash ..................................................................... | 900 | |
| | Accumulated DepreciationXMachine ..................................... | 14,700 | |
| | Loss on Disposal of Plant Assets ....................................... | 300 | |
| |    Machine ........................................................ | | 15,900 |
| *d.* | Machine (New) ........................................................ | 18,600 | |
| | Accumulated DepreciationXMachine ..................................... | 14,700 | |
| |    Machine (Old) ................................................. | | 15,900 |
| |    Cash ........................................................... | | 17,400 |

## MATCHING

Referring to the terms listed below, place the appropriate letter next to the corresponding description.

| | | | | | |
|---|---|---|---|---|---|
| *a.* | Amortization | *g.* | Goodwill | *m.* | Materiality concept |
| *b.* | Copyright | *h.* | Patent | *n.* | Natural resources |
| *c.* | Depletion | *i.* | Wasting asset | *o.* | Intangible assets |
| *d.* | Leasehold improvement | *j.* | Lease | *p.* | Leasehold |
| *e.* | Trademark | *k.* | Operating lease | *q.* | Research and |
| *f.* | Capital lease | *l.* | Franchise | | development costs |

_____ 1. A noncurrent asset classification that includes assets, having no physical existence that are valued because of the advantages or exclusive rights they provide.

_____ 2. A symbol, design, brand name, or any other indicator of easy and ready recognition attributed to the product.

_____ 3. An estimate, usually expressed in terms of cost, of the service potential of an intangible asset that expired in a period.

_____ 4. The intangible value attached to a firm resulting from the ability of its management to produce above-average earnings.

_____ 5. An exclusive privilege conferred on the owner that protects his or her writings, designs, and literary productions from unauthorized reproduction.

_____ 6. The amount of cost assigned to a natural resource extracted, mined, or harvested in a period.

_____ 7. A contract in which a lessor grants a lessee the right to operate or use property for a stated period of time in exchange for stipulated payments.

_____ 8. Allows the accountant to deal with unimportant items in a theoretically incorrect manner.

_____ 9. A privilege granted by the federal government to an inventor giving the exclusive right to manufacture, lease, sell, or otherwise benefit from an invention.

_____ 10. The agreement that allows the owner (operator) of a local fast-food restaurant to use the McDonald's name.

_____ 11. Examples are ore bodies, mineral deposits, oil reserves, and timber stands.

_____ 12. A lease that is, in effect, an installment purchase of an asset.

_____ 13. Another name for a depletible natural resource.

_____ 14. All leases that do not meet the criteria for a capital lease.

_____ 15. The account to which the down payment, other than the first period's rent, on a long-term operating lease is debited.

_____ 16. Costs incurred in a planned search for new knowledge and in translating such knowledge to produce a new product or process.

_____ 17. Any physical alteration to leased property from which benefits are expected beyond the current accounting period.

---

## COMPLETION AND EXERCISES

1. A truck is purchased by the Irvine Company on April 1, 1998, for $15,000, with an estimated useful life of five years and an estimated salvage value of $3,000. The company uses the double-declining-balance method of depreciation. If the truck is sold on December 31, 1999, for $8,000, what is the amount of gain or loss on the sale?

2. A machine is purchased on August 1, 1998, for $12,400 with an estimated useful life of six years and an estimated salvage value of $920. The company uses the sum-of-the-years'-digits method of depreciation. The machine is exchanged for a similar machine with a cash price of $20,000 on December 31, 1999, and the company received a trade-in allowance of $6,000. Prepare the entry to record the exchange.

3. A gain or loss on the sale of a plant asset is determined by comparing the asset's

_____ _____ with its _____ _____.

4. A machine that cost $72,000 and has an Accumulated Depreciation account balance of $27,000 is sold for $24,600. There is a (gain/loss) _____ on the sale of $ _____.

5. Prepare the journal entry if the plant asset described below is sold for $11,700 and depreciation has been recorded to the date of sale. (Omit explanation.)

Cost of asset ...............................................$22,500
Accumulated depreciation ...................... 10,510

| Date | Account Titles and Explanation | Post. Ref. | Debit | Credit |
|------|-------------------------------|------------|-------|--------|
|  |  |  |  |  |
|  |  |  |  |  |
|  |  |  |  |  |
|  |  |  |  |  |
|  |  |  |  |  |

6. What entry is required to record the retirement of the machine described below? (Omit explanation.)

Cost ............................................................$31,800
Accumulated depreciation ...................... 30,000
Estimated value of salvaged materials.... 1,800

| Date | Account Titles and Explanation | Post. Ref. | Debit | Credit |
|------|-------------------------------|------------|-------|--------|
|  |  |  |  |  |
|  |  |  |  |  |
|  |  |  |  |  |
|  |  |  |  |  |
|  |  |  |  |  |

7. Assume that a building costing $150,000 is completely destroyed by fire. Depreciation accumulated to the date of destruction amounts to $65,000. What journal entry is required to record the destruction if $40,000 is expected to be recovered from an insurance company? (Omit explanation.)

| Date | Account Titles and Explanation | Post. Ref. | Debit | Credit |
|------|-------------------------------|------------|-------|--------|
|  |  |  |  |  |
|  |  |  |  |  |
|  |  |  |  |  |
|  |  |  |  |  |
|  |  |  |  |  |
|  |  |  |  |  |

8. Assume that factory equipment costing $40,000 and having an up-to-date Accumulated Depreciation account balance of $32,500 is exchanged for an automobile. In addition to the factory equipment, cash of $13,500 is given in exchange for an automobile. The automobile has a cash price of $15,000. What journal entry is required to record the exchange? (Omit explanation.)

| Date | Account Titles and Explanation | Post. Ref. | Debit | Credit |
|------|-------------------------------|-----------|-------|--------|
|      |                               |           |       |        |
|      |                               |           |       |        |
|      |                               |           |       |        |
|      |                               |           |       |        |
|      |                               |           |       |        |
|      |                               |           |       |        |
|      |                               |           |       |        |

9. Assume that $340,800 cash and an old machine that cost $267,200 and has an up-to-date Accumulated Depreciation account balance of $160,000 are exchanged for a similar new machine that has a cash price of $480,000. What entry is required to record this exchange? (Omit explanation.)

| Date | Account Titles and Explanation | Post. Ref. | Debit | Credit |
|------|-------------------------------|-----------|-------|--------|
|      |                               |           |       |        |
|      |                               |           |       |        |
|      |                               |           |       |        |
|      |                               |           |       |        |
|      |                               |           |       |        |

10. Assume that $30,720 cash and an old delivery truck that cost $18,560 and has an up-to-date Accumulated Depreciation account balance of $16,400 are exchanged for a new delivery truck that has a cash price of $32,000. What entry is required to record this exchange? (Omit explanation.)

| Date | Account Titles and Explanation | Post. Ref. | Debit | Credit |
|------|-------------------------------|-----------|-------|--------|
|      |                               |           |       |        |
|      |                               |           |       |        |
|      |                               |           |       |        |
|      |                               |           |       |        |
|      |                               |           |       |        |
|      |                               |           |       |        |
|      |                               |           |       |        |
|      |                               |           |       |        |

11. _____ is caused by the physical removal of a quantity of natural resources.

12. What are the forms of the two different possible entries for recording periodic depletion?

| Date | Account Titles and Explanation | Post. Ref. | Debit | | Credit | |
|---|---|---|---|---|---|---|
| | | | | | | |
| | | | | | | |
| | | | | | | |
| | | | | | | |
| | | | | | | |
| | | | | | | |

13. Hendrick Company paid $1,218,000 for the mineral rights, estimated at 7,000,000 tons, in a certain tract of land. In its first year of operations, Hendrick Company extracted 320,000 tons of minerals and sold 310,000 tons. The depletion cost per ton is _____, and the depletion cost to be charged to expense in the first year of operations is _____.

14. Specialized machinery was installed at the site of an oil reserve. The machinery has an estimated physical life of 25 years. The oil reserve is expected to be productive for 30 more years. The machinery should be depreciated over _____ years.

15. What are intangible assets?

_____

_____

_____

_____

16. _____ is an estimate, usually expressed in terms of cost, of the services received from an intangible asset in a period.

17. Over what period of time should patents be amortized?

_____

_____

_____

_____

18. _____ is an intangible value attached to a business because its management is able to produce above-average earnings per dollar of investment.

19. Research and development costs should be _____ as incurred.

20. On July 1, 1998, the first day of its fiscal year, Corry Co. leased a warehouse for five years at an annual rental of $12,000. The warehouse has an estimated life of 30 years.

Corry Co. paid the first and fifth years' rent on July 1. This is a(n) _____ lease.

The first year's rent of $12,000 should be debited to _____ _____; the fifth year's rent should be debited to _____.

21. Bruce Co. leased a computer-controlled photoengraving machine on December 31, 1998. The lease runs for four years, which is the estimated useful life of the machine, and calls for four annual payments on December 31 of $8,000. The estimated salvage value of the machine is zero. The lease is a(n) _____ lease. The leased property is recorded as an _____ and the lease obligation as a _____. The property is depreciated over _____ _____.

22. On January 1, 1998, Wilson bought an oil well for $780,000. He has no right to any land value after the oil is pumped. It is estimated that there are 1,000,000 barrels of oil in the ground. In 1998, he pumped and sold oil for $36 per barrel showing total credit sales of $3,600,000. Journalize entries for 1998 relating to the oil well.

| | | | | | | | |
|---|---|---|---|---|---|---|---|
| | | | | | | | |
| | | | | | | | |
| | | | | | | | |
| | | | | | | | |
| | | | | | | | |
| | | | | | | | |
| | | | | | | | |
| | | | | | | | |
| | | | | | | | |
| | | | | | | | |
| | | | | | | | |
| | | | | | | | |
| | | | | | | | |
| | | | | | | | |
| | | | | | | | |

23. Make the necessary general journal entries required in the following transactions for Bentsen Company.
    a.  Purchased a patent for $90,000.
    b.  Amortized the above patent for one full year. Bentsen Company received exclusive rights to the patent for 12 years, but the patent is expected to have economic value for only 10 years.

| | | | | | | | |
|---|---|---|---|---|---|---|---|
| | | | | | | | |
| | | | | | | | |
| | | | | | | | |
| | | | | | | | |
| | | | | | | | |
| | | | | | | | |

24. Gephardt Co. acquired Machine 1 on July 1, 1998, for $21,000. Machine I was traded in on Machine II on December 31, 1999. For depreciation purposes, machines of this type are expected to have useful lives of five years and no salvage value. Use straight-line depreciation and no salvage value for Machine I. Data regarding the trade-in is shown below: (Assume depreciation has already been recorded to December 31, 1999.)

|  | Cash Price | Cash Paid |
|---|---|---|
| Machine II | $24,000 | $10,500 |

Journalize in the space below the entry required on December 31, 1999, to record the exchange.

|  |  |  |  |  |  |  |  |
|---|---|---|---|---|---|---|---|
|  |  |  |  |  |  |  |  |
|  |  |  |  |  |  |  |  |
|  |  |  |  |  |  |  |  |
|  |  |  |  |  |  |  |  |
|  |  |  |  |  |  |  |  |
|  |  |  |  |  |  |  |  |
|  |  |  |  |  |  |  |  |
|  |  |  |  |  |  |  |  |
|  |  |  |  |  |  |  |  |

25. Total Assets Turnover indicates the efficiency with which a company uses its assets to generate _____.

## TRUE-FALSE QUESTIONS

Indicate whether each of the following statements is true or false by inserting a capital "T" or "F" in the blank space provided.

_____ 1. A loss generally will be recorded on the sale of a plant asset if the sales price is less than the asset's book value.

_____ 2. The total depreciation recorded on a plant asset before its retirement can never exceed the asset's cost.

_____ 3. Natural resources are generally recorded at cost, including the cost of exploration and development.

_____ 4. In calculating depletion for a period, the residual value of acquired land containing an ore deposit should be deducted from the total purchase price.

_____ 5. All recorded intangible assets are subject to amortization.

_____ 6. Goodwill is recorded by accountants only if it is purchased.

_____ 7. A patent should be amortized over 40 years.

_____ 8. Because it has an indefinite life, a trademark need not be amortized.

_____ 9. A capital lease has no effect on the balance sheet.

_____ 10. Intangible assets should be amortized over the longer of their economic life or legal life.

_____ 11. The Patent account should be debited for the cost of the first successfully defended patent infringement suit if an outside law firm was retained.

_____ 12. If a fully-depreciated asset continues to be used, management can continue to take depreciation.

_____ 13. An operating lease is a lease that transfers to the lessee virtually all advantages and risks of ownership of property.

_____ 14. Trademarks and trade names should be recorded at their fair market value and amortized over their legal life.

_____ 15. If a franchise is purchased for a lump sum, the amount is recorded as an asset and amortized over 40 years or its useful life, whichever is shorter.

_____ 16. A copyright's legal life is 50 years and it gives its owner protection against writings and literary productions being reproduced without authorization.

_____ 17. Before disposing of a plant asset, depreciation to the date of sale or disposition must be recorded in the journal.

_____ 18. If a company purchases a competing patent to ensure revenue-generating capability of a previously owned patent, the cost of the purchased patent should be expensed in the period of purchase.

_____ 19. When dissimilar plant assets are exchanged, the asset received would normally be recorded at the cash price of the new asset or the fair market value of the asset given up plus cash paid.

_____ 20. According to generally accepted accounting principles, when similar assets are exchanged, the new asset will be recorded at the book value of the old asset plus the cash paid or the cash price of the asset received, whichever is lower.

_____ 21. If removal costs exceed the proceeds from salvage, such removal costs increase the loss or reduce the gain recognized on disposal of a plant asset.

_____ 22. Accumulated Depletion is a contra account to an asset reported in the natural resources section of the balance sheet.

_____ 23. M Industries has average total assets of $750,000 and net sales of $1,500,000. The company's total assets turnover is 50%.

_____ 24. Modern technology eliminates the need to use estimates for the measurement of oil and gas reserves.

## MULTIPLE CHOICE QUESTIONS

For each of the following questions, indicate the best answer by circling the appropriate letter.

1. On August 15, 1998, Tyler, Inc. traded in a word processor for a newer model. The cost of the old machine was $1,040 and its book value (adjusted to Aug. 15, 1998), was $312. The new machine had a cash price of $2,600 but was acquired for $2,080 plus the old machine. The new asset should be recorded at:
   A. $2,080
   B. $2,392
   C. $2,496
   D. $2,600
   E. None of these (must know fair value of the old machine at date of trade-in).

2. Which of the following accounts is not a plant asset?
   A. Delivery Equipment
   B. Shop Supplies on Hand
   C. Buildings
   D. Furniture & Fixtures
   E. Automobiles

3. Natural resources such as timberstands, mineral deposits, and oil reserves, which are known as wasting assets, are carried in the accounts at cost less accumulated:
   A. depreciation.
   B. depletion.
   C. usage.
   D. deterioration.
   E. None of these.

4. Company Q received exclusive rights to a patent for 15 years, but it is expected to have value for only 5 years. The patent cost is $92,000. The entry to record the amortization for one full year is:

A. Patent Amortization Expense ........................................................ 18,400
    Patents ..................................................................................... 18,400

B. Patent Amortization Expense .................................................... 6,133
    Patents ................................................................................. 6,133

C. Patents ............................................................................... 92,000
    Cash ...................................................................................... 92,000

D. Patents written off ................................................................. 92,000
    Patents ..................................................................................... 92,000

E. None of the above.

The following information relates to questions 5 and 6. On August 1 of the current fiscal year Wayne Angell traded an old computer for a new one with a cash price of $2,250. He received a trade-in allowance of $375 and paid the balance in cash. The following information about the old computer is obtained from the account in the office equipment ledger: cost, $1,200; accumulated depreciation at December 31, the close of the previous fiscal period, $960; monthly depreciation, $12.

5. The recorded cost of the new computer will be:
A. $2,115
B. $1,875
C. $2,031
D. $2,250
E. None of the above.

6. The gain or loss on the exchange will be:
A. Gain, $135
B. Loss, $165
C. Gain, $219
D. Gain, $225
E. None of the above.

7. The Neal Company bought a truck on July 1, 1998, for $18,400. The company uses the straight-line method of depreciation. It is estimated that this truck will have a salvage value of $3,680 at the end of its estimated useful life of 8 years. The book value of this truck on the December 31, 1999, balance sheet is:
A. $18,400
B. $17,480
C. $9,200
D. $15,640
E. $14,720

8. A mine having an estimated 600,000 tons of available ore is purchased for $120,000. If 30,000 tons of ore are mined and sold during the first year, the amount of depletion included as expense for the year is:
A. $120,000
B. $12,000
C. $6,000
D. $4,000
E. None of the above.

9. On January 2, 1995, Gordon Cameras purchased office equipment at a cost of $6,960 that had an estimated life of six years with no salvage value. On March 1, 1999, the equipment was sold for $1,740 cash. At the close of the annual accounting period on December 31, 1998, the accounts showed the following:

| | |
|---|---|
| Office Equipment | $6,960 |
| Accumulated DepreciationXOffice Equipment | 4,640 |

The proper entries (to the nearest dollar) to be made on March 1, 1999, assuming the straight-line method, are:

A.
| | | |
|---|---|---|
| Cash | 1,740 | |
| Accumulated DepreciationXOffice Equipment | 4,640 | |
| Loss on Disposal of Plant Assets | 580 | |
| Office Equipment | | 6,960 |

B.
| | | |
|---|---|---|
| Depreciation Expense | 193 | |
| Accumulated DepreciationXOffice Equipment | | 193 |
| | | |
| Cash | 1,740 | |
| Accumulated DepreciationXOffice Equipment | 4,833 | |
| Loss on Disposal of Plant Assets | 387 | |
| Office Equipment | | 6,960 |

C.
| | | |
|---|---|---|
| Depreciation Expense | 193 | |
| Accumulated DepreciationXOffice Equipment | | 193 |
| | | |
| Cash | 1,740 | |
| Accumulated DepreciationXOffice Equipment | 4,640 | |
| Loss on Disposal of Plant Assets | 580 | |
| Office Equipment | | 6,960 |

D.
| | | |
|---|---|---|
| Depreciation Expense | 1,160 | |
| Accumulated DepreciationXOffice Equipment | | 1,160 |
| | | |
| Cash | 1,740 | |
| Accumulated DepreciationXOffice Equipment | 5,800 | |
| Office Equipment | | 6,960 |
| Gain on Disposal of Plant Assets | | 580 |

E. None of these.

10. If a mine having an estimated 2,000,000 tons of available ore is purchased for $900,000, the depletion charge per ton of ore mined is:
 A. $7.20
 B. $0.90
 C. $0.45
 D. $18.00

11. If a fully depreciated asset is still in use:
 A. the cost should be adjusted to market value.
 B. prior years' depreciation should be adjusted.
 C. the cost and accumulated depreciation should remain in the ledger and no more depreciation should be taken.
 D. part of the depreciation should be reversed.
 E. it should be written off the books.

12. How is the book value of a plant asset determined?
    A. By deducting the accumulated depreciation from the balance of the asset account.
    B. By deducting the current depreciation expense from the amount in the asset account.
    C. By adding the accumulated depreciation to the balance of the asset account.
    D. By deducting the accumulated depreciation from the sales value of the asset.
    E. None of these.

13. Accumulated depreciation is debited for:
    A. loss of cash.
    B. the write-off of a fully depreciated asset.
    C. the yearly depreciation expense.
    D. None of these.

14. At the beginning of its fiscal year on July 1, 1995, a company purchased office equipment costing $10,800. On September 1, 1999, the equipment was sold for $2,250 cash. Depreciation expense was recorded to fiscal year-end on June 30, 1999, using a six-year life and straight-line depreciation with no expected salvage value. The correct entry to record the sale on September 1, 1999, is:

| | | | |
|---|---|---:|---:|
| A. | Depreciation Expense | 300 | |
| | Accumulated DepreciationXOffice Equipment | | 300 |
| | Cash | 2,250 | |
| | Accumulated DepreciationXOffice Equipment | 7,500 | |
| | Loss on Sale of Plant Assets | 1,050 | |
| | Office Equipment | | 10,800 |
| B. | Depreciation Expense | 450 | |
| | Accumulated DepreciationXOffice Equipment | | 450 |
| | Cash | 2,250 | |
| | Accumulated DepreciationXOffice Equipment | 7,500 | |
| | Loss on Sale of Office Equipment | 1,050 | |
| | Office Equipment | | 10,800 |
| C. | Depreciation Expense | 300 | |
| | Accumulated DepreciationXOffice Equipment | | 300 |
| | Loss on Sale of Plant Assets | 1,350 | |
| | Cash | 2,250 | |
| | Accumulated DepreciationXOffice Equipment | 7,200 | |
| | Office Equipment | | 10,800 |
| D. | Cash | 22,500 | |
| | Accumulated DepreciationXOffice Equipment | 7,200 | |
| | Gain on Sale of Plant Assets | | 18,900 |
| | Accumulated DepreciationXOffice Equipment | | 10,800 |

    E. None of these.

# SOLUTIONS

*Matching*

| | |
|---|---|
| 1. o | 10. l |
| 2. e | 11. n (or i) |
| 3. a | 12. f |
| 4. g | 13. i |
| 5. b | 14. k |
| 6. c | 15. p |
| 7. j | 16. q |
| 8. m | 17. d |
| 9. h | |

*Completion and Exercises*

1. Gain of $1,700
   Depreciation taken:

   1998 40% x  $15,000 x 9/12  =  $4,500
   1999 40% x ($15,000 - 4,500)  =   4,200
   　　　　　　　　　　　　　　　　　$8,700

   $15,000　　　　　　$8,000  Sales price
   - 8,700　　　　　　- 6,300
   $ 6,300  Book value  $1,700  Gain

2. $21,981
   Depreciation taken:
   8/1/98-8/1/99:　　　　　6/21 x ($12,400 - $920)  = $3,280
   8/1/99-12/31/99: ($12,400 - $920) x 5/21 x 5/12  =  1,139*
   　　　　　　　　　　　　　　　　　　　　　　　　$4,419

| | | |
|---|---|---|
| Machine (new) | 20,000 | |
| Accumulated DepreciationXMachine | 4,419 | |
| Loss on Disposal of Plant Asset | 1,981 | |
| 　Machine (old) | | 12,400 |
| 　Cash ($20,000 - $6,000) | | 14,000 |

   *Rounded

3. book value (cost less accumulated depreciation); sales price
4. loss; $20,400, calculated as [($72,000 - $27,000) - $24,600]

| | | |
|---|---|---|
| 5. Cash | 11,700 | |
| Accumulated DepreciationXPlant Assets | 10,510 | |
| Loss on Disposal of Plant Assets | 290 | |
| 　Plant Assets | | 22,500 |
| | | |
| 6. Salvaged Materials | 1,800 | |
| Accumulated DepreciationXMachinery | 30,000 | |
| 　Machinery | | 31,800 |
| | | |
| 7. Receivable from Insurance Company | 40,000 | |
| Fire Loss | 45,000 | |
| Accumulated DepreciationXBuilding | 65,000 | |
| 　Building | | 150,000 |

8. Automobiles .......................................................................................... 15,000
   Accumulated DepreciationXFactory Equipment ................................... 32,500
   Loss on Disposal of Plant Assets ............................................................ 6,000
       Factory Equipment ........................................................................ 40,000
       Cash .................................................................................................. 13,500
       [Loss on disposal is difference between book value of $7,500
       ($40,000 - $32,500), and trade-in allowance of $1,500 ($15,000 - $13,500)]

9. Machinery (new) ................................................................................... 448,000
   Accumulated DepreciationXMachinery ................................................ 160,000
       Machinery (old) .............................................................................. 267,200
       Cash .................................................................................................. 340,800

10. Delivery Trucks (new) ......................................................................... 32,000
    Accumulated DepreciationXDelivery Trucks ...................................... 16,400
    Loss on Disposal of Plant Assets ......................................................... 880
        Delivery Trucks (old) ..................................................................... 18,560
        Cash .................................................................................................. 30,720
        [Loss on disposal is difference between book value of $2,160
        ($18,560 - $16,400), and trade-in allowance of $1,280 ($32,000 - $30,720)]

11. Depletion
12. Depletion ........................................................................................ xxx
        Natural Resource ............................................................................. xxx

    Depletion ........................................................................................ xxx
        Accumulated Depletion .................................................................. xxx
13. $0.174 ($1,218,000 / 7,000,000 tons); 53,940 ($0.174 x 310,000 tons sold).
14. 25 (because useful life of machinery is shorter than life of oil reserve)
15. Intangible assets are noncurrent, nonphysical assets acquired for use in business
    operations rather than for resale. They provide business advantages and exclusive
    rights or privileges to their owners.
16. Amortization
17. Patents should be amortized over the shorter of their legal life of 17 years or their
    estimated useful life.
18. Goodwill
19. expensed
20. operating; Prepaid Rent (or Rent Expense); Leasehold
21. capital; asset; liability; four years (the useful life to the lessee)

22. Oil Deposits ......................................................................................... 780,000
        Cash .................................................................................................. 780,000

    Accounts Receivable ............................................................................3,600,000
        Sales .................................................................................................. 3,600,000

    Depletion Expense* .............................................................................. 78,000
        Accumulated DepletionXMineral Deposits .................................... 78,000
      *   $780,000 / 1,000,000 barrels = $0.78 per barrel
        $3,600,000 / $36 = 100,000 barrels
        ($0.78 x 100,000 = $78,000 depletion)

| 23. *a.* | Patents .................................................................................. | 90,000 | |
| | Cash .................................................................................. | | 90,000 |
| | | | |
| *b.* | Patent Amortization Expense ............................................. | 9,000 | |
| | Patents .............................................................................. | | 9,000 |

| 24. | Machine II ................................................................................... | 24,000 | |
| | Accumulated Depreciation ($21,000 / 5) x 1.5 ........................... | 6,300 | |
| | Loss on Disposal of Plant Assets ............................................... | 1,200* | |
| | Machine I ................................................................................ | | 21,000 |
| | Cash ........................................................................................ | | 10,500 |

```
    *  Book value:    $21,000 - $6,300    =  $14,700
       Trade-in:      $24,000-$10,500     =   13,500
       Loss                                  $ 1,200
```

25. Sales

## True-False Questions

1. T
2. T
3. T Then depletion is recorded so that the cost is allocated over the time periods benefited.
4. T
5. T
6. T
7. F Patents should be amortized over the shorter of their economic or legal life of 17 years.
8. F A trademark should be amortized over its economic life or 40 years, whichever is shorter.
9. F A capital lease is a lease that transfers to the lessee virtually all rewards and risks that accompany ownership of property. The lessee must record the leased property as an asset and the lease obligation as a liability.
10. F It is the shorter of their economic or legal life rather than the longer.
11. T
12. F No more depreciation can be taken on a fully depreciated plant asset.
13. F This describes a capital lease.
14. F Trademarks and trade names should be recorded at cost and amortized over their economic life or 40 years, whichever is shorter.
15. T
16. F A copyright's legal life is equal to the life of the creator plus 50 years.
17. T
18. F The cost of a purchased patent used for protection of an existing patent should be debited to the Patents account and amortized over the remaining useful life of the existing patent.
19. T
20. T This prevents a gain from being recorded.
21. T
22. T
23. F The company's total assets turnover is 200%, ($1,500,000/$750,000).
24. F For example, oil and gas reserves cannot be measured exactly.

1. B  $312 book value + $2,080 cash paid = $2,392
2. B  Shop supplies on hand is a current asset.
3. B
4. A
5. C  $1,200 - [$960 + 7 ($12)] = $156 Book value: $375 trade-in - $156 = $219 gain;
     $2,250 - $219 = $2,031 valuation of the new machine
6. E  No gain is recorded on exchanges of similar assets.
7. D  ($18,400 - $3,680 salvage value) / 8 years = $1,840 per yr.;
     $1,840 x 12 years = $2,760 accumulated depreciation balance;
     $18,400 cost - $2,760 accumulated depreciation = $15,640 book value
8. C  ($120,000 / 600,000 = $.20; $.20 x 30,000 = $6,000)
9. B
10. C  $900,000/2,000,000 tons = $0.45
11. C
12. A
13. B
14. A  $10,800 / 6 = $1,800 per yr.; $1,800 x 4 = $7,200 (depr. to 6/30/97). $1,800 x 1/6 =
     $300 (depr. for July and August). $7,200 + $300 = $7,500 (accumulated depreciation).

# CHAPTER 12

# STOCKHOLDERS' EQUITY: CLASSES OF CAPITAL STOCK

## Learning Objectives

1. *State the advantages and disadvantages of the corporate form of business.*
2. *List the values commonly associated with capital stock and give their definitions.*
3. *List the various kinds of stock and describe the differences between them.*
4. *Present in proper form the stockholders' equity section of a balance sheet.*
5. *Account for the issuances of stock for cash and other assets.*
6. *Determine book values of both preferred and common stock.*
7. *Analyze and use the financial results — return on average common stockholders' equity.*

## REFERENCE OUTLINE

---

## CHAPTER OUTLINE

---

THE CORPORATION
1. A corporation is an entity recognized by law as possessing an existence separate and distinct from its owners — it is a separate legal entity.
   a. Is endowed with many of the rights and obligations possessed by persons.
   b. Can enter into contracts in its own name; buy, sell, or hold property; borrow money; hire and fire employees; and sue and be sued.

*Learning Objective 1:*
*State the advantages and disadvantages of the corporate form of business.*

ADVANTAGES OF THE CORPORATE FORM OF BUSINESS
2. Advantages of corporations include:
   a. Ownership is easily transferred on a stock exchange, where owners cannot usually dictate to whom shares can or cannot be sold.
   b. Stockholders have limited liability and are not personally responsible for the corporation's debts.
   c. Since a corporation is a legal entity separate and distinct from the owners, the death of a stockholder has no effect on the continuous existence of the corporation.
   d. A corporation raises capital easily by issuing shares of stock to many investors.
   e. Stockholders as owners do not usually operate the corporation; instead professional managers are employed.
   f. Owners do not have the power to bind the corporation to business contracts, thus preventing owners from jeopardizing other owners through poor decision making.

DISADVANTAGES OF THE CORPORATE FORM OF BUSINESS
3. Disadvantages of the corporation include:
   a. A corporation's net income is taxed twice —
      (1) Corporation is taxed once on its income.
      (2) Stockholders must include dividends on their individual tax returns.
   b. Corporations are subject to greater governmental regulations and control than are single proprietorships and partnerships.
   c. Corporate managers can be unfairly retained because they can use corporate funds to solicit votes from stockholders.
   d. Because creditors cannot look to the personal assets of stockholders for satisfaction of debts, the amount of creditor capital loaned to a corporation may be limited.

INCORPORATING
4. The precise requirements that must be met by the incorporators are enumerated in the various state acts.

a. The laws of each state view a corporation organized in that state as a domestic corporation, and a corporation organized in any other state as a foreign corporation.

ARTICLES OF INCORPORATION

5. Articles of incorporation comprise the application for the charter and include information regarding the types and amounts of stock to be issued.
   a. A charter is the contract between the state and the incorporators and their successors that permits them to operate as a corporation.
   b. Generally the following information is contained in the articles of incorporation:
      (1) Name of corporation.
      (2) Location of principal offices.
      (3) Purposes of business.
      (4) Number of shares of stock authorized, class or classes of shares, and voting and dividend rights of each class of shares.
      (5) Value of assets paid in by the original incorporators.
      (6) Limitations on authority of the management and owners of the corporation.

BYLAWS

6. The board of directors adopts bylaws, which are rules or regulations to govern the conduct of corporate affairs.
   a. The bylaws contain, along with other information, provisions for the following:
      (1) the place, date, and manner of calling the annual stockholders' meeting.
      (2) the number of directors and the method for electing them.
      (3) the duties and powers of the directors.
      (4) the method for selecting officers of the corporation.

ORGANIZATION COSTS

7. Costs of organizing a corporation, such as state incorporation fees and legal fees, should be debited to an Organization Costs account and reported on the balance sheet as an intangible asset.

DIRECTING THE CORPORATION

8. The corporation is managed through the delegation of authority in a line from the stockholders to the directors to the officers.
9. Stockholders do not have the right to participate actively in the management of the business unless they serve as directors and/or officers. However, they do have the following basic rights:
   a. Dispose of their shares of stock.
   b. Purchase new issues of stock of the class owned in proportion to their holdings at the new issue date. (This is the preemptive right.)
   c. Share in earnings when declared as dividends.
   d. Receive a proportionate share of undistributed assets in excess of creditors' claims at the time of liquidation.
   e. Share in management by voting at stockholders' meetings. This right may be signed over to another in a proxy.
10. The board of directors is elected by the stockholders. The board's duties include:
   a. Appointing administrative officers and delegating to them the execution of the policies established by the board.
   b. Authorizing contracts.
   c. Declaring dividends.
   d. Establishing executive salaries.
   e. Granting authorization to borrow money.

## DOCUMENTS, BOOKS, AND RECORDS RELATING TO CAPITAL STOCK

11. Numerous records and documents are related to capital stock. A stock certificate is a printed or engraved document serving as evidence of ownership of a certain number of shares of stock. When a stockholder sells stock, the stock certificate is cancelled, and a new one is issued to the new owner.

## STOCKHOLDERS' LEDGER

12. Corporations maintain a stockholders' ledger showing the number of shares of stock currently held by each stockholder. Corporations employ stock transfer agents, usually a bank or trust company, to transfer stock between buyers and sellers. For control purposes, stock transfer agents send new certificates to a stock registrar, usually another bank, that maintains separate records of the shares outstanding.

## THE MINUTES BOOK

13. A minutes book records actions taken at stockholders' and board of directors' meetings, such as declaration of dividends, and is the written authorization for borrowing funds or purchasing expensive assets. The minutes book contains a variety of data, including the following:

    *a.* A copy of the corporate charter.
    *b.* A copy of the bylaws.
    *c.* Dividends declared by the board of directors.
    *d.* Authorization for the acquisition of major assets.
    *e.* Authorization for borrowing.
    *f.* Authorization for increases or decreases in capital stock.

*Learning Objective 2:*
*List the values commonly associated with capital stock and give their definitions.*

## PAR VALUE AND NO-PAR CAPITAL STOCK

14. Each share of stock may or may not have a par or stated value attached to it.

## PAR VALUE STOCK

15. Par value is the arbitrary amount specified in the charter and assigned to each share and is the amount credited to the capital stock account for each share issued.

## NO-PAR STOCK WITH A STATED VALUE

16. Stated value is a value assigned to no-par value stock by the board of directors and is the amount credited to the capital stock account for each share issued.

## NO-PAR STOCK WITHOUT A STATED VALUE

17. No-par stock may be without a stated value, in which case the entire amount received is credited to the capital stock account.

## OTHER VALUES COMMONLY ASSOCIATED WITH CAPITAL STOCK

18. Besides par or stated value, there are several other values commonly associated with capital stock.

## MARKET VALUE

19. Market value is the price at which the shares are selling on the open market.

## BOOK VALUE

20. Book value is the amount per share that each stockholder would receive if the corporation were liquidated without incurring any further expenses and if assets were sold and liabilities liquidated at their recorded amounts.

## LIQUIDATION VALUE

21. Liquidation value is the amount a stockholder will receive if a corporation discontinues operations and liquidates by selling its assets, paying its liabilities, and distributing the remaining cash to stockholders.

## REDEMPTION VALUE

22. Redemption value is the amount at which the corporation will redeem preferred stock if it chooses to do so. This is the same as the call price.

*Learning Objective 3:*
*List the various kinds of stock and describe the differences between them.*

## CAPITAL STOCK AUTHORIZED AND OUTSTANDING

23. Capital stock authorized is the number of shares of stock the corporation is authorized to issue; the charter specifies the par value, if any, to be attached to each share.
    a. All authorized shares need not be issued immediately.
    b. Outstanding stock is stock that has been authorized, issued, and is currently held by stockholders.

## CLASSES OF CAPITAL STOCK

24. The two ordinary classes of stock that may be issued are common and preferred.

## COMMON STOCK

25. Common stock represents the residual equity in the corporation; all other claims must be settled before the common stockholders' claims.

## PREFERRED STOCK

26. Preferred stock may be preferred as to dividends and/or assets, and its dividend return is usually fixed.

## TYPES OF PREFERRED STOCK

27. Preferred stock has many features, including the following.
    a. Preferred as to dividends. If it is, it may be:
       (1) Cumulative or noncumulative.
           (a) Cumulative—all dividends in arrears must be paid before dividends can be paid on common.
           (b) Noncumulative—a dividend passed need not be paid in any future year.
    b. Preferred as to assets in the event of liquidation.
       (1) A liquidation value may be stated in the stock contract.
    c. Convertible or nonconvertible.
       (1) Stock may be convertible into specified numbers of shares of common stock at the stockholders' option.
    d. Callable if the issuing corporation can require the stockholders to surrender their shares, often at a call price.

## STOCK PREFERRED AS TO DIVIDENDS

28. Stock preferred as to dividends means that the preferred stockholders are entitled to a specified dividend per share before any dividend on common stock is paid.
    a. Noncumulative preferred stock's right to receive a dividend expires if the dividend is not declared.
    b. Cumulative preferred stock is preferred stock for which the right to receive a dividend accumulates if the dividend is not paid.
    c. Dividends in arrears are cumulative unpaid dividends; these are not shown as liabilities on the balance sheet because they are not legal liabilities until declared by the board of directors.

## STOCK PREFERRED AS TO ASSETS

29. Most preferred stock receives preference as to assets if the corporation is dissolved or liquidated.

## CONVERTIBLE PREFERRED STOCK

30. Convertible preferred stock is attractive because it allows stockholders to convert their shares into common stock of the issuing corporation.

## CALLABLE PREFERRED STOCK

31. Preferred stock may be callable at the option of the issuing corporation, which requires that the stockholders surrender their stock to the company if the option is exercised.

*Learning Objective 4:*
*Present in proper form the stockholders' equity section of a balance sheet.*

## BALANCE SHEET PRESENTATION OF STOCK

32. The two main elements of the stockholders' equity section of the corporation's balance sheet are: paid-in capital and retained earnings.
    a. Paid-in capital results from cash and other assets invested by owners.
    b. Retained earnings represents accumulated earnings and is increased by net income and decreased by a net loss and dividends declared and paid to stockholders.

*Learning Objective 5:*
*Account for the issuances of stock for cash and other assets.*

## STOCK ISSUANCES FOR CASH

33. When stock is issued for cash, the Cash account is debited. The account(s) credited depend on the issue price and whether the stock is par or no-par, with or without a stated value.

## ISSUANCE OF PAR VALUE STOCK FOR CASH

34. If the stock is par value, the credit to the stock account is at par value times the number of shares issued.
    a. If the issue price is above par value, the excess is credited to Paid-In Capital in Excess of Par Value.
    b. Paid-In Capital in Excess of Par Value is part of the paid-in capital contributed by the stockholders and is shown separately in the stockholders' equity section of the balance sheet for each class of stock issued.

## ISSUANCE OF NO-PAR, STATED VALUE STOCK FOR CASH

35. When stock with no-par value but with stated value is issued, the credit to the stock account is at stated value times the number of shares issued.
    a. If the issue price is above stated value, the excess is credited to Paid-In Capital in Excess of Stated Value.
    b. The stated or legal capital of a corporation issuing stated value shares is generally equal to the aggregate of the stated value of the shares issued.

## ISSUANCE OF NO-PAR STOCK WITHOUT A STATED VALUE FOR CASH

36. When stock without par value or stated value is issued, the entire amount received is credited to the capital stock account.

## CAPITAL STOCK ISSUED FOR PROPERTY OR SERVICES

37. When stock is issued for property or services, it is recorded at the fair value of either the property or the services received, or the shares of stock issued, whichever is more clearly evident.

## BALANCE SHEET PRESENTATION OF PAID-IN CAPITAL IN EXCESS OF PAR (OR STATED) VALUE—COMMON OR PREFERRED

38. The amounts received in excess of stated or par value are carried in a separate stockholders' equity account as Paid-In Capital in Excess of Par (or Stated) Value—Common (or Preferred).

*Learning Objective 6:*
*Determine book values of both preferred and common stock.*

BOOK VALUE

39. Total book value is equal to stockholders' equity.
    a. Book value of preferred stock is equal to the liquidation value plus any dividends in arrears and/or currently payable. These dividends in arrears are expressed in per share terms.
    b. Book value of common stock is what remains after all amounts assignable to preferred stock issues are deducted from total stockholders' equity.

*Learning Objective 7:*
*Analyze and use the financial results – return on average common stockholders' equity.*

ANALYZING AND USING THE FINANCIAL RESULTS—RETURN ON AVERAGE COMMON STOCKHOLDERS' EQUITY

40. The return on average common stockholders' equity equals net income available to common stock divided by average common stockholders' equity. If preferred stock is outstanding, the numerator is net income minus the annual preferred dividend, and the denominator is the average total book value of common stock. If no preferred stock is outstanding, the numerator is net income and the denominator is average stockholders' equity.

41. The return on average common stockholders' equity is an important measure of the income-producing ability of the company.

---

## DEMONSTRATION PROBLEM

---

On January 6 of the current year, Brooks Corporation was organized with an authorization of 25,000 shares of 7 percent cumulative preferred stock, $60 par, and 50,000 shares of $30 par common stock.

The following selected transactions occurred during the first year of operations:

Jan. 31: Issued 200 shares of preferred stock to an attorney in payment of a bill for $12,000 of legal fees for organizing the corporation.

Jan. 31: Issued 10,000 shares of common stock at par for cash.

Feb. 8: Issued 20,000 shares of common stock in exchange for land, buildings, equipment, and patents with fair market values of $153,600, $302,400, $114,000, and $40,800, respectively.

Required:
a. Record general journal entries for the above transactions.
b. Prepare the stockholders' equity section of the balance sheet as of December 31, the end of the current year. A loss of $13,080 was incurred for the year.

*a.*

## GENERAL JOURNAL

| Date | | Account Titles and Explanation | Post. Ref. | Debit | | | Credit | | |
|------|--|-------------------------------|-----------|-------|--|--|--------|--|--|
| | | | | | | | | | |
| | | | | | | | | | |
| | | | | | | | | | |
| | | | | | | | | | |
| | | | | | | | | | |
| | | | | | | | | | |
| | | | | | | | | | |
| | | | | | | | | | |
| | | | | | | | | | |
| | | | | | | | | | |
| | | | | | | | | | |
| | | | | | | | | | |
| | | | | | | | | | |
| | | | | | | | | | |
| | | | | | | | | | |
| | | | | | | | | | |
| | | | | | | | | | |
| | | | | | | | | | |
| | | | | | | | | | |
| | | | | | | | | | |
| | | | | | | | | | |
| | | | | | | | | | |
| | | | | | | | | | |
| | | | | | | | | | |
| | | | | | | | | | |

*b.* _____

| | | | | | | | | | |
|--|--|--|--|--|--|--|--|--|--|
| | | | | | | | | | |
| | | | | | | | | | |
| | | | | | | | | | |
| | | | | | | | | | |
| | | | | | | | | | |
| | | | | | | | | | |
| | | | | | | | | | |
| | | | | | | | | | |
| | | | | | | | | | |

## SOLUTION TO DEMONSTRATION PROBLEM

### BROOKS CORPORATION

a.

| | | | |
|---|---|---|---|
| Jan. 31 | Organization Costs ....................................................... | 12,000 | |
| | Preferred Stock, 7 percent ....................................... | | 12,000 |
| | (200 shares @ $60) | | |

| | | | |
|---|---|---|---|
| Jan. 31 | Cash ......................................................................... | 300,000 | |
| | Common Stock ......................................................... | | 300,000 |
| | (10,000 shares @ $30) | | |

| | | | |
|---|---|---|---|
| Feb. 8 | Land ......................................................................... | 153,600 | |
| | Buildings .................................................................. | 302,400 | |
| | Equipment ................................................................ | 114,000 | |
| | Patents ..................................................................... | 40,800 | |
| | Common Stock (20,000 shares @ $30) ..................... | | 600,000 |
| | Paid-In Capital in Excess of Par Value — Common | | 10,800 |

b. *Stockholders' equity*
Paid-in capital:

| | | | |
|---|---|---|---|
| Preferred stock, $60 par value, 7 percent cumulative, (25,000 shares authorized, 200 shares issued and outstanding) | | | $ 12,000 |
| Common stock, $30 par (50,000 shares authorized, 30,000 shares issued and outstanding) ........................................ | $900,000 | | |
| Paid-in capital in excess of par value — common ........................ | 10,800 | | 910,800 |
| Total paid-in capital ................................................................... | | | $922,800 |
| Retained earnings ....................................................................... | | | (13,080) |
| Total stockholders' equity ..................................................... | | | $909,720 |

## MATCHING

Referring to the terms listed below, place the appropriate letter next to the corresponding description.

*a.* Call premium (on preferred stock)
*b.* Liquidation value
*c.* Cumulative preferred stock
*d.* Organization costs
*e.* Common stock
*f.* Code of regulations (bylaws)
*g.* Minutes book
*h.* Capital stock authorized
*i.* Preemptive right
*j.* Par value

_____ 1. The stock that a corporation is entitled to issue as designated in its charter.

_____ 2. An intangible asset consisting of the various costs incurred in bringing a corporation into existence.

_____ 3. The record book in which actions taken at a stockholders' and board of directors' meetings are recorded.

_____ 4. The right to receive a basic dividend each year accumulates if not paid.

_____ 5. The right of stockholders to subscribe to additional shares of the same class of stock they hold in any subsequent issuance of new shares.

_____ 6. Shares of stock representing the residual equity in the corporation.

_____ 7. The difference between the amount at which a corporation may call its preferred stock for redemption and the par value of the stock.

_____ 8. A set of rules or regulations adopted by the board of directors of a corporation to govern the conduct of corporate affairs within the general laws of the state and the policies and purposes stated or implied in the corporate charter.

_____ 9. The amount to be paid per share of preferred stock upon liquidation of the corporation.

_____ 10. An arbitrary amount assigned to each share of a given class of stock and printed on the stock certificate.

## COMPLETION AND EXERCISES

1. How can a corporation determine the number of shares of stock outstanding? _____

_____

_____

2. A corporation may issue preferred stock for the following reasons:

   *a.* _____

   *b.* _____

   *c.* _____

3. The evidence of ownership issued to a stockholder is called a _____ _____ .

4. Most state corporation laws require a minimum of _____ incorporators.

5. The law of each state views a corporation in that state as a _____ corporation and a corporation organized in any other state as a _____ corporation.

6. The _____ is the contract between the state and the incorporators and their successors.

7. The application for a charter is known as the _____ _____ _____ .

8. When does a corporation come into existence?

_____

_____

9. Organization costs are classified on the balance sheet as an _____ asset.

10. What is the source of the authority of the board of directors?

_____

11. A _____ is a document of authority, signed by the stockholder, giving another person the authority to vote the stockholders' shares.

12. From whom do the officers of a corporation derive their authority?

_____

13. What is another name for the code of regulations of a corporation?

_____

14. What is meant by capital stock authorized?

_____

_____

_____

15. What is meant by capital stock outstanding?

_____

_____

16. What are the two ordinary classes of capital stock that may be issued by a corporation?

a. _____

b. _____

17. What is meant when common stock is referred to as the residual equity in a corporation?

_____

_____

18. What is the meaning of par value?

_____

_____

_____

19. What are the advantages of the corporate form of business?

a. _____

b. _____

c. _____

d. _____

e. _____

20. A corporation is an artificial, invisible, intangible being or person created by _____.

21. The balance sheet of May 31 of the Caldwell Corporation is as follows (no dividends are in arrears or are currently payable):

| | | |
|---|---|---|
| Total assets | | $395,280 |
| Liabilities | | $125,280 |
| Preferred stock (500 shares outstanding, 10 percent non-cumulative $125 par value, $125 liquidation value) | $ 62,500 | |
| Common stock (10,000 shares outstanding, no-par value) | 156,250 | |
| Retained earnings | 51,250 | 270,000 |
| Total liabilities and stockholders' equity | | $395,280 |

a. The book value of the preferred stock is $ _____.

b. The book value of the common stock is $ _____.

22. A company issued 100 shares of $150 par value common stock for a parcel of land. No cash price was fixed for the land, but similar parcels in the vicinity had recently sold for $18,000. Prepare the entry for this stock issuance.

| | | Debit | Credit |
|---|---|---|---|
| | | | |
| | | | |
| | | | |
| | | | |
| | | | |

23. If a corporation is obligated to pay arrearages for prior years on preferred stock before paying dividends to the common stockholders, the preferred stock would be called

_____ preferred stock.

24. On May 4, a corporation issued for cash 200,000 shares of its no-par common stock at $2.10 per share. Prepare the entry for the sale under each of the unrelated assumptions:

a. The common stock has no stated or legal value assigned to it.

b. The board voted to place a one dollar per share stated value on the no-par stock.

| Date | Account Titles and Explanation | Post. Ref. | Debit | Credit |
|---|---|---|---|---|
| a. | | | | |
| | | | | |
| | | | | |
| b. | | | | |
| | | | | |
| | | | | |

25. What is the amount of the credit to the capital stock account for a corporation issuing capital stock without par or stated value?

_____

_____

26. Give the entries if a corporation issued 2,000 shares of $36 par value common stock for $42 a share and if it issued on the same date 1,000 shares of stock in exchange for land.

| | | | | | | | | | | | |
|---|---|---|---|---|---|---|---|---|---|---|---|
| | | | | | | | | | | | |
| | | | | | | | | | | | |
| | | | | | | | | | | | |
| | | | | | | | | | | | |
| | | | | | | | | | | | |
| | | | | | | | | | | | |
| | | | | | | | | | | | |
| | | | | | | | | | | | |
| | | | | | | | | | | | |
| | | | | | | | | | | | |

27. When property or services are received for capital stock, what value is placed on the exchange?

_____

_____

28. The _____ _____ contains supporting detail for the stock accounts contained in the general ledger.

29. The _____ _____ is a written record of the action taken at official meetings of the board of directors and at stockholders' meetings.

30. What is meant by the liquidation value of stock?

_____

_____

_____

31. When only common stock is outstanding, how is book value per share calculated?

_____

_____

32. From the following information, compute the book value per share of both preferred and common stock.

Preferred stock, 6 percent cumulative, par value $60; liquidation value $60
1,000 shares authorized, issued and outstanding ............................................. $ 60,000
Common stock, without par or stated value; 20,000 shares authorized,
18,000 shares issued and outstanding ................................................ 151,200
Retained earnings ....................................................................................... 112,800
Total stockholders' equity .......................................................................... $324,000

Note: Two years dividends are in arrears on the preferred stock, including those for the current year.

|  | Total | | | Per Share | | |
|---|---|---|---|---|---|---|
|  |  |  |  |  |  |  |
|  |  |  |  |  |  |  |
|  |  |  |  |  |  |  |
|  |  |  |  |  |  |  |
|  |  |  |  |  |  |  |
|  |  |  |  |  |  |  |
|  |  |  |  |  |  |  |
|  |  |  |  |  |  |  |
|  |  |  |  |  |  |  |
|  |  |  |  |  |  |  |
|  |  |  |  |  |  |  |

## TRUE-FALSE QUESTIONS

Indicate whether each of the following statements is true or false by inserting a capital "T" or "F" in the blank space provided.

_____ 1. Shares of preferred stock and shares of common stock both represent ownership in a corporation, and both always confer the same rights and privileges.

_____ 2. A conversion of callable, convertible preferred stock can only occur if the holders of the stock have initiated the conversion.

_____ 3. Through the use of a proxy, a stockholder gives another person authority to vote his or her shares at a stockholders' meeting.

_____ 4. When a corporation liquidates, stockholders have the right to receive the undistributed assets that are in excess of the claims of creditors.

_____ 5. The application for a charter is known as a code of regulations.

_____ 6. Cash dividends received by a stockholder are normally taxable to the stockholder.

_____ 7. A corporation cannot borrow money in its own name, but must secure funds through the president.

_____ 8. The par value of a share of capital stock is no indication of the market value or of the book value of the share of stock.

_____ 9. The par value of a share of common stock must be $100.

_____ 10. The assignment by the board of directors of a stated value to each share of stock that is without par value results in the receipt of a uniform price per share for the stock.

_____ 11. Stockholders whose stock is preferred as to assets in the event of corporate liquidation are entitled to receive the par value of their shares before any amounts are distributed to creditors or common stockholders.

_____ 12. If one expected a business to have a very long life, one would prefer the corporate form of organization for an enterprise, rather than a partnership.

_____ 13. One may favor the corporate form of organization for a quite risky business enterprise primarily because of the ease with which the corporation's shares can be transferred.

_____ 14. A corporation may conduct business only in the state in which it is incorporated.

_____ 15. Items that may influence the selection of the state of incorporation include the powers granted a corporation, the taxes levied against it, and the reports required of it.

_____ 16. The assignment of a par value to each share of stock results in the receipt of a uniform price per share for the stock.

_____ 17. The issuance of par value stock at a price less than the par value may create a contingent liability on stockholders to creditors of the corporation.

_____ 18. When shares of stock are issued for equipment, the exchange may be recorded at the fair market value of the equipment.

_____ 19. The minutes book is a special journal containing the debit and credit entries for transactions authorized by the board of directors.

_____ 20. Issuing corporations are typically not directly involved in the daily buying and selling of their shares on organized stock exchanges.

_____ 21. The number of a corporation's authorized shares of stock may never exceed the number of its shares that are issued and outstanding.

_____ 22. When shares of stock are issued for property other than cash, the exchange cannot be recorded at the fair market value of the shares issued.

_____ 23. The limited liability feature of corporations may limit their ability to raise creditor capital.

_____ 24. A stock that is preferred as to dividends might not receive dividends in a period even though the common stockholders do.

_____ 25. Convertible preferred stock is always exchanged for common stock on a one-to-one ratio.

_____ 26. The life of a corporation may be perpetual, or its existence may be limited by its charter.

_____ 27. A corporation can buy, sell, or hold real or personal property.

_____ 28. It is often difficult to dispose of shares of capital stock, except for corporations whose stock is closely held.

_____ 29. Corporate existence is not affected by death, incapacity, or withdrawal of a stockholder.

_____ 30. Liquidation value is the amount at which a corporation has the right to redeem its preferred stock.

_____ 31. A corporation can sue and be sued.

_____ 32. Creditors of the corporation have a claim to the personal assets of stockholders if corporate assets are insufficient to satisfy their claims.

_____ 33. The rights of stockholders include the power to bind the corporation to contracts.

_____ 34. Return on Average Common Stockholders' Equity is an important measure of the income-producing ability of the corporation.

# MULTIPLE CHOICE QUESTIONS

For each of the following questions, indicate the best answer by circling the appropriate letter.

1. Which of the following is not an advantage of the corporate form of organization?
   A. Continuity of Life
   B. Government Supervision
   C. Separate Legal Entity
   D. No Mutual Agency

2. The amount per share that a corporation agrees to pay if it elects to call its stock for retirement is known as:
   A. Stated Value.
   B. Par Value.
   C. Market Price.
   D. Redemption Price.

3. Given the following information: Capital Stock, $12,000 ($12 par). Premium on Common Stock, $30,000, Retained Earnings, $60,000. Assuming only one class of stock, the book value per share is:
   A. $102
   B. $42
   C. $12
   D. $60
   E. None of the above.

4-5. Nova Corporation's balance sheet lists: 7 percent preferred stock, $450,000, Premium on preferred stock, $60,000, Common stock, $750,000, Discount on common stock, $30,000, and Retained Earnings, $180,000.

4. What is the amount of paid-in capital attributable to the preferred stock?
   A. $180,000
   B. $510,000
   C. $720,000
   D. $1,410,000

5. What is the amount of paid-in capital attributable to the common stock?
   A. $180,000
   B. $510,000
   C. $720,000
   D. $1,410,000

6-7. The Lee Corporation had the following two classes of capital stock outstanding as of December 31, 1999.

| | |
|---|---|
| 6 percent preferred, $150 par, 1,000 shares outstanding ................. | $150,000 |
| Common stock, $150 par, 5,000 shares outstanding ........................ | $750,000 |

On December 31, 1999, the Board of Directors declared $90,000 in cash dividends for 1999. Indicate the total dollar amount of the $90,000 that would go to preferred and common stock under each of the following independent cases:

6. If the preferred stock is noncumulative, the total to preferred is:
   A. $90,000
   B. $9,000
   C. $15,000
   D. $18,000
   E. None of the above

7. If the preferred stock is cumulative and dividends are in arrears since 1997, the total to preferred is:
   A. $45,000
   B. $18,000
   C. $27,000
   D. $9,000

---

## SOLUTIONS

### Matching

| | | | |
|---|---|---|---|
| 1. | h | 6. | e |
| 2. | d | 7. | a |
| 3. | g | 8. | f |
| 4. | c | 9. | b |
| 5. | i | 10. | j |

### Completion and Exercises

1. A corporation can determine the number of shares outstanding by summing the shares shown on the open stubs or stubs without certificates attached in the stock certificate book.
2. A company may issue preferred stock for the following reasons:
   a. To avoid the use of bonds that have fixed interest charges that must be paid regardless of the company's profitability.
   b. To avoid issuing so many additional shares of common stock that earnings per share will be less in the current year than in prior years.
   c. To avoid diluting the common stockholders' control of the corporation, since preferred stockholders have no voting rights.
3. stock certificate
4. three
5. domestic; foreign
6. charter
7. articles of incorporation
8. when the articles of incorporation are approved and the charter is granted
9. intangible
10. the stockholders
11. proxy
12. the board of directors
13. the bylaws
14. the number of shares and par value, if any, per share of each class of stock that the corporate charter will permit to be issued
15. the shares authorized, issued, and currently held by stockholders
16. (a) preferred stock; (b) common stock
17. This means that all other claims rank ahead of the claims of the common stockholders.
18. Par value is an arbitrarily assigned dollar amount appearing on stock certificates that serves as the basis for the credit to the capital stock account.
19. (a) transferable shares; (b) limited liability; (c) continuous existence; (d) opportunity to employ professional management (e) separation of owners and entity
20. law
21. a. Preferred stock
      Book value of $125 equals liquidation value since no preferred dividends are in arrears.

b. Common stock
   $270,000
   - 62,500
   $207,500 / 10,000 shares = $20.75

| 22. | Land ......................................................................................... | 18,000 | |
| | Common Stock .......................................................................... | | 15,000 |
| | Paid-In Capital in Excess of Par Value — Common Stock ....... | | 3,000 |

23. cumulative

| 24. a. | Cash ........................................................................................ | 420,000 | |
| | Common Stock .......................................................................... | | 420,000 |
| b. | Cash ........................................................................................ | 420,000 | |
| | Common Stock .......................................................................... | | 200,000 |
| | Paid-In Capital in Excess of Stated Value — Common ............ | | 220,000 |

25. The entire amount received for the stock.

| 26. | Cash ........................................................................................ | 84,000 | |
| | Common Stock .......................................................................... | | 72,000 |
| | Paid-In Capital in Excess of Par — Common ........................... | | 12,000 |
| | To record issuance of common stock. | | |
| | Land ....................................................................................... | 42,000 | |
| | Common Stock .......................................................................... | | 36,000 |
| | Paid-In Capital in Excess of Par — Common ........................... | | 6,000 |
| | To record issuance of common stock for land. | | |

27. The fair market value of the property or services received or of the stock issued, whichever is more clearly evident.

28. stockholders' ledger

29. minutes book

30. The liquidation value is the amount a stockholder would receive if a corporation were to discontinue operations and liquidate by selling its assets, paying its liabilities, and distributing the remaining cash among the stockholders.

31. Book value per share is calculated by dividing stockholders' equity by the number of shares outstanding.

32.

| | Total | Per Share |
|---|---|---|
| Total stockholders' equity ....................................................... | $324,000 | |
| Book value of preferred stock (1,000 shares): | | |
| Liquidation value ................................................................. $60,000 | | |
| Dividends (two years at $3,600) ....................................... 7,200 | 67,200 | $67.20 |
| Book value of common stock (18,000 shares) ....................... | $256,800 | $14.27 |

## True-False Questions

1. F  Shares of preferred stock and of common stock do not usually confer the same rights and privileges, although both represent ownership in the corporation.

2. F  A corporation can often force conversion of its preferred stock. If the market price of the preferred is largely a reflection of the market value of the common shares into which it can be converted, and if this market price is higher than the call price of the preferred, an investor would be foolish not to convert the preferred when it is called.

3. T  A proxy grants such authority.

4. T The stockholders do receive the undistributed assets that are in excess of creditors' claims.
5. F The application for a charter is known as the articles of incorporation.
6. T Stockholders are taxed on the dividends received in addition to the corporation's net income being subject to tax; this double taxation is one of the disadvantages of corporations.
7. F A corporation can borrow money in its own name.
8. T Par value is merely an arbitrary amount specified in the charter.
9. F Par value may be any amount.
10. F The assignment of a stated value to stock without par value results in a uniform amount per share being credited to the capital stock account, but shares issued at different times are still likely to be issued at different prices because of changing market conditions. Any excess over the stated value is credited to a paid-in-capital account.
11. F The claims of the creditors rank ahead of the claims of the stockholders, even those stockholders whose stock is preferred as to assets.
12. T Continuous existence is one of the main advantages of the corporation, not the partnership. The corporate form of business organization is better suited for businesses that are long-lived.
13. F Limited liability is the primary reason one would prefer the corporate form of business organization in a situation involving considerable risk
14. F A corporation is incorporated in only one state, but it need not restrict its business activities to that state.
15. T Such factors must be considered when deciding on the state of incorporation.
16. F The assignment of a par value to stock results in a uniform amount per share being credited to the capital stock account; but shares issued at different times are still likely to be issued at different prices because of changing market conditions. Any excess over the par value is credited to a paid-in capital account.
17. T Stock issued at a discount (at a price less than its par value) may create and carry a contingent liability on stockholders to creditors of the corporation for the amount of the discount.
18. T An exchange of shares of stock for property other than cash may be recorded at the fair market value of the property received if this value is more clearly evident than the value of the shares issued.
19. F The minutes book is not a journal, and the information contained in it is not in debit and credit entry form.
20. T These changes or trades are usually made by stockholders and other investors and do not directly involve the company.
21. F The number of authorized shares may exceed the number of shares issued and outstanding.
22. F An exchange of shares of stock for property other than cash may be recorded at the fair market value of the shares issued if this value is more clearly evident than the value of the property received.
23. T The limited liability feature may limit a corporation's ability to raise creditor capital.
24. F Holders of stock preferred as to dividends must receive dividends before common shareholders.
25. F The ratio may vary and is not always on a one-to-one basis.
26. T A corporation's life may be either unlimited or limited by its charter.
27. T A corporation may participate in all of these activities.
28. F Stock of a corporation is generally traded on a stock exchange, and there is usually easy transfer of ownership.

29. T  Because a corporation is a legal entity separate and distinct from the owners, it has continuous existence.

30. F  Redemption value is the amount at which preferred stock may be redeemed by the corporation. Liquidation value is the amount a stockholder will receive if a corporation goes out of business, sells its assets, pays its liabilities, and distributes the remaining cash among the stockholders.

31. T  A corporation is a separate legal entity and has many of the rights and obligations of a natural person.

32. F  Stockholders have limited liability and are not personally responsible for the corporation's debts.

33. F  Stockholders do not have the power to bind the corporation to business contracts.

34. T

## Multiple Choice Questions

1. B  Corporations are subject to greater supervision and regulation because they are created by law and are separate legal entities.

2. D  Redemption price is also known as the call price.

3. A  Adding the Capital Stock ($12,000) plus Premium on Common Stock ($30,000) plus Retained Earnings ($60,000) gives a total of $102,000. Dividing $102,000 by the 1,000 shares outstanding ($12,000/$12 par) gives a book value of $102.

4. B  The paid-in capital attributable to preferred stock is the total of the Preferred Stock account and the Premium on Preferred Stock account ($450,000 + $60,000). Retained earnings are not part of paid-in capital.

5. C  The paid-in capital attributable to common stock is the total of the Common Stock account ($750,000) less the Discount on Common Stock ($30,000) equals $720,000. Retained earnings are not part of paid-in capital.

6. B  Preferred stockholders would receive 6 percent x $150,000 = $9,000.

7. C  If the preferred stock is cumulative and dividends are in arrears since 1997, 3 years x $9,000 or $27,000 must first be paid to preferred stockholders before common stockholders would receive any dividends.

# CHAPTER 13

# CORPORATIONS: PAID-IN CAPITAL, RETAINED EARNINGS, DIVIDENDS, AND TREASURY STOCK

*Learning Objectives*

1. *Identify the different sources of paid-in capital and describe how to present them on a balance sheet.*
2. *Account for a cash dividend, a stock dividend, a stock split, and a retained earnings appropriation.*
3. *Account for the acquisition and reissuance of treasury stock.*
4. *Describe the proper accounting treatment of discontinued operations, extraordinary items, and changes in accounting principles.*
5. *Define prior period adjustments and show their proper presentation in the financial statements.*
6. *Analyze and use the financial results — earnings per share and price-earnings ratio.*

## REFERENCE OUTLINE

---

## CHAPTER OUTLINE

---

*Learning Objective 1:*
*Identify the different sources of paid-in capital and describe how to present them on a balance sheet.*

### PAID-IN (OR CONTRIBUTED) CAPITAL

1. Paid-in capital consists of the contributed capital of a corporation with separate accounts established for each source of paid-in capital.
2. Paid-in capital arises from sale of stock, stock dividends, treasury stock transactions, and donations.

### PAID-IN CAPITAL—STOCK DIVIDENDS

3. Paid-In Capital—Stock Dividends may be created when a corporation distributes additional shares of stock instead of cash to its present stockholders.

### PAID-IN CAPITAL—TREASURY STOCK TRANSACTIONS

4. Paid-In Capital—Treasury Stock Transactions results when a corporation reacquires shares of its own outstanding capital stock at one price and later reissues them at a higher price.

### PAID-IN CAPITAL—DONATIONS

5. Paid-In Capital—Donations results from the donation of assets to the corporation, such as a gift of land from a city for locating a company's plant in its community.

### RETAINED EARNINGS

6. Stockholders' equity generally consists of two elements: Paid-In Capital and Retained Earnings.
7. Retained earnings result from the difference between a corporation's net income earned from the date of incorporation to the present and the dividends declared during the same period.
   a. Net income increases retained earnings.
   b. Net losses reduce retained earnings.
   c. Dividends reduce retained earnings.
   d. A debit balance in Retained Earnings represents a deficit.

### PAID-IN CAPITAL AND RETAINED EARNINGS ON THE BALANCE SHEET

8. Unless the balance sheet is highly condensed, the details regarding Paid-In Capital are described, such as number of shares of stock authorized, issued, and outstanding and the sources of paid-in capital.

*Learning Objective 2:*
*Account for a cash dividend, a stock dividend, a stock split, and a retained earnings appropriation.*

### DIVIDENDS

9. Dividends are distributions of earnings made by a corporation to its stockholders.
   a. The declaration date is the date on which the board of directors declares the dividend. This date is recorded in the minutes book.
   b. The date of record is the date used to determine to whom the dividends will be paid.
   c. The date of payment is the date on which the actual payment is made.
   d. After original issuance, stock of a company is traded on secondary markets. Companies often keep database programs that keep up with these trades between investors. These programs are used to determine stockholders on the date of record.

## CASH DIVIDENDS

10. Cash is normally distributed, but other types of assets may be distributed.
    a. Dividends are generally distributed from retained earnings.
       (1) When the dividend is declared, Retained Earnings (or Dividends) is debited and Dividends Payable is credited.
       (2) When the dividend is paid, the payable is debited and the appropriate asset account (usually cash) is credited.
    b. After a cash dividend is declared and notice is given to stockholders, it cannot be rescinded unless all stockholders agree to such action.
    c. Companies try to maintain an established dividend level from year to year. Investors often interpret decreases in dividends as a sign that a company is not as profitable. This interpretation is not always an accurate one.

## STOCK DIVIDENDS

11. Stock dividends involve the distribution of additional shares of capital stock.
    a. Stock dividends have no effect on the total amount of stockholders' equity because retained earnings are decreased by the same amount that paid-in capital is increased.
    b. Stock dividends do not affect the individual stockholders' percentage of ownership in the corporation.
    c. Stock dividends are declared for several reasons, which include the following:
       (1) Retained earnings may have become large relative to total stockholders' equity, or the corporation may wish a larger permanent capitalization.
       (2) The firm may wish to decrease the market price of its shares.
       (3) The firm may wish to increase the number of shares outstanding.
       (4) The corporation may lack sufficient cash to pay a cash dividend, and a stock dividend is used to silence stockholders' demands for dividends.

12. A small stock dividend occurs when there is a distribution of less than 20 to 25 percent of the previously outstanding shares. To record the declaration of a small stock dividend:
    a. A Stock Dividend Distributable account is credited for the par or stated value, if any, of the shares or for the total amount of shares without par or stated value.
    b. A Paid-In Capital—Stock Dividends account is credited for any amount above par or stated value.
    c. The Retained Earnings account is debited for the total fair market value of the shares issued.
    d. When the dividend is issued, the Stock Dividend Distributable account is debited and a capital stock account is credited.
    e. The stock dividend distributable is part of the stockholders' equity.

13. A large stock dividend occurs when there is a distribution of shares greater than 20 to 25 percent of the previously outstanding shares. Par value per share is not changed.
    a. A large stock dividend has the purpose of causing a large reduction in the market price per share of outstanding stock.
    b. A large stock dividend is recorded at par or stated value.

## STOCK SPLITS

14. A stock split is a distribution of some multiple of outstanding shares (e.g., 2 for 1, 3 for 1, etc.) for which the corporation receives no assets.
    a. The purpose of a stock split is to reduce the market price per share of the outstanding stock.
    b. In the usual stock split, the number of shares outstanding is increased, while the par value per share is decreased.

## LEGALITY OF DIVIDENDS

15. The legality of a dividend generally depends on the amount of retained earnings available for dividends.

## LIQUIDATING DIVIDENDS

16. Dividends from contributed capital, called liquidating dividends, are allowed in certain cases.

## RETAINED EARNINGS APPROPRIATIONS

17. A retained earnings appropriation represents a segregation of retained earnings.
    a. An appropriation is created—
       (1) By the board of directors, voluntarily or in accordance with the provisions of certain contracts.
       (2) To restrict the distribution of retained earnings as dividends because of the need to reinvest earnings or the need to fulfill an expected obligation.
       (3) By debiting Retained Earnings and crediting an appropriately titled appropriation account.
    b. Appropriations are usually returned intact to Retained Earnings when their purpose has been satisfied.

## RETAINED EARNINGS APPROPRIATIONS ON THE BALANCE SHEET

18. The appropriations are shown in the balance sheet in the stockholders' equity section as a part of total retained earnings.
    a. Rather than establishing a separate ledger account for retained earnings appropriations, footnote explanations often are used.
    b. Creation of a retained earnings appropriation does not reduce stockholders' equity; it only restricts a portion of retained earnings for specific reasons.

## STATEMENT OF RETAINED EARNINGS

19. The statement of retained earnings is a formal statement showing net income or loss, dividends, and appropriations that changed the retained earnings balance.

## STATEMENT OF STOCKHOLDERS' EQUITY

20. Corporations usually include these four financial statements in their annual reports:
    a. Balance sheet
    b. Income statement
    c. Statement of stockholders' equity (in place of a statement of retained earnings)
    d. Statement of cash flows
21. A statement of stockholders' equity summarizes the transactions affecting the accounts in the stockholders' equity section of the balance sheet during a stated period of time.

*Learning Objective 3:*
*Account for the acquisition and reissuance of treasury stock.*

## TREASURY STOCK

22. Treasury stock is capital stock that has been issued and then reacquired by the issuing corporation. It has not been canceled and may be reissued.
    a. Treasury stock may be reacquired by purchase or through donation by stockholders.
    b. Dividends are not paid on treasury stock, nor is the stock voting stock.
    c. In many states the cost of treasury stock may not exceed the amount of retained earnings at the date the shares are reacquired.
       (1) This law protects creditors by preventing the corporation from using funds to reacquire their own stock instead of paying its debts when the corporation is in financial difficulty.
       (2) In these states, an amount of retained earnings equal to the cost of the treasury stock is legally unavailable for dividends until the stock is reissued.

## ACQUISITION AND REISSUANCE OF TREASURY STOCK

23. When outstanding shares are acquired by purchase, a treasury stock account is debited for the cost of the shares.
24. Reissues are credited to a treasury stock account.
   a. If the reissue price is above cost, the difference is credited to Paid-In Capital— Common (Preferred) Treasury Stock Transactions.
   b. If the reissue price is less than cost, the difference is debited to Paid-In Capital— Common (Preferred) Treasury Stock Transactions if it contains a credit balance; otherwise, it is debited to Retained Earnings.
25. When outstanding shares are acquired by donation, only a memo entry is made. When the shares are later sold, the credit is to Paid-in-Capital— Donations.

## TREASURY STOCK ON THE BALANCE SHEET
26. Treasury stock is shown in the balance sheet at cost and as a deduction from the sum of total paid-in capital and retained earnings.

## STOCKHOLDERS' EQUITY ON THE BALANCE SHEET
27. The stockholders' equity section of the balance sheet shows the following:
   a. Amount of capital assigned to shares outstanding.
   b. Capital contributed for outstanding shares in addition to that assigned to the shares.
   c. Other forms of paid-in capital.
   d. Retained earnings, appropriated and unappropriated.

*Learning Objective 4:*
*Describe the proper accounting treatment of discontinued operations, extraordinary items, and changes in accounting principles.*

## NET INCOME—INCLUSIONS AND EXCLUSIONS
28. The net income for a period includes discontinued operations, the net tax effect of extraordinary items, and the cumulative effects on prior years' earnings of an accounting change. Prior period adjustments are adjustments to retained earnings and are not a factor in determining net income.

## DISCONTINUED OPERATIONS
29. A discontinued operation occurs when a business segment, usually unprofitable, is sold or abandoned.
   a. Information regarding a discontinued segment is shown in a special section of the income statement.
   b. The income or loss, net of tax effect, from the segment's operations for the portion of the current year before it was discontinued is shown.
   c. The gain or loss, net of tax effect, on disposal of the segment is shown.

## EXTRAORDINARY ITEMS
30. Extraordinary items are gains or losses that are unusual in nature and that occur infrequently. They are to be reported, net of their tax effects, if any, in the income statement. A common cause of an extraordinary gain is the early voluntary retirement of debt.

## CHANGES IN ACCOUNTING PRINCIPLE
31. Changes in accounting principle are changes in accounting methods, such as a change from FIFO to LIFO. The cumulative effects on prior years' income (net of tax) must be shown in the income statement.

*Learning Objective 5:*
*Define prior period adjustments and show their proper presentation in the financial statements.*

## PRIOR PERIOD ADJUSTMENTS
32. Prior period adjustments consist almost entirely of corrections of errors in previously published financial statements. Corrections of these errors are to be reported net of their

tax effects, if any, in the statement of retained earnings as adjustments to the beginning retained earnings balance.

ACCOUNTING FOR TAX EFFECTS

33. Items shown as discontinued operations, extraordinary items, changes in accounting principle, and prior period adjustments are shown net of their tax effects according to *FASB Statement No. 96.*

*Learning Objective 6:*
*Analyze and use the financial results – earnings per share and price-earnings ratio.*

ANALYZING AND USING THE FINANCIAL RESULTS—EARNINGS PER SHARE AND PRICE-EARNINGS RATIO

34. Earnings per share is calculated only for common shares.
   *a.* Earnings per share (EPS) is calculated as income available to common stockholders divided by the weighted-average number of common shares outstanding.
   *b.* Income available to common stockholders is net income less any dividends on preferred stock.
   *c.* The regular normal preferred dividend (not a dividend in arrears, however) is deducted to arrive at income available to common stockholders, whether or not declared, but only declared dividends are deducted on noncumulative preferred stock.
   *d.* Earnings per share is calculated for major categories of income, such as income from continuing operations, discontinued operations, extraordinary items, and accounting changes.

35. The price-earnings ratio equals the current market price per share of common stock divided by earnings per share. The price-earnings ratio provides an index on whether a stock is relatively cheap or expensive compared to other stocks.

---

### DEMONSTRATION PROBLEM

The following entries represent selected transactions that occurred during the year for Hynes Company.

Jan. 12   Purchased 2,000 shares of the company's own common stock at $36. There were 45,000 shares of $20 par common stock outstanding prior to the 2,000 share purchase.

Mar. 5   The board of directors declared a $10 per share semiannual dividend on the 5,000 shares of preferred stock and $4 per share dividend on the common stock to stockholders of record on March 15, payable on March 25.

Mar. 25   Paid the cash dividends.

May 10   Received cash for the sale of 700 shares of treasury stock at $42.

Sept. 5   The board of directors again declared $10 per share dividend on the outstanding preferred stock and $6 per share dividend on the common stock. The board also voted a 4 percent common stock dividend on the common stock outstanding. The fair market value of the common stock to be issued is estimated at $32 per share. The date of record for all dividends is October 1, and the date of payment is October 10.

Oct. 10   Paid the cash dividends and issued the stock certificates for the common stock dividend.

Required: Prepare the necessary journal entries to record the above transactions.

| Date | Account Titles and Explanation | Post. Ref. | Debit | Credit |
|------|-------------------------------|------------|-------|--------|
|  |  |  |  |  |
|  |  |  |  |  |
|  |  |  |  |  |
|  |  |  |  |  |
|  |  |  |  |  |
|  |  |  |  |  |
|  |  |  |  |  |
|  |  |  |  |  |
|  |  |  |  |  |
|  |  |  |  |  |
|  |  |  |  |  |
|  |  |  |  |  |
|  |  |  |  |  |
|  |  |  |  |  |
|  |  |  |  |  |
|  |  |  |  |  |
|  |  |  |  |  |
|  |  |  |  |  |
|  |  |  |  |  |
|  |  |  |  |  |
|  |  |  |  |  |
|  |  |  |  |  |
|  |  |  |  |  |
|  |  |  |  |  |
|  |  |  |  |  |
|  |  |  |  |  |
|  |  |  |  |  |
|  |  |  |  |  |
|  |  |  |  |  |
|  |  |  |  |  |
|  |  |  |  |  |
|  |  |  |  |  |
|  |  |  |  |  |
|  |  |  |  |  |
|  |  |  |  |  |
|  |  |  |  |  |
|  |  |  |  |  |
|  |  |  |  |  |
|  |  |  |  |  |
|  |  |  |  |  |
|  |  |  |  |  |
|  |  |  |  |  |
|  |  |  |  |  |
|  |  |  |  |  |

## HYNES COMPANY

| | | | |
|---|---|---|---|
| January 12 | Treasury Stock—Common (2,000 x $36) ................................. | 72,000 | |
| | Cash ......................................................................................... | | 72,000 |
| | | | |
| March 5 | Retained Earnings .................................................................. | 222,000 | |
| | Dividends Payable ............................................................. | | 222,000 |
| | $10 x 5,000 shares = $ 50,000 | | |
| | $4 x 43,000 shares = <u>172,000</u> | | |
| | <u>$222,000</u> | | |
| | | | |
| March 25 | Dividends Payable ................................................................. | 222,000 | |
| | Cash ......................................................................................... | | 222,000 |
| | | | |
| May 10 | Cash ......................................................................................... | 29,400 | |
| | Paid-In Capital—Common Treasury Stock Transactions | | 4,200 |
| | Treasury Stock—Common ................................................ | | 25,200 |
| Sept. 5 | Retained Earnings .................................................................. | 312,200 | |
| | Dividends Payable ............................................................. | | 312,200 |
| | $10 x 5,000 shares = $ 50,000 | | |
| | $6 x 43,700 shares = <u>262,200</u> | | |
| | <u>$312,200</u> | | |
| | | | |
| | Retained Earnings (1,748 shares x $32) ................................. | 55,936 | |
| | Stock Dividend Distributable—Common (1,748 x $20) . | | 34,960 |
| | Paid-in Capital—Stock Dividends (1,748 x $12) ............. | | 20,976 |
| | 43,700 x 4% = 1,748 shares | | |
| | | | |
| Oct. 10 | Dividends Payable ................................................................. | 312,200 | |
| | Cash ......................................................................................... | | 312,200 |
| | | | |
| | Stock Dividend Distributable—Common ........................... | 34,960 | |
| | Common Stock ................................................................... | | 34,960 |

# MATCHING

Referring to the terms listed below, place the appropriate letter next to the corresponding description.

a. Liquidating dividends
b. Extraordinary items
c. Treasury stock
d. Net-of-tax effect
e. Date of declaration of dividends

f. Stock dividends
g. Appropriation of retained earnings
h. Paid-in capital — treasury stock transactions
i. Prior period adjustments

j. Stock dividend distributable
k. Common stock
l. Date of record
m. Price-earnings ratio

_____ 1. An account created as a voluntary or contractual restriction on retained earnings and designed to inform readers of the existence of the restriction.

_____ 2. Dividends that are a return of contributed capital, not a distribution to be charged to retained earnings.

_____ 3. An account created when a corporation acquires shares of its own outstanding capital stock at one price and later reissues them at a higher price.

_____ 4. The date on which the board of directors formally states the intention of the corporation to pay a dividend.

_____ 5. Material adjustments that have an income or loss effect and result from accounting errors made in prior accounting periods.

_____ 6. A dividend payable in additional shares of the declaring corporation's stock.

_____ 7. Used for discontinued operations, extraordinary items, prior period adjustments, and accounting changes whereby items are shown at the dollar amounts remaining after deducting the effects on such items of income tax obligations payable currently.

_____ 8. Shares of capital stock issued and reacquired by the issuing corporation that have not been formally canceled or retired and are available for reissue.

_____ 9. Gains and losses that are unusual in nature and nonrecurring.

_____ 10. A stockholders' equity account credited for the par or stated value of the shares to be distributed when a stock dividend is declared.

_____ 11. Current market price per share of common stock divided by earnings per share.

# COMPLETION AND EXERCISES

1. A corporation has $200,000 of common stock ($20 par) outstanding. In July a stock dividend of one share for each five shares was issued. In November of the same year a 40 cent cash dividend per share is paid to the stockholders. The total amount of cash dividends paid to the stockholders is _____.

2. A company was authorized to issue 3,000 shares of no-par value common stock for which the directors voted to assign a stated value of $20 per share. In addition, the following transactions occurred for which you are asked to prepare journal entries.

   May 1  Received a donation of 400 shares of the company's stock.
   10  Reacquired 100 shares of its stock at $24 per share. These shares were originally issued at $22 per share.
   20  Sold the donated treasury stock for $34 per share.
   28  Sold, for $30 per share, 70 shares of the treasury stock reacquired May 10.

| Date | Account Titles and Explanation | Post. Ref. | Debit | Credit |
|------|-------------------------------|------------|-------|--------|
|      |                               |            |       |        |
|      |                               |            |       |        |
|      |                               |            |       |        |
|      |                               |            |       |        |
|      |                               |            |       |        |
|      |                               |            |       |        |
|      |                               |            |       |        |
|      |                               |            |       |        |
|      |                               |            |       |        |
|      |                               |            |       |        |
|      |                               |            |       |        |
|      |                               |            |       |        |

3. The date of _____ is established by the board to determine which individual stockholders are entitled to any dividends that have been declared.

4. When a corporation reacquires some of its own previously issued and fully paid stock, which it does not cancel or reissue, such stock is termed _____ stock.

5. The periodic payments made by a corporation to its stockholders are known as _____.

6. The _____ value is the price at which a share of stock is bought or sold at a particular moment.

7. What is treasury stock?

_____

_____

_____

8. When treasury stock is reissued, the excess of reissue price over cost is credited to ____

_____

_____

9. A separate paid-in capital account is used for each _____ of capital.

10. A liquidating dividend returns a portion of the corporation's _____ capital to its stockholders.

11. An appropriation of retained earnings does not involve segregating a sum of _____.

12. The statement that summarizes part of the change in stockholders' equity (that part brought about by net income and the payment of dividends) is called the _____ _____ _____ _____.

13. Dividends paid in cash are usually debited to _____ _____.

14. What effect do stock dividends have on the total amount of stockholders' equity?

_____

_____

_____

15. When a corporation receives assets as donated capital, at what amount is the transaction recorded?

_____

16. Differentiate between small stock dividends and large stock dividends and the value used in recording each type of dividend.

_____

_____

_____

_____

17. *a.* A corporation that is being sued wishes to establish a retained earnings appropriation for $100,000. Show the required entry.

| Date | Account Titles and Explanation | Post. Ref. | Debit | Credit |
|------|-------------------------------|------------|-------|--------|
|      |                               |            |       |        |
|      |                               |            |       |        |

*b.* If the final judgment is for $50,000, show the entries for paying the judgment and closing the appropriation.

| Date | Account Titles and Explanation | Post. Ref. | Debit | Credit |
|------|-------------------------------|------------|-------|--------|
|      |                               |            |       |        |
|      |                               |            |       |        |
|      |                               |            |       |        |
|      |                               |            |       |        |
|      |                               |            |       |        |

18. What are the two major elements of stockholders' equity in a corporation?

_____

19. When the Retained Earnings account has a debit balance it is called a _____.

20. What is the purpose of creating a retained earnings appropriation?

_____

_____

_____

21. On January 1, 1999, the Appropriation for Plant Expansion and Retained Earnings accounts for Southeast, Inc., appeared as follows:

| | |
|---|---|
| Appropriation for Plant Expansion ................................................................... | $ 108,000 |
| Retained Earnings ............................................................................................... | 1,140,000 |

The essential facts that related to retained earnings during the year are as follows:

| | |
|---|---|
| Cash dividends declared ..................................................................................... | $204,000 |
| Increase in appropriation for plant expansion ............................................. | 60,000 |
| Net income for year ............................................................................................ | 492,000 |
| Stock dividends declared ................................................................................... | 228,000 |

Prepare a statement of retained earnings for the current year. (Use the form on the next page.)

22. Prepare the necessary general journal entries required in the following transactions of Jackson Company:
   a. Increased the retained earnings appropriation for plant expansion by $10,000.
   b. The Board of Directors declared a regular quarterly dividend of $5 per share. 12,000 shares have been issued but 2,000 shares have been acquired as treasury stock and are still retained.
   c. The dividends were paid.
   d. The par value per share of the common stock outstanding was reduced from $50 par to $25; each stockholder received two new shares for each old share held.

| | | | | | | | | | |
|---|---|---|---|---|---|---|---|---|---|
| | | | | | | | | | |
| | | | | | | | | | |
| | | | | | | | | | |
| | | | | | | | | | |
| | | | | | | | | | |
| | | | | | | | | | |
| | | | | | | | | | |
| | | | | | | | | | |
| | | | | | | | | | |
| | | | | | | | | | |
| | | | | | | | | | |
| | | | | | | | | | |

23. An item that has a material income or loss effect and is unusual and nonrecurring is called an _____ _____ and is reported in the _____ _____ net of its _____ _____.

24. A material adjustment that is characterized primarily as a correction of an error in a previously published financial statement is called a _____ _____ _____. It is reported in the _____ _____ _____ _____, net of its _____ _____.

25. Changes in accounting principle are changes in _____ _____, which are reported in the _____ _____, net of their tax effects.

Paper for Question 21

26. Whether an item is unusual and nonrecurring is to be determined by reference to the

_____ in which the firm operates. Thus, a loss on the sale of a plant asset

probably _____ (would/would not) be classified as an extraordinary item.

27. From the following information on the Gregory Corporation, prepare an income statement for the year 1999.

| | |
|---|---|
| Expenses (not including federal income taxes) .................... | $25,000,000 |
| Revenues ................................................................................ | 29,000,000 |
| Loss from earthquake ............................................................ | 540,000 |

Assume a 50 percent federal income tax rate. The earthquake causing the loss was the first experienced in the area in which the company operates.

| | | | | | | | |
|---|---|---|---|---|---|---|---|
| | | | | | | | |
| | | | | | | | |
| | | | | | | | |
| | | | | | | | |
| | | | | | | | |
| | | | | | | | |
| | | | | | | | |
| | | | | | | | |

28. From the following information pertaining to Klein Corporation, prepare the stockholders' equity section of the balance sheet. The information is as of December 31, 1999.

| | |
|---|---|
| Total retained earnings ........................................................... | $606,000 |
| Preferred stock—$60 par value; authorized 5,000 shares; issued and outstanding 3,000 shares | |
| Common stock—$6 par value; 1,000,000 shares authorized; 600,000 shares issued | |
| Retained earnings appropriated for pending litigation ..... | $150,000 |
| Cost of treasury stock held—common ................................. | $108,000 |
| Number of shares of treasury stock held ........................... | 15,000   shares |
| Paid-in capital in excess of par value—common ............... | $810,000 |
| Paid-in capital from treasury stock transactions ................ | $ 30,000 |
| Paid-in capital from stock dividend ..................................... | $396,000 |

(Use the form on the next page.)

|  |  |  |  |  |  |  |  |  |  |
|---|---|---|---|---|---|---|---|---|---|
|  |  |  |  |  |  |  |  |  |  |
|  |  |  |  |  |  |  |  |  |  |
|  |  |  |  |  |  |  |  |  |  |
|  |  |  |  |  |  |  |  |  |  |
|  |  |  |  |  |  |  |  |  |  |
|  |  |  |  |  |  |  |  |  |  |
|  |  |  |  |  |  |  |  |  |  |
|  |  |  |  |  |  |  |  |  |  |
|  |  |  |  |  |  |  |  |  |  |
|  |  |  |  |  |  |  |  |  |  |
|  |  |  |  |  |  |  |  |  |  |
|  |  |  |  |  |  |  |  |  |  |
|  |  |  |  |  |  |  |  |  |  |
|  |  |  |  |  |  |  |  |  |  |
|  |  |  |  |  |  |  |  |  |  |
|  |  |  |  |  |  |  |  |  |  |
|  |  |  |  |  |  |  |  |  |  |
|  |  |  |  |  |  |  |  |  |  |
|  |  |  |  |  |  |  |  |  |  |
|  |  |  |  |  |  |  |  |  |  |
|  |  |  |  |  |  |  |  |  |  |
|  |  |  |  |  |  |  |  |  |  |
|  |  |  |  |  |  |  |  |  |  |
|  |  |  |  |  |  |  |  |  |  |
|  |  |  |  |  |  |  |  |  |  |
|  |  |  |  |  |  |  |  |  |  |
|  |  |  |  |  |  |  |  |  |  |
|  |  |  |  |  |  |  |  |  |  |

29. Todd Company's common stock has a par value of $100 per share, which was issued at $110 per share; it has no preferred stock. It reacquired 400 shares at a cost of $137 per share on January 5. On July 10 the company sold half of the shares for $150 per share. Later on December 8 the company sold the remaining shares for $125 per share.

Required: Prepare journal entries to record the above transactions.

|  |  |  |  |  |  |  |  |  |  |  |  |  |
|--|--|--|--|--|--|--|--|--|--|--|--|--|
|  |  |  |  |  |  |  |  |  |  |  |  |  |
|  |  |  |  |  |  |  |  |  |  |  |  |  |
|  |  |  |  |  |  |  |  |  |  |  |  |  |
|  |  |  |  |  |  |  |  |  |  |  |  |  |
|  |  |  |  |  |  |  |  |  |  |  |  |  |
|  |  |  |  |  |  |  |  |  |  |  |  |  |
|  |  |  |  |  |  |  |  |  |  |  |  |  |
|  |  |  |  |  |  |  |  |  |  |  |  |  |

30. The King Company has authorized and outstanding 10,000 shares of $150 par value common stock. On June 1, 1999, the King Company declared a dividend of $3 per share to stockholders of record date on June 15, 1999, to be paid on July 15, 1999. Give the appropriate entries.

|  |  |  |  |  |  |  |  |  |  |  |  |  |
|--|--|--|--|--|--|--|--|--|--|--|--|--|
|  |  |  |  |  |  |  |  |  |  |  |  |  |
|  |  |  |  |  |  |  |  |  |  |  |  |  |
|  |  |  |  |  |  |  |  |  |  |  |  |  |
|  |  |  |  |  |  |  |  |  |  |  |  |  |
|  |  |  |  |  |  |  |  |  |  |  |  |  |
|  |  |  |  |  |  |  |  |  |  |  |  |  |
|  |  |  |  |  |  |  |  |  |  |  |  |  |
|  |  |  |  |  |  |  |  |  |  |  |  |  |

31. EPS equals the earnings available to common shareholders divided by the _____-_____ _____ ____ _____ _____ _____.

32. The price-earnings ratio equals the current market price per share divided by _____ .

## TRUE-FALSE QUESTIONS

Indicate whether each of the following statements is true or false by inserting "T" or "F" in the blank space provided.

_____ 1. Basically, the Retained Earnings account balance reflects the excess of the company's aggregate net income since its formation over all dividends distributed and aggregate net losses.

_____ 2. The Retained Earnings account describes one source of corporate capital and is properly classifiable as paid-in capital in the stockholders' equity section of the balance sheet.

_____ 3. Since treasury stock has been issued once, it may be reissued without violating the preemptive rights of the stockholders.

_____ 4. Dividend restrictions are preferably shown by parenthetical comments in the balance sheet or by balance sheet footnotes.

_____ 5. It is not necessary to make a distinction between common stock and retained earnings.

_____ 6. Treasury stock is an asset only if management intends to reissue it in the near future.

_____ 7. A retained earnings appropriation account is established by a debit to Retained Earnings and a credit to the appropriation account being set up.

_____ 8. The establishment of a retained earnings appropriation reduces the total stockholders' equity shown in the balance sheet.

_____ 9. The payment of a cash dividend increases a corporation's current liabilities.

_____ 10. The date of declaration is the date used to determine to whom a dividend will be paid.

_____ 11. The declaration and issuance of a stock dividend does not change the total amount of stockholders' equity in the corporation.

_____ 12. The balance in the Treasury Stock account basically represents the cost of a company's own stock that was issued and then reacquired.

_____ 13. When treasury stock is purchased, the amount of issued stock is reduced.

_____ 14. A purchase of treasury stock does not affect stockholders' equity.

_____ 15. Dividends are expenses since they decrease the stockholders' equity.

_____ 16. No-par stock may be more valuable than par value stock.

_____ 17. At the date of record of a cash dividend, an entry is made on the books of the corporation debiting Retained Earnings and crediting Dividends Payable for the total amount of dividends declared.

_____ 18. Par value, rather than market value, is used to indicate the legal capital of a corporation.

_____ 19. A "deficit" is an expression indicating a debit balance in the Common Stock account.

_____ 20. A statement of retained earnings for the current period itemizes revenues, expenses, and the net income or net loss for the period.

_____ 21. When treasury stock is purchased, the Retained Earnings account is reduced.

_____ 22. The par value of a share of stock is usually of more significance than book value or market value.

_____ 23. A loss suffered from destruction by a tornado of a firm's manufacturing plant is probably an extraordinary item.

_____ 24. A stock dividend declared from retained earnings reduces the retained earnings balance and permanently capitalizes a portion of the retained earnings.

_____ 25. Damage suffered by a Florida citrus grower's orange crop from a heavy frost would probably be reported as an extraordinary item.

_____ 26. The Paid-In Capital—Donations account is not the most common source of dividend distributions.

_____ 27. The retained earnings of a corporation are a part of its paid-in capital or capital surplus.

_____ 28. The entire proceeds from the disposal of donated treasury stock are credited to Gain From Donated Stock Transactions.

_____ 29. Stock dividends do not affect total stockholders' equity.
_____ 30. Treasury stock includes all the corporation's stock described in the company's articles of incorporation.
_____ 31. The Dividends account is closed to Income Summary at the end of the period.
_____ 32. If the Income Summary account shows a credit balance of $3,000 after all income and expense accounts have been closed, and the Dividends account shows a debit balance of $500, the net income is $2,500.
_____ 33. The date of declaration is the date when the liability for dividends becomes effective for the corporation.
_____ 34. At the time a company issues bonds payable, the board of directors may take action to disclose that a portion of retained earnings is unavailable for dividends.
_____ 35. Companies often use database computer programs to maintain records of trades between investors.
_____ 36. Companies are not concerned with prior years' dividend levels.

## MULTIPLE CHOICE QUESTIONS

For each of the following questions, indicate the best answer by circling the appropriate letter.

Questions 1-2. Stockholders of Pitts Co. donated 500 shares of no-par common stock to the corporation. The corporation issued these shares for cash at $40 per share.

1. The entry made for the receipt of the stock is:
   A. Common Stock Receivable
         Paid-In Capital-Donations
   B. Donated Stock
         Common Stock
   C. No entry made
   D. Memo entry made

2. The entry made for the issue of the stock described in 1 is:
   A. Cash
         Paid-In Capital-Donations
   B. Cash
         Common Stock
   C. Donated Receivable
         Common Stock
   D. No entry made
   E. Memo entry made

3. The balance sheet of the Perry Co. showed Common Stock (20,000 shares authorized) $50 par, $500,000; Paid-In Capital—Common Stock $80,000; and Retained Earnings, $300,000. The board of directors declared a 10 percent stock dividend when the market price of the stock was $90 a share. The credit(s) to the journal entry to record the declaration of the dividend is (are):
   A. Stock Dividend Distributable ................................................................. 50,000
      Paid-In Capital—Common Stock Dividend ..................................... 40,000
   B. Common Stock ........................................................................................... 50,000
      Paid-In Capital—Common Stock Dividend ..................................... 40,000
   C. Retained Earnings .................................................................................... 90,000
   D. Common Stock ........................................................................................... 50,000

4. An individual stockholder is entitled to any dividends that have been declared on stock owned, provided the stock is held on the:
   A. payment date.
   B. purchase date.
   C. date of record.
   D. None of the above.

5. An entry to increase the appropriation for plant expansion is:
   A. Dr. Appropriation for Plant Expansion
      Cr. Retained Earnings
   B. Dr. Retained Earnings
      Cr. Appropriation for Plant Expansion
   C. Dr. Retained Earnings
      Cr. Capital Contributed from Plant Expansion
   D. Dr. Appropriation for Plant Expansion
      Cr. Cash

6. Kirk Co. Issued 50,000 shares of $40 par value common stock and subsequently acquired 1,000 shares, which it now holds as treasury stock. If the board of directors declares a cash dividend of $2 per share, what will be the total amount of the dividend?
   A. $100,000
   B. $98,000
   C. $102,000
   D. None of these

7. The amount that a preferred stockholder will be entitled to receive per share if a corporation dissolves is known as:
   A. book value.
   B. redemption value.
   C. liquidation value.
   D. par value.
   E. market value.

8. Treasury stock should be shown on the balance sheet as a:
   A. reduction of the corporation's stockholders' equity.
   B. sundry asset.
   C. current asset.
   D. fixed asset.
   E. current liability.

9. The Board of Directors declared the regular quarterly dividend of $10 per share. The company had issued 12,000 shares, but now holds 2,000 shares as treasury stock. The entry for the dividend declaration is:
   A. Dr. Retained Earnings .................................................................... 100,000
      Cr. Dividends Payable ................................................................. 100,000
   B. Dr. Dividends Payable .................................................................. 100,000
      Cr. Cash .......................................................................................... 100,000
   C. Dr. Dividends Payable .................................................................. 120,000
      Cr. Cash .......................................................................................... 120,000
   D. Dr. Retained Earnings .................................................................... 120,000
      Cr. Dividends Payable ................................................................. 120,000
   E. A and B above

10. The par value of a company's 1,000 shares of common stock outstanding has been reduced from $100 par to $50; an additional 1,000 shares are issued to stockholders. The entry is:

A. Dr. Retained Earnings .................................................................................... 50,000
    Cr. Common Stock .................................................................................... 50,000

B. Dr. Dividend Payable .................................................................................... 100,000
    Cr. Common Stock .................................................................................... 100,000

C. Dr. Retained Earnings.................................................................................... 50,000
    Cr. Contributed Capital from Reduction in Par Value of Stock ................ 50,000

D. None of these

11-13. A company's 20,000 shares of $100 par value common stock outstanding were issued at $110 per share. It now reacquired 400 shares of its own stock at a cost of $137 per share.

11. The entry to record the reacquisition is:

A. Dr. Premium on stock ................................................................................ 14,800
    Dr. Treasury stock .................................................................................... 40,000
    Cr. Cash .................................................................................................... 54,800

B. Dr. Premium on stock ................................................................................ 10,800
    Dr. Treasury stock .................................................................................... 44,000
    Cr. Cash .................................................................................................... 54,800

C. Dr. Treasury stock .................................................................................... 54,800
    Cr. Cash .................................................................................................... 54,800

D. Dr. Paid-in Capital — Treasury Stock Transaction ..................................... 14,800
    Dr. Treasury Stock .................................................................................... 40,000
    Cr. Cash .................................................................................................... 54,800

12. The entry when the company reissued half of the shares for $150 per share is:

A. Dr. Cash .................................................................................................... 30,000
    Cr. Treasury stock — Common ................................................................ 27,400
    Cr. Paid-In Capital — Common Treasury Stock Transactions ................... 2,600

B. Dr. Cash .................................................................................................... 30,000
    Cr. Treasury Stock — Common ................................................................ 30,000

C. Dr. Cash .................................................................................................... 30,000
    Cr. Treasury Stock — Common ................................................................ 27,400
    Cr. Retained earnings .............................................................................. 2,600

D. Dr. Cash .................................................................................................... 27,400
    Cr. Treasury stock — Common ................................................................ 27,400

13. The company reissued the remaining treasury shares for $125 per share. The entry is:

A. Dr. Cash .................................................................................................... 25,000
    Cr. Treasury stock — Common ................................................................ 25,000

B. Dr. Cash .................................................................................................... 25,000
    Dr. Paid-In Capital — Common Treasury Stock Transaction ................... 2,400
    Cr. Treasury Stock — Common ................................................................ 27,400

C. Dr. Cash .................................................................................................... 25,000
    Dr. Retained earnings .............................................................................. 2,400
    Cr. Treasury Stock — Common ................................................................ 27,400

D. None of these

14. Atlantic Co. has been authorized to issue 200,000 shares of $50 par common stock. On May 10, ten years ago, it issued 10,000 shares; on July 20, four years later, it issued 6,000 shares; and on April 2 of the current year it reacquired 400 shares. On May 1 of the current year, a five-for-one stock split occurred in which the par value was decreased to $10. What is the number of shares outstanding after the last transaction?
   A. 202,000
   B. 200,000
   C. 80,000
   D. 78,000
   E. 250,000

15. Alpha Company declared a stock dividend amounting to 1,000 shares of common stock. (10 percent of its outstanding shares). If at the declaration date the par value is $10 per share, the book value is $18 per share and the market value is $20 per share, what will be the amount debited to Retained Earnings in recording the dividend distributable?
   A. $10,000
   B. $18,000
   C. $20,000
   D. None of these

16. The Long Island Lighting Company is a public utility that provides electric and gas service to more than 1 million customers in three Long Island counties. A recent annual report includes the following information: Earnings per common share, $2.15; high and low market price during the fourth quarter, 27 3/4 to 23 1/4. If the high price per share represented the price on December 31, what was the price-earnings ratio?
   A. 10.8 times
   B. 12.9 times
   C. 1.19 times
   D. 0.08 times

---

## SOLUTIONS

### Matching

| | | | |
|---|---|---|---|
| 1. | g | 7. | d |
| 2. | a | 8. | c |
| 3. | h | 9. | b |
| 4. | e | 10. | j |
| 5. | i | 11. | m |
| 6. | f | | |

### Completion and Exercises

1. $4,800; 10,000 shares outstanding x 20% = 2,000 shares in stock dividend.
   10,000 shares + 2,000 shares = 12,000; 12,000 x $0.40 = $4,800 dividend.

2. May 1  Memorandum: Received donation of 400 shares common stock

| | | | |
|---|---|---|---|
| 10 | Treasury Stock ............................................................................... | 2,400 | |
| | Cash ............................................................................... | | 2,400 |
| 20 | Cash ............................................................................... | 13,600 | |
| | Paid-In Capital – Donations ............................................... | | 13,600 |
| 28 | Cash ............................................................................... | 2,100 | |
| | Treasury Stock ............................................................... | | 1,680 |
| | Paid-In Capital – Common Treasury Stock Transactions ........ | | 420 |

3. record

4. treasury
5. dividends
6. market
7. Treasury stock is stock that has been issued and then reacquired by the issuing corporation.
8. Paid-In Capital—Common (Preferred) Treasury Stock Transactions.
9. source
10. permanent (or contributed)
11. cash
12. statement of retained earnings
13. retained earnings
14. They have no effect. They usually increase paid-in capital and decrease retained earnings by the same amount.
15. The fair market value of the asset received
16. Small stock dividends are of less than 20 to 25 percent of the previously outstanding stock and are assumed to have little effect on the market value of the shares. Small stock dividends are recorded at present market value of outstanding shares. Large stock dividends are those over 20 to 25 percent of the previously outstanding shares. Since large stock dividends are assumed to reduce the market value of the stock, they are accounted for at their par or stated value.

17. *a.* Retained Earnings ................................................................. 100,000
   Appropriation for Possible Losses from Lawsuit ....................              100,000
   To record Retained Earnings Appropriation.

   *b.* Loss from Lawsuits .............................................................. 50,000
      Cash ...................................................................................              50,000
   To record payment of court award judgment.

   Appropriation for Possible Losses from Lawsuits ........................ 100,000
   Retained Earnings .................................................................              100,000
   To eliminate appropriation of Retained Earnings.

18. Paid-in capital and retained earnings
19. deficit
20. To inform stockholders that a certain amount of the assets brought into the corporation through the earning process is not to be distributed as dividends.

21.
**SOUTHEAST, INC.**
**Statement of Retained Earnings**
**For the Year Ended December 31, 1999**

Appropriated:
  Appropriated for plant expansion,
    balance January 1, 1999 ................................................. $108,000
  Additional appropriation ................................................    60,000
  Retained earnings appropriated, December 31, 1999............           $168,000
Unappropriated:
  Balance, January 1, 1999 ..................................... $1,140,000
  Net income for year .............................................    492,000   $1,632,000
  Cash dividends declared ....................................... $  204,000
Stock dividends declared .........................................    228,000
Appropriation for plant expansion .........................     60,000    492,000
Retained earnings unappropriated, December 31, 1999 ..........         1,140,000
Total retained earnings, December 31, 1999 .............................         $1,308,000

22. *a.* Retained Earnings ................................................. 10,000
   Appropriation for Plant Expansion ........................ 10,000
   *b.* Retained Earnings ................................................. 50,000
   Dividends Payable ...................................................... 50,000
   *c.* Dividends Payable .................................................. 50,000
   Cash ........................................................................... 50,000
   *d.* Memo:
   Increased shares to 20,000 shares outstanding and reduced par value to
   $25 per share.
23. extraordinary item; Income Statement; tax effects
24. prior period adjustment; statement of retained earnings; tax effects
25. accounting methods; income statement
26. environment; would not
27.

**GREGORY CORPORATION**
**Income Statement**
**For the Year Ended December 31, 1999**

| | | |
|---|---:|---:|
| Revenues .................................................................................. | | $29,000,000 |
| Expenses ................................................................................. | $25,000,000 | |
| Federal income taxes ($4,000,000 x 50%) ............................... | 2,000,000 | 27,000,000 |
| Net income before extraordinary items ................................. | | $ 2,000,000 |
| Loss from earthquake (net of tax effect of $270,000) ............ | | 270,000 |
| Net income ............................................................................. | | $ 1,730,000 |

28.

**KLEIN CORPORATION**
**Partial Balance Sheet**
**December 31, 1999**

| | | | |
|---|---:|---:|---:|
| Stockholders' Equity: | | | |
| Paid-in capital:........................................................................ | | | |
| Preferred stock—$60 par value; 5,000 shares authorized, | | | |
| 3,000 shares issued and outstanding ............................................ | | | $ 180,000 |
| Common stock—$6 par value; 1,000,000 shares authorized, | | | |
| 600,000 shares issued and outstanding of which 15,000 shares | | | |
| are held in treasury ............................................................ | | | 3,600,000 |
| Paid-in capital in excess of par value:....................................... | | | |
| From common stock issuances ............................................ | | $810,000 | |
| From capitalization of retained earnings through | | | |
| stock dividends ................................................................. | | 396,000 | |
| From treasury stock transactions ....................................... | | 30,000 | 1,236,000 |
| Total paid-in capital .......................................................... | | | $5,016,000 |
| Retained Earnings: | | | |
| Appropriated for pending litigation ................................... | | $150,000 | |
| Unappropriated (restricted to the extent of $108,000, the cost of | | | |
| treasury shares held) ........................................................ | | 456,000 | 606,000 |
| ................................................................................ | | | $5,622,000 |
| Less: Treasury stock—common 15,000 shares at cost ..................... | | | 108,000 |
| Total Stockholders' Equity .......................................................... | | | $5,514,000 |

**29.**

**TODD COMPANY**

| | | | | | |
|---|---|---|---|---|---|
| January | 5 | Treasury Stock—Common | ..................................................... | 54,800 | |
| | | Cash | .............................................................................. | | 54,800 |
| | | | | | |
| July | 10 | Cash | .............................................................................. | 30,000 | |
| | | Treasury Stock—Common | ................................................. | | 27,400 |
| | | Paid-In Capital—Common Treasury Stock Transactions | | | 2,600 |
| | | | | | |
| December | 8 | Cash | .............................................................................. | 25,000 | |
| | | Paid-in Capital—Common Treasury Stock Transactions . | | 2,400 | |
| | | Treasury Stock—Common | ................................................. | | 27,400 |

**30.**

| | | | | | |
|---|---|---|---|---|---|
| June | 1 | Retained Earnings | ............................................................. | 30,000 | |
| | | Dividends Payable | ........................................................... | | 30,000 |

Dividends declared: $3 on 10,000 shares, payable
July 15, 1999, to stockholders on June 15, 1999.

| | | | | | |
|---|---|---|---|---|---|
| June | 15 | No entry | | | |
| | | | | | |
| July | 15 | Dividends Payable | ............................................................ | 30,000 | |
| | | Cash | .............................................................................. | | 30,000 |

Paid the dividend declared on June 1, 1999.

31. Weighted-average number of common shares outstanding
32. EPS

*True-False Questions*

1. T
2. F  Although a source of corporate capital, retained earnings do not represent paid-in capital, that is, capital contributed by the owners. Retained earnings are classified separately from paid-in capital within the stockholders' equity section.
3. T  It may be reissued without violating the preemptive rights.
4. T
5. F  Stockholders' equity generally consists of two elements—paid-in capital, which includes common stock, and retained earnings.
6. F  Treasury stock is never an asset because a corporation cannot own part of itself.
7. T
8. F  Setting up a retained earnings appropriation does not reduce the total stockholders' equity. It merely earmarks a portion of that equity to indicate that assets brought into the corporation through the earnings process are to be used for a specific purpose.
9. F  The declaration of a cash dividend increases a firm's current liabilities. The payment of the cash dividend decreases current liabilities.
10. F  The date of record is the date used to determine to whom the dividends will be paid. The date of declaration is the date the liability for dividends payable becomes effective.
11. T  The usual stock dividend merely decreases retained earnings and increases paid-in capital by an equal amount. Thus, there is no change in total stockholders' equity.
12. T
13. F  The amount of issued stock is not reduced; instead, the amount of outstanding shares is reduced. Treasury stock is not automatically canceled when it is purchased because the board of directors may intend to reissue it.
14. F  Treasury stock reduces total stockholders' equity.
15. F  Dividends are distributions of earnings and are not expenses.

16. T  No-par stock may be more valuable; but par or no-par is not the crucial factor. The market value which reflects many economic factors is a better indication of a stock's worth.

17. F  No entry is made on the date of record; this date merely determines which stockholders are to receive the dividend.

18. T

19. F  A deficit is a debit balance in the Retained Earnings account.

20. F  A Retained Earnings Statement shows the changes in the Retained Earnings account during a stated period of time. These changes include additions such as net income and deductions such as dividends declared and net losses.

21. F  Retained Earnings is not reduced; but the amount of retained earnings available for distribution as cash dividends is usually restricted by an amount equal to the cost of the treasury stock.

22. F

23. T  Such losses are likely to be unusual in nature and nonrecurring.

24. T  A stock dividend declared from retained earnings permanently capitalizes a portion of retained earnings by transferring an amount from retained earnings to paid-in capital.

25. F  Such damage occurs too frequently to be considered nonrecurring.

26. T  The usual source of dividend distributions is the Retained Earnings account.

27. F  The paid-in capital of a corporation includes capital contributed by stockholders or others. It does not include retained earnings.

28. F  Proceeds from donated treasury stock are credited to a paid-in capital account rather than a gain account that affects net income.

29. T

30. F  Treasury stock does not include all authorized stock; only the stock that has been issued and reacquired.

31. F  The Dividends account is closed to Retained Earnings. An alternative treatment is to debit Retained Earnings at the time dividends are declared and not use a Dividends account.

32. F  The net income would be $3,000; dividends are not expenses and are instead distributions of income to stockholders.

33. T

34. T  The board of directors may appropriate retained earnings at the time bonds are issued.

35. T

36. F  Companies try to maintain prior years' dividend levels.

*Multiple Choice Questions*

1. D  At the time the donated shares were received, a memo entry would be made.

2. A  At the time of sale of donated shares, Paid-In Capital – Donations is credited.

3. A  At the time of the stock dividend declaration, there are 10,000 shares of stock outstanding. This means that 1,000 shares are to be distributed as a stock dividend; 1,000 shares x $50 par = $50,000 credited to Stock Dividend Distributable. Because the market value of the stock is $90 at the time of declaration, Paid-In Capital – Stock Dividend is credited for $40,000.

4. C

5. B  The correct entry to increase the appropriation for plant expansion is to debit Retained Earnings and to credit Appropriation for Plant Expansion.

6. B  50,000 - 1,000 shares reacquired as treasury stock = 49,000 shares outstanding, on which $2 dividend per share is being paid.

7. C

8. A

9. A 12,000 shares - 2,000 shares reacquired as treasury shares = 10,000 shares outstanding, on which $10 dividends are being paid. The correct entry is to debit Retained Earnings, and to credit Dividends Payable on the date of declaration.

10. D This is a stock split, and none of the entries listed is correct. A memo entry could be made or Common Stock, $100 par, would be debited and Common Stock, $50 par, would be credited.

11. C The Treasury Stock account is debited at cost, which is 400 shares x $137 per share.

12. A The Treasury Stock account is credited for the cost of the shares (200 shares x $137 per share). The difference between the cost and the amount received is credited to Paid-In Capital—Common Treasury Stock Transaction.

13. B The amount received is less than the cost of the treasury shares. The Treasury Stock—Common account is credited for the cost and the difference is debited to the Paid-In Capital—Common Treasury Stock Transactions, since that account has a credit balance.

14. D (10,000 + 6,000 - 400) x 5 = 78,000 shares outstanding.

15. C Market value is used, which is $20 x 1,000 shares = $20,000 debited to Retained Earnings.

16. B Calculated as 27 3/4 divided by $2.15 = 12.9 times.

# CHAPTER 14
# STOCK INVESTMENTS: COST, EQUITY, CONSOLIDATIONS, AND INTERNATIONAL ACCOUNTING

## Learning Objectives

1. *Report stock investments and distinguish between the cost and equity methods of accounting for stock investments.*
2. *Prepare journal entries to account for short-term stock investments and for long-term stock investments of less than 20%.*
3. *Prepare journal entries to account for long-term stock investments of 20% to 50%.*
4. *Describe the nature of parent and subsidiary corporations.*
5. *Prepare consolidated financial statements through the use of a consolidated statement work sheet.*
6. *Identify the differences between purchase accounting and pooling of interests accounting.*
7. *Describe the uses and limitations of consolidated financial statements.*
8. *Analyze and use the financial results – dividend yield on common stock and payout ratio.*
9. *Discuss the differences in international accounting among nations (Appendix).*

## REFERENCE OUTLINE

---

## CHAPTER OUTLINE

### STOCK INVESTMENTS

1. The motivation for making an investment in another company and the relative size of the investment determine the method of accounting for the stock investment.

2. Corporations invest funds in the securities of other corporations for any one of three reasons:
   a. To earn revenue on otherwise idle cash.
   b. To ensure a supply of a required raw material.
   c. To expand their business operations.

*Learning Objective 1:*
*Report stock investments and distinguish between the cost and equity methods of accounting for stock investments.*

### COST AND EQUITY METHODS

3. The two methods of accounting for investments in common stock are the cost and the equity methods. The Accounting Principles Board has identified the circumstances under which each method must be used.

4. Using the cost method, the investor records the investment at the price paid at acquisition and does not subsequently adjust the investment account balance for its share of the investee's reported income, losses, and dividends.

5. Using the equity method, the investor company subsequently adjusts the investment account periodically for the investor's share of the investee's earnings, losses, and dividends.

*Learning Objective 2:*
*Prepare journal entries to account for short-term stock investments and for long-term stock investments of less than 20%.*

### ACCOUNTING FOR SHORT-TERM STOCK INVESTMENTS AND FOR LONG-TERM STOCK INVESTMENTS OF LESS THAN 20%

6. The cost method is used for long-term investments if the company owns less than 20% of the outstanding stock of the investee company and does not exercise significant influence over the company.

7. The equity method is used for long-term investments if the purchasing company owns from 20% to 50% of the outstanding stock of the investee company or owns less than 20% but still exercises significant influence over the investee company.

8. The cost method is used for all short-term stock investments.

9. The cost or equity method can be used for investments of more than 50%; the application of consolidation procedures yields the same result.

COST METHOD FOR SHORT-TERM INVESTMENTS AND FOR LONG-TERM INVESTMENTS OF LESS THAN 20%

10. Using the cost method, stock investments are recorded at cost.
    a. If the stock is purchased as a short-term investment, either trading securities or available-for-sale securities is debited. If they were bought for sale in the "near term" they are trading securities. If not, they are available-for-sale securities.
    b. If the stock is purchased as a long-term investment, the Available-for-Sale Securities account is debited.

ACCOUNTING FOR CASH DIVIDENDS RECEIVED

11. Under the cost method, cash dividends are debited to Cash or Dividends Receivable and credited to Dividend Revenue.

STOCK DIVIDENDS AND STOCK SPLITS

12. Income is not recognized on the receipt of stock dividends.
13. When an investor receives more shares in a stock dividend or a stock split, the investor would note the number of shares received and the reduction in the per-share cost.

SALE OF TRADING SECURITIES OR AVAILABLE-FOR-SALE SECURITIES

14. Gain or loss on the sale of securities is the difference between the net proceeds received and the carrying value of the shares sold. The gain is credited to Realized Gain on Sale of Trading Securities or Realized Gain on Sale of Available-for-Sale Securities.

SUBSEQUENT VALUATION OF STOCK INVESTMENTS UNDER THE FAIR MARKET VALUE METHOD

15. The treatment differs for trading and available-for-sale securities. Trading securities and available-for-sale securities are considered to be two separate investment portfolios, and the fair market value is applied independently to each portfolio.

TRADING SECURITIES

16. Trading securities are valued at the fair market value. When stock is to be written down, an unrealized loss account entitled Unrealized Loss on Trading Securities is debited and Trading Securities is credited.
17. The unrealized loss on trading securities is shown on the income statement as a deduction in arriving at net income.

AVAILABLE-FOR-SALE SECURITIES

18. Available-for-sale securities are valued at the fair market value. The reduction in value is debited to an unrealized loss account, which is shown as a deduction to total stockholders' equity or to total paid-in capital.
19. If a loss on an individual noncurrent security is determined to be permanent, it is recorded as a realized loss and deducted in determining net income.

*Learning Objective 3:*
*Prepare journal entries to account for long-term stock investments of 20% to 50%.*

EQUITY METHOD FOR LONG-TERM INVESTMENTS OF BETWEEN 20% AND 50%

20. When the equity method is used, the investor recognizes its share of the purchased company's income, regardless of whether dividends are received.
    a. This treatment recognizes that the purchasing company may exercise influence over the declaration of dividends and manipulate its own income by influencing the investee's decision to declare or not declare dividends.
    b. When the subsidiary company reports income, the investor company debits Investment in Subsidiary Company and credits Income from Subsidiary Company.

c. If the subsidiary incurs a loss, the parent company debits Loss of Subsidiary Company and credits Investment in Subsidiary Company for its share of the loss.

(1) The Loss of Subsidiary Company account is closed to Income Summary.

(2) The incurrence of a subsidiary loss reduces the investor's equity in the investee.

d. When a subsidiary pays a cash dividend, the parent company debits Cash and credits the Investment in Subsidiary Company account, thereby reducing the parent's equity in the subsidiary.

## REPORTING FOR STOCK INVESTMETNS OF MORE THAN 50%

21. Companies may expand by purchasing a major portion, or all, of another company's outstanding voting stock.

a. Both companies remain separate legal entities.

b. Purchases of such large portions of stock usually occur because the investor company seeks to ensure a source of raw materials (such as oil), desires to enter a new industry, or wishes to receive income on the investment.

*Learning Objective 4:*
*Describe the nature of parent and subsidiary corporations.*

## PARENT AND SUBSIDIARY CORPORATIONS

22. A parent company is one that owns more than 50 percent of the outstanding voting common stock of another corporation.

23. A subsidiary company is the corporation acquired and controlled by the parent company.

24. Consolidated financial statements must be prepared when the following two conditions exist:

a. One company owns a majority (which is more than 50 percent) of the outstanding voting common stock of another company, and

b. Unless control is likely to be temporary or if it does not rest with the majority owner (e.g., the company is in legal reorganization or bankruptcy).

   (Previously, a condition was that the two companies were not in markedly dissimilar businesses).

25. Consolidated statements are the financial statements that result from combining the parent's financial statement amounts with those of its subsidiaries (after certain eliminations have been made).

## ELIMINATIONS

26. Elimination entries are required so that the assets, liabilities, stockholders' equity, revenues, expenses, and dividends will appear as if the parent and its subsidiaries taken together constitute a single economic enterprise.

a. To avoid double counting assets and stockholders' equity, the parent company's investment account and the subsidiary's capital accounts must be eliminated.

b. Intercompany debt and other intercompany balances must also be eliminated.

c. Elimination entries are made only on a consolidated statement work sheet; they are not posted to the parent's or the subsidiary's accounts.

*Learning Objective 5:*
*Prepare consolidated financial statements through the use of a consolidated statement work sheet.*

## CONSOLIDATED BALANCE SHEET AT TIME OF ACQUISITION

27. A consolidated statement work sheet is needed to combine assets and liabilities of a parent company and its subsidiaries.

a. This informal statement includes the elimination entries necessary to show the parent and its subsidiaries as one economic enterprise.

b. The first two columns of the work sheet show individual assets, liabilities, and stockholders' equity of the corporations involved.
c. The next columns (debit and credit) show the eliminations that are needed to offset intercompany items.
d. A final column shows the amounts that will appear on the consolidated balance sheet.

ACQUISITION OF SUBSIDIARY AT BOOK VALUE

28. If the investment in the subsidiary is acquired at book value and it represents 100 percent ownership, the elimination entry required is to debit Common Stock and debit Retained Earnings of the subsidiary and to credit Investment in Subsidiary Company at the original cost at the date of acquisition.

ACQUISITION OF SUBSIDIARY AT A COST ABOVE OR BELOW BOOK VALUE

29. Subsidiaries may be acquired at a cost greater than or less than book value.
    a. Where cost exceeds book value because of expected above-average earnings, the excess is labeled goodwill on the consolidated balance sheet.
    b. When the cost exceeds book value because assets of the subsidiary are undervalued, the asset values should be increased to the extent of the excess.
30. A parent may acquire a subsidiary at less than its book value.
    a. Any excess of book value over cost must be used first to reduce proportionately the value of the noncurrent assets acquired (except long-term investments in marketable securities).
    b. If the noncurrent assets are reduced to zero, any remaining dollar amount should be reported as a deferred credit on the consolidated balance sheet.

ACQUISITION OF LESS THAN 100% OF SUBSIDIARY

31. When a parent acquires less than 100% of a subsidiary, minority stockholders or a minority interest exists.
    a. The minority stockholders have an interest in the subsidiary's net assets and share the subsidiary's earnings with the parent company.
    b. When a consolidated balance sheet is prepared for a partially owned subsidiary, all of the subsidiary's stockholders' equity is still eliminated.

ACCOUNTING FOR INCOME, LOSSES, AND DIVIDENDS OF A SUBSIDIARY

32. Either the cost or equity method of accounting may be used by a parent company for its investment in a subsidiary.
    a. The investment account is eliminated during the consolidation process.
    b. Results are identical after consolidation.

CONSOLIDATED FINANCIAL STATEMENTS AT A DATE AFTER ACQUISITION

33. Using the equity method, the parent company records its share of the subsidiary company's earnings by debiting Investment in Subsidiary Company and crediting Income of Subsidiary Company for income.
    a. The balance in the investment account differs after acquisition from its balance on the date of acquisition.
    b. Under the equity method, the amounts eliminated on the consolidated statement work sheet will differ from year to year.

*Learning Objective 6:*
*Identify the differences between purchase accounting and pooling of interests accounting.*

## PURCHASE VERSUS POOLING OF INTERESTS

34. *APB Opinion No. 16* separates business combinations into two categories: purchases and poolings of interests.

    a. A purchase is a business combination in which cash, other assets, or debt securities are given up in exchange for a subsidiary's outstanding voting common stock. A purchase also occurs when common stock is exchanged for common stock and the resulting business combination does not satisfy the conditions specified in *APB Opinion No. 16*.

    b. A pooling of interests occurs when common stock is exchanged for common stock and the resulting business combination satisfies all of the conditions specified in *APB Opinion No. 16*.

35. The purchase method of accounting is used for business combinations classified as purchases.

    a. The parent company's investment is recorded at the amount of cash given up or at the fair market value of the assets or stock given up, or the fair market value of the stock received, whichever is the most clearly and objectively determinable.

    b. The subsidiary's retained earnings at date of acquisition do *not* become part of consolidated retained earnings.

    c. Only that portion of the subsidiary's net earnings which arises after the date of acquisition is included in consolidated net earnings.

36. The pooling of interests method of accounting is used for business combinations classified as poolings of interests.

    a. The parent company records its investments at the book value of the subsidiary's net assets with the result that there can be no goodwill or deferred credit from consolidation.

    b. The subsidiary's retained earnings on the date of acquisition become part of consolidated retained earnings.

    c. All the subsidiary's net income for the year of acquisition is included in consolidated net income.

*Learning Objective 7:*
*Describe the uses and limitations of consolidated financial statements.*

## USES AND LIMITATIONS OF COLSOLIDATED STATEMENTS

37. Consolidated financial statements are of primary importance to the parent company's stockholders, managers, and directors, while the subsidiary's individual financial statements are more important to the subsidiary's creditors and minority stockholders.

38. Consolidated financial statements are of limited use to creditors and minority stockholders of the subsidiary.

*Learning Objective 8:*
*Analyze and use the financial results – dividend yield on common stock and payout ratio.*

## ANALYZING AND USING THE FINANCIAL RESULTS—DIVIDEND YIELD ON COMMON STOCK AND PAYOUT RATIO

39. Dividend Yield on Common Stock =

$$\frac{\text{Dividend per Share of Common Stock}}{\text{Current Market Price per Share}}$$

    a. This ratio is used as a tool to compare stocks.

40. Payout Ratio on Common Stock =

$$\frac{\text{Dividend per Share of Common Stock}}{\text{Earnings per Share (EPS)}}$$

   a. This ratio provides an index of whether a company pays out a large percentage of earnings as dividends or reinvests most of its earnings.

APPENDIX: INTERNATIONAL ACCOUNTING

*Learning Objective 9:*
*Discuss the differences in international accounting among nations (Appendix).*

WHY ACCOUNTING PRINCIPLES AND PRACTICES DIFFER AMONG NATIONS

41. Even though business is truly international, accounting principles and reporting practices differ among countries.
   a. The degree of development of the accounting profession and the general level of education of a country influence accounting practices and procedures used.
   b. Accounting differences often stem from the various legal or political systems of nations.

ATTEMPTED HARMONIZATION OF ACCOUNTING PRACTICES

42. Several organizations are working to achieve greater understanding and harmonization of different accounting practices. These organizations include:
   a. Organization for Economic Cooperation and Development (OECD)
   b. European Economic Community (EEC)
   c. International Accounting Standards Committee (IASC)
   d. International Federation of Accountants (IFAC)

FOREIGN CURRENCY TRANSLATION

43. Foreign currency translation has two main components:
   a. Accounting for transactions in a foreign currency.
   b. Translating the foreign currency in financial statements of foreign enterprises into a different, common currency.

ACCOUNTING FOR TRANSACTIONS IN A FOREIGN CURRENCY

44. One approach to recording purchases when the exchange rate in effect on the purchase date and payment date differ is to regard the purchase and settlement of the invoice as two separate transactions. This is known as the time-of-transaction method. The transactions are recorded at two different exchange rates.

45. The "time-of-settlement" method regards the transaction and its settlement as a single event.

TRANSLATING FINANCIAL STATEMENTS

46. Two methods are used to translate financial statements: the current-rate approach and the current/historical-rates approach.
   a. Under the current-rate approach, all assets and liabilities are translated at the current rate.
   b. Under the current/historical-rates approach, some items are translated at the current rate and others at the historical rates.

INVENTORIES

47. The basis for determining cost (and whether cost, once determined, should be increased or decreased to reflect the market value of the inventories) causes variations in accounting for inventories.

## DETERMINATION OF COST

48. FIFO, LIFO, and average cost are the three principal bases used for inventory costing, but other methods are also used in some countries.

## MARKET VALUE OF INVENTORIES

49. Valuing inventories at the lower-of-cost-or-market is the predominant method; however, the interpretation of market value differs among countries.

## ACCOUNTING FOR THE EFFECTS OF CHANGING PRICES

50. Since several countries are concerned about the loss of relevance of historical-cost financial reporting in inflationary environments, they have adopted either the constant dollar or current-cost approach to account for inflation.

---

### DEMONSTRATION PROBLEM

The Pep Company acquired all of the outstanding voting common stock of the Smith Company on July 1, 1999, for $300,000. The balance sheets for the two companies on the date of acquisition were as shown below:

| Assets | Pep Company | Smith Company |
|---|---|---|
| Cash | $ 23,000 | $ 15,000 |
| Accounts receivable | 45,000 | 38,900 |
| Notes receivable | 35,000 | 7,000 |
| Merchandise Inventory | 60,000 | 25,000 |
| Investment in Smith Company | 300,000 | |
| Building, net | 150,000 | 156,000 |
| Land | 80,000 | 100,000 |
| Total assets | $693,000 | $341,900 |
| *Liabilities and Stockholders' Equity* | | |
| Accounts payable | $ 65,000 | $ 56,700 |
| Notes payable | 36,000 | 13,000 |
| Common stock—$25 par | 300,000 | 150,000 |
| Retained earnings | 292,000 | 122,200 |
| Total liabilities and stockholders' equity | $693,000 | $341,900 |

Pep management believes that the building of Smith and the land on which it is located are undervalued by $5,000 and $10,000, respectively. The remainder of the excess of cost over book value is due to superior earnings potential.

On July 1, 1999, when the acquisition occurred, Smith borrowed $3,000 from Pep Company on a note.

Required:

a. Prepare a work sheet for a consolidated balance sheet on the date of acquisition.
b. Prepare a consolidated balance sheet for July 1, 1999.

a.

| Accounts | Pep Co. | | | Smith Co. | | | Eliminations | | | | | | Consolidated Amounts | | |
|---|---|---|---|---|---|---|---|---|---|---|---|---|---|---|---|
| | | | | | | | Debit | | | Credit | | | | | |
| Assets | | | | | | | | | | | | | | | |
| | | | | | | | | | | | | | | | |
| | | | | | | | | | | | | | | | |
| | | | | | | | | | | | | | | | |
| | | | | | | | | | | | | | | | |
| | | | | | | | | | | | | | | | |
| | | | | | | | | | | | | | | | |
| | | | | | | | | | | | | | | | |
| | | | | | | | | | | | | | | | |
| | | | | | | | | | | | | | | | |
| | | | | | | | | | | | | | | | |
| | | | | | | | | | | | | | | | |
| | | | | | | | | | | | | | | | |
| | | | | | | | | | | | | | | | |
| | | | | | | | | | | | | | | | |
| | | | | | | | | | | | | | | | |
| | | | | | | | | | | | | | | | |
| | | | | | | | | | | | | | | | |
| | | | | | | | | | | | | | | | |
| | | | | | | | | | | | | | | | |
| Liabilities and Stockholders' Equity | | | | | | | | | | | | | | | |
| | | | | | | | | | | | | | | | |
| | | | | | | | | | | | | | | | |
| | | | | | | | | | | | | | | | |
| | | | | | | | | | | | | | | | |
| | | | | | | | | | | | | | | | |
| | | | | | | | | | | | | | | | |
| | | | | | | | | | | | | | | | |
| | | | | | | | | | | | | | | | |
| | | | | | | | | | | | | | | | |
| | | | | | | | | | | | | | | | |
| | | | | | | | | | | | | | | | |

b.

# SOLUTION TO DEMONSTRATION PROBLEM

a.

## PEP COMPANY AND SUBSIDIARY SMITH COMPANY
### Work Sheet for Consolidated Balance Sheet
### July 1, 1999

| Accounts | Pep Co. | Smith Co. | Eliminations Debit | Eliminations Credit | Consolidated Amounts |
|---|---|---|---|---|---|
| *Assets:* | | | | | |
| Cash ............................... | 23,000 | 15,000 | | | 38,000 |
| Accounts receivable................. | 45,000 | 38,900 | | | 83,900 |
| Notes receivable........................ | 35,000 | 7,000 | | (b)   3,000 | 39,000 |
| Merchandise Inventory............ | 60,000 | 25,000 | | | 85,000 |
| Investment in Smith Co............ | 300,000 | | | (a)300,000 | |
| Building, net ............................. | 150,000 | 156,000 | (a)   5,000 | | 311,000 |
| Land........................................ | 80,000 | 100,000 | (a)  10,000 | | 190,000 |
| Goodwill................................... | | | (a)  12,800 | | 12,800 |
| | 693,000 | 341,900 | | | 759,700 |
| *Liabilities and Stockholders' Equity:* | | | | | |
| Accounts payable...................... | 65,000 | 56,700 | | | 121,700 |
| Notes payable........................... | 36,000 | 13,000 | (b)   3,000 | | 46,000 |
| Common stock—$25 par.......... | 300,000 | 150,000 | (a)150,000 | | 300,000 |
| Retained earnings .................... | 292,000 | 122,200 | (a)122,200 | | 292,000 |
| | 693,000 | 341,900 | 303,000 | 303,000 | 759,700 |

# PEP COMPANY AND SUBSIDIARY SMITH COMPANY
## Consolidated Balance Sheet
### July 1, 1999

*Assets*

| | | |
|---|---:|---:|
| Current assets: | | |
| Cash | | $ 38,000 |
| Accounts receivable | 83,900 | |
| Notes receivable | 39,000 | |
| Merchandise Inventory | 85,000 | |
| Total current assets | | $ 245,900 |
| Plant and equipment: | | |
| Building, net | $ 311,000 | |
| Land | | 190,000 |
| Total plant and equipment | | 501,000 |
| Goodwill | | 12,800 |
| Total assets | | $ 759,700 |

*Liabilities and Stockholders' Equity*

| | | |
|---|---:|---:|
| Current liabilities: | | |
| Accounts payable | | $ 121,700 |
| Notes payable | | 46,000 |
| Total liabilities | | $167,700 |
| Stockholders' equity: | | |
| Common stock—$25 par | $ 300,000 | |
| Retained earnings | 292,000 | |
| Total stockholders' equity | | 592,000 |
| Total liabilities and stockholders' equity | | $ 759,700 |

---

## MATCHING

Referring to the terms listed below, place the appropriate letter next to the corresponding description. Some terms might not be used.

| | | | | | |
|---|---|---|---|---|---|
| a. | Parent company | e. | Consolidated statement work sheet | j. | Equity method |
| b. | Consolidated statements | f. | Goodwill | k. | Cost method |
| c. | Subsidiary company | g. | Journal entires | l. | Pooling of interest |
| d. | Elimination entries | h. | Majority interest | m. | Purchase |
| | | i. | Minority interest | n. | Trading securities |

_____ 1. A corporation acquired and controlled by another company.

_____ 2. An informal statement on which elimination entries are shown.

_____ 3. A company that owns more than 50 percent of the outstanding voting common stock of another company.

_____ 4. Debit and credit combinations that are made in a parent's and subsidiaries' accounting records.

_____ 5. Intangible value attached to a business resulting from above-average earnings prospects.

_____ 6. Statements that result from combining the parent's and subsidiaries' financial statement amounts.

_____ 7. Debit and credit combinations that are made only on a consolidated statement work sheet.

_____ 8. Using this method, the Investment in Subsidiary Company remains at its acquisition price.

_____ 9. Claims of stockholders who own more than 50 percent of a subsidiary's outstanding voting common stock.

_____ 10. Claims of stockholders who own less than 50 percent of a subsidiary's outstanding voting common stock.

_____ 11. Using this method, the Investment in Subsidiary Company is adjusted for losses and income of the subsidiary.

_____ 12. Occurs when common stock is exchanged for common stock and certain other conditions are met.

_____ 13. Shares of common stock of another company that will be sold in the "near-term."

---

## COMPLETION AND EXERCISES

1. When a corporation invests in common or preferred stocks of other corporations, what constitutes the cost of the securities?

_____

_____

2. If a cash dividend of $8,000 is declared on securities held as investments in one period but paid in the next period, what is the entry required at the end of the first period?

| Date | Account Titles and Explanation | Post. Ref. | Debit | Credit |
|------|-------------------------------|------------|-------|--------|
|      |                               |            |       |        |
|      |                               |            |       |        |
|      |                               |            |       |        |

3. How is a stock dividend treated on securities held as investments?

_____

_____

_____

4. Securities may be written down below cost when their _____ _____ _____ is less than their _____ for a portfolio of securities classified as trading securities and for a portfolio classified as available-for-sale securities.

5. The account, Unrealized Loss on Available-for-Sale Securities, would be shown as

_____

6. On December 31, 1998, Ace Co. had a portfolio of trading securities that has a total cost of $84,000. During 1999 the following occurred:

    Purchased 100 shares of Mox Co. common stock at $50, plus a commission of $150.

    Received 20 shares of Kahn Co. common stock as a stock dividend.

    Sold 200 shares of Lee Co. common stock at $40, less commissions and other charges of $200. Cost of securities sold was $4,000.

    Cash dividends received, $5,600.

    At the end of 1999, the fair market value of the securities in the portfolio was $3,200 less than their cost.

    Prepare the necessary entries for 1999.

| Date | Account Titles and Explanation | Post. Ref. | Debit | Credit |
|------|-------------------------------|-----------|-------|--------|
|      |                               |           |       |        |
|      |                               |           |       |        |
|      |                               |           |       |        |
|      |                               |           |       |        |
|      |                               |           |       |        |
|      |                               |           |       |        |
|      |                               |           |       |        |
|      |                               |           |       |        |
|      |                               |           |       |        |
|      |                               |           |       |        |
|      |                               |           |       |        |
|      |                               |           |       |        |
|      |                               |           |       |        |
|      |                               |           |       |        |
|      |                               |           |       |        |
|      |                               |           |       |        |
|      |                               |           |       |        |
|      |                               |           |       |        |
|      |                               |           |       |        |
|      |                               |           |       |        |
|      |                               |           |       |        |
|      |                               |           |       |        |

| | | | | | | | | | |
|---|---|---|---|---|---|---|---|---|---|
| | | | | | | | | | |
| | | | | | | | | | |
| | | | | | | | | | |
| | | | | | | | | | |
| | | | | | | | | | |
| | | | | | | | | | |
| | | | | | | | | | |
| | | | | | | | | | |
| | | | | | | | | | |
| | | | | | | | | | |
| | | | | | | | | | |
| | | | | | | | | | |
| | | | | | | | | | |
| | | | | | | | | | |
| | | | | | | | | | |
| | | | | | | | | | |
| | | | | | | | | | |
| | | | | | | | | | |

7. A parent company owns _____ _____ _____ _____ of the outstanding voting common stock of another company, which is referred to as a _____ _____ .

8. Consolidated financial statements must be prepared when the following circumstances exist:

   a. _____

   _____

   b. _____

   _____

   _____

9. Elimination entries are made only on a _____ _____

   _____ _____ .

10. The cost of an investment in a subsidiary may exceed the investment's book value for either or both of the following reasons:

   a. _____

   _____

b. _____

_____

11. When the cost of an investment exceeds its underlying book value and none of the subsidiary's assets is considered to be undervalued, the excess of cost over book value is labeled _____ on the consolidated balance sheet.

12. What is the elimination entry needed if on the date of acquisition the parent company loaned the subsidiary company $5,000 on a note receivable?

| | | | | | | | | | |
|---|---|---|---|---|---|---|---|---|---|
| | | | | | | | | | |
| | | | | | | | | | |
| | | | | | | | | | |
| | | | | | | | | | |
| | | | | | | | | | |
| | | | | | | | | | |

13. A minority interest appears on the consolidated balance sheet when _____

_____

14. Using the equity method, earnings of a subsidiary _____ the balance of the investment account, while losses incurred by a subsidiary _____ the investment account balance. Dividends paid by a subsidiary _____ the investment account balance.

15. When Goodwill is recorded on the books, what happens to it?

_____

(See Chapter 11 for review.)

16. According to *APB Opinion No. 16*, business combinations can be classified into two categories:

(a) _____ and (b) _____ _____ _____. A _____

_____ _____ is a business combination that results when common

stock is exchanged for common stock and the conditions specified in *APB Opinion No. 16* are

satisfied. All other business combinations are classified as _____.

17. Add Company acquired 100 percent of the outstanding voting common stock of City Company for $500,000. On the date of acquisition, City Company's stockholders' equity consists of common stock, $400,000, and retained earnings, $85,000. What journal entry should be made by Add Company to record the above transaction?

| | | | | | | | | | |
|---|---|---|---|---|---|---|---|---|---|
| | | | | | | | | | |
| | | | | | | | | | |
| | | | | | | | | | |
| | | | | | | | | | |

18. Refer back to Question 18. Assume that a consolidated statement work sheet is prepared on the date of acquisition. What elimination entry must be made? (The subsidiary's tangible assets are not overvalued or undervalued.)

_____

_____

_____

_____

19. The Lewis Company acquired 40 percent of the outstanding voting common stock of the Corley Company for $670,000 on January 2, 1999. During 1999, the Corley Company had net income of $96,000 and paid out $47,000 in dividends on common stock. What journal entries should be made by Lewis Company to record the above events assuming it uses the equity method?

| | | | | | | | | | | |
|---|---|---|---|---|---|---|---|---|---|---|
| | | | | | | | | | | |
| | | | | | | | | | | |
| | | | | | | | | | | |
| | | | | | | | | | | |
| | | | | | | | | | | |
| | | | | | | | | | | |
| | | | | | | | | | | |
| | | | | | | | | | | |
| | | | | | | | | | | |
| | | | | | | | | | | |
| | | | | | | | | | | |
| | | | | | | | | | | |
| | | | | | | | | | | |
| | | | | | | | | | | |
| | | | | | | | | | | |
| | | | | | | | | | | |

20. Under the purchase method of accounting, a parent company records an investment in a subsidiary at the

_____

_____

_____

_____

_____

_____

21. Under the pooling of interests method, what portion of the subsidiary's net income is included in consolidated net income for the year of acquisition?

_____

_____

22. Under the pooling of interests method, an investment in a subsidiary is recorded at the _____

_____

23. Assume that the amount paid by a parent corporation for the stock of a subsidiary is either more or less than the book value of the subsidiary interest.

   a. If the cost exceeds the book value:

      1. Where will the amount be reported on the consolidated balance sheet?

      _____

      _____

      2. Into what account on the work sheet is the excess classified?

      _____

   b. If the book value exceeds the cost:

      1. What is the most logical explanation?

      _____

      _____

      2. In this case, what is the correct treatment?

      _____

24. The consolidated financial statements are of primary importance to _____

_____

25. The creditors and minority stockholders of a subsidiary are primarily interested in the _____

_____

financial statements.

26. Tinker Company acquired 82 percent of the outstanding voting common stock of Morton Company for $402,000. On the date of acquisition, the minority interest in Morton Company amounts to $90,000. The book value of Tinker Company's investment in Morton Company is _____. What is the relationship between the cost and the book value of the investment? _____

_____

27. On January 1, 1999, the Paul Company acquired 75 percent of the outstanding voting common stock of the Sowell Company for $148,000. Also on January 1, 1999, the Sowell Company borrowed $12,000 from the Paul Company. The debt is evidenced by a note. Complete the consolidated statement work sheet shown below. The subsidiary's tangible assets are neither overvalued nor undervalued.

## PAUL COMPANY AND SUBSIDIARY SOWELL COMPANY
### Work Sheet for Consolidated Balance Sheet
### January 1, 1999

| Accounts | Paul Company | Sowell Company | Eliminations Debit | Eliminations Credit | Consolidated Amounts |
|---|---|---|---|---|---|
| *Assets:* | | | | | |
| Cash ............................................. | 36,000 | 18,000 | | | |
| Notes receivable ......................... | 12,000 | | | | |
| Accounts receivable, net .......... | 29,000 | 19,000 | | | |
| Merchandise inventory ............. | 34,000 | 27,000 | | | |
| Investment in Sowell Co. ......... | 148,000 | | | | |
| Equipment, net ........................... | 47,000 | 50,000 | | | |
| Buildings, net ............................. | 83,000 | 74,000 | | | |
| Land ............................................. | 28,000 | 22,000 | | | |
| | 417,000 | 210,000 | | | |
| *Liabilities and Stockholders' Equity:* | | | | | |
| Notes payable ............................. | | 12,000 | | | |
| Accounts payable ....................... | 26,000 | 10,000 | | | |
| Common stock ............................. | 250,000 | 110,000 | | | |
| Retained earnings ...................... | 141,000 | 78,000 | | | |
| | 417,000 | 210,000 | | | |

28. Using the consolidated statement work sheet prepared for Question 18, prepare a consolidated balance sheet in the space provided below.

29. The dividend yield on common stock is equal to the dividend per share of common stock divided by the

_____ _____ _____ _____ _____ .

30. Last year, Company C paid a $2 dividend per share on its common stock and had earnings per share of $10. The current market price of Company C's common stock is $25. Company C's payout ratio on common stock is _____%.

31. (Appendix) The temporal method is an example of one of the methods used to _____ financial statements.

## TRUE-FALSE QUESTIONS

Indicate whether each of the following statements is true or false by inserting a capital "T" or "F" in the blank space provided.

_____ 1. A loss resulting from a permanent decline in fair market value on available-for-sale securities is reported on the income statement.

_____ 2. Upon the receipt of stock dividends, an investor debits an asset account and credits a revenue account.

_____ 3. Even when the parent and subsidiary are not engaged in similar or related businesses, consolidated financial statements must usually be prepared.

_____ 4. In the consolidating process of preparing financial statements for the parent and its subsidiaries, elimination entries are made in the subsidiary's respective journals.

_____ 5. One of the purposes of consolidated financial statements is to show a parent and its subsidiaries as one economic enterprise.

_____ 6. The reason that the elimination entry is needed crediting the Investment in Subsidiary Company is that if both the investment account and the subsidiary's assets appear on the consolidated balance sheet, the same resources will be counted twice.

_____ 7. When a subsidiary is acquired at a cost above its book value and its assets are undervalued, Goodwill is recognized in the elimination entries.

_____ 8. When a parent company pays less than book value of the subsidiary's net assets, it generally indicates that the parent has acquired a "bargain" purchase.

_____ 9. Even though minority stockholders own less than 50 percent of the subsidiary's outstanding voting common stock, they share in subsidiary earnings with the parent company.

_____ 10. There is lack of agreement among accountants as to whether the minority interest is a liability or a part of stockholders' equity.

_____ 11. When a subsidiary pays dividends, both the parent company and the minority stockholders share in the dividends.

_____ 12. When a subsidiary is acquired at a cost less than its book value and its assets are overvalued, the Accounting Principles Board requires that the excess of book value over cost be used to reduce proportionately the value of the noncurrent assets acquired.

_____ 13. Under the equity method, when a subsidiary incurs a loss, the parent company debits a loss account and credits an investment account for the parent's share of the loss.

_____ 14. Consolidated statements are of great use to creditors and minority stockholders of the subsidiary because these creditors can look to the parent company for payment.

_____ 15. When the purchase method is used, and cost exceeds book value because depreciable assets are undervalued, more depreciation will be recorded under the purchase method than under the pooling of interests method.

_____ 16. Under the equity method, when a subsidiary reports net income, the parent company debits the investment account and credits a revenue account for the parent's share of the net income.

_____ 17. Subsidiary creditors are more interested in the consolidated statements than in the individual financial statements of the subsidiary.

_____ 18. The payout ratio on common stock provides an index of whether a company pays out a large percentage of earnings as dividends or reinvests most of its earnings.

_____ 19. (Appendix) There is no organization that ensures compliance with international accounting standards.

## MULTIPLE CHOICE QUESTIONS

For each of the following questions indicate the best answer by circling the appropriate letter.

1. The book value of stock is:

   A. Accumulated depreciation less the related plant asset's original cost.
   B. Total stockholders' equity.
   C. Net assets.
   D. The price at which the corporation's stock is selling on the market.
   E. B and C above.

2. Lewis Company acquired all of the stock of Downs Company for $200,000. The entry needed is:

   A. Investment in Lewis Company ......................................... 200,000
          Cash ................................................................................        200,000

   B. Investment in Downs Company ....................................... 200,000

|                        |         | 200,000 |
|------------------------|---------|---------|
| C.  Cash ..............................................................................................  | 200,000 |         |
|         Investment Income  .......................................................... |         | 200,000 |
|                        |         |         |
| D.  Cash  .............................................................................................. | 200,000 |         |
|         Investment in Downs Company  ................................................. |         | 200,000 |

E.  None of the above.

3.  If the following balances exist prior to the preparation of a consolidated balance sheet, what elimination entry is needed if the parent owns 100 percent of the subsidiary?

|                                      | Parent Company | Subsidiary Company |
|--------------------------------------|----------------|--------------------|
| Common Stock...........................................  | 340,000        | 50,000             |
| Investment in Subsidiary Company  ...... | 75,000         |                    |
| Retained Earnings............................. ......  | 180,000        | 25,000             |

A.  Investment in Subsidiary Company  ................................................. 75,000
        Retained earnings .........................................................................        25,000
        Common Stock ...............................................................................        50,000

B.  Common Stock .............................................................................. 390,000
        Retained Earnings.........................................................................        205,000
        Investment in Subsidiary Company  .............................................        185,000

C.  Retained Earnings........................................................................ 25,000
        Common Stock ............................................................................... 50,000
        Investment in Subsidiary Company  .............................................        75,000

D.  Gain from Elimination of Subsidiary Company ............................. 75,000
        Investment in Subsidiary Company  .............................................        75,000

E.  None of the above.

4.  Q Company acquired 100 percent ownership of O Company for $100,000 after evaluating its assets and finding that its building is undervalued by $1,000 and that its prospects of above-industry earnings are good. Q Company management attaches $7,500 value to these earnings prospects. O Company's Common Stock has a balance of $62,500 and its Retained Earnings has a balance of $29,000. Q Company's Common Stock has a balance of $90,000 and its Retained Earnings has a balance of $32,500. The elimination entry needed is:

A.  Investment in O Company  ........................................................... 100,000
        Retained Earnings.........................................................................        10,000
        Common Stock ...............................................................................        90,000

| B. | Common Stock | 152,500 | |
| | Retained Earnings | 64,000 | |
| | Investment in O Company | | 100,000 |
| | Goodwill | | 116,500 |

| C. | Common Stock | 62,500 | |
| | Retained Earnings | 29,000 | |
| | Building | 1,000 | |
| | Goodwill | 7,500 | |
| | Investment in O Company | | 100,000 |

| D. | Common Stock | 62,500 | |
| | Retained Earnings | 29,000 | |
| | Investment in O Company | | 91,500 |

| E. | Common Stock | 62,500 | |
| | Retained Earnings | 29,000 | |
| | Excess of Cost Over Book Value | 8,500 | |
| | Investment in O Company | | 100,000 |

5. P Company purchased 70 percent of Subsidiary Company's stock for $90,000 at a time when Subsidiary Company's Common Stock balance was $90,000 and its Retained Earnings balance was $30,000. P Company attributed any excess to the excellent prospects of above-average earnings. The *credits* needed in the elimination entry are:

| A. | Investment in Subsidiary Company | 90,000 |
| | Minority Interest | 36,000 |
| B. | Goodwill | 6,000 |
| | Investment in Subsidiary Company | 90,000 |
| C. | Minority Interest | 50,000 |
| | Investment in Subsidiary Company | 90,000 |
| D. | Common Stock | 90,000 |
| | Retained Earnings | 30,000 |
| E. | Goodwill | 90,000 |
| | Investment in Subsidiary Company | 90,000 |

---

## SOLUTIONS

---

*Matching*

| 1. | c | 8. | k |
| 2. | e | 9. | h |
| 3. | a | 10. | i |
| 4. | g | 11. | j |
| 5. | f | 12. | l |
| 6. | b | 13. | n |
| 7. | d | | |

*Completion and Exercises*

1. The cost of the securities is the actual price of the securities plus any brokerage fee.

2. Dividends Receivable.................................................... 8,000
   Dividend Revenue................................................... 8,000

3. A notation is made of the larger number of shares held and the smaller per share cost.

4. Fair market value; cost

5. A deduction from total stockholders' equity or from total paid-in capital.

6. Trading Securities ...................................................... 5,150
   Cash .......................................................... 5,150
   Note: Received 20 shares of Kahn Co. common stock as a stock dividend.
   Cash ............................................................ 7,800
   Trading Securities ............................................. 4,000
   Realized Gain on Sale of Trading Securities ...................... 3,800
   Cash ............................................................ 5,600
   Dividend Revenue ............................................... 5,600
   Unrealized Loss on Trading Securities ........................... 3,200
   Trading Securities ............................................ 3,200

7. More than 50 percent (a majority); subsidiary company.

8. (a) one company owns more than 50 percent of the outstanding voting common stock of another company and (b) control is not likely to be temporary or does not rest with someone other than the majority owner. (e.g., company is in legal reorganization or bankruptcy.)

9. Consolidated statement work sheet

10. a. The parent may think the subsidiary's assets are undervalued.
    b. The parent may believe the subsidiary's earnings prospects justify paying a price greater than book value.

11. goodwill

12. Note Payable ........................................................ 5,000
    Note Receivable .................................................. 5,000

13. a parent owns less than 100 percent of a subsidiary

14. increase; decrease; decrease

15. Goodwill is required to be amortized over a period not to exceed 40 years.

16. (a) purchases; (b) poolings of interests; pooling of interests; purchases

17. Investment in City Company ......................................... 500,000
    Cash .......................................................... 500,000

| 18. Common Stock | 400,000 | |
| Retained Earnings | 85,000 | |
| Goodwill | 15,000 | |
| Investment in City Company | | 500,000 |

| 19. Investment in Corley Company | 670,000 | |
| Cash | | 670,000 |
| To record investment of 40 percent in subsidiary. | | |

| Investment in Corley Company | 38,400 | |
| Income from Corley Company | | 38,400 |
| To record 40 percent of subsidiary's income. | | |

| Cash | 18,800 | |
| Investment in Corley Company | | 18,800 |
| To record 40% of dividends paid by subsidiary. | | |

20. amount of cash given up, or at the fair market value of the assets or stock given up, or the fair market value of the stock received, whichever can be the most clearly and objectively determined.

21. all the subsidiary's net income for the year of acquisition

22. book value of the subsidiary's net assets

23. a.  1.  In the asset section, usually as the last item on the consolidated balance sheet.
    2.  Goodwill.
   b.  1.  Some of the subsidiary's assets are overvalued
    2.  The excess of book value over cost should be used to reduce proportionately the value of the noncurrent assets acquired. If noncurrent assets are reduced to zero, the remaining dollar amount should be classified as a deferred credit.

24. The stockholders, managers, and directors of the parent company

25. Subsidiary's

26. $410,000 (or $90,000 ÷ 0.18 = $500,000; $500,000 – $90,000 = $410,000)
    Book value exceeds cost by $8,000 (or $410,000 – $402,000).

**27.**

## PAUL COMPANY AND SUBSIDIARY SOWELL COMPANY
### Work Sheet for Consolidated Balance Sheet
### January 1, 1999

| Accounts | Paul Company | Sowell Company | Eliminations Debit | Eliminations Credit | Consolidated Amounts |
|---|---|---|---|---|---|
| *Assets:* | | | | | |
| Cash | 36,000 | 18,000 | | | 54,000 |
| Notes receivable | 12,000 | | | (b) 12,000 | |
| Accounts receivable, net | 29,000 | 19,000 | | | 48,000 |
| Merchandise inventory | 34,000 | 27,000 | | | 61,000 |
| Investment in Sowell Co. | 148,000 | | | (a) 148,000 | |
| Equipment, net | 47,000 | 50,000 | | | 97,000 |
| Buildings, net | 83,000 | 74,000 | | | 157,000 |
| Land | 28,000 | 22,000 | | | 50,000 |
| Goodwill | | | (a) 7,000 | | 7,000 |
| | 417,000 | 210,000 | | | 474,000 |
| *Liabilities and Stockholders' Equity:* | | | | | |
| Notes payable | | 12,000 | (b) 12,000 | | |
| Accounts payable | 26,000 | 10,000 | | | 36,000 |
| Common stock | 250,000 | 110,000 | (a) 110,000 | | 250,000 |
| Retained earnings | 141,000 | 78,000 | (a) 78,000 | | 141,000 |
| Minority interest | | | | (a) 47,000 | 47,000 |
| | 417,000 | 210,000 | 207,000 | 207,000 | 474,000 |

**28.**

## PAUL COMPANY AND SUBSIDIARY SOWELL COMPANY
### Consolidated Balance Sheet
### January 1, 1999

*Assets*

Current assets:
Cash ................................................................................................ $ 54,000
Accounts receivable, net .......................................................... 48,000
Merchandise Inventory ............................................................. 61,000
    Total current assets ............................................................ $163,000
Plant and equipment:
Equipment, net ........................................................................... $ 97,000
Buildings, net .............................................................................. 157,000
Land ............................................................................................... 50,000
    Total plant and equipment .............................................. 304,000
Goodwill ............................................................................................... 7,000
    Total assets ............................................................................ $474,000

*Liabilities and Stockholders' Equity*

Current liabilities:
Accounts payable .............................................................................. $ 36,000
Minority interest ............................................................................... 47,000
Stockholders' equity:

| | | |
|---|---|---|
| Common stock ............................................................................ | $250,000 | |
| Retained earnings ....................................................................... | 141,000 | |
| Total stockholders' equity .................................................. | | 391,000 |
| Total liabilities and stockholders' equity ............................ | | $474,000 |

29. Current market price per share

30. 20%

31. translate

## True-False Questions

1. **T** When a loss is realized, it must be recognized in the income statement.

2. **F** Income is not recognized upon the receipt of stock dividends.

3. **T** Since the parent and subsidiary are controlled by a central management, the parent is required to prepare combined financial statements.

4. **F** Elimination entries are not made in the accounting records of the parent or the subsidiary; they are made only on a consolidated statement work sheet.

5. **T**

6. **T**

7. **F** Goodwill is recognized only when there are prospects of above-average earnings; in this case, the asset amounts should be increased to their fair market value.

8. **F** It generally means that the subsidiary's assets are overvalued.

9. **T** Minority stockholders share in subsidiary earnings.

10. **T**

11. **T** Minority stockholders share dividends with the parent company.

12. **T**

13. **T**

14. **F** Creditors and minority stockholders of the subsidiary cannot look to the parent for payment.

15. **T** The book value of the depreciable assets will be higher under the purchase method than under the pooling of interests method.

16. **T** The debit to the investment account increases the parent's equity in the subsidiary company.

17. **F** Subsidiary creditors cannot look to parent company investments as a means to satisfy their debts a result they are more interested in a subsidiary's individual financial statements.

18. T

19. T

*Multiple Choice Questions*

1. E

2. B

3. C

4. C

5. A   The complete journal entry is:

| | | |
|---|--:|--:|
| Common Stock ............................................................................. | 90,000 | |
| Retained Earnings ...................................................................... | 30,000 | |
| Goodwill ..................................................................................... | 6,000 | |
|     Investment in Subsidiary Company ............................................... | | 90,000 |
|     Minority Interest (30% × $120,000) ....................................................... | | 36,000 |

# CHAPTER 15

# LONG-TERM FINANCING: BONDS

## Learning Objectives

1. *Describe the features of bonds and tell how bonds differ from shares of stock.*
2. *List the advantages and disadvantages of financing with long-term debt and prepare examples showing how to employ financial leverage.*
3. *Prepare journal entries for bonds issued at face value.*
4. *Explain how interest rates affect bond prices and what causes a bond to sell at a premium or a discount.*
5. *Apply the concept of present value to compute the price of a bond.*
6. *Prepare journal entries for bonds issued at a discount or a premium.*
7. *Prepare journal entries for bond redemptions and bond conversions.*
8. *Describe the ratings used for bonds.*
9. *Analyze and use the financial results — times interest earned ratio.*
10. *Explain future value and present value concepts and make required calculations (Appendix).*

## REFERENCE OUTLINE

## CHAPTER OUTLINE

### BONDS PAYABLE

*Learning Objective 1:*
*Describe the features of bonds and tell how bonds differ from shares of stock.*

1. Bonds are a common form of long-term financing and are a written instrument in the form of an unconditional promise, made under seal, wherein the borrower promises to pay a specified sum at a determinable future date and interest at a stated rate and on stated dates.
2. The bond certificate is physical evidence of the debt.
3. The borrower agrees to pay the face or principal amount of the bond on a specific maturity date and usually periodic interest at a specified rate on the face value at stated dates.

### COMPARISON WITH STOCK

4. Bonds differ from stock in the following ways:
   a. A bond is a debt, while stock represents ownership.
   b. Bonds have maturity dates, while stock does not mature.
   c. Bonds require stated periodic interest payments by the company; dividends to stockholders are payable only when declared.
   d. Bond interest is deductible by the issuer in computing both net income and taxable income, while dividends are not deductible in either computation.

### SELLING (ISSUING) BONDS

5. An investment firm or banker, called an underwriter, usually sells a bond issue.
   a. The trustee usually is a bank or trust company that represents the bondholders.
   b. A bond indenture is the contract or loan agreement under which the bond is issued.

### CHARACTERISTICS OF BONDS

6. All bonds have these two characteristics:
   a. They promise to pay cash or other assets.
   b. They come due or mature.
7. In other respects, bonds may differ as to features such as the following:
   a. Secured bonds are secured by a pledge against real estate, machinery, merchandise, investments, or personal property.
   b. Debenture bonds are unsecured bonds issued against the general credit of the corporation.
   c. Registered bonds are those for which interest is paid to the owner by check.
   d. Bearer bonds are unregistered and are assumed to be the property of the holder (or bearer).

e. Coupon bonds carry detachable coupons that are to be clipped and presented for payment of interest due.

f. Term bonds mature on the same date as all other bonds in a given bond issue.

g. Serial bonds mature in installments through time.

h. Callable bonds contain a provision that gives the issuer the right to call (buy back) the bonds before their maturity date.

i. Convertible bonds may be converted at the bondholder's option and under stated conditions into stock of the issuing corporation.

j. Junk bonds with high interest rates were issued in the 1980s to finance corporate restructurings.

8. Bonds may be issued with stock warrants that allow the holder to purchase shares of stock at a fixed price for some stated period of time.

a. A bond with nondetachable warrants is virtually the same as a convertible bond.

b. Detachable warrants allow bondholders to keep their bonds and still purchase shares of stock through exercise of the warrants.

*Learning Objective 2:*
*List the advantages and disadvantages of financing with long-term debt and prepare examples showing how to employ financial leverage.*

ADVANTAGES OF ISSUING DEBT

9. The advantages of issuing bonds when additional long-term funds are needed include the following:

a. Stockholder ownership is not shared with the bondholders.

b. The interest rate may be less than the dividend rate on the capital stock of the firm.

c. Interest is deductible for tax purposes, whereas dividends are not.

d. If borrowed funds can generate net income greater than their interest cost (favorable financial leverage), corporate earnings per share are enhanced, to the benefit of the stockholders.

e. A company is said to be trading on the equity when it issues bonds or is employing other financial leverage such as issuing preferred stock or long-term notes.

DISADVANTAGES OF ISSUING DEBT

10. Under certain conditions, there are also disadvantages to issuing bonds:

a. The interest expense represents a contractual obligation that must be paid if default on the loan is to be avoided.

b. The ability of the company to absorb losses prior to becoming insolvent is reduced.

c. If the borrowed funds generate net income less than their interest cost (unfavorable financial leverage), the additional amount of interest paid over the amount earned reduces the corporate earnings per share available. This reduction is to the detriment of the stockholders.

d. A bond indenture may require a certain amount of working capital and place limitations on dividends and additional borrowings.

*Learning Objective 3:*
*Prepare journal entries for bonds issued at face value.*

ACCOUNTING FOR BONDS ISSUED AT FACE VALUE

11. The bonds authorized may all be issued at one time, or a portion at one date and the remainder later, as a source of future funds.

BONDS ISSUED AT FACE VALUE ON AN INTEREST DATE

12. When the bonds are issued at face value on an interest date, Cash is debited for the amount received and Bonds Payable is credited for the face value on the bonds issued.

# BONDS ISSUED AT FACE VALUE BETWEEN INTEREST DATES

13. If bonds are issued at face value between interest dates, the sales price must include accrued interest.
    a. The issuing company will debit Cash and credit Bonds Payable and Bond Interest Payable.
    b. At the next interest payment date, Bond Interest Payable and Bond Interest Expense are debited and Cash is credited.

*Learning Objective 4:*
*Explain how interest rates affect bond prices and what causes a bond to sell at a premium or a discount.*

# BOND PRICES AND INTEREST RATES

14. If the interest rate on the bonds is lower than that demanded by the investors (the market rate), the bonds will be issued at a discount.
15. If the interest rate on the bonds is higher than that demanded by the investors (the market rate), the bonds will be issued at a premium.

*Learning Objective 5:*
*Apply the concept of present value to compute the price of a bond.*

# COMPUTING BOND PRICES

16. The issue price comprises the sum of the present values of the principal due at maturity and the interest to be paid periodically; the interest rate involved being that demanded by the investors for bonds of that risk category. Use the tables in the Appendix at the end of the text to calculate bond prices.

*Learning Objective 6:*
*Prepare journal entries for bonds issued at a discount or a premium.*

# BONDS ISSUED AT A DISCOUNT

17. If bonds are issued at a discount:
    a. The discount, the difference between the face value and the issue price, is debited to a Discount on Bonds Payable or Bonds Payable—Discount account.
    b. The discount represents a cost of using funds to the borrower and represents additional interest earnings to the investor.
    c. The total cost of borrowing is the sum of the total periodic interest payments plus the total discount.
    d. The discount is allocated or amortized, on the effective interest rate basis or on a straight-line basis, over the remaining life of the bonds. The discount account is credited, and Interest Expense is debited.
    e. When a balance sheet is prepared, the remaining balance of the discount account is shown as a deduction from bonds payable.

# BONDS ISSUED AT A PREMIUM

18. If bonds are issued at a premium:
    a. The premium, the difference between the face value and the issue price, is credited to a Premium on Bonds Payable or Bonds Payable—Premium account.
    b. The premium represents a reduction in the cost of using funds to the borrower and represents a reduction in interest earnings to the investor.
    c. The total cost of borrowing is the total periodic interest payments minus the total premium.
    d. The premium is allocated or amortized, on the effective interest rate basis or on a straight-line basis, over the remaining life of the bonds. The premium account is debited, and Interest Expense is credited.

e.    When a balance sheet is prepared, the remaining balance of the premium account is shown as an addition to bonds payable.

DISCOUNT/PREMIUM AMORTIZATION

19.    The bond interest expense recorded each period differs from the cash payment for bond interest if bonds are issued at a premium or discount.

20.    Two methods are available for amortizing a discount or premium on bonds: straight-line method and effective interest rate method.

    a.    Under the straight-line method, interest expense is recorded at a constant amount.

    b.    Under the effective interest rate method, interest expense for any period is equal to the effective (market) rate of interest at date of issuance times the carrying value of the bonds at the beginning of that interest period.

21.    A discount or premium amortization schedule aids in preparing entries for interest expense.

*Learning Objective 7:*
*Prepare journal entries for bond redemptions and bond conversions.*

REDEEMING BONDS PAYABLE

22.    Redemption of bonds (or extinguishment of debt) may occur in the following ways:

    a.    Paid at maturity.

    b.    Called.

    c.    Purchased in the market and retired.

23.    When bonds are redeemed in total at maturity by direct payment from the cash of the issuing company, the journal entry is to debit Bonds Payable and credit Cash for the face amount.

SERIAL BONDS

24.    Serial bonds mature over several dates and avoid the burden of redeeming an entire bond issue at one time.

    a.    The amount maturing the next year is reported as a current liability.

    b.    The entry to retire a serial bond is to debit Serial Bonds Payable and credit Cash.

BOND REDEMPTION OR SINKING FUNDS

25.    Bond redemption funds or sinking funds are required in bond indentures to reduce the risk of default at maturity date. Cash deposited with the sinking fund trustee can only be used to redeem bonds.

    a.    The entry to record a payment to the trustee is a debit to Sinking Fund and a credit to Cash.

    b.    When bonds are redeemed out of the sinking fund, Bonds Payable and Bond Interest Expense on bonds redeemed are debited and Sinking Fund is credited.

    c.    Expenses paid by the trustee are debited to Sinking Fund Expenses and credited to Cash.

CONVERTIBLE BONDS

26.    Bonds may be convertible into shares of the issuer's common stock.

    a.    The entry made when bonds are converted is to debit Bonds Payable and credit Common Stock. Any unamortized discount or premium on the bonds is closed out.

    b.    A Paid-in Capital account is established for the difference.

*Learning Objective 8:*
*Describe the ratings used for bonds.*

## BOND RATING SERVICES

27. Bonds are rated as to their riskiness.
    a. The two leading bond rating services are Moody's Investors Service and Standard & Poor's Corporation.
    b. As a company's prospects change over time, the ratings of its outstanding bonds change because of the higher or lower probability that the company can pay the interest and principal on the bonds when due.
    c. The ratings of these two services appear daily in such sources as The Wall Street Journal.

*Learning Objective 9:*
*Analyze and use the financial results – times interest earned ratio.*

## ANALYZING AND USING THE FINANCIAL RESULTS—TIMES INTEREST EARNED RATIO

28. The times interest earned ratio indicates the ability of a company to meet required interest payments when due.
    a. The ratio is found by dividing Income Before Interest and Taxes by Interest Expense.
    b. The higher the ratio, the greater the ability to meet interest payments. [E15-9]

*Learning Objective 10:*
*Explain future value and present value concepts and make required calculations (Appendix).*

## APPENDIX—FUTURE VALUE AND PRESENT VALUE

29. Future value and present value concepts deal with the time value of money.

## THE TIME VALUE OF MONEY

30. The time value of money concept is based on the preference for having a dollar today rather than a dollar at some future date because:
    a. there is risk that the future dollar will never be received.
    b. if the dollar is on hand now it can be invested resulting in an increase in total dollars possessed in the future.

## FUTURE VALUE

31. The future value of an investment is the amount to which a sum of money invested today will grow in a stated time period at a specified interest rate.
    a. Simple interest is interest on principal only.
    b. Compound interest is interest on principal and on interest of prior periods.

## FUTURE VALUE OF AN ANNUITY

32. An annuity is a series of equal cash flows spaced equally in time.

## PRESENT VALUE

33. The present value concept is useful in determining the price of a bond and in amortizing a premium or accumulating a discount.

34. Present value is the current worth of a future cash receipt and is essentially the reverse of future value.

## PRESENT VALUE OF AN ANNUITY

35. An annuity is a series of equal cash flows spaced equally in time; semiannual interest payments on a bond form a frequently encountered annuity.

# DEMONSTRATION PROBLEM

On May 1, Macbeth issued $100,000, 5-year, 8% bonds at a price to yield a 10% annual effective rate. Interest is to be paid on May 1 and November 1. The fiscal year is the calendar year.

Required:

a. Prepare the entries for purchase of the bonds.

b. Using the effective interest rate method, present entries to recognize the interest incurred for the first six months.

c. Prepare entries to accrue interest and record discount amortization at year-end.

## GENERAL JOURNAL

| Date | Account Titles and Explanation | Post. Ref. | Debit | Credit |
|------|-------------------------------|------------|-------|--------|
|      |                               |            |       |        |
|      |                               |            |       |        |
|      |                               |            |       |        |
|      |                               |            |       |        |
|      |                               |            |       |        |
|      |                               |            |       |        |
|      |                               |            |       |        |
|      |                               |            |       |        |
|      |                               |            |       |        |
|      |                               |            |       |        |
|      |                               |            |       |        |
|      |                               |            |       |        |
|      |                               |            |       |        |
|      |                               |            |       |        |
|      |                               |            |       |        |
|      |                               |            |       |        |
|      |                               |            |       |        |
|      |                               |            |       |        |
|      |                               |            |       |        |
|      |                               |            |       |        |
|      |                               |            |       |        |
|      |                               |            |       |        |
|      |                               |            |       |        |
|      |                               |            |       |        |

# SOLUTION TO DEMONSTRATION PROBLEM

a. May 1 Present value of the promise to pay principal is $100,000 x the present value of $1 due in 10 periods at 5%. Using Table A.3
$100,000 x .61391................................................................ $61,391.00

Present value of the promise to pay periodic interest is $4,000 times the present value of an annuity of $1 for 10 periods at 5% — $4,000 x 7.72173 from Table A.4.............................. 

30,886.92
$92,277.92

The discount is $100,000 – $92,277.92 = $7,722.08

| | | |
|---|---|---|
| Cash..................................................................... | 92,277.92 | |
| Discount on Bonds Payable ................................... | 7,722.08 | |
| Bonds Payable........................................................ | | 100,000.00 |

b. November 1

| | | |
|---|---|---|
| Bond Interest Expense ......................................... | 4,613.90 | |
| Discount on Bonds Payable .............................. | | 613.90 |
| Cash........................................................................ | | 4,000.00 |

($92,277.92 x 10% x ½ = $4,613.90; $4,613.90 – $4,000.00 = $613.90 discount amortization)

c. December 31

| | | |
|---|---|---|
| Bond Interest Expense ......................................... | 1,548.20 | |
| Discount on Bonds Payable .............................. | | 214.87 |
| Bond Interest Payable ........................................ | | 1,333.33 |

($92,891.82 x 10% x 2/12 = $1,548.20;
$1,548.20 – $1,333.33 = $214.87 discount amortization)

---

# MATCHING

Referring to the terms listed below, place the appropriate letter next to the corresponding description.

| | | | | | |
|---|---|---|---|---|---|
| a. | Bond | f. | Convertible bonds | k. | Serial bonds |
| b. | Bond indenture | g. | Effective interest rate method | l. | Trustee |
| c. | Call premium | h. | Favorable financial leverage | m. | Underwriter |
| d. | Carrying value | i. | Market rate of interest | n. | Unsecured bond |
| e. | Coupon bonds | j. | Registered bond | o. | Times interest earned ratio |

_____ 1. Bonds that mature over several dates.

_____ 2. A debenture bond.

_____ 3. A bond in which the name of the owner appears on the bond certificate.

_____ 4. The addition to earnings of the owners from earning more with borrowed funds than the interest that must be paid for their use.

_____ 5. The $50 above face value per bond that a company paid when it redeemed all of a bond issue before its maturity date.

_____ 6. The bank or trust company selected to act for the bondholders.

_____ 7. The investment banking firm that aids a company in marketing a bond issue.

_____ 8. Bonds on which interest is paid by a means other than checks.

_____ 9. The rate of interest a bond is sold to yield.

_____ 10. The theoretically correct way of computing periodic interest expense on a bond.

_____ 11. Bonds that can be exchanged for shares of the issuer's stock.
_____ 12. Face value of a bond issue, plus unamortized premium.
_____ 13. Substantially the same as a note.
_____ 14. The contract containing all of the provisions under which bonds were issued.
_____ 15. Income before interest and taxes divided by interest expense.

## COMPLETION AND EXERCISES

1.  Favorable financial leverage exists when borrowed funds can generate net income
    _____ than their interest cost.

2.  If the interest rate on the bonds is higher than the market rate of interest for bonds of that
    risk category, the bonds will be issued at a _____.

3.  Outland Company issued on January 1, 1999, $100,000, 10-year, 10% bonds at an effective
    rate of 8%. The interest payment is made on January 1 and July 1 every year.
    Required:
    a.  What is the entry to record the sale of the bonds on January 1, 1999?
    b.  Give the entry for the first interest payment. (Use straight-line amortization.)
    c.  When may the straight-line method be used?

| a. | | | | | | | |
|---|---|---|---|---|---|---|---|
| | | | | | | | |
| | | | | | | | |
| | | | | | | | |
| | | | | | | | |
| | | | | | | | |
| | | | | | | | |
| b. | | | | | | | |
| | | | | | | | |
| | | | | | | | |
| | | | | | | | |
| c. | | | | | | | |
| | | | | | | | |
| | | | | | | | |

4. Present entries, in general journal form, to record the selected transactions of Timon Company described below.

    a. Issued $1,000,000 of 10-year, 9% bonds at 101-1/2. The interest is paid semiannually.
    b. The payment of semiannual interest; the amortization of bond premium for this period is $750.
    c. Redemption of bonds at 101. The bonds were carried at $1,012,000 at the time of the redemption.

| a. | | | | |
|----|---|---|---|---|
| | | | | |
| | | | | |
| | | | | |
| | | | | |
| b. | | | | |
| | | | | |
| | | | | |
| | | | | |
| | | | | |
| c. | | | | |
| | | | | |
| | | | | |
| | | | | |

5. On August 1, 1999, Kelley Company issued for cash, at 100 plus accrued interest, $1,000,000 of 10-year, 9% bonds, dated January 1, 1999, which call for semi-annual interest payments on January 1 and July 1. What entries are necessary at issuance, and at December 31, 1999 (the accounting year-end)?

| | | | | |
|----|---|---|---|---|
| | | | | |
| | | | | |
| | | | | |
| | | | | |
| | | | | |

2. What is the first six months' journal entry to record interest under these conditions?

a.

b.

c. 1.

2.

| Date | Account Titles and Explanation | Post. Ref. | Debit | Credit |
|------|-------------------------------|------------|-------|--------|
|      |                               |            |       |        |
|      |                               |            |       |        |

19. a. On August 1, 1998, Titus Company issued for cash, at 100 plus accrued interest, $150,000 of five-year, 8% bonds, dated January 1, 1998, that call for semiannual interest payments on January 1 and July 1. What entries are necessary at issuance, and at December 31, 1998 (the accounting year-end)?

b. Assume instead that Titus Company issued the bonds on January 1, 1998, for cash of $162,780 — a price that yields 6%. Give the entries for 1998, including the December 31 adjusting entries. (Use the effective interest rate method.)

20. Baxter Company plans to issue $100,000 face value of 10%, 10-year bonds that are dated January 31, 1999. These bonds have semiannual interest payments and mature on January 31, 2009.

Required: (Round all amounts to the nearest dollar)

a. At what price should the bonds sell if they are priced to yield 12%?

b. Determine the first six months' interest expense assuming the bonds are issued at the price determined in (a).

c. If, instead, the bonds are priced to yield 6%, at what price should the bonds sell?

d. Assuming the bonds are sold to yield a 6% yield, what is the first six months' journal entry to record interest on the books of the issuer?

a.

b.

c.

| Date | Account Titles and Explanation | Post. Ref. | Debit | Credit |
|------|-------------------------------|-----------|-------|--------|
|  |  |  |  |  |
|  |  |  |  |  |
|  |  |  |  |  |

d.

| Date | Account Titles and Explanation | Post. Ref. | Debit | Credit |
|------|-------------------------------|-----------|-------|--------|
|  |  |  |  |  |
|  |  |  |  |  |
|  |  |  |  |  |
|  |  |  |  |  |
|  |  |  |  |  |

21. a. Prove that a $10,000 face value bond, bearing interest at 10%, payable semiannually, and maturing in 4 years, will sell for $10,000 if sold to yield ten percent.

|  |  |  |
|--|--|--|
|  |  |  |
|  |  |  |
|  |  |  |
|  |  |  |

b. If the same bond is issued to yield 8%, what price will it bring?

|  |  |  |
|--|--|--|
|  |  |  |
|  |  |  |
|  |  |  |
|  |  |  |

c. Give the entry to record the issuance of the bonds to yield 8% and the entry to record the first six months' interest expense.

| Date | Account Titles and Explanation | Post. Ref. | Debit | Credit |
|------|-------------------------------|-----------|-------|--------|
|  |  |  |  |  |
|  |  |  |  |  |
|  |  |  |  |  |
|  |  |  |  |  |
|  |  |  |  |  |
|  |  |  |  |  |

d. Compute the present value of the bonds sold to yield 8% with 6 periods (3 years) of life remaining.

| | | | | |
|---|---|---|---|---|
| | | | | |
| | | | | |
| | | | | |
| | | | | |
| | | | | |

22. The times interest earned ratio is equal to _____ _____ _____ _____ _____ divided by _____ _____.

**(The remaining questions are based on the chapter Appendix.)**

23. Interest is compounded whenever the amount of _____ for a period is computed and is added to the _____ to serve as the basis for computing interest for the next period.

24. The future value of $10,000 five years from now if invested at 6% compounded annually is _____.

25. If the interest in Question 24 had been compounded semiannually, what would the future value have been? _____

26. Present value is the _____ of future value.

27. Prove that Question 26 is true by showing that the present value of $13,382.30 (the answer to Question 24) to be received five years from now at 6% is $10,000. (Hint: Multiply $13,382.30 by the reciprocal of the factor used to answer Question 24.)

28. What is the present value of an annuity of $2,000 to be received at the end of each of the next ten years at 8% interest?

---

## TRUE-FALSE QUESTIONS

Indicate whether each of the following statements is true or false by inserting a capital "T" or "F" in the blank space provided.

_____ 1. Another term for determining present values is discounting.

_____ 2. The carrying value of bonds payable is the face value of the bonds plus any unamortized discount or less any unamortized premium.

_____ 3. Provisions in many bond indentures call for periodic payments to be made to a bond redemption fund, often called a petty cash fund.

_____ 4. Buyers of bearer bonds incur more risk through possible loss than do buyers of registered bonds.

_____ 5. Financial leverage is said to be favorable for an organization when borrowed funds are used to increase total assets of the organization.

_____ 6. Investors will be less attracted to bonds offering a coupon rate greater than the market rate for such bonds and will generally only buy these at a discount.

_____ 7. Unfavorable financial leverage may result from trading on the equity.

_____ 8. Favorable financial leverage may result from trading on the equity.

_____ 9. If bond interest is accrued, but not paid at the end of the accounting period, an adjusting entry should be made on the books of the issuer.

_____ 10. The recommended amortization procedure is the effective interest rate method, also referred to as the interest method.

_____ 11. When Premium on Bonds Payable is amortized, an entry crediting this account is needed.

_____ 12. Under the interest method of amortization, interest expense is recorded at a constant amount.

_____ 13. A bond may have a life of 50 years and call for quarterly interest payments.

_____ 14. When bonds are redeemed before maturity and the original sales price was above face value, the entry required to record the redemption is to debit Bonds Payable and credit Cash for the call price.

_____ 15. A bond is likely to be called and redeemed with funds secured from new borrowing after a period of rising interest rates.

_____ 16. The contract rate of interest is used to determine the amount of interest payable currently.

_____ 17. Bonds may be made more attractive by adding the convertible feature to them, which allows the bondholder to convert the bonds into shares of the issuer's common stock.

_____ 18. The amount a bond sells for above face value is called a discount.

_____ 19. Convertible bonds can be exchanged for other bonds issued by the same borrower.

_____ 20. Bonds are rated as to their riskiness.

# MULTIPLE CHOICE QUESTIONS

For each of the following questions indicate the best answer by circling the appropriate letter.

1. The contract rate:

   A. is stated in the bond indenture and printed on the face of each bond.

   B. is also called the coupon, nominal, or stated rate.

   C. is the minimum rate of interest investors are willing to accept on bonds of a particular risk category.

   D. All of the above.

   E. (A) and (B) above.

Questions 2-4. On April 30, 1999, Dee Co. issued $100,000 of 10-year, 9% bonds dated April 30 for $94,000 to yield 12%. Interest is payable semiannually on April 30 and October 31. Present the entries in general journal form to record the following transactions.

2. Issuance of the bonds:

   A. Investment in Bonds .................................................................. 94,000
          Cash ..................................................................................            94,000

   B. Cash ........................................................................................ 100,000
          Bonds Payable .................................................................         100,000

   C. Cash ........................................................................................ 94,000
          Discount on Bonds Payable ............................................ 6,000
          Bonds Payable .................................................................         100,000

   D. Cash ........................................................................................ 94,000
          Premium on Bonds Payable ............................................. 6,000
          Bonds Payable .................................................................         100,000

3. Accrual of interest and amortization of bond discount on October 31, 1999, using the effective interest rate method is:

| | | | |
|---|---|---|---|
| A. | Interest Expense ................................................................................... | 4,500 | |
| | Premium on Bonds Payable ............................................................... | 1,140 | |
| | Interest Payable ........................................................................ | | 5,640 |
| B. | Interest Expense ................................................................................... | 5,640 | |
| | Interest Payable ........................................................................ | | 4,500 |
| | Discount on Bonds Payable ............................................................ | | 1,140 |
| C. | Interest Expense ................................................................................... | 6,000 | |
| | Discount on Bonds Payable ............................................................ | | 6,000 |
| D. | Interest Expense ................................................................................... | 9,000 | |
| | Interest Payable ........................................................................ | | 9,000 |

4. Deposit of $6,000 in a bond sinking fund:

| | | | |
|---|---|---|---|
| A. | Sinking Fund ........................................................................................ | 6,000 | |
| | Cash .............................................................................................. | | 6,000 |
| B. | Investment in Bonds ........................................................................... | 6,000 | |
| | Cash .............................................................................................. | | 6,000 |
| C. | Cash ....................................................................................................... | 6,000 | |
| | Sinking Fund ............................................................................... | | 6,000 |
| D. | Investment in Bonds ........................................................................... | 6,000 | |
| | Bond Sinking Fund Income ........................................................... | | 6,000 |

5. When bonds are issued between interest dates at face value, the following is true:

A. One reason for the delay may be due to higher interest rates on the bond than anticipated.

B. Interest starts to accrue at the date of the bond sale.

C. Investors purchasing such bonds after they begin to accrue interest have an option whether they pay for the accrued interest.

D. The entry on the books of the issuer is a debit to Cash, a credit to Bonds Payable and a credit to Bond Interest Payable.

E. All of the above.

6. If $100,000 of 10% bonds bearing semiannual interest are sold to yield an effective interest rate of 12%, the following is true:

A. The bonds are issued at a discount.

B. The bonds are issued at a premium.

C. The Cash ledger account will be debited for $100,000.

D. The discount amortized each period will be the difference between the carrying value of the bonds × 6% and $5,000.

E. A and D.

7. Miller Corporation has a bond issue of $10,000 outstanding, on which there is an unamortized premium of $3,000. The corporation exercises its option of calling the bonds at 102. The entry is:

A. Bonds Payable ........................................................................... 10,000
   Premium on Bonds Payable ...................................................... 3,000
     Cash ........................................................................................ 13,000
B. Bonds Payable ........................................................................... 10,000
   Premium on Bonds Payable ...................................................... 3,000
     Cash ........................................................................................ 10,200
     Interest Revenue .................................................................. 2,800
C. Bonds Payable ........................................................................... 10,000
   Loss on Bond Redemption ....................................................... 200
     Cash ........................................................................................ 10,200
D. Bonds Payable ........................................................................... 10,000
   Premium on Bonds Payable ...................................................... 3,000
     Cash ........................................................................................ 10,200
     Gain on Bond Redemption .................................................. 2,800

Question 8-10. Smith Corporation issued $1,000,000 of 9%, 10-year convertible bonds for $985,000 to yield 10% on March 1, 1998; interest is payable March 1 and September 1. The conversion clause in the indenture granted the bondholders the right to convert the bonds after March 1, 2000, into shares of the company's common stock at the rate of 150 shares of $5 par value common stock for each $1,000 bond. The corporation completed the following transactions:

8. On September 1, 1998, Smith Corporation paid the interest on the bonds and amortized the discount. The entry using the effective interest rate method is:

A. Cash ........................................................................................ 985,000
   Discount on Bonds Payable ...................................................... 15,000
     Bonds Payable ...................................................................... 1,000,000
B. Bond Interest Expense .............................................................. 49,250
     Discount on Bonds Payable .................................................. 4,250
     Cash ........................................................................................ 45,000
C. Bond Interest Expense .............................................................. 45,000
     Cash ........................................................................................ 45,000
D. Bond Interest Expense .............................................................. 45,000
     Discount on Bonds Payable .................................................. 4,250
     Bond Interest Payable .......................................................... 40,750
E. Bond Interest Expense .............................................................. 49,250
     Discount on Bonds Payable .................................................. 1,250
     Cash ........................................................................................ 48,000

9. On March 1, 1999, after the semiannual interest on the bonds had been paid, Smith Corporation converted bonds having a face value of $300,000 to common stock. Assume that the unamortized discount on the converted bonds at this time totaled $1,538. The entry is:

A. Bonds Payable ................................................................................... 300,000
    Common Stock .............................................................................                                     300,000

B. Bonds Payable ................................................................................... 300,000
    Discount on Bonds Payable ................................................................. 75,000
    Common Stock................................................................................. 225,000

C. Bonds Payable ................................................................................... 300,000
    Discount on Bonds Payable ................................................................. 1,538
    Paid-in Capital in Excess of Par Value—Common Stock ............. 73,462
    Common Stock ................................................................................. 225,000

D. None of these.

10. On July 1, 2000, Smith Corporation purchased on the open market and retired bonds having a $100,000 face value. The total cash outlay was $97,500. Assume that the unamortized discount on the bonds retired was $900.

A. Bonds Payable ................................................................................... 100,000
    Cash .............................................................................................. 97,500
    Gain on Bond Redemption ................................................................. 2,500

B. Bonds Payable ................................................................................... 97,500
    Cash .............................................................................................. 97,500

C. Bonds Payable ................................................................................... 100,000
    Cash .............................................................................................. 97,500
    Discount on Bonds Payable ................................................................. 2,500

D. Bonds Payable ................................................................................... 100,000
    Discount on Bonds Payable ................................................................. 900
    Gain on Bond Redemption ................................................................. 1,600
    Cash .............................................................................................. 97,500

E. None of these.

11. What is (are) the credit(s) in the journal entry to record the issuance of $1,000,000 face value of 10-year 12% bonds dated October 31, 1998, at 103 (a price that yields 11%)? Interest is payable semiannually on October 31 and April 30.

A. Cash................................................................................................. 1,030,000
B. Premium on Bonds Payable ................................................................. 30,000
    Bonds Payable ................................................................................. 1,000,000
C. Bonds Payable ................................................................................... 1,000,000
D. Discount on Bonds Payable ................................................................. 30,000
    Bonds Payable ................................................................................. 1,000,000

12. What is the entry to record amortization of premium and interest payment on the above bonds on April 30, 1999?

A. Interest Expense ............................................................ 3,350

    Premium on Bonds Payable ..........................................     3,350

B. Premium on Bonds Payable ...................................... 3,350

    Interest Expense ............................................................ 60,000

    Cash .............................................................................     63,350

C. Interest Expense ............................................................ 60,000

    Premium on Bonds Payable ..........................................     60,000

D. Premium on Bonds Payable ...................................... 3,350

    Interest Expense ............................................................ 56,650

    Cash .............................................................................     60,000

---

# SOLUTIONS

## Matching

| | | | |
|---|---|---|---|
| 1. | k | 9. | i |
| 2. | n | 10. | g |
| 3. | j | 11. | f |
| 4. | h | 12. | d |
| 5. | c | 13. | a |
| 6. | l | 14. | b |
| 7. | m | 15. | o |
| 8. | e | | |

## Completion and Exercises

1. greater

2. premium

3. a. Present value of principal: $100,000 × .45639 .............................. $ 45,639.00

    Present value of interest payments:

      $5,000 × 13.59033 ...................................................................... 67,951.65

    Total price (present value) .......................................................... $113,590.65

    Cash ........................................................................................ 113,590.65

      Bonds Payable ...........................................................................     100,000.00

      Premium on Bonds Payable ..........................................................     13,590.65

   b. Bond Interest Expense .......................................................... 4,320.47

    Premium on Bonds Payable .......................................................... 679.53

      Cash ........................................................................................     5,000.00

   c. The straight-line method may be used only when it does not differ materially from the effective interest rate method. The effective interest rate method is theoretically correct.

| | | | | |
|---|---|---|---|---|
| 4. a. | Cash ........................................................................................... | | 1,015,000 | |
| |     Bonds Payable ...................................................................... | | | 1,000,000 |
| |     Premium on Bonds Payable ................................................. | | | 15,000 |
| b. | Interest Expense ................................................................... | | 44,250 | |
| | Premium on Bonds Payable ............................................... | | 750 | |
| |     Cash .................................................................................... | | | 45,000 |
| c. | Bonds Payable ....................................................................... | | 1,000,000 | |
| | Premium on Bonds Payable ............................................... | | 12,000 | |
| |     Gain on Bond Redemption ................................................. | | | 2,000 |
| |     Cash .................................................................................... | | | 1,010,000 |

| | | | | |
|---|---|---|---|---|
| 5. | Aug. 1, 1999 | Cash ........................................................................ | 1,007,500 | |
| | |     Bonds Payable ............................................... | | 1,000,000 |
| | |     Interest Payable ............................................ | | 7,500 |
| | Dec. 31, 1999 | Interest Expense ................................................... | 37,500 | |
| | |     Interest Payable ............................................ | | 37,500 |

| | | | | |
|---|---|---|---|---|
| 6. | Jan. 1, 1999 | Cash ........................................................................ | 1,067,952 | |
| | |     Bonds Payable ............................................... | | 1,000,000 |
| | |     Premium on Bonds Payable ......................... | | 67,952 |
| | July 1, 1999 | Interest Expense ($1,067,952 × .04) .................... | 42,718 | |
| | | Premium on Bonds Payable ............................. | 2,282 | |
| | |     Cash ................................................................ | | 45,000 |
| | Dec. 31, 1999 | Interest Expense [($1,067,952 – $2,282) × .04] .. | 42,627 | |
| | | Premium on Bonds Payable ............................. | 2,373 | |
| | |     Interest Payable ............................................ | | 45,000 |

7. plus; minus

8. effective interest rate

9. accrued interest

10. secured; debenture; bearer

11. principal; interest

| | |
|---|---|
| 12. Present value of principal: $1,000 × .45639 ................................................................ | $  456.39 |
|     Present value of interest: $40 × 13.59033 ................................................................. | 543.61 |
|         Total present value .......................................................................................... | $1,000.00 |

| | |
|---|---|
| 13. Present value of principal: $10,000 × .45639 ............................................................. | $4,563.90 |
|     Present value of interest: $300 × 13.59033 ................................................................ | 4,077.10 |
|         Total price (present value) .............................................................................. | $8,641.00 |

14. Cash ......................................................................................... 8,641.00
 Discount on Bonds Payable ...................................................... 1,359.00
  Bonds Payable ................................................................... 10,000.00
 Interest Expense ($8,641.00 × .04) ........................................ 345.64
  Discount on Bonds Payable ............................................... 45.64
  Cash .................................................................................. 300.00

15. Present value of principal: $10,000 × .47464 .................................................. $4,746.40
 Present value of interest: $300 × 13.13394 .................................................... 3,940.18
  Total present value .................................................................................... $8,686.58

16. $45.58; discount amortized

17. sinking fund

18. LEED COMPANY

  a.  Price to yield 10% (5% per period)
      Present value of principal ($200,000 × .37689) ............................ $ 75,378
      Present value of interest ($12,000 × 12.46221) ............................. 149,547
      Present value (price to be offered) ............................................... $224,925
  b.  First period's interest expense is $224,925 × 5% ......................... $ 11,246
  c.  1. Price to yield 14% (7% per period)
      Present value of principal ($200,000 × .25842) ........................ $ 51,684
      Present value of interest ($12,000 × 10.59401) ........................ 127,128
      Present value (price to be offered) ............................................. $178,812
    2. Interest Expense ($178,812 × 7%) ............................................. 12,517
      Cash ...................................................................................... 12,000
      Discount on Bonds Payable ...................................................... 517

19. a.  Aug. 1, 1998    Cash .............................................. 151,000.00
                          Bonds Payable ......................................... 150,000.00
                          Interest Payable (8% × $150,000 × 1/12) 1,000.00
        Dec. 31, 1998   Interest Expense ............................... 5,000.00
                          Interest Payable ........................................ 5,000.00
    b.  Jan. 1, 1998    Cash .............................................. 162,780.00
                          Bonds Payable ......................................... 150,000.00
                          Premium on Bonds Payable .................. 12,780.00
        July 1, 1998    Interest Expense ($162,780.00 × .03) ............. 4,883.40
                          Premium on Bonds Payable ..................... 1,116.60
                          Cash ........................................................ 6,000.00
        Dec. 31, 1998   Interest Expense [($162,780.00 − $1,116.80) × .03] 4,849.90
                          Premium on Bonds Payable ......................... 1,150.10
                          Interest Payable ...................................... 6,000.00

20. a.  Price to yield 12% (6% per period)
        Present value of principal ($100,000 × .31180) ............................ $31,180.00
        Present value of interest ($5,000 × 11.46992) ............................. _57,349.60_
        Present value (price to be offered) ....................................... $88,529.60
    b.  First period's interest expense is ($88,529.60 × 6%) ................... $ 5,311.78
    c.  Price to yield 6% (3% per period)
        Present value of principal ($100,000 × .55368) ........................... $ 55,368.00
        Present value of interest ($5,000 × 14.87747) ............................ _74,387.35_
        Present value (price to be offered) ...................................... $129,755.35
    d.  Interest Expense ($129,755.35 × 3%) ..................................... 3,892.66
        Premium on Bonds Payable ............................................... 1,107.34
            Cash .............................................................................   5,000.00

21. a.  Present value of principal ($10,000 × .67684) ............................ $ 6,768.40
        Present value of interest ($500 × 6.46321) ............................... _3,231.60_
            Total present value .................................................. $10,000.00
    b.  Present value of principal ($10,000 × .73069) ............................ $ 7,306.90
        Present value of interest ($500 × 6.73274) ............................... _3,366.37_
            Total price (present value) .......................................... $10,673.27
    c.  Cash ................................................................. 10,673.27
        Premium on Bond Payable ...............................................    673.27
            Bonds Payable ...................................................... 10,000.00
        Interest Expense ($10,673.27 × .04) ................................... 426.93
        Premium on Bonds Payable .............................................. 73.07
            Cash ..............................................................    500.00
    d.  Present value of principal ($10,000 × .79031) ............................ $ 7,903.10
        Present value of interest (500 × 5.24214) ................................ _2,621.07_
            Total present value .................................................. $10,524.17

22. Income before interest and taxes; interest expense

23. interest; principal

24. $13,382.30. This can be found by looking in Table A.1 at the factor in the 5 periods row and 6% column (which is 1.33823). Multiply this factor times $10,000, and the answer is $13,382.30.

25. $13,439.20. This is found by looking at the factor in Table A.1 in the 10 periods row and 3% column (since there are 10 semiannual periods and the interest rate is 3% per period). 1.34392 × $10,000 = $13,439.20.

26. reciprocal

27. $13,382.30 × (1/1.33823) = $10,000

    Of course, this could also be found by using: $13,382.30 × 0.74726 = $10,000. Note that 1/1.33823 = 0.74726

28. $2,000 × 6.71008 = $13,420.16. The factor of 6.71008 is found in the 10 periods row and 8% column.

## True-False Questions

1. T

2. F  The carrying value of bonds payable is the face value of the bonds less any unamortized discount or plus any unamortized premium.

3. F  The bond indenture may call for periodic payments to be made to a sinking fund, not a petty cash fund which is established for small expenditures.

4. T  If the bond is lost and it is a bearer bond, the finder can cash in the bond when due.

5. F  Favorable financial leverage occurs when the borrowed funds are used to increase earnings per share of common stock.

6. F  Investors will be attracted to such bonds and will bid up the price of such bonds above the face value and the bonds will sell at a premium.

7. T

8. T

9. T

10. T

11. F  A debit is needed to amortize Premium on Bonds Payable.

12. F  Interest expense is a constant amount under the straight-line procedure.

13. T

14. F  Bonds Payable is debited for the face value, any unamortized premium on bonds payable is debited, Cash is credited for the call price, and the difference is either a gain or loss on bond redemption.

15. F  Such a redemption is likely to happen in a period of declining interest rates.

16. T

17. T

18. F  A premium is the amount a bond sells for above face value.

19. F  The bonds may be converted into shares of the issuer's common stock.

20. T  Moody's and Standard & Poor's are the two leading bond rating services.

## Multiple Choice Questions

1. E

2. C Bonds Payable is credited for the face value of the bonds, and the discount is recorded as a debit of $6,000 (or $94,000 sales price − $100,000 face value).

3. B Using the effective interest rate method, Interest Expense is debited for $5,640 ($94,000 × 12% × 1/2) Interest Payable is credited for $4,500 (or $100,000 × 9% × 1/2); the difference is a credit to Discount on Bonds Payable of $1,140.

4. A

5. D One reason for the delay may be due to lower interest rates than expected. Interest starts to accrue from the date of the bonds, and investors are required to pay for the accrued interest.

6. E

7. D

8. B Bond Interest Expense is debited for $49,250, which is 10% × $985,000 × 1/2. Cash is credited for $45,000, which is 9% × $1,000,000 × 1/2. The difference is credited to Discount on Bonds Payable.

9. C

10. D

11. B

12. D Interest expense is debited for $56,650 (or $1,030,000 × 11% × 1/2), and Cash is credited for $60,000 (or $1,000,000 × 12% × 1/2). The difference is a debit to Premium on Bonds Payable.

# CHAPTER 16
# ANALYSIS USING THE STATEMENT OF CASH FLOWS

## Learning Objectives

1. *Explain the purposes and uses of the statement of cash flows.*
2. *Describe the content of the statement of cash flows and where certain items would appear on the statement.*
3. *Describe how to calculate cash flows from operating activities under both the direct and indirect methods.*
4. *Prepare a statement of cash flows under both the direct and indirect methods, showing cash flows from operating activities, investing activities, and financing activities.*
5. *Analyze a statement of cash flows of a real company.*
6. *Analyze and use the financial results — cash flow per share of common stock, cash flow margin, and cash flow liquidity ratios.*
7. *Use a working paper to prepare a statement of cash flows (Appendix).*

## REFERENCE OUTLINE

# CHAPTER OUTLINE

*Learning Objective 1:*
*Explain the purposes and uses of the statement of cash flows.*

## PURPOSES OF THE STATEMENT OF CASH FLOWS

1.  A statement of cash flows reports the flow of cash into and out of a business in an accounting period.
    a.  Reports on cash receipts and cash disbursements of an entity.
    b.  Reports on the entity's investing and financing activities for the period.
    c.  Such a statement is required each time a balance sheet and an income statement are presented.

## USES OF THE STATEMENT OF CASH FLOWS

2.  The statement of cash flows summarizes the effects on cash of the operating, investing, and financing activities of a company for a period.
    a.  The statement of cash flows reports on past management decisions on such matters as issuance of capital stock or the sale of long-term bonds.
    b.  Cash flow information is available only in bits and pieces from the other financial statements.

## MANAGEMENT USES

3.  A statement of cash flows provides feedback to management on results of past management decisions.
    a.  It may reveal that the flow of cash from operations is large enough to make proposed external financing unnecessary.
    b.  It may show why cash shortages, if any, exist.
    c.  It may cause management to change its dividend policy to conserve funds.

## INVESTOR AND CREDITOR USES

4.  The statement may provide creditors and investors with valuable information on the:
    a.  Enterprise's ability to generate positive future net cash flows.
    b.  Enterprise's ability to pay debts.
    c.  Enterprise's ability to pay dividends.
    d.  Enterprise's need for external financing.
    e.  Reasons for differences between net income and associated cash receipts and payments.
    f.  Effects on an enterprise's financial position of its cash investing and financing transactions during the period.

*Learning Objective 2:*
*Describe the content of the statement of cash flows and where certain items would appear on the statement.*

## INFORMATION IN THE STATEMENT OF CASH FLOWS

5.  The statement of cash flows presents cash receipts and cash disbursements in three major categories: operating, investing, and financing cash flows.
    a.  Operating activities include the cash effects of transactions and other events that enter into the determination of income.
        (1) Cash received from operating activities includes cash received from (1) producing and selling goods and providing services, (2) interest from making loans, (3) dividends from investments in equity securities, (4) the sale of trading securities, and (5) other sources that are not from investing and financing activities.
        (2) Cash paid for operating activities includes cash paid (1) to acquire inventory, (2) to other suppliers and employees for other goods and services, (3) to lenders and other

creditors for interest, (4) for purchase of trading securities, and (5) other cash payments not considered investing or financing activities.

    b.  Investing activities generally include transactions involving the acquisition or disposal of noncurrent assets.

        (1)  Cash received from investing activities includes cash received from (1) the sale of property, plant, and equipment, (2) the sale of available-for-sale and held-to-maturity securities; and (3) the collection of loans made to others.

        (2)  Cash paid for investing activities includes cash paid to (1) purchase plant, property, and equipment, (2) purchase available-for-sale and held-to-maturity securities, and (3) to make loans to others.

    c.  Financing activities generally include the cash effects of transactions and other events involving creditors and owners.

        (1)  Cash received from financing activities includes cash received from issuing capital stock and bonds, mortgages, notes, and from other short- or long-term borrowing.

        (2)  Cash paid for financing activities includes cash paid for cash dividends, the purchase of treasury stock, and repayments of amounts borrowed.

**A SEPARATE SCHEDULE FOR SIGNIFICANT NONCASH INVESTING AND FINANCING ACTIVITIES**

6.  Investing and financing activities that do not involve actual cash flows must be reported in a separate schedule.

*Learning Objective 3:*
*Describe how to calculate cash flows from operating activities under both the direct and indirect methods.*

**CASH FLOWS FROM OPERATING ACTIVITIES**

7.  Cash flows from operating activities can be calculated using either the direct or indirect method.

    a.  The direct method deducts only those expenses using cash from those revenues yielding cash.

    b.  The indirect method starts with net income and adjusts it for items that affected reported net income but did not involve cash.

        (1)  Analyze changes that occurred in current accounts other than cash. Net income must be adjusted for differences between accrual basis and cash basis accounting.

           (a)  Add decreases and subtract increases in accounts receivable, inventories, prepaid expenses, and other current assets (except cash).

           (b)  Add increases and deduct decreases in accounts payable, accrued liabilities, and other current liabilities.

        (2)  Add back expenses or losses that did not reduce cash; examples are depreciation expense and loss from sale of noncurrent assets.

        (3)  Deduct noncash credits or revenues; examples are gains from the sale of noncurrent assets and income recorded for investments accounted for by the equity method.

        (4)  The residual is net cash flow from operating activities.

    c.  The FASB encourages the use of the direct method, but permits the use of the indirect method.

*Learning Objective 4:*
*Prepare a statement of cash flows under both the direct and indirect methods, showing cash flows from operating activities, investing activities, and financing activities.*

**STEPS IN PREPARING STATEMENT OF CASH FLOWS**

8.  The first step is to determine cash flows from operating activities and present these items in the "Cash flows from operating activities" section.

9. The second step is to analyze all noncurrent accounts for charges resulting from investing and financing activities.

10. The third step involves arranging the information in the format required for the statement of cash flows.

## STEP 1: DETERMINING CASH FLOWS FROM OPERATING ACTIVITIES – DIRECT METHOD

11. The income statement must be converted from the accrual basis to the cash basis.
    a. Changes in balance sheet accounts that are related to items on the income statement are considered.
    b. Generally, an increase in a current asset (other than cash) decreases cash inflow or increases cash outflow.
    c. An increase in a current liability increases cash inflow or decreases cash outflow.

## ALTERNATIVE STEP 1: DETERMINING CASH FLOWS FROM OPERATING ACTIVITIES – INDIRECT METHOD

12. Using the indirect method, certain adjustments are necessary to convert net income to cash flows from operating activities.
    a. Changes that occurred in current accounts other than cash must be analyzed for their effects on cash.
    b. To convert accrual basis net income to cash basis net income, add decreases in current assets and deduct increases in current assets, then add increases in current liabilities and deduct decreases in current liabilities.
    c. Add back expenses or losses that did not reduce cash; examples are depreciation expense and loss from sale of noncurrent assets.
    d. Deduct noncash credits or revenues; examples are gains from sale of noncurrent assets and income recorded for investments accounted for by the equity method.

## STEP 2: ANALYZING THE NONCURRENT ACCOUNTS AND ADDITIONAL DATA

13. Analyze noncurrent accounts and additional data for causes of the change in cash. Examine the difference between the amount in noncurrent accounts at the beginning of the period and the amount at the end of the period.
    a. Begin by reviewing the Retained Earnings account, so that net income and dividend amounts can be determined.
    b. Classify the differences as either "cash flows from investing activities" or "cash flows from financing activities."

## STEP 3: ARRANGING INFORMATION IN THE STATEMENT OF CASH FLOWS

14. The three major sections of a completed statement of cash flows are:
    a. Cash flows from operating activities.
    b. Cash flows from investing activities.
    c. Cash flows from financing activities.

15. The format in the operating activities section differs for the direct and indirect methods.

16. The direct method adjusts each item in the income statement to a cash basis.

17. The indirect method makes these same adjustments but makes them to net income rather than to each item in the income statement.

*Learning Objective 5:*
*Analyze a statement of cash flows of a real company.*

## ANALYSIS OF THE STATEMENT OF CASH FLOWS

18. An illustration of analyzing the 1996 statement of cash flows of the Colgate-Palmolive Company is included in the text. You should work through that illustration carefully to see how the statement of cash flows is used for analysis and decision making. This same

company is used in the next chapter to illustrate the complete analysis and interpretation of all of the financial statements.

## COLGATE-PALMOLIVE COMPANY'S STATEMENTS OF CASH FLOWS

19. Consolidated statements of cash flows for the years 1996, 1995, and 1994 are shown in illustration 16.6.

## MANAGEMENT'S DISCUSSION AND ANALYSIS

20. Information from Colgate-Palmolive's 1996 Annual Report regarding Liquidity and Capital Resources is included.

## EXPLANATION OF ITEMS IN COLGATE-PALMOLIVE COMPANY'S STATEMENTS OF CASH FLOWS

21. The Colgate-Palmolive Company uses the indirect method of calculating net cash provided by operations.
22. Information regarding the Colgate-Palmolive Company's investing activities and financing activities is included in the text.

## USE OF THE CASH FLOW INFORMATION FOR DECISION MAKING

23. Management, stockholders, and creditors use the information in the statement of cash flows for decision making.

*Learning Objective 6:*
*Analyze and use the financial results – cash flow per share of common stock, cash flow margin, and cash flow liquidity ratios*

## ANALYZING AND USING THE FINANCIAL RESULTS—CASH FLOW PER SHARE OF COMMON STOCK, CASH FLOW MARGIN, AND CASH FLOW LIQUIDITY RATIOS

24. Further analysis of the statement of cash flows is provided by the use of three ratios.
25. The *cash flow per share of common stock ratio* is equal to Net Cash Provided by Operating Activities divided by Average Number of Shares of Common Stock Outstanding. This ratio indicates the company's ability to pay dividends and liabilities.
26. The *cash flow margin ratio* is equal to Net Cash Provided by Operating Activities divided by Net Sales. This ratio indicates the company's ability to turn sales revenue into cash.
27. The *cash flow liquidity ratio* is equal to the total of Cash, Marketable Securities, and Net Cash Provided by Operating Activities divided by Current Liabilities. This ratio is a test of a company's short-term, debt-paying ability.

*Learning Objective 7:*
*Use a working paper to prepare a statement of cash flows (Appendix).*

## APPENDIX—USE OF A WORKING PAPER TO PREPARE A STATEMENT OF CASH FLOWS

28. A working paper may be used to assist in preparing a statement of cash flows.
29. Enter the beginning account balances in the first column and the ending account balances in the fourth column.
30. Enter entries for analyzing transactions in the second and third columns. The entries serve two purposes: (a) they explain the change in each account and (b) they classify the changes into operating, investing, and financing activities.
31. Use the bottom portion of the working paper to prepare the statement of cash flows.
32. Use of a working paper makes the process quite mechanical. We believe that preparing the statement without the use of a working paper will enable you to better understand and use the statement of cash flows.

## DEMONSTRATION PROBLEM

The 1999 and 1998 year-end balance sheet of Gibson, Inc., carried these debit and credit amounts:

| | Debits | |
|---|---|---|
| | 1999 | 1998 |
| Cash | $ 12,000 | $ 7,500 |
| Accounts receivable, net | 12,000 | 18,000 |
| Merchandise inventory | 33,000 | 27,000 |
| Equipment | 42,000 | 39,000 |
| Totals | $ 99,000 | $ 91,500 |

Credits

| | 1999 | 1998 |
|---|---|---|
| Accumulated depreciation, equipment | $ 9,000 | $ 10,500 |
| Accounts payable | 12,000 | 15,000 |
| Taxes payable | 9,000 | 6,000 |
| Common stock, $20 par value | 40,500 | 37,500 |
| Paid-in capital in excess of par value | 1,500 | |
| Retained earnings | 27,000 | 22,500 |
| Totals | $ 99,000 | $ 91,500 |

Analysis of the 1999 income statement and accounts revealed:

1. Equipment costing $9,000 was purchased.
2. Fully depreciated equipment that cost $6,000 was discarded, and its cost and accumulated depreciation were removed from the accounts.
3. The company's equipment was depreciated $4,500 during the year.
4. The company's income statement showed $15,000 net income for 1999.
5. One hundred fifty shares of the company's common stock were issued at $30 per share.
6. Dividends totaling $10,500 were declared and paid during the year.

Required:

Prepare a statement of cash flows under the indirect method.

b.

**GIBSON, INC.**
**Statement of Cash Flows**
**For the Year Ended December 31, 1999**

## SOLUTION TO DEMONSTRATION PROBLEM

### GIBSON, INC.
### Statement of Cash Flows
### For Year Ended December 31, 1999

*Cash flows from operating activities:*

| | | |
|---|---:|---:|
| Net income | | $ 15,000 |
| Adjustments to reconcile net income to net cash provided by operating activities: | | |
| Decrease in accounts receivable | 6,000 | |
| Increase in merchandise inventory | (6,000) | |
| Decrease in accounts payable | (3,000) | |
| Increase in taxes payable | 3,000 | |
| Depreciation | 4,500 | |
| Cash provided by operating activities | | $ 19,500 |

*Cash flows from investing activities:*

| | | |
|---|---:|---:|
| Purchase of equipment | $ (9,000) | |
| Net cash used by investing activities | | (9,000) |

*Cash flows from financing activities:*

| | | |
|---|---:|---:|
| Sale of common stock | $ 4,500 | |
| Paid dividends | (10,500) | |
| Net cash used by financing activities | | (6,000) |
| Net increase in cash | | $ 4,500 |

---

## MATCHING

Referring to the terms listed below, place the appropriate letter next to the corresponding description.

a. Direct method
b. Financing activities
c. Indirect method
d. Investing activities
e. Cash flows from operating activities

f. Noncash charges/expenses
g. Noncash credits/revenues
h. Operating activities
i. Separate schedule
j. Statement of cash flows

k. Statement of changes in financial position
l. Working capital
m. Cash flow margin ratio
n. Cash flow per share of common stock outstanding

_____ 1. Generally include the cash effects of transactions and other events that enter into the determination of net income.

_____ 2. Replaced by the statement of cash flows.

_____ 3. Reports the flow of cash into and out of a business in a given period.

_____ 4. Current assets minus current liabilities.

_____ 5. Include obtaining resources from owners and providing them with a return on their investment and obtaining resources from creditors and repaying or otherwise settling the debt.

_____ 6. Shows significant financing and investing activities that did not affect cash.

_____ 7. A way of determining cash flows from operating activities that starts with net income and adjusts for expenses and revenues that do not affect cash.

_____ 8. Include lending money and collecting the principal on those loans; acquiring and selling or disposing of securities of other companies; and acquiring or disposing of property, plant, and equipment.

_____ 9. Deducts from cash sales only those operating expenses that consumed cash.

_____ 10. Revenues and gains included in arriving at net income that do not provide cash.

_____ 11. Expenses and losses that are added back to net income because they do not actually use cash of the company.

_____ 12. Net cash provided by operating activities divided by the average number of shares of common stock outstanding.

_____ 13. Net cash provided by operating activities divided by net sales.

_____ 14. Cash generated by the regular operations of a business; usually computed as net income plus or minus the effects of other current assets and current liabilities on cash flows, plus noncash expenses deducted in arriving at net income, minus noncash revenues included, less certain gains and plus any losses that are included in the total proceeds received from sale of fixed assets.

## COMPLETION AND EXERCISES

1. The increases and decreases in the individual current asset and current liability accounts are reflected in the aggregate as a change in the company's _____

   _____.

2. A statement of cash flows shows the _____ of the net change in cash between two dates.

3. The former statement of changes in financial position generally defined "funds" as

   _____ _____.

4. Deterioration in the company's _____ position due to inadequate planning by management leads to a company's inability to meet short-run financial requirements.

5. The main source of cash of a business enterprise is usually

   _____ _____.

6. What are three main sources of cash that result from financing or investing activities?

   a. _____

   b. _____

   c. _____

7. What are four main uses of cash that result from operating, financing, or investing activities?

a. _____

b. _____

c. _____

d. _____

8. What is a "noncash financing or investing activity"?

_____

_____

_____

9. From the following condensed income statement show how these items would be presented in a statement of cash flows prepared under the indirect method.

| | | |
|---|---|---|
| Sales ............................................................................................ | | $162,500 |
| Expenses (except depreciation and amortization) ............................ | | 113,750 |
| | | $ 48,750 |
| | | |
| Depreciation ................................................................................ | $16,250 | |
| Amortization of patent ................................................................. | 6,500 | 22,750 |
| Net Income ................................................................................. | | $ 26,000 |

| | | | | | | | | | | | |
|---|---|---|---|---|---|---|---|---|---|---|---|
| | | | | | | | | | | | |
| | | | | | | | | | | | |
| | | | | | | | | | | | |
| | | | | | | | | | | | |
| | | | | | | | | | | | |
| | | | | | | | | | | | |
| | | | | | | | | | | | |
| | | | | | | | | | | | |
| | | | | | | | | | | | |

10. This question concerns the adjustment or conversion procedure used to adjust accrual basis net income to obtain the cash flows from operating activities. Add the plus or minus signs to complete the table in the space.

Accrual basis net income + or – Changes in other current asset and current liability accounts:

a. _____     Expenses and losses not reducing cash

b. _____     Revenues and gains not producing cash

   = Cash flows from operating activities

11. The current assets and current liabilities sections for 1999 and 1998 are given below for Carter Corporation.

|  | December 31 | |
| --- | --- | --- |
|  | 1999 | 1998 |
| Current Assets: | | |
| Cash | $11,000 | $ 8,250 |
| Accounts receivable (net) | 23,100 | 20,625 |
| Inventories | 28,160 | 26,180 |
| Prepaid expenses | 1,210 | 1,375 |
| Total Current Assets | $63,470 | $56,430 |
| Current Liabilities: | | |
| Accounts payable | $14,300 | $12,650 |
| Notes payable | 17,050 | 19,250 |
| Accrued liabilities | 13,750 | 12,650 |
| Total Current Liabilities | $45,100 | $44,550 |

Using these current accounts and the following information, prepare a statement of cash flows for the Carter Corporation for 1999 under the indirect method.

| | |
| --- | --- |
| Net income for 1999 | $44,000 |
| Depreciation expense | $16,500 |

An analysis of changes in noncurrent accounts revealed the following:

a. Sold equipment for $2,750; original cost, $11,000, accumulated depreciation, $8,800.
b. Purchased equipment for $13,750.
c. Sold capital stock; 55 shares at $50 per share.
d. Purchased land and building for $34,210.
e. Paid cash dividends of $11,000.

12. An adequate working capital position does not ensure an adequate _____ position for meeting payments.

13. The income statement does not measure net cash flows from operating activities because it is prepared on a(n) _____ basis.

14. Assume an income statement shows sales of $243,750. The Accounts Receivable balance was $21,000 on January 1 and $16,500 on December 31. Given only this information, how much cash was collected from customers?

15. The income statement shows that cost of goods sold for the year amounted to $187,500. Accounts payable on January 1 were $27,000, and on December 31 they were $31,500. Inventory was $30,000 on January 1 and $35,000 on December 31. Given only this information how much was cost of goods sold on a cash basis?

16. To derive the cash flow from operating activities for the period under the direct method, net income on an accrual basis must be converted to net income on a _____ basis.

17. Cash flows from operating activities equals net income on an accrual basis

plus decreases in (a) _____.

plus increases in (b) _____.

minus decreases in (c) _____.

and minus increases in (d) _____.

plus (e) _____.

minus (f) _____.

18. The cash flow liquidity ratio is equal to cash, marketable securities, and net cash provided by operating activities divided by _____ _____.

19. Automatic Data Processing, Inc. (ADP) is one of the largest companies in the world dedicated to providing computerized transactions processing, data communication, and information services. The following data were taken from its 1996 Annual Report (all amounts in thousands):

| | |
|---|---|
| Net cash flows from operating activities ............................................. | $644,054 |
| Cash and cash equivalents ................................................................ | $314,416 |
| Marketable securities ....................................................................... | $321,743 |
| Current liabilities ............................................................................. | $835,613 |
| Net sales ........................................................................................... | $3,566,597 |
| Average number of shares of common stock outstanding ................ | 288,967 shares |

*Required*: Calculate the following three ratios:

a.  The cash flow per share of common stock outstanding ratio
b.  The cash flow margin ratio
c.  The cash flow liquidity ratio

a.  _____ =

b.  _____ =

c.  _____ =

---

## TRUE-FALSE QUESTIONS

Indicate whether each of the following statements is true or false by inserting a capital "T" or "F" in the blank space provided.

_____  1.  When a building is purchased by issuing bonds, the transaction would not be reported in the statement of cash flows or in a separate schedule.

_____  2.  The excess of total assets over total liabilities is called working capital.

_____  3.  When a statement of cash flows is prepared, dividends paid are reported as an investing activity.

_____  4.  The indirect method of computing cash flows from operating activities adjusts net income rather than each income statement item to a cash basis.

_____  5.  A corporation may elect not to prepare a statement of cash flows.

_____  6.  The statement of cash flows explains how changes in noncurrent assets reported on last year's balance sheet and this year's balance sheet affect cash flows.

_____  7.  If accounts receivable increased from $12,000 to $15,000 during the year and if sales amounted to $100,000 for the year, cash receipts from customers amounted to $103,000.

_____  8.  A company must publish a statement of cash flows for each period for which it publishes an income statement.

_____ 9. The amount of goodwill amortized in a period is added back to net income under the indirect method.

_____ 10. The most important reason for preparing a statement of cash flows is to compute the change in cash.

_____ 11. Depreciation provides cash for replacing plant assets; and this is the reason depreciation is shown as an inflow of cash on the statement of cash flows.

_____ 12. If a company issues its common stock for equipment, this transaction would not be disclosed on the statement of cash flows or in a separate schedule.

_____ 13. Borrowing of funds through the use of a mortgage would not be reflected on a statement of cash flows because it involves a long-term liability.

_____ 14. A stock split would be reported in a separate schedule.

_____ 15. The former statement of changes in financial position presented information on the flow of financial resources into and out of a business.

_____ 16. The former statement of changes in financial position generally defined "funds" as working capital.

_____ 17. When net income is used as a starting point in measuring cash flows from operating activities, there is no need to add depreciation expense to net income.

_____ 18. The collection of accounts receivable is a financing activity.

_____ 19. Capital stock issued as a stock dividend is reported in a statement of cash flows.

_____ 20. Collections of loans are a financing activity.

_____ 21. If capital stock is split three for one, this transaction is reported on a statement of cash flows.

_____ 22. Cash received from the issuance of long-term debt is a financing activity.

_____ 23. Any reputable company has a cash flow liquidity ratio of greater than 1.0.

# MULTIPLE CHOICE QUESTIONS

For each of the following questions indicate the best answer by circling the appropriate letter.

Using the following information, answer questions 1-3 concerning a statement of cash flows.

    a.  The company reported $35,000 of net income for 1999.
    b.  The company recorded $7,000 depreciation on its store equipment.
    c.  Store equipment that cost $2,800 and had depreciated $1,400 was sold for $700.
    d.  Fully depreciated store equipment that cost $4,900 was discarded.
    e.  $5,600 of new store equipment was purchased during the year.
    f.  $6,720 of cash dividends were declared and paid during the year.
    g.  A 1,000-share stock dividend was declared and distributed at a time when the stock was selling for $15 per share.

1. Which of the above data will be used to determine cash flows from operating activities?

    A.  1, 5, 6
    B.  1, 2, 3
    C.  5, 3, 2
    D.  1, 2, 7
    E.  2, 3

2. Which of the above data will be used to determine cash flows from investing activities?

    A.  7
    B.  1, 2, 3
    C.  6
    D.  3, 5
    E.  4, 5

3. Which of the above data will be used to determine cash flows from financing activities?

    A.  4, 5
    B.  1, 2, 3
    C.  6
    D.  6, 7
    E.  7

Questions 4-6. How would the following transactions be shown on a statement of cash flows?

4. Treasury stock was purchased for $6,500 cash during the year.

    A.  Shown as a positive cash flow from investing activities.
    B.  Shown as a negative cash flow from investing activities.
    C.  Shown as a negative cash flow from financing activities.
    D.  Not shown on the statement.
    E.  Shown as an operating activity item.

5. Equipment was purchased for $41,250 during the year.

   A. Shown as a negative cash flow from investing activities.
   B. Shown as a negative cash flow from financing activities.
   C. Shown as a negative cash flow from operating activities.
   D. Shown as a positive cash flow from financing activities.
   E. Not shown on the statement.

6. A five-year, 6% mortgage note payable for $87,500 was issued to the bank to acquire additional land and a building from a contractor.

   A. Shown in a separate schedule.
   B. Not shown at all since cash was not affected.
   C. Shown as a cash flow from operating activities.
   D. (A) and (C) are both correct.
   E. None of the above statements is correct.

7. Which of the following is true concerning depreciation, amortization of patents, amortization of bond discount, interest expense, and salary expense?

   A. All are added to income to determine cash flows from operating activities.
   B. Only interest and salary expense are added to income to determine cash flows from operating activities.
   C. Depreciation, amortization of patents, and bond discounts are added to income to determine cash from operating activities.
   D. Only depreciation and interest expense are added to income to determine cash flows from operating activities.

8. Indicate the effect on the statement of cash flows if fully depreciated office equipment costing $4,800 was discarded, and its cost and accumulated depreciation were removed from the books.

   A. The transaction would be shown as an investing activity.
   B. The transaction would be shown as a financing activity.
   C. The transaction would be shown in determining cash flows from operating activities.
   D. The transaction would not be shown on a statement of cash flows.

9. Machinery with a cost of $13,500 and accumulated depreciation of $11,970 was sold for $1,800 cash. How would the proceeds of sale be reported in the statement of cash flows?

   A. Cash flows from investing activities; Sale of machinery of $270
   B. Cash flows from financing activities; $1,800
   C. Would be shown as a decrease in a current asset.
   D. Cash flows from investing activities; Sale of machinery of $1,800
   E. Not shown on statement of cash flows.

10. A corporation issued $2,000,000 of 10-year bonds for cash at 95. How would the transaction be shown on the statement of cash flows?

    A. Positive cash inflow from financing activities, $1,900,000
    B. Positive cash inflow from financing activities, $2,000,000
    C. Negative cash flow from investing activities, $1,900,000
    D. Negative cash flow from investing activities, $2,000,000

E. Not shown on the statement of cash flows.

11. A company paid the following dividends during the year:

Cash Dividends ............................................................................................... $6,000
Stock Dividends ............................................................................................ 15,000

The correct statement concerning a statement of cash flows is:

A. Neither dividend is shown on the statement.
B. Both dividends are shown on the statement.
C. Cash dividends are shown, while stock dividends are not shown.
D. Stock dividends are shown while cash dividends are not.
E. None of the above statements is true.

12. On a statement of cash flows, the correct statement concerning a gain of $1,440 from the sale of a patent is:

A. The gain appears as an investing activity of $1,440.
B. The gain is used to adjust the income reported.
C. The gain does not appear on the statement.
D. None of the above statements is true.

13. You are given the following data concerning the Land account:

Land

| Date | Explanation | Debit | Credit | Balance |
|------|-------------|-------|--------|---------|
| July 1 | Balance ............................................................ | | | 337,500 |
| Aug. 8 | Sold for $75,000 cash ...................................... | | 45,000 | 292,500 |
| Sept. 1 | Purchased for cash ......................................... | 37,500 | | 330,000 |
| Oct. 31 | Purchased for cash | 112,500 | | 442,500 |

The above data would be shown on the statement of cash flows as:

A. Cash flows from investing activities; sale of land, $75,000.
B. Cash flows from investing activities; sale of land, $45,000.
C. Cash flows from financing activities; purchase of land, $37,500.
D. Cash flows from financing activities; purchase of land, $112,500.
E. None of the above is correct.

*Matching*

| | | | |
|---|---|---|---|
| 1. | h | 8. | d |
| 2. | k | 9. | a |
| 3. | j | 10. | g |
| 4. | l | 11. | f |
| 5. | b | 12. | n |
| 6. | i | 13. | m |
| 7. | c | 14. | e |

*Completion and Exercises*

1.  working capital

2.  causes

3.  working capital

4.  cash

5.  profitable operations (net income)

6.  (a) capital stock issues;  (b) bond or other long-term debt issues;  (c) sales of noncurrent assets

7.  (a) net loss existing after adjustment for noncash items;  (b) dividends paid;  (c) debt repayment;
    (d) purchase of noncurrent assets

8.  A noncash financing or investing activity is one that neither provides nor consumes cash.

9.  *cash flows from operating activities:*

    Net income ............................................................................................ $26,000
        Adjustments to reconcile net income to net cash provided by operating activities:
            Depreciation .................................................................... $16,250
            Amortization of patent ................................................... 6,500

10. a.  +

    b.  −

11.

**CARTER CORPORATION**

**Statement of Cash Flows**

**For the Year Ended December 31, 1999**

*Net cash flow from operating activities:*

| | | |
|---|---:|---:|
| Net income | $ 44,000 | |
| Adjustments to reconcile net income to net cash provided by operating activities: | | |
| Increase in accounts receivable | (2,475) | |
| Increase in inventories | (1,980) | |
| Decrease in prepaid expenses | 165 | |
| Increase in accounts payable | 1,650 | |
| Decrease in notes payable | (2,200) | |
| Increase in accrued liabilities | 1,100 | |
| Depreciation | 16,500 | |
| Gain on sale of equipment | (550) | |
|     Net cash flow provided by operating activities | | $56,210 |

*Cash flows from investing activities:*

| | | |
|---|---:|---:|
| Sale of equipment | $ 2,750 | |
| Purchase of equipment | (13,750) | |
| Purchase of land and building | (34,210) | |
|     Net cash used by investing activities | | (45,210) |

*Cash flows from financing activities:*

| | | |
|---|---:|---:|
| Sale of capital stock | $ 2,750 | |
| Payment of dividends | (11,000) | |
|     Net cash used by financing activities | | (8,250) |
| Net increase in cash | | $2,750 |

12. cash

13. accrual

| | |
|---|---:|
| 14. Sales on accrual basis | $243,750 |
|     Add decrease in Accounts Receivable | 4,500 |
|     Cash collected from customers | $248,250 |

| | |
|---|---:|
| 15. Cost of goods sold on accrual basis | $187,500 |
|     Deduct increase in Accounts Payable | 4,500 |
| | $183,000 |
|     Add increase in inventory | 5,000 |
|     Cost of goods sold on a cash basis | $188,000 |

16. cash

17. (a) current assets; (b) current liabilities; (c) current liabilities; (d) current assets; (e) noncash expenses and losses; (f) noncash revenues and gains.

18. current liabilities

19. a. 644,054/288,967 shares = 2.23 per share

    b. 644,054/$3,566,597 = 18.06%

    c. 1,280,213/835,613 = 1.53 times

### True-False Questions

1. F  This transaction is a significant investing activity and must be reported in a separate schedule.

2. F  Working capital is the difference between current assets and current liabilities.

3. F  Dividends paid are shown as a financing activity.

4. T

5. F  The Financial Accounting Standards Board specified that a statement of cash flows is required for each period for which an income statement and balance sheet are presented.

6. T

7. F  Cash receipts from customers would total $97,000.

8. T

9. T

10. F

11. F  Depreciation is not a source of cash for replacing plant assets; depreciation is shown as a noncash capital expense and is added to net income.

12. F  According to the FASB, a firm must disclose all significant financing and investing activities regardless of whether cash is used. The transaction is significant even if it did not change the amount of cash and would be reported in a separate schedule.

13. F  Cash is increased, and this transaction would be reported on a statement of cash flows.

14. F  A stock split is not considered to be a significant financing or investing activity.

15. T

16. T

17. F

18. F  The collection of accounts receivable is an exchange of one current asset (cash) for another current asset (accounts receivable). The net change in accounts receivable affects the cash flows from operating activities.

19. F   This transaction does not involve cash.

20. F   Collections of loans are an investing activity.

21. F

22. T

23. F   The text showed four reputable companies' cash flow liquidity ratios, all of which were less than 1.0.

*Multiple Choice Questions*

1.  B

2.  D

3.  C

4.  C

5.  A

6.  A

7.  C   Interest expense and salaries expense, unlike the other expenses listed, involve an outflow of cash.

8.  D   There would be no effect on cash because Accumulated Depreciation would be debited for the same amount that Office Equipment would be credited. If significant, this item would be shown on a separate schedule.

9.  D

10. A

11. C

12. B

13. A

CHAPTER 17
# ANALYSIS AND INTERPRETATION
# OF FINANCIAL STATEMENTS

Learning Objectives

1. *Describe and explain the objectives of financial statement analysis.*
2. *Describe the sources of information for financial statement analysis.*
3. *Calculate and explain changes in financial statements using horizontal analysis, vertical analysis, and trend analysis.*
4. *Perform ratio analysis on financial statements using liquidity ratios, long-term solvency ratios, profitability tests, and market tests.*
5. *Describe the considerations used in financial statement analysis.*

## REFERENCE OUTLINE

---

## CHAPTER OUTLINE

*Learning Objective 1:*
*Describe and explain the objectives of financial statement analysis.*

OBJECTIVES OF FINANCIAL STATEMENT ANALYSIS

1. A company's financial statements are analyzed internally by management and externally by investors, creditors, and regulatory agencies.
   a. Management's analysis of financial statements primarily relates to parts of the company. Management is able to obtain specific, special-purpose reports in order to aid in decision making.
   b. External users focus their analysis of financial statements on the company as a whole. They must rely on the general-purpose financial statements that companies publish.

FINANCIAL STATEMENT ANALYSIS

2. Financial statements are issued primarily to communicate useful financial information to interested parties to aid them in making decisions regarding a company.
   a. Analysis of the statements usually clarifies and magnifies their significance.
   b. The purpose of statement analysis is to establish and present the relationships and trends found in the data contained in the statements.
3. Comparisons or relationships are among the types of analysis that may be performed on a company's financial statements.
   a. Comparative financial statements present financial data for a number of accounting periods for the same firm, and the analysis commonly includes the following:
      (1) Absolute increases and decreases in individual items.
      (2) Percentage increases and decreases in individual items.
         (a) Such percentage analysis facilitates analysis of widely varying dollar amounts.

(b) Both dollar and percentage changes should be presented.

(3) Percentages of single items to an aggregate total.

(4) Trend percentages.

(5) Ratios of significant figures.

    (a) Horizontal analysis is the calculation of dollar or percentage changes in the statement items or totals.

    (b) For trend percentages, a base year is selected and comparisons are made to the base year.

    (c) Vertical analysis consists of the study of a single financial statement by expressing each item on the statement as a percentage of a significant total.

    (d) Common size statements show no absolute amounts, only percentages.

    (e) Financial analysts draw their information from annual reports, SEC reports, business publications, and credit agencies.

*Learning Objective 2:*
*Describe the sources of information for financial statement analysis.*

PUBLISHED REPORTS

4. Published reports are one source of financial information. Published reports include consolidated financial statements, explanatory notes, letters to stockholders, reports of independent accountants, and management's discussion and analysis (MDA).

GOVERNMENT REPORTS

5. Government reports are another source of financial information and include Form 10-K, Form 10-Q, and Form 8-K. These reports are available to the public for a small charge.

FINANCIAL SERVICE INFORMATION, BUSINESS PUBLICATIONS, NEWSPAPERS, AND PERIODICALS

6. Financial Service Information, Newspapers, and Periodicals offer meaningful financial information to external users. Moody's, Standard and Poor's, Dun and Bradstreet, Inc., and Robert Morris Associates are all firms that provide useful industry information. Business publications, such as *The Wall Street Journal* and *Forbes*, also report industry financial news.

*Learning Objective 3:*
*Calculate and explain changes in financial statements using horizontal analysis, vertical analysis, and trend analysis.*

HORIZONTAL AND VERTICAL ANALYSIS: AN ILLUSTRATION

7. *Financial statements are used in horizontal and vertical analysis to provide management with relationships that can be used in decision making. Investors and creditors can use such relationships in deciding whether to invest or loan money to a firm.*

ANALYSIS OF A BALANCE SHEET

8. An analysis of the balance sheet may reveal that assets have increased or decreased and how any asset increase has been financed.

ANALYSIS OF STATEMENTS OF INCOME AND RETAINED EARNINGS

9. An analysis of the statements of income and retained earnings focuses on any increase or decrease in gross margin, changes in expenses and revenues, and changes in retained earnings.

TREND PERCENTAGES

10. Trend percentages are referred to as index numbers and are used for comparison of financial information over time to a base year. The following steps are involved.

    a. A base year is selected.

    b. The amounts appearing on the base year financial statements are assigned a weight of 100 percent.

    c. Amounts shown on the other years' financial statements are expressed as a percentage of base year amounts.

11. Trend analysis indicates changes that are taking place in a firm and highlights direction of the changes.

*Learning Objective 4:*
*Perform ratio analysis on financial statements using liquidity ratios, long-term solvency ratios, profitability tests, and market tests.*

## RATIO ANALYSIS

12. Ratios can be broadly classified as liquidity ratios, equity or long-term solvency ratios, profitability tests, and market tests.

## LIQUIDITY RATIOS

13. Liquidity ratios are used to indicate a company's debt-paying ability and are designed to show the company's general capacity to meet maturing current liabilities and its ability to generate cash to pay these liabilities.

## CURRENT, OR WORKING CAPITAL, RATIO

14. The current, or working capital, ratio (total current assets ÷ total current liabilities) helps measure the firm's ability to meet maturing current liabilities.
    a. Working capital is equal to the excess of current assets over current liabilities.
    b. Current assets are cash and any other assets reasonably expected to be realized in cash, or sold, or consumed in the course of normal operations during the normal operating cycle or one year, whichever is longer.

## ACID-TEST (OR QUICK) RATIO

15. The acid-test or quick ratio (quick assets ÷ current liabilities) is a more severe test of immediate debt-paying ability.
    a. Quick assets include cash, net receivables, and marketable securities. They are those assets that are cash or can be converted into cash quickly.
    b. The quality of the receivables and marketable securities needs to be considered before determining whether or not the existing ratio is adequate.

## CASH FLOW LIQUIDITY RATIO

16. The cash flow liquidity ratio [(cash + marketable securities + net cash provided by operating activities)/current liabilities] is another approach for measuring short-term liquidity.
    a. Cash and marketable securities are highly "liquid" assets.
    b. Net cash provided by operating activities shows the amount of cash generated from operating activities and, thus, the ability of a company to sell inventory and collect accounts receivable.

## ACCOUNTS RECEIVABLE TURNOVER

17. Turnover ratios express the number of times during the period that an asset or group of assets was disposed of or converted into another asset or group of assets and generally measures the efficiency with which the assets are used.
    a. Accounts receivable turnover = Net credit sales (or net sales) ÷ Net accounts receivable (preferably the average of end-of-month or end-of-week balances).
       (1) A high ratio usually means that the accounts have a relatively short average life.
       (2) The ratio size depends on credit and collection policies and general business conditions.
       (3) Generally, a high ratio is desirable. But one should be careful when attempting to increase it so as not to discourage future sales.

NUMBER OF DAYS' SALES IN ACCOUNTS RECEIVABLE

18. The number of day's sales in accounts receivable is also called the average life (or collection period) of accounts receivable: the number of days in the year divided by accounts receivable turnover ratio.

INVENTORY TURNOVER

19. Inventory turnover = Cost of goods sold ÷ Average inventory for the period.
    a. The ratio indicates the rapidity of inventory turnover.
    b. The smaller the inventory required, the smaller the capital needed to produce a given volume of sales.
    c. A rapid turnover tends to prevent the accumulation of obsolete items.
    d. Shortages may result if the inventory is too small.

TOTAL ASSETS TURNOVER

20. Total assets turnover = Net sales ÷ Average total assets during the period.
    a. It is a measure of the efficiency of the use of the capital invested in assets to generate sales.
    b. Specific problems can be identified only by computing the turnover of specific assets.

EQUITY, OR LONG-TERM SOLVENCY, RATIOS

21. Equity or long-term solvency ratios indicate the financial structure of a company by showing the relationship between debt and equity financing.

EQUITY (OR STOCKHOLDERS' EQUITY) RATIO

22. Stockholders and creditors are the two basic sources of assets, but in ratio analysis, the term equity refers only to stockholders' equity.
    a. Equity ratio = Stockholders' equity ÷ Total assets (or total equities)
    b. This ratio indicates the proportion of total equities (or total assets) that is provided by stockholders on any given date.

STOCKHOLDERS' EQUITY TO DEBT (DEBT TO EQUITY) RATIO

23. The stockholders' equity to debt ratio expresses the relative equities of stockholders and creditors and may be inverted and called the debt to equity ratio.
    a. Stockholders invest capital and permit earnings to be retained.
    b. Creditors provide both long-term and short-term funds.

PROFITABILITY TESTS

24. In judging profitability, two areas of concern are: (1) the relationships of items on the income statement that indicate a company's ability to recover costs and expenses, and (2) the relationship of income to some balance sheet measure, which indicates the relative ability to earn income on assets employed.

RATE OF RETURN ON OPERATING ASSETS

25. Rate of return on operating assets = Operating margin × Turnover of operating assets.

26. Operating margin = Net operating income/Net sales.

27. Turnover of operating assets = Net sales ÷ Operating assets.

28. Therefore, the rate of return on operating assets also equals net operating income divided by operating assets.
    a. Net operating income excludes losses or gains from discontinued operations, extraordinary items, cumulative effect of changes in accounting principle, and nonoperating revenues and expenses.
    b. Operating assets are all those assets actively used in producing operating revenue.

29. This ratio is the best measure of earnings performance without regard to the sources of assets.

30. High turnover tends to be associated with low margin; low turnover with high margin.
31. In order to survive, companies must attain a minimum level of earning power, but this minimum can be achieved in many different ways.

NET INCOME TO NET SALES (RETURN ON SALES) RATIO

32. Net income to net sales measures the proportion of the sales dollar that remains after deduction of all expenses; it is computed as Net income/Net sales.

RETURN ON AVERAGE COMMON STOCKHOLDERS' EQUITY

33. An important measure of the income-producing ability of a company is the relationship of return on average common stockholders' equity, which is also referred to as return on equity (ROE).

CASH-FLOW MARGIN

34. The cash-flow margin measures the ability of a company to translate sales into cash.
    a.  It is important to measure the amount of cash generated from every dollar of sales.
    b.  It is cash that a company needs to service debt, pay dividends, and invest in new capital assets.

EARNINGS PER SHARE OF COMMON STOCK

35. Stockholders are interested in net income as a percentage of average stockholders' equity and in earnings per share of common stock.
    a.  If preferred stock is outstanding, a portion of net income must be assigned to these shares before earnings per share of common stock outstanding is computed.
    b.  Generally accepted accounting principles require that EPS be reported on the face of the income statement.
36. If shares were issued for assets during the year, the average number of shares outstanding during the year must be computed by recognizing the various dates on which the shares were issued.
37. Since stock dividends or stock splits do not increase invested capital, all that is required is a restatement of all prior calculations of EPS using the increased number of shares.
38. According to *APB Opinion 15*, a company with a complex capital structure must compute and present basic EPS and diluted EPS data.

TIMES INTEREST EARNED RATIO

39. The times interest earned ratio = Income before interest and income taxes (IBIT) ÷ Interest for the period; it provides an indication of the likelihood that interest payments will continue to be met.

TIMES PREFERRED DIVIDENDS EARNED RATIO

40. Number of times preferred dividends are earned = Net income after income taxes ÷ Annual preferred dividends.

MARKET TESTS

41. Certain ratios, using information from the financial statements and information about market prices, help investors assess the merits of stocks in the market place.

EARNINGS YIELD ON COMMON STOCK

42. Earnings yield on common stock = Earnings per share of common stock ÷ Current market price per share of common stock.

PRICE-EARNINGS RATIO

43. If the ratio is inverted, it becomes the price-earnings ratio. Thus, price-earnings ratio = Current market price per share of common stock ÷ Earnings per share of common stock.

## PAYOUT RATIO ON COMMON STOCK

44. Payout ratio on common stock = Dividends per share of common stock ÷ Earnings per share; it indicates the percentage of the earnings that were paid out as dividends.

## DIVIDEND YIELD ON COMMON STOCK

45. Dividend yield on common stock = Dividends per share of common stock ÷ Current market price per share of common stock.

## DIVIDEND YIELD ON PREFERRED STOCK

46. Dividend yield on preferred stock = Dividends per share of preferred stock ÷ Current market price per share of preferred stock.

## CASH FLOW PER SHARE OF COMMON STOCK

47. Cash flow per share of common stock = Net cash provided by operating activities ÷ Average number of shares of common stock outstanding.

*Learning Objective 5:*
*Discuss the considerations used in financial statement analysis.*

## FINAL CONSIDERATIONS IN FINANCIAL STATEMENT ANALYSIS

48. Ratios should be used only as clues that focus attention on certain relationships that might require further investigation.

## NEED FOR COMPARABLE DATA

49. The data used should be comparable in terms of the accounting practices followed.

## INFLUENCE OF EXTERNAL FACTORS

50. External factors such as general business conditions may exert great influence on the firm's operations and should be taken into consideration when interpreting the statements.

51. Comparability of financial statements may be seriously impaired by fluctuations in the general price level or in specific prices.

## NEED FOR COMPARATIVE STANDARDS

52. Relationships between financial statement items become much more meaningful when appropriate standards are available for comparison.

---

## DEMONSTRATION PROBLEM

---

1. Common-size percentages are often used to compare the statements of companies of unequal size. The condensed income statements of Companies A and B are given below. Enter in the spaces provided the amounts expressed in common-size percentages.

### COMPANY A AND COMPANY B
### Income Statements for Year Ended December 31, 2000

| | Dollar Amounts | | Common-Size Percentages | |
|---|---|---|---|---|
| | Company A | Company B | Company A | Company B |
| Sales | $ 450,000 | $ 525,000 | _____ % | _____ % |
| Cost of goods sold | 261,000 | 210,000 | _____ % | _____ % |
| Gross margin | $ 189,000 | $ 315,000 | _____ % | _____ % |
| Selling expenses | $ 81,000 | $ 89,250 | _____ % | _____ % |
| Administrative Expenses | 45,000 | 52,500 | _____ % | _____ % |
| Total operating expenses | $ 126,000 | $ 141,750 | _____ % | _____ % |
| Income | $ 63,000 | $ 173,250 | _____ % | _____ % |

2. After expressing the amounts of the income statements in common-size percentages, examine them and write in this space (_____) the name of the company that operated more efficiently.

---
## SOLUTION TO DEMONSTRATION PROBLEM
---

1.

### COMPANY A AND COMPANY B
### Income Statements for Year Ended December 31, 2000

|  | Dollar Amounts | | Common-Size Percentages | |
|---|---|---|---|---|
|  | Company A | Company B | Company A | Company B |
| Sales.......................................... | $ 450,000 | $ 525,000 | 100% | 100% |
| Cost of goods sold............................. | 261,000 | 210,000 | 58% | 40% |
| Gross margin ....................................... | $ 189,000 | $ 315,000 | 42% | 60% |
| Selling expenses ................................. | $ 81,000 | $ 89,250 | 18% | 17% |
| Administrative Expenses.................... | 45,000 | 52,500 | 10% | 10% |
| Total operating expenses ................... | $ 126,000 | $ 141,750 | 28% | 27% |
| Income | $ 63,000 | $ 173,250 | 14% | 33% |

2. Company B operated more efficiently.

---
## MATCHING
---

Referring to the terms listed below, place the appropriate letter next to the corresponding description.

a. Working capital ratio
b. Equity ratio
c. Dividend yield on preferred stock
d. Earnings yield on common stock
e. Accounts receivable turnover
f. Total assets turnover

g. Earning power percentage
h. Payout ratio on common stock
i. Acid-test ratio
j. Earnings per share of common stock
k. Price-earnings ratio
l. Net operating income
m. Times preferred dividends earned ratio

n. Times interest earned ratio
o. Return on average common stockholders' equity
p. Inventory turnover
q. Net income to net sales
r. Cash flow liquidity ratio

_____ 1. Cost of goods sold divided by average inventory.

_____ 2. Same as current ratio.

_____ 3. Current market price per share of common stock divided by earnings per share.

_____ 4. Net income divided by average common stockholders' equity.

_____ 5. Dividends per share of common stock divided by earnings per share.

_____ 6. Net income divided by annual preferred dividends.

_____ 7. Shows number of times interest is earned.

_____ 8. Net income divided by net sales.

_____ 9. Annual preferred dividend per share divided by current market price per share of preferred stock.

_____ 10. Net sales divided by average total assets.

_____ 11. Operating revenues less operating expenses.

_____ 12. Earnings available to common stockholders divided by weighted-average number of common shares outstanding.

_____ 13. Current earnings per share divided by current market price per share of common stock.

_____ 14. Same as rate of return on operating assets.

_____ 15. "Liquid" assets plus net cash provided by operating activities divided by current liabilities.

_____ 16. Quick assets divided by current liabilities.

_____ 17. This ratio, when divided into the number of days in the year, shows the number of days' sales in accounts receivable.

_____ 18. Shows the proportion of total assets provided by stockholders.

*Completion and Exercises*

1. A company has sales of $1,287,000 per year. Its average accounts receivable balance is $235,500.
   a. What is the average number of days an average account receivable is outstanding?

   _____

   b. Assuming released funds can be invested at 12 percent, how much could the company earn by reducing the collection period of the accounts receivable to 40 days? _____

   _____

   c. What assumption must you make in order for this earnings calculation to be correct?

   _____

   _____

2. A company paid bond interest of $15,000, incurred federal income taxes of $36,000, and had net earnings (after-taxes) of $69,000. How many times was the bond interest earned? _____

3. Statement analysis is the selection and use of data presented in the financial statements to establish significant _____ and _____.

4. What are comparative financial statements? _____

   _____

   _____

5. What are net assets? _____ _____ – _____ _____

   = _____ _____.

6. What is the definition of working capital? _____ _____ –

   _____ _____.

7. How is the current ratio computed? _____ _____ ÷ _____

   _____.

8. What is the purpose of the current ratio? _____

   _____

   _____

   _____

9. Does the payment of a current liability leave the current ratio unchanged? _____

   Why? _____

   _____

   _____

   _____

   _____

10. If a company borrows money from a bank on a one-year note, what effect does this have on the working capital of a company? _____ Why? _____

   _____

   _____

   _____

11. What items are included in "quick assets" for the purpose of computing the acid-test or

quick ratio? _____

_____

_____

12. _____ and _____ are the two sources of assets for a business

enterprise.

13. How is the cash flow liquidity ratio computed?( _____ + _____ _____

+ _____ _____ _____ _____ _____ _____ )

÷ _____ _____

14. How is the equity ratio computed? _____ _____ ÷ _____ _____ .

15. Fill in the blank spaces below.

|  | December 31 | | Increase or Decrease | |
|  | 2000 | 1999 | 2000 Dollars | 1999 Percentage |
| --- | --- | --- | --- | --- |
| Current Assets: |  |  |  |  |
| Cash | $ 121,500 | $ 108,000 | _____ | _____ |
| Accounts receivable, net | 238,500 | 180,000 | _____ | _____ |
| Inventories | 207,000 | 189,000 | _____ | _____ |
| Prepaid expenses | 58,500 | 81,000 | _____ | _____ |
|  | $ 625,500 | $ 558,000 | _____ | _____ |

16. What do turnover ratios express and what do they measure? _____

_____

_____

_____

_____

_____

17. What can be interpreted from the accounts receivable turnover ratio? _____

_____

_____

_____

_____

_____

18. What does the inventory turnover ratio show? _____

_____

_____

_____

_____

19. What does the total assets turnover show? _____

_____

_____

_____

_____

20. The price-earnings ratio is computed by dividing the _____ _____

_____ per share _____ _____ _____ by

_____ per share.

21. The dividend yield on stock is computed by dividing _____ per share by

_____ _____ per share.

22. The payout ratio is equal to _____ _____ _____

÷ _____ _____ _____.

23. Compute the requested figures for 2000 from the financial statements of the George
Company presented on the following pages. (Assume all assets are operating assets.)
a. Accounts receivable turnover = _____ ÷ _____ = _____.

b. Average collection period of accounts receivable = _____ ÷ _____

= _____.

c. Inventory turnover = _____ ÷ _____ = _____.

d. Total asset turnover = _____ ÷ _____ = _____.

e. Net income to net sales = _____ ÷ _____ = _____.

f. Rate of return on operating assets = _____ × _____

= _____.

g. Return on average common stockholders' equity = _____ ÷ _____

= _____.

h. Earnings per share of common stock = _____ ÷ _____

= _____.

i. Number of times interest is earned = _____ ÷ _____

    = _____.

j. Current ratio = _____ ÷ _____ = _____.

k. Acid-test ratio = _____ ÷ _____ = _____.

l. Price-earnings ratio = _____ ÷ _____ = _____.

m. Dividend yield on common stock = _____ ÷ _____

    = _____.

n. Payout ratio on common stock = _____ ÷ _____

    = _____.

o. Equity ratio = _____ ÷ _____ = _____.

p. Working capital = _____ − _____ = _____.

## GEORGE COMPANY
### Comparative Balance Sheets
### December 31, 2000 and 1999

| | December 31 | |
| --- | --- | --- |
| | 2000 | 1999 |
| *Assets* | | |
| Current assets: | | |
| Cash | $ 63,000 | $ 54,000 |
| Accounts receivable | 86,400 | 75,600 |
| Merchandise inventory | 91,800 | 84,600 |
| Prepaid expenses | 9,000 | 7,200 |
| Total Current Assets | $250,200 | $221,400 |
| Plant and equipment (net) | 333,600 | 300,000 |
| Intangible assets | 15,600 | 18,000 |
| Total assets | $599,400 | $539,400 |
| *Liabilities and Stockholders' Equity* | | |
| Liabilities: | | |
| Current liabilities | $129,600 | $126,000 |
| 9% first-mortgage bonds | 162,000 | 162,000 |
| Total liabilities | $291,600 | $288,000 |
| Stockholders' equity: | | |
| 6% preferred stock, par $60, 500 shares authorized and outstanding | $ 30,000 | $ 30,000 |
| Common stock, par $12, 9,000 shares authorized and outstanding | 108,000 | 108,000 |
| Paid-in capital in excess of par value | 20,400 | 20,400 |
| Retained earnings | 149,400 | 93,000 |
| Total stockholders' equity | $307,800 | $251,400 |
| Total liabilities and stockholders' equity | $599,400 | $539,400 |

## GEORGE COMPANY

### Income Statement

### For the Year Ended December 31, 2000

| | | |
|---|---:|---:|
| Sales | | $1,107,000 |
| Less: Sales returns and allowances | | 27,000 |
| Net sales | | $1,080,000 |
| Cost of goods sold: | | |
| Beginning inventory | | $ 84,600 |
| Purchases | | 684,000 |
| Goods available for sale | | $ 768,600 |
| Less: Ending inventory | | 91,800 |
| Cost of goods sold | | 676,800 |
| Gross margin | | $ 403,200 |
| Operating expenses | | 277,020 |
| Net operating income | | $ 126,180 |
| Interest expense | | 14,580 |
| Income before federal income taxes | | $ 111,600 |
| Income taxes | | 36,000 |
| Net Income after Income Taxes | | $ 75,600 |

Assume market price per share of common stock at December 31, 2000, was $36.

24. Donna Company had 1,000 shares of 6 percent Cumulative Preferred Stock, $150 par value, issued and outstanding during all of 1999. It started 1999 with 100,000 shares of $45 par value common stock outstanding and issued 40,000 shares for cash on September 30. Net income for 1999 was $834,000. Compute the earnings per share of common stock for 1999.

25. The Thomas Company had 50,000 shares of common stock outstanding on January 1, 1999. On July 1, 1999, it issued 25,000 additional shares for cash. The income available for common stockholders for 1999 was $225,000. What amount of earnings per share of common stock should the company report?

26. The following data were taken from the balance sheet at the end of the current year. Determine (a) working capital, (b) current ratio, and (c) acid-test ratio. Present figures used in your computations.

| | |
|---|---:|
| Cash | $503,400 |
| Marketable securities | 144,000 |
| Accounts receivable | 678,000 |
| Notes receivable, short-term | 48,000 |
| Merchandise inventory | 777,000 |
| Prepaid expenses | 29,400 |
| Accounts payable | 936,000 |
| Income tax payable | 204,000 |
| Accrued liabilities payable | 120,000 |

# TRUE-FALSE QUESTIONS

Indicate whether each of the following statements is true or false by inserting a capital "T" or "F" in the blank space provided.

_____ 1. A company with an equity ratio of .75:1 has three times as much stockholders' equity as debt.

_____ 2. The best measure of the ability of a company to use assets efficiently is its return on average common stockholders' equity.

_____ 3. A company with an accounts receivable turnover of four has approximately 90 days' sales that are uncollected.

_____ 4. Prepaid expenses are included in calculating the quick ratio.

_____ 5. A company that has a negative margin may be quite profitable if it has a high turnover of total assets.

_____ 6. Comparative statements consist of the financial statements of two companies recast into the same format.

_____ 7. Inter-company analysis of financial statements may be aided if the balance sheet amounts are expressed as percentages of total assets.

_____ 8. A company may be quite profitable and yet find it difficult to pay its accounts payable.

_____ 9. An EPS amount typically is calculated for both preferred and common shares.

_____ 10. If EPS for 1999 was $4, and a 100 percent stock dividend was distributed in 2000, the revised EPS for 1999 is $2.

_____ 11. Common-size statements provide information so that readers can determine the dollar amounts of increases and decreases in accounts from the previous year.

_____ 12. Trend percentages are calculated by first assigning a weight of 100 percent to the amounts appearing on the base year financial statements and comparing later periods with these amounts.

_____ 13. Earnings per share are often increased if a company introduces larger portions of debt into its capital structure.

_____ 14. If a company's common stock balance was $120,000, retained earnings was $180,000, and bonds payable was $90,000 (and these were the only balances in its equity accounts), its stockholders' equity/debt ratio would be 1.50:1.

_____ 15. A low stockholders' equity ratio is desirable to creditors because of the protection provided to them.

_____ 16. Operating assets are all assets actively used in producing operating revenues and would include land rented to another company.

_____ 17. Net operating income excludes extraordinary items, interest revenue, and interest expense.

_____ 18. The net income to net sales ratio includes the effects of extraordinary items and interest charges.

_____ 19. Net income to average common stockholders' equity can be referred to as return on equity—R.O.E.

_____ 20. In calculating earnings per share of common stock, the preferred dividends must be declared before they can correctly be subtracted from net income in the numerator.

_____ 21. A potential investor should rely entirely on percentages or ratio analysis because each of these methods is useful in uncovering potential strengths and weaknesses.

_____ 22. Cash flow margin measures the ability of a company to meet its short-term debt obligations.

_____ 23. A payout ratio on common stock of 80 percent means that the company paid out 80 percent of the earnings per share in interest to creditors.

_____ 24. The net income to net sales ratio is not affected by the methods used to finance the company's assets.

_____ 25. A low stockholders' equity ratio is desirable to stockholders if borrowed funds can be put to work earning more than their cost.

_____ 26. If a company increases its portion of debt in its capital structure and a loss occurs, the loss is magnified when determining earnings per share.

# MULTIPLE CHOICE QUESTIONS

For each of the following questions indicate the best answer by circling the appropriate letter.

Questions 1-3: Consider each of the following transactions separately and state the effect of each transaction on working capital, the current ratio, and the acid-test ratio. Assume the current ratio is 1:1 before these transactions occurred.

1.  Purchased merchandise on account, $210,000:

    A.  No effect on working capital, decrease both current ratio and acid-test ratio.
    B.  No effect on working capital or current ratio, decrease acid-test ratio.
    C.  No effect on all three items.
    D.  Decreases all three items.
    E.  Increases working capital, decrease current and acid-test ratios.

2.  Paid cash for office supplies, $9,000:

    A.  Increase working capital and current ratio, decrease acid-test ratio.
    B.  No effect on all three items.
    C.  No effect on working capital and current ratio, decrease acid-test ratio.
    D.  Decrease all three items.

3.  Paid short-term portion of notes payable, $60,000:

    A.  Decreases working capital, current ratio, and acid-test ratios.
    B.  Increases working capital, no effect on currrent and acid-test ratios.
    C.  Increases working capital, decreases current and acid-test ratios.
    D.  No effect on all three items.
    E.  No effect on working capital, increases current ratio and acid-test ratio.

Questions 4-5. The following data were abstracted from the balance sheet of Roy Company:

| | |
|---|---:|
| Cash | $34,000 |
| Marketable securities | 16,000 |
| Accounts and notes receivable, net | 46,000 |
| Merchandise inventory | 61,000 |
| Prepaid expenses | 3,000 |
| Accounts and notes payable, short term | 64,000 |
| Accrued liabilities | 16,000 |

4.  The current ratio is:

    A.  1:2
    B.  2:1
    C.  1.2:1
    D.  3:1
    E.  4:1

5.   The acid-test ratio is:

A.  1:2
B.  2:1
C.  1.2:1
D.  3:1
E.  4:1

Questions 6-8: The balance sheet for Bryan Co. at the end of the current fiscal year indicated the following:

| | |
|---|---:|
| Total current liabilities (noninterest bearing) ........................................ | $300,000 |
| Bonds payable, 5% (issued in 1999, due in 20 years) ......................... | 600,000 |
| Preferred 6% stock, $200 par ................................................................. | 240,000 |
| Common stock, $20 par ........................................................................... | 480,000 |
| Premium on common stock ...................................................................... | 120,000 |
| Retained earnings ...................................................................................... | 420,000 |

Income before income taxes was $180,000 and income taxes were $78,000 for the current year:

6.   The rate earned on common stockholders' equity is:

A.  7 percent.
B.  8.6 percent.
C.  9.1 percent.
D.  8.1 percent.
E.  6.1 percent.

7.   The stockholders' equity to debt ratio is:

A.  4:1
B.  2.1:1
C.  0.7:1
D.  1.2:1
E.  1.4:1

8.   The number of times preferred dividends were earned is:

A.  7.1
B.  8.6
C.  9.1
D.  8.1
E.  6.1

Questions 9-11: In the following questions express the following income statements' amounts in common-size percentages:

## RING COMPANY

### Income Statement for Year Ended December 31, 1999

| | |
|---|---:|
| Sales ................................................................................................. | $45,000 |
| Cost of goods sold ........................................................................ | 29,340 |
| Gross profit from sales ................................................................ | $15,660 |
| Operating expenses ...................................................................... | 10,800 |
| Net income ................................................................................... | $ 4,860 |

9.  Cost of goods sold expressed in a common-size percentage is:

   A.  66 percent.
   B.  100 percent.
   C.  65.2 percent.
   D.  6.03 percent.

10. Operating expenses expressed in a common-size percentage are:

   A.  69 percent.
   B.  24 percent.
   C.  28 percent.
   D.  2.22 percent.

11. Net income expressed in a common-size percentage is:

   A.  100 percent.
   B.  31 percent.
   C.  12 percent.
   D.  10.8 percent.

12. A company showed the following for a fiscal year ended December 31.

| | |
|---|---:|
| Accounts Receivable, January 1 ............................................... | $36,000 |
| Accounts Receivable, December 31 ........................................... | 48,000 |
| Gross Sales ...................................................................................... | 240,000 |
| Sales Returns and Allowances ................................................... | 30,000 |
| Net Sales .......................................................................................... | 210,000 |

The accounts receivable turnover is:

   A.  5.257 times per year.
   B.  5.83 times per year.
   C.  5 times per year.
   D.  4.375 times per year.
   E.  4.6 times per year.

13. Which of the following transactions would result in an increase in the current ratio assuming that the ratio presently is 2:1?

   A. Customer paid her accounts receivable.
   B. Merchandise was purchased on account.
   C. Paid a long-term debt.
   D. Paid a 90-day note payable.
   E. None of the above transactions would increase the present current ratio.

14. Booie Company's records reveal the following:

| | |
|---|---:|
| Income before interest and taxes | $960,000 |
| Less interest on bonds | 96,000 |
| Balance | $864,000 |
| Income taxes at 45 percent | 388,800 |
| Income after taxes | $475,200 |
| Less preferred dividends | 32,640 |
| Income available for common stockholders | $442,560 |

   The number of times the interest is earned is:

   A. 2.20 times.
   B. 2.02 times.
   C. 10 times.
   D. 11.11 times.
   E. 12.5 times.

15. What would be the effect of the following transaction on working capital?

   Received $250 from a customer in payment of his account.
   A. Increased current assets, thus increase in working capital.
   B. Decreased working capital.
   C. No effect.

# SOLUTIONS

## Matching

| | | | | | |
|---|---|---|---|---|---|
| 1. | p | 7. | n | 13. | d |
| 2. | a | 8. | q | 14. | g |
| 3. | k | 9. | c | 15. | r |
| 4. | o | 10. | f | 16. | i |
| 5. | h | 11. | l | 17. | e |
| 6. | m | 12. | j | 18. | b |

## Completion and Exercises

1.  a.  $1,287,000/$235,500 = 5.46; 365 ÷ 5.46 = 67 days

    b.  $235,500 ÷ 67 = $3,515
       67 days – 40 days = 27 less days
       27 × $3,515 = $94,905 released funds
       $94,905 × 12% = $11,389

    c.  You must assume that sales will not be reduced by the action you take to reduce the collection period for accounts receivable.

2.  ($69,000 + $36,000 + $15,000)/$15,000 = $120,000/$15,000 = 8 times

3.  Relationships; trends

4.  Comparative financial statements are those that present the statements of the same company for each of two or more accounting periods.

5.  Total assets – Total liabilities = Net assets

6.  Current assets – Current liabilities

7.  Current assets ÷ Current liabilities

8.  The purpose of the current ratio is to measure the immediate debt-paying ability and the strength of the working capital position of a company.

9.  Not usually. If the current ratio is greater than one, the payment of a current liability will increase the current ratio. If the current ratio is less than one, the payment of a current liability will reduce the current ratio. Only if the ratio is equal to one will it remain unchanged.

10. None. The borrowing increases Cash (current asset) and Notes Payable (current liability) by the same amount.

11. The "quick assets" consist of cash, net receivables, and martketable securities.

12. Stockholders; creditors

13. Cash + Marketable Securities + Net cash provided by operating activities ÷ Current Liabilities.

14. Stockholders' equity ÷ Total assets (or Total equities)

15.

*Increase or Decrease**
*2000 over 1999*

| Dollars | Percentage |
|---|---|
| $13,500 | 13 |
| 58,500 | 33 |
| 18,000 | 10 |
| 22,500* | 28* |
| $67,500 | 12 |

16. Turnover ratios express the number of times during a period that an asset or group of assets is disposed of or converted into another asset or group of assets. Turnover ratios measure the efficiency with which the asset or assets are used.

17. The accounts receivable turnover ratio shows the average age of accounts receivable. A high turnover ratio means that funds are freed quickly for investment elsewhere. A low turnover rate means that funds are "tied up" in accounts receivable.

18. The inventory turnover ratio indicates the rapidity with which inventories are sold and replenished. The higher the turnover, the smaller the amount of capital needed to produce a given amount of sales.

19. The total assets turnover shows the relationship between dollar volume of sales and total assets as a measure of the efficiency of the use of capital invested in the assets.

20. Current market price; of common stock; earnings

21. Dividends; market price

22. Dividends per share ÷ Earnings per share

23. a. $1,080,000 ÷ $81,000 = 13.3 times

b. 365/13.3 = 27 days approximately

c. $676,800 ÷ $88,200 = 7.67

d. $1,080,000 ÷ $569,400 = 1.9

e. $75,600 ÷ $1,080,000 = 7 percent

f. $126,180/$1,080,000 × $1,080,000/$599,400 = 21.1%
or $126,180/$599,400 = 21.1%

g. Net income – Preferred dividend/Average book value of common stock
($75,600 – $1,800)/( [($307,800 – $31,800) + ($251,400 – $31,800)] ÷ 2)
$73,800/$247,800 = 30%

h. $73,800/9,000 = $8.20 ($75,600 – $1,800 preferred dividends = $73,800)

i. $126,180/$14,580 = 8.65$ times

j. $250,200/$129,600 = 1.93:1$

k. $149,400/$129,600 = 1.15:1$

l. $36/$8.20 = 4.39$ times

m. $1.93/$36 = 5.36\%$. Net income – Increase in retained earnings = Dividends paid
= $75,600 – $56,400 = $19,200; 19,200 – $1,800 (Preferred dividends)
= Dividends on common stock = $17,400.
$17,400 ÷ 9,000 = $1.93 Dividends per share of common stock.

n. $1.93 ÷ $8.20 = 23.54\%$

o. $307,800 ÷ $599,400 = 51.4\%$

p. $250,200 – $129,600 = $120,600$

24. ($834,000 – $9,000)/[.75 (100,000) + .25(140,000)] = $825,000/110,000 shares = $7.50 per share

25. $225,000/[.50 (50,000) + .50(75,000)] = $225,000/62,500 shares = $3.60 per share

26. a.
| | |
|---|---:|
| Current Assets | $ 2,179,800 |
| Current Liabilities | −1,260,000 |
| Working Capital | $ 919,800 |

b. CA/CL = $2,179,800/$1,260,000 = 1.73:1

c.
| | |
|---|---:|
| Cash | $ 503,400 |
| Mkt. Sec. | 144,000 |
| A/R | 678,000 |
| N/R | 48,000 |
| | $ 1,373,400 |

$1,373,400/$1,260,000 = 1.09:1

## True-False Questions

1. T  The equity ratio is equal to stockholders' equity divided by total assets.

2. F  Return on average common stockholder's equity measures what a company earned for its stockholders from all sources.

3. T  365/4 = approximately 90 days.

4. F  The numerator of the quick ratio only includes Cash, net receivables, and marketable securities.

5. F  A high turnover cannot compensate for a negative margin.

6. F  Comparative financial statements present the same company's financial statements for two or more successive periods in side-by-side columns.

7. T

8. T The accrual net income shown on the income statement is not cash basis income and does not indicate the cash flow.

9. F Earnings per share is calculated for common shares only.

10. T A 100 percent stock dividend doubles the number of shares of stock outstanding, which reduces in half the earnings per share.

11. F Common-size statements show no absolute amounts, only percentages.

12. T Trend percentages are computed by dividing nonbase amounts by the base year amounts and then multiplying the result by 100.

13. T When a company finances activities by issuing debt, higher EPS often results. This procedure is known as favorable financial leverage.

14. F The stockholders' equity/debt ratio is 3.33:1 ($300,000/$90,000).

15. F A high stockholders' equity ratio would be desirable to creditors because of its protection.

16. F Land rented to another company is a nonoperating asset, but the definition of operating assets is correct.

17. T Net operating income excludes losses or gains from discontinued operations, extraordinary items, cumulative effect of changes in accounting principle, nonoperating revenues, such as interest revenue, and nonoperating expenses, such as interest expense.

18. T Net income includes extraordinary items and interest charges.

19. T

20. F Preferred dividends are subtracted whether declared or not.

21. F A potential investor should not rely entirely on any single percentage or ratio analysis.

22. F Cash flow margin is a profitability ratio that measures the ability of a company to translate sales into cash.

23. F A payout ratio on common stock of 80 percent means that the company paid out 80 percent of the earnings per share in dividends.

24. F For instance, interest expense resulting from debt financing is deducted in determining net income.

25. T Net income is reduced by issuing bonds instead of common stock, but there are fewer shares outstanding, so earnings per share might increase.

26. T The loss is magnified when determining earnings per share because there are fewer shares to spread the loss over.

## Multiple Choice Questions

1. B

2. C

3. D

4. B    $34,000 + $16,000 + $46,000 + $61,000 + $3,000 = $160,000 current assets
        $64,000 + $16,000 = $80,000 current liabilities
        $160,000/$80,000 = 2:1

5. C    $34,000 + $16,000 + $46,000 = $96,000 quick assets;
        $96,000 quick assets/$80,000 current liabilities = 1.2:1

6. B    $102,000 net income – $14,400 preferred dividends = $87,600;
        $87,600/$1,020,000 common stockholders' equity = 8.6%

7. E    $1,260,000 stockholders' equity ÷ $900,000 total debt = 1.4:1

8. A    $102,000 net income/$14,400 preferred dividends = 7.1 times

9. C

10. B

11. D

12. C    $210,000 net sales/$42,000 average accounts receivable = 5 times

13. D

14. C    $960,000/$96,000 = 10 times

15. C